THE JIM CROW ROUTINE

THE
JIM CROW
ROUTINE

Everyday Performances of Race, Civil Rights,
and Segregation in Mississippi

Stephen A. Berrey

The University of North Carolina Press CHAPEL HILL

This book was published with the assistance of the Authors Fund of the University of North Carolina Press.

© 2015 The University of North Carolina Press
All rights reserved
Designed by Alyssa D'Avanzo
Set in Miller by codeMantra, Inc.
Manufactured in the United States of America

The paper in this book meets the guidelines for permanence and durability of the Committee on Production Guidelines for Book Longevity of the Council on Library Resources.

The University of North Carolina Press has been a member of the Green Press Initiative since 2003.

Cover illustration: In a juke joint on a Saturday afternoon in Clarksdale, Mississippi, 1939 (Courtesy of the Library of Congress, Prints and Photographs Division, LC-USF34-052479)

Complete cataloging information can be obtained online at the Library of Congress catalog website.
ISBN 978-1-4696-2093-0 (pbk.: alk. paper)
ISBN 978-1-4696-2094-7 (ebook)

For Emily, and for my parents,
Bob and Bonnie

CONTENTS

ILLUSTRATIONS

ACKNOWLEDGMENTS

In the process of writing this book, I have benefited from the support, advice, and encouragement of many people. My interest in history crystallized around issues of race during my undergraduate years, and I am particularly appreciative of Jean Allman, LeeAnn Whites, and Robert Collins, who introduced me to histories that are fascinating, disturbing, and complex. At the University of Tennessee, I was fortunate to learn what it meant to "do" history from Cynthia Fleming, Stephen Ash, and Susan Becker. I am particularly grateful to Beth Haiken, who provided encouragement when I needed it most, and to Jim Cobb, who taught us that good research deserves good writing (and I hope that some of those lessons are reflected in this book). For their camaraderie during those days and since, thanks to Brad Austin, Jeff Bremer, Melinda Pash, and Kris Ray. The research for this book began when I was at the University of Texas, and Neil Foley was the ideal adviser. His guidance and enthusiasm for the project were instrumental in the early stages of this work. I am also grateful to others who guided me through this process, including James Sidbury, Toyin Falola, Gunther Peck, Michael Stoff, Robert Olwell, and Ted Gordon. For their professional advice and friendship, which made my time in Austin more enjoyable, I am especially grateful to Howard Miller and the late Robin Kilson. Austin truly was a wonderful place to be in graduate school, and I appreciated the friendship and intellectual support of Ethan Blue, Ernie Capello, Ed Donovan, Andrew Falk, Rebecca Montes-Donovan, Clint Starr, and John Troutman.

In writing this book, I have had the good fortune to be surrounded by great colleagues at two institutions. During my time at Indiana University, Ilana Gershon's suggestion that I check out Erving Goffman's work on performance would eventually change how I thought about the entire project. Matt Guterl was and continues to be supportive of my work in multiple ways. Thanks also to Valerie Grim, Michael Martin, Khalil Muhammad, Amrita Myers, Micol Seigel, and Vernon Williams. The University of Michigan has proven to be an excellent place to write a book, in no small measure because of the support I have received from my colleagues in the Department of American Culture and the Department of History. For various suggestions and advice along the way, thanks to Evelyn Alsultany, Amy Sara Carroll, Bruce Conforth, Jay Cook, Matthew Countryman, Angela Dillard, Greg Dowd, Geoff Eley, Kevin Gaines, Colin Gunckel, Rima Hassouneh, Kali Israel, Martha Jones, Scott Kurashige, Matt Lassiter, Anthony Mora, Gina Morantz-Sanchez, Dan Ramirez, Sherie Randolph, Penny Von Eschen, and Stephen Ward. In addition, Brandi Hughes, Elise Lipkowitz, and Hussein Fancy have been great readers and sounding boards and even better friends. This project benefited from the feedback I received during my year as a fellow in Michigan's Eisenberg Institute. The book was made immeasurably better from the manuscript workshop for junior faculty, an incredible program in which colleagues and external readers gave up their time to read and comment on the manuscript. For their participation, thanks to Matt Lassiter, Matthew Countryman, Grace Hale, Mark Simpson-Vos, Gina Morantz-Sanchez, Michelle McClellan, Greg Dowd, Brandi Hughes, Geoff Eley, Elise Lipkowitz, and Yeidy Rivero.

At various stages, this book has been shaped by suggestions and input from many people, including Dan Berger, John Dittmer, Jane Dailey, Jim Grossman, Robin D. G. Kelley, Tera Hunter, Joe Crespino, Hasan Jeffries, Donna Murch, Paul Ortiz, Jim Cobb, Brenda Gayle Plummer, Kari Frederickson, Charles Reagan Wilson, Pete Daniel, Laurie Green, Steve Estes, Hannah Rosen, and Michael V. Williams. Numerous others have read versions of the manuscript in part or in whole and offered valuable feedback, including Grace Hale, Matt Lassiter, Matthew Countryman, Martha Jones, Jason Morgan Ward, Anthony Mora, Melinda Pash, Brandi Hughes, and Matt Guterl. Special thanks go to Elise Lipkowitz and Hussein Fancy for their regular feedback and for holding me accountable every week without fail. I am especially grateful to Yeidy Rivero for reading the manuscript in every form it has taken and for providing both advice and friendship.

In conducting research, my work has been aided by generous support from various institutions. A fellowship at the James Weldon Johnson Institute at Emory University came at a crucial time and provided me with a sabbatical year to complete revisions. At an earlier stage I benefited from a grant from the John Hope Franklin Research Center for African and African American History and Culture at Duke University.

Both the University of Texas and the Eisenberg Institute at the University of Michigan provided fellowship support.

Knowledgeable and helpful archivists and librarians made the research easier and more enjoyable. I am grateful to the staffs at the Mississippi Department of Archives and History in Jackson, the Southern Historical Collection at the Wilson Library at the University of North Carolina at Chapel Hill, the Rare Book and Manuscript Library at Duke University, the Center for Oral History and Cultural Heritage and the William David McCain Library and Archives (named for one of the men instrumental in keeping African Americans out of that institution in the late 1950s and early 1960s) at the University of Southern Mississippi, the Margaret Walker Center at Jackson State University, and the L. Zenobia Coleman Library at Tougaloo College. I appreciate the help I have received from Jan Hillegas, who has been an invaluable source of information on Mississippi and the civil rights movement. For their assistance in organizing my research, I am thankful for the efforts of two students I recruited from my seminar on race and culture, Korbin Felder and Jeanine Gonzalez. A thanks also goes to Michelle Manno for her timely assistance in the book's final stages. I have especially appreciated the interest, commitment, and editorial skill from editor Mark Simpson-Vos and the staff at the University of North Carolina Press.

Writing is often a lonely enterprise, and I have been fortunate to have some welcome distractions from that process from friends and family. I am thankful especially for the support of my late father and my mother, Bob and Bonnie, and my siblings, K. D., Mark, and Susan. I met Emily Richmond when I was deep into the revising process, and as I was finishing this book we were getting engaged and then married. I have regularly taken advantage of her talents as a writer and editor. I have no doubt also taken advantage of her patience and good humor. On a daily basis, she is a reminder of how rich and full life is away from this book. For all the clarity she has brought to my writing, she has brought even more clarity to my life. And for that, I am grateful every day.

THE JIM CROW ROUTINE

DE SOTO
BENTON
ALCORN
TISHOMINGO
TUNICA
MARSHALL
TIPPAH
TATE
PRENTISS
UNION
PANOLA
LAFAYETTE
•Oxford
LEE
•Tupelo
PONTOTOC
ITAWAMBA
COAHOMA
•Clarksdale
QUITMAN
YALOBUSHA
CALHOUN
CHICKASAW
MONROE
TALLAHATCHIE
BOLIVAR
SUNFLOWER
LEFLORE
•Money
GRENADA
WEBSTER
CLAY
•Greenwood
MONTGOMERY
•Greenville
CARROLL
Starkville•
•Columbus•
WASHINGTON
HUMPHREYS
HOLMES
CHOCTAW
OKTIBBEHA
LOWNDES
ATTALA
•Lexington
WINSTON
NOXUBEE
SHARKEY
•Yazoo City
LEAKE
YAZOO
NESHOBA
KEMPER
ISSAQUENA
MADISON
WARREN
NEWTON
LAUDERDALE
•Vicksburg
SCOTT
Meridian
•
★Jackson
HINDS
RANKIN
CLAIBORNE
SMITH
JASPER
CLARKE
COPIAH
SIMPSON
JEFFERSON
COVINGTON
•Laurel
•Natchez
LAWRENCE
JEFFERSON
DAVIS
JONES
WAYNE
ADAMS
FRANKLIN
LINCOLN
WILKINSON
AMITE
•McComb
MARION
•Hattiesburg
GREENE
LAMAR
FORREST
PIKE
WALTHALL
PERRY
GEORGE
PEARL RIVER
STONE
HANCOCK
HARRISON
JACKSON
Gulfport•
•Biloxi

0   50   100 MILES

INTRODUCTION
Living Jim Crow

The novelist Richard Wright, who was born on a plantation near Natchez, Mississippi, and spent much of his childhood in Jackson, Mississippi, and Memphis, Tennessee, recounted how he navigated a dangerous racial world in the 1937 essay, "The Ethics of Living Jim Crow." Two experiences in particular highlight the racialized nature of his daily existence. In the first, Wright described how he borrowed books from a whites-only public library. He approached the librarian with a note—ostensibly written by a white patron—that read, "Please let this nigger boy have the following books." As the librarian retrieved the books, Wright explained, he stood "hat in hand, looking as unbookish as possible." The second moment came on an elevator full of white people. Wright had an armful of packages, and as he boarded, a white man reached up and removed Wright's hat. Wright then faced a dilemma. If he had thanked the man, it would have conveyed that they were social equals, a risky breach of racial etiquette that he believed could provoke a violent reaction. The appropriate Jim Crow response—the one that Wright assumed the white passengers expected—was for him to offer a side-glance and a grin, which he found distasteful and demeaning. Confronted with these two unappealing options, Wright struck upon a third one: "I immediately—no sooner than my hat was lifted—pretended that my packages were about to spill, and appeared deeply distressed with keeping them in my arms." The distraction freed him from having to acknowledge the white man.[1]

In each of these seemingly uneventful moments, Wright was performing race. In his words, he "pretended," he "appeared," and he tried "looking" a particular way. His two enactments, though, were quite different. In the library, he took on the expected role of blackness, portraying deference and meekness for entrance into a world of knowledge formally closed to black Southerners. The future novelist tried to look "unbookish" for an audience—the library clerk—and Wright believed he could gain access to the books only if the clerk accepted the authenticity

1

of his performance and believed that he really was running an errand for a white man. In the elevator, Wright explicitly rejected the deferential role he had chosen to play in the library. Before these white spectators, whom Wright assumed would inflict physical violence on him for the wrong performance, he chose to enact clumsiness and to use his body to appear "deeply distressed" about his packages. In these two episodes, Wright painted a portrait of a Jim Crow world of audiences and actors. It was a world in which blacks and whites regularly interacted in spaces where they were close enough to see, hear, and touch each other. Each entered these spaces expected to play a particular role, to adhere to a particular racial routine. But, as Wright revealed, the script could be manipulated and revised, altering the boundaries and meanings of those spaces and altering the meanings of whiteness and blackness for individual subjects.

Later, and perhaps somewhat less obviously, Wright's written narrative also served as a discursive performance related to, but distinct from, the physical enactments in the library and elevator. The story allowed for another opportunity to frame the events, to draw the reader's attention to some elements—such as a hat or a subtle grin—and even to revise the events. Thus, the witnesses in the elevator may have seen a moment of clumsiness rather than a black man refusing to play the expected deferential role. For an audience of national readers, however, Wright's actions became performances of deception and cleverness. In addition, in the retelling, Wright could include hypothetical or imagined outcomes, such as the white man beating the black man for giving the wrong response. We do not know how the white man or others on the elevator would have reacted, but in the retelling, Wright positioned violence at the center of an encounter that ultimately did not include any actual physical aggression. Finally, Wright's published essay may have represented one of many versions of these events. Perhaps he discussed it with friends or others, and, depending on the audience, he may have framed these moments to emphasize caution or cunning or something else. Regardless, both Wright's experience and his retelling of it reveal the deeply performative nature of Jim Crow in the everyday realm and the multiple meanings and readings embodied in even the most mundane interactions between African Americans and whites.

The term "Jim Crow" commonly refers to a system that preserved white supremacy from the late nineteenth century to the mid-twentieth century. Laws, customs, and force maintained this racialized structure.

Jim Crow's most familiar features—segregated spaces, racial discrimination, disfranchisement, and lynching—functioned together to solidify and extend white political and economic power.[2] Although Jim Crow is more closely associated with the South, it was a national institution in which the practices and policies that protected white privilege varied by region.[3] And while scholars have most often understood Jim Crow as a legal and political system, it was also, as Richard Wright's experiences suggest, a cultural one that revolved around daily performances of race.[4]

The Jim Crow Routine explores race relations and the everyday culture of race in Mississippi from the 1930s to the early 1960s, and it addresses two broad questions: How did blacks and whites "live Jim Crow" in their daily lives? How did these experiences change as state-mandated segregation was coming to an end in the 1950s? It answers these questions by focusing on interracial interactions in the physical spaces of the everyday realm—elevators, sidewalks, buses, stores, homes, and elsewhere—and on the stories African Americans and whites told about these interactions in laws, newspapers, public speeches, published sources, and elsewhere. In the mid-1950s, as African Americans increasingly embraced another form of racial performance—one of public protest—and as white segregationists fought in vain to save their racial system, the daily racial routines and the narratives about them changed. In place of the informal encounters that defined Wright's experience on the elevator, Mississippi officials, including politicians, local officials, members of the private Citizens' Council organization, and agents of the state-run Mississippi State Sovereignty Commission, centralized and formalized the ways they policed racial lines. They turned to legal measures and practices that concealed racial intent and shifted political authority from the local to the state level. At roughly the same time, white segregationists also adjusted how they talked about race in public, transitioning from an emotionally charged and overtly racialized discourse to a more subtle and sophisticated language marked outwardly by reason, science, and statistics. These developments informed the nature of race relations in a post–Jim Crow world. The routine and how that routine changed, then, is at the center of this exploration.

The word "routine" is generally associated with a regular practice or action that is so well known by an individual that it is followed with little conscious thought. Routine implies regularity and mundaneness and suggests movement. The routine is something that the individual or individuals *do*, a set of practices put into motion. Routine is tied to repetition and predictability, and when an action is done enough times—rehearsed—it is then consistently carried out in the same way, or in nearly the same way, each time. In this regard, a routine can also be understood as a daily performance. In this book, the racial routine refers to the set of daily practices that guided the interactions between blacks and whites in Mississippi in the final decades of Jim Crow. The routines came from customs, laws, previous experiences, and beliefs about race, and they indicated how blacks and whites were *expected* to interact. At the same time, if routines suggested predictability, they could also be revised. To put it another way, on a daily basis, Jim Crow and the meanings of whiteness and blackness were ever in the process of being made, unmade, and remade in the racial interactions between blacks and whites.

Spotlighting the racial routines tells a story about Mississippi that is different from the ones we usually encounter in public memory and even in the scholarship. Mississippi is best known not for subtlety but for drama, not for delicate interactions on elevators but for staging more lynchings than any other state.[5] In the civil rights era, it is perhaps best known for the murders of Emmett Till, Medgar Evers, James Chaney, Michael Schwerner, and Andrew Goodman, among many others. As these episodes have painted Mississippi as a place of extremism, they have also contributed more broadly to a notion of Southern exceptionalism, with the region imagined as more racist and violent than the rest of the country.[6] While scholars have rightly devoted much attention to the dramatic racial moments in the South, a focus on the routines reveals other truths about how race functioned in daily life and how race changed in Mississippi and, in fact, throughout the nation in the civil rights era.

With its emphasis on the performative nature of the everyday realm, this study makes four interventions into the histories of Jim Crow, the black freedom struggle, and racial change in the post–World War II years. First, an examination of the regular interactions in Mississippi positions Jim Crow as a system of cultural exchange and power that was at once subtle and dynamic, intimate and volatile.[7] Studies of the Jim Crow South have tended to target the early period (roughly the 1880s to the 1910s), an era when the postemancipation gains made by African Americans were rolled back by a tide of white supremacy manifested in mob violence, the passage of new racially restrictive laws, the formal marking of racial spaces, and public speeches regularly warning of an uncontrolled black threat.[8] Accordingly, an emphasis on the blunt and direct features of the early period often stands in for the entire Jim Crow era, glossing over the more subtle ways race functioned in a later period and neglecting how, as Richard Wright's actions illustrate, African Americans also made and remade physical spaces and altered expected racial practices.[9] To be sure, throughout the Jim Crow years and into the 1960s, whites held a material advantage, and many dramatic demonstrations of their authority influenced race relations. At the same time and especially in the later decades, white supremacy was—to borrow a description from Jane Dailey, Glenda Elizabeth Gilmore, and Bryant Simon—less "an overwhelming force" than "a precarious balancing act, pulled in all directions by class, gender, and racial tensions."[10] Nowhere was this balancing act more prevalent than in the daily interactions between blacks and whites. On a daily basis, they worked out Jim Crow's limits and its excesses, pulling Jim Crow in one direction or another. In this regard, each encounter in the everyday realm was ripe with political meaning and energy. Attention to these interactions similarly demonstrates that Jim Crow in the South was manifested not only in overt and violent moments but also in insidious and hidden ones. Emphasis on the routines also provides opportunities to think comparatively and nationally about race, especially as scholars of the urban North and West have more fully considered the subtle and less visible dynamics of Jim Crow.[11]

Second, the story of African Americans negotiating the daily performative expectations created by Jim Crow's white architects is part of the larger story of the black freedom struggle. A significant body of scholarship has argued that a long civil rights movement materialized around critical national developments in the 1930s and 1940s, including the radical organizing of the New Deal years, an emerging climate of racial liberalism that inspired civil rights reforms, and the changing relationship between the federal government and the South and between the federal government and citizens. Studies of these early years of the movement have focused especially on the role of national and regional organizations, such as the NAACP and the Southern Conference for Human Welfare, on the court battles and collective action of various groups, and on labor organizing outside the South.[12] The everyday routines explored in this book tell their own story about this long freedom struggle. In the years before local people attended civil rights meetings, joined demonstrations, and registered to vote, black Mississippians laid a foundation of militancy and self-definition in their regular responses to Jim Crow and the stories they told about those encounters.[13] A focus on the routines of African Americans connects their daily performances and narratives—about deference, about sly deception, and often about militancy—to the performances of public protest in the 1950s and 1960s.

Third, attention to Jim Crow routines in the 1950s reveals that white Mississippi officials responded to the desegregation challenge by adjusting their own racial practices and discourses. Early studies often described the segregationist response as one of "massive resistance," a term that initially referred to a limited legal strategy to prevent school desegregation.[14] As a term that came to describe the entire defense of Jim Crow, however, massive resistance not only implied a united white Southern populace, but it also suggested a straightforward response linked to overtly racist rhetoric and the tactics of bold defiance. A more recent generation of scholars has instead found a diversity of responses and attitudes among white Southerners. In Atlanta, white responses to desegregation, notes Kevin Kruse, varied by class, by time, and by the racial composition of the neighborhood.[15] In suburban Atlanta and Charlotte, white citizens defended segregation practices not through a racialized rhetoric but rather through a class-based discourse that invoked racial innocence.[16] Similarly, focusing on the electoral realm in Mississippi, Joseph Crespino contends that segregationists, and especially racially moderate politicians, "initiated a subtle and strategic accommodation" that positioned the state within a national "conservative counterrevolution."[17] Collectively, this scholarship captures a diverse white South and reveals the dynamic and flexible nature of segregationists. In this study, I build on this work to illustrate the deeper shifts within the racial culture of the everyday realm. Attention to how Mississippi segregationists—including hardliners—adapted their racial routines tells a story of a sophisticated transition into a post–Jim Crow world.[18] Before losing the battle over state-sanctioned segregation, Mississippi officials were already adopting racial practices and discourses that would have been familiar in any region of the nation.

Fourth, Mississippi's turn to state-enforced racial control should be situated within national transformations in policing and criminalization in the post–World War II years. In the urban North and

West, even as civil rights activists found some support for overturning discriminatory practices, other developments would substantially reshape race relations. At the local level, the war years witnessed an upsurge in racial tensions, related in part to a steadily increasing migration of black Southerners into Northern cities and hardening racial attitudes within white populations. In New York City, officials expanded the authority of the police, leading to a dramatic increase in police brutality and deaths of African Americans.[19] Oakland, California, endured similar shifts, and law enforcement agencies responded by formalizing their systems, turning to modern equipment, and involving more individuals in the policing process, such as judges, probation officers, and child guidance specialists. As historian Donna Murch contends, Oakland reflected a national trend toward "legalistic" policing in which the authority and reach of the police steadily extended into people's everyday lives.[20] These measures would have an especially adverse effect on nonwhite and poor populations. Not only were these groups more likely to be targeted, but these policing practices also fueled public discourses that criminalized them and positioned them as a threat to law and order.[21]

In the mid-1950s, in response to racial challenges in their state, Mississippi officials adopted similar strategies around policing and criminalization. Officials increasingly relied on state agents and law enforcement officials and adopted new laws designed to conceal racial practices within the legal structure. In defending Jim Crow, segregationists also tapped into a nationally familiar language of black criminality. While these efforts did not save segregation, in another sense the transition to a new racial language and more centralized practices succeeded. The Jim Crow stage was not torn down, it was simply refashioned with blacks and whites cast in different but still unequal roles. Since the 1950s, even as the media steadfastly portrayed the South—and in particular Mississippi—as more racist and more violent than the rest of the nation, Mississippi had turned to racial discourses and practices that would have been familiar in any region of the country. Ultimately, then, in terms of the black freedom struggle and the transition to a post–Jim Crow world, some aspects of the Mississippi experience were unique, as a great deal of violence accompanied the processes of racial change. In other critical ways, however, Mississippi was part of, not aberrant to, the larger racial transformations of modern America.

THE CONCEPT OF performance anchors my discussion of racial routines in Mississippi.[22] Various intellectuals and scholars have alluded to theatrical elements to make sense of relations between the races. From Paul Laurence Dunbar's 1896 poem "We Wear the Mask" to Ralph Ellison's 1952 novel *Invisible Man*, many great works of the African American literary canon depict a racial system in which blacks were expected to play a particular role around whites, such as to grin and lie in the presence of whites in order to conceal their true feelings. African Americans played the part in the name of self-protection, but such enactments could also have a psychological effect, rendering the black individual virtually invisible.[23] In the 1930s, sociologist Bertram Wilbur Doyle relied on the concept of racial etiquette to describe "the behavior that is expected and accepted when white and colored persons meet or associate."[24] Doyle's work, which considered relations during and after enslavement, was especially innovative in that it was one of the few studies at the time or since to recognize that Jim Crow established rules of interaction for both races.[25] Since the 1930s, scholars have regularly returned to dramaturgical metaphors to illustrate racial interactions.[26] I draw on these discussions in this study, but I also extend the concept of performance further to analyze race relations in Mississippi.

Influenced by the work of Erving Goffman, I consider here the detailed ways in which Jim Crow created roles and expectations for both blacks and whites. In the 1950s, Goffman, a sociologist, embraced the terminology of the theater to explain how individuals interacted in daily life. He used the term "performance" to refer "to all the activity of an individual which occurs during a period marked by his continuous presence before a particular set of observers and which has some influence on the observers."[27] In essence, Goffman contended that whenever two or more people were present, each individual presented himself in a specific way to make an impression on the other person or persons, and those other persons constituted the audience who interpreted that expression. The expression included verbal lines as well as tones, gestures, clothing, and other props. In these encounters, the observer was both an audience member and a participant who likewise was expressing himself and making an impression on the other individual. The role of an individual varied by context because an individual was likely to present himself differently if the audience member was, for instance, a close friend, a judge in a courtroom, a stranger at a bar, or a priest in a confessional.

Goffman noted that the various ways of presenting oneself were not random but rather followed a "pre-established pattern of action," what he calls a "part" or a "routine" and what we may think of as an expected way of acting in a given situation that is agreed upon by the participants and audience.[28] Individuals, then, enter an interaction with an expectation for how to perform and with an expectation for how the other individual will perform. Goffman's concept captures a world governed by scripts and routines. Yet if that metaphor suggests stasis, with everyone following predetermined roles, other aspects of these encounters point to something much more dynamic. As Goffman noted, while interactions revolve around expected routines, the "performance is a delicate, fragile thing that can be shattered by very minor mishaps."[29]

The shattering of an expected performance might come from someone playing the wrong part such as knowingly or unknowingly delivering the wrong lines. For example, Richard Wright saying "thank you" to a white man would have been the wrong line and, based on the script, a mishap. The fragility of the performance can also be broken through intentional manipulation or misrepresentation. That is, the performer can dupe the audience as Wright did when he pretended that his packages were falling. Accordingly, the notion of performance is useful not only because it can reveal how race worked and how racial expectations informed the daily lives for both blacks and whites, but it can also reveal the ways in which this racial system continually had to be remade, with seemingly infinite possibilities for mishaps and manipulation. Certainly, white people and black people did not enter these interactions as social equals, and the consequences for mishaps and manipulation could be far more severe for African Americans. At the same time, on a daily basis, the Jim Crow balancing act tilted one way or another in response to even the most minor and mundane of mishaps and manipulations on the part of black people and white people. The concept of performance, then, sheds light on the expectations and the disruptions that defined these encounters and regularly re-created Jim Crow. It similarly provides a means for understanding how the racial routines changed in the civil rights era.[30]

In my exploration of Mississippi, I consider two types of performance, one physical and the other narrative. The physical performance refers to the in-person interactions between blacks and whites. The stage, with its physical construction of racially specific signs and barriers (props), materialized wherever blacks and whites interacted, including even "segregated" spaces such as libraries, schools, and buses, as well as spaces with no or few visible racial barriers such as elevators, sidewalks, and homes. Blacks and whites entered these stages with scripts—anticipated lines and stage directions for what to say and how to move—derived from laws, customs, community instruction, and previous experience. In these encounters, the audience members were also participants, with each observing and reacting to the performance of the other.

The narrative performance refers to the stories black Mississippians, white Mississippians, and others told about race and the South. Examples include published accounts, such as Wright's essay on living Jim Crow, David L. Cohn's book-length essay explaining the "Delta Negro," and newspaper coverage of lynchings and racial conflicts, as well as oral accounts of African Americans sharing stories about white violence and black militancy and the propaganda brochures and speeches from segregationist organizations.[31] Especially important by the 1950s, these narratives also came from the national media—via photographs, articles, and television footage—as well as from civil rights activists and segregationists. Each told particular stories about race and the South to local and national audiences. These narrative performances, like the physical ones, imagined particular roles and scripts for blacks and whites, and these stories also had an audience, whether it was the local community or the national public. Unlike the physical encounter, however, in these enactments the narrator had more control over the characters. Depending on who was telling the story, blacks could be imagined as contented servants, as criminals, as victims, or as heroes. Whites, meanwhile, could be imagined in these narratives as violent racists, as paternalists, or as victims. The various stories about race and the South represented competing narratives within a larger battle to explain and legitimate a particular vision of the world, and they were as important in defining a Jim Crow world as were the daily enactments in physical space. Both the physical and the narrative forms of these interactions are central to understanding everyday race relations in Mississippi in the 1930s, 1940s, and 1950s.

On these Jim Crow stages, individual physical and narrative performances came together and contributed to a much larger production. That production, I contend, revolved around interracial intimacy. No doubt, Jim Crow Mississippi was a violent place, and some individuals espoused a rhetoric of racial hatred and preferred complete racial separation.[32] But at its ideological core, Jim Crow was a world of intimacy, of blacks and whites living within the same society as (unequal) members of a larger family. Mississippi was not alone in this regard. Across the South in the late nineteenth century, even as white Southerners erected racial barriers, from Virginia to Tennessee to Mississippi, they also passed laws and enforced customs that preserved a great deal of interaction between the races. These interactions depended on performances and were tied to two idealized racial roles that emerged from a longer cultural tradition in the state and the region. The white person assumed the part of the master, as a paternalist who protected, disciplined, and cared for black people. The black person played the role of the loving servant who was always loyal to white people and who preferred segregation.[33] These expected performances regulated interactions through various forms of physical intimacy. A working-class white man cutting in front of a black man in a line at a store was not the same thing as a wealthy white woman interacting with her black maid, and yet both encounters were intimate. Jim Crow created regular opportunities for performances of an intimacy intertwined with white supremacy. Of course, not everyone could play or wanted to play these roles, and one finds competing visions of this imagined world, especially within the black community. Nonetheless, this idea of an interracial intimacy drove the daily experiences of blacks and whites in Jim Crow's final decades.[34]

As the daily production of an interracial intimacy anchored the Jim Crow performance, other racial performances disrupted these roles in the late 1950s. Both the enactments of protest staged by African Americans and national media narratives that showed angry, hateful white Southerners physically attacking black Southerners undermined stories of intimacy and harmony. Segregationists responded by adjusting the racial routines of the everyday realm. In place of a racial system regulated primarily in the informal interactions between white citizens and black citizens, officials centralized the process and expanded the roles for police officers, state investigative agents, politicians, lawyers, judges, and other official agents of the state. These performances of race and authority reflected a more formalized racial system where the law and the legal structure became more important. The changing racial roles also produced other racial narratives, which tapped into a longer tradition from Reconstruction and, before that, from slavery, of linking blackness to deviance.[35] Stories defined by interracial intimacy competed with stories that suggested distance and that imagined African Americans not as loyal family members but as ungrateful and immoral and as criminal threats to the white population. Unlike the earlier narratives of intimacy, the emerging post–Jim Crow narratives imagined blacks and whites at odds with each other and especially positioned black people and black criminality as a danger to the nation. These narratives drew on national discourses, and they demonstrated a national convergence in public conversations about race. In this way, practices and discourses preserved white privilege and racial disparities in new forms. The emerging racial system brought together diverse white populations across regional lines—framed, for example, through fears of black criminality and opposition to affirmative action—just as the old Jim Crow routines had served to gloss over differences among whites in the South and within Mississippi.

THE JIM CROW STAGE and its performances established a fairly standard set of expected behaviors for blacks and for whites across a diverse state. From the 1930s to the 1950s, the black population and the white population in Mississippi were nearly equal, with blacks barely constituting a majority (50.2 percent) in 1930 and whites holding on to a slim majority (50.7 percent) a decade later.[36] With only twelve towns with populations greater than 10,000 people as of 1940, Mississippi was the most rural state in the South, and that ruralness informed the state's economic and political life.[37] The largest percentage of African Americans were in the Mississippi-Yazoo Delta, and in some counties blacks comprised an overwhelming majority.[38] The Delta stretches approximately one hundred miles along the Mississippi River from Memphis to the north and Vicksburg and Jackson to the south, bulging in the middle. Initially, this swampy, tree-covered landscape concealed a rich black soil, and, once cleared, it supported massive cotton production. That labor-intensive work required a large workforce, which initially came from enslaved labor and after emancipation shifted to sharecropping by both black farmers and white farmers. The region was one of extremes, of a wealthy and politically powerful planter elite alongside impoverished sharecroppers, where one of the nation's most ardent and powerful segregationists—Senator James Eastland—lived within a few miles of sharecropper-turned-civil-rights-leader Fannie Lou Hamer.[39] Because of the rich and extensive available sources, the Delta figures a little more prominently than other regions in the following pages.

Evidence from other areas, however, illustrates that the performative nature of Jim Crow informed race relations throughout the state.

In the hill region to the north and east of the Delta, the black population was much smaller. This region, spanning from the hills in the north to the pinelands in the south, featured soil much less fertile than that of the Delta. The population included many small landowning farmers, tenant farmers, and poor whites. These differences in agricultural labor in the two regions regularly played out within the political realm, with Delta planters in alliance with commercial and industrial elites against the small farmers in the east. Thus, class-based tension and struggles over political and economic power often marked the relationship between the Delta and the hills.[40] In spite of the relatively fewer number of African Americans in the east, substantial black communities and institutions emerged in larger towns in the pinelands and became important sites for civil rights organizing, including in Hattiesburg, Laurel, and Meridian.

Jackson, the capital and the largest city in the state, grew rapidly in the last three decades of Jim Crow, increasing from about 23,000 people in 1920 to nearly 100,000 by 1950. It also had the largest black community in the state, much of it centered around the Farish Street District, home of numerous black businesses and professionals where African Americans had some independence from white influence, a relatively typical Southern urban pattern.[41] The city was home to the most widely circulating newspapers in the state, including, in the 1950s, the *Clarion-Ledger* and the *Jackson Daily News*, both owned by forceful advocates of segregation, and the racially more moderate *State Times*, which began operations in 1955. In addition, the *Jackson Advocate*, the largest circulating black-owned newspaper in the state, had, at least until the late 1950s, a reputation for being critical of segregation.[42] Into the 1960s, Jackson remained a relatively small city, but it was large enough to provide greater autonomy for its African American citizens than did other parts of the state.

The southwest corner of Mississippi, along the Louisiana border, had a much greater ratio of white residents to black residents than Jackson and the Delta. Nonetheless, this area supported a significant number of black landowners, who had a measure of economic independence from local white elites. Accordingly, as a means of control over relatively independent African Americans, this region had a well-earned reputation for racial vigilantism. The White Caps, a vigilante group engaged in terrorism and night riding, formed in this region in the late nineteenth century. In the 1950s, the Ku Klux Klan was especially strong here, and in the 1960s, the Americans for the Preservation of the White Race, a group claiming to be nonviolent but engaged in harassment, formed in Natchez.[43] Last, the area along the Gulf Coast, including Biloxi and Gulfport, was, in the post–World War II era, in the process of transforming itself into a destination for tourists. Relative to other parts of the state, it had a reputation for racial moderation. It was nonetheless the scene of Mack Charles Parker's lynching in 1959, and it was also the site for important local civil rights organizing in the 1960s.[44]

On this diverse landscape, Mississippi's history in the last decades of Jim Crow and the civil rights years is a complicated one. Similar to the rest of the South and the nation, World War II represented a turning point for civil rights efforts in the state, including an upswing in local activism often led by returning military veterans.[45] A decade later as groups across the country steadily mobilized against Jim Crow practices, national civil rights organizations generally avoided Mississippi, preferring instead to make inroads first in places that seemed less severe and less violent. Nonetheless, despite these harsh realities, within the state, black Mississippians and their allies were organizing and planning.[46] Many of them, drawing on a long tradition, embraced an ideology of armed self-defense.[47] Even as the state had earned a reputation for racial violence, it was also a place where African Americans took up guns and sometimes fought back, a dramatic performance of aggression that can be positioned alongside the subtler daily enactments, such as juggling packages on an elevator. In various ways, then, African Americans challenged Jim Crow norms and altered relations between the races. In this regard, too, Jim Crow Mississippi was a place of extremes and seeming contradictions.

Amid the complexities of this state, an exploration of daily racial performances and routines has posed a number of challenges related to sources. One approach to researching the everyday realm and its relationship to social movements is to search out what James C. Scott refers to as the "hidden transcripts," that is, the challenges to domination that are hidden within the realm of everyday culture, including in songs, gestures, jokes, stories, and elsewhere.[48] In terms of historical research, this notion of transcripts can be useful not only for looking for resistance but also for understanding the routines and the expectations and disruptions that are both visible and hidden within the movements and interactions of daily life. Most historical studies of Mississippi in the 1950s have emphasized political movements for racial change and have thus relied on the records of major figures and organizations. My approach, in contrast, has been to cast a wider net and search not only for evidence of the dramatic events but also for the evidence of the more mundane workings of the racial system, such as how blacks and whites interacted while waiting in line at a store or riding an elevator, or in how white individuals spoke fondly of a black domestic worker. I certainly examine the more dramatic events, such as the death of Emmett Till, the arrest of the Freedom Riders, and the 1954 shootings by African American Eddie Noel, but in each case my interest has been primarily in how black Mississippians and white Mississippians talked about and made sense of these events. In examining the newspapers, the language of various laws, published stories from the period, propaganda materials from segregationists, and surveillance records, I have paid particular attention to how various authors described and imagined the racial routines of their daily lives.

Oral history, an especially useful source, requires additional explanation. Even as they have become central to studies of the civil rights movement, oral histories are nonetheless tricky historical records. If the goal is to secure specific facts—what happened when and where—memories of participants have proven to be unreliable.[49] Beyond issues of forgetting or remembering details incorrectly, oral histories can also be influenced by subsequent events or by the present moment in which they are conducted. For example, oral histories of civil rights activists conducted in the 1970s during the women's rights movement included lengthy discussions of sexism within civil rights organizations. Those issues were downplayed in later interviews. Additionally, black women were much less likely than white women to mention sexism in organizations.[50]

Alongside these concerns, however, oral histories have a number of strengths that outweigh the limitations of more traditional sources.[51] Sometimes they can reveal the historical silences left by other sources, and that is especially true for groups—such as the oppressed, the poor, and the illiterate—who are underrepresented or misrepresented in traditional sources found in the archives.[52] When, for example, media scholar Steven Classen was investigating the local black response to the Jackson television station's coverage of racial issues in the 1960s, he was surprised to find little evidence of protest in the archives, including in the records of the Federal Communications Commission. It was only when he talked to individuals in the community that he learned of an extensive series of protests against the station during these years.[53] More than detail or nuance, then, oral histories can compel us to reconsider the accepted narrative. Another strength of oral histories is that even when the historical facts are remembered incorrectly, interviews with historical participants can reveal other, deeper truths, such as reflecting larger themes of thought for an era. That is, the individual can summarize her or his experience and identify patterns and impressions across a particular period.[54] In this regard, oral histories are ideal for exploring the everyday realm and for uncovering patterns in how black Mississippians and white Mississippians imagined Jim Crow.

In conducting research for this project, I read or listened to more than 600 previously collected interviews with historical participants. Approximately 200 of them were particularly useful in shedding light on everyday racial routines. To mitigate some of the potential weaknesses of these sources, I adopted a diverse approach. I examined interviews with African Americans and whites. Some of them were activists or segregationist leaders while others were ordinary citizens. The interview subjects vary greatly in terms of age at the time of the interview, the date and place of birth, class, education, and vocation. Mirroring the range of experiences of the interviewees was the variations among the interviewers and the projects that inspired the oral histories. The dates of the interviews span from the 1970s to the early 2000s. There were black and white interviewers, including professors, graduate students, undergraduates, and even high school students. These interviews were conducted for historical projects with varied agendas, including the civil rights movement in Mississippi or in specific counties, the Jim Crow experience for black Mississippians, the cultural and social history of a specific neighborhood or county, the political history of the segregation defense, and white reactions and resistance to integration. Where possible, I have substantiated broad themes and specific details that emerge from the oral histories. I have also found that the errors or skewed themes in the oral histories can be useful. For example, within the oral histories, accounts of black militancy are overwhelmingly about black males fighting back, even as other accounts of the period suggest that militancy was prevalent across gender lines.[55] Rather than ignore those discrepancies or throw out the evidence of militancy, I found these gender implications invaluable in illustrating how these participants made sense of their racial world.

WITH AN INTEREST IN the everyday performances that defined the last decades of Jim Crow in Mississippi, the book begins by explaining how these racial stages were constructed within the legal and cultural realms. I first explore the laws and customs that came together to produce a physical and conceptual world of signs and barriers. Examining how white and black Mississippians moved through this world, I argue that these boundaries conditioned specific performances of whiteness and blackness attached to an ideology of interracial intimacy, though participants sometimes adhered to and sometimes disrupted the script. Next, I assess stories about race and violence from whites and from African Americans to consider the narrative performances that gave meaning to the Jim Crow world. Those stories, which often functioned as competing narratives, emerged from actual lynchings and killings by whites or by blacks and from fictionalized, or imagined, acts of aggression and militancy.

The next three chapters spotlight the 1950s to address how race changed and how the civil rights movement and the end of state-mandated segregation generated new racial performances and new racial narratives, particularly around animosity and black criminality. I first consider racial surveillance, broadly defined as the ways in which segregationists monitored racial lines. By the late 1950s, an informal and highly personal system tied to the daily interactions was being replaced by a much more formal and secretive system that depended on professionals and official agents of the state, and much of the surveillance activity revolved initially around the Mississippi State Sovereignty Commission, a state-funded organization created in 1956 to preserve segregation. Building on these transformations in how officials literally watched black citizens in daily life, the next chapter addresses the state's growing reliance on arrests and new laws during the civil rights era as both a response to increased activism and a new approach to policing racial lines. The police and the law would each play an expanded role in a post–Jim Crow world. In the final chapter, I return to narrative performances and consider the stories about race and the South being told during the civil rights era. Competing claims about race and the South produced a segregationist narrative that positioned not only African Americans but all "nonwhite" groups in the United States and beyond as a threat to the nation and to white civilization.

In recent years, public interest in the civil rights movement has steadily grown, and much is at stake in how the 1950s and 1960s is remembered as an era of racial change. Some have narrowly pointed to the movement's successes, such as the end of legal segregation and increases in black voting, and have suggested that the South and the nation have overcome their racial past. Numerous politicians, critics, and others have simultaneously celebrated the civil rights movement and argued that affirmative action and voter protection laws are no longer necessary. This narrative of a "postracial" America overlooks the ways in which racism changed and survived the legal demise of Jim Crow. It misses the persistence of racial violence and racial inequalities, especially in terms of criminalization and mass incarceration. Indeed, misperceptions of Jim Crow racism and the movement that challenged it point to a continuing need to revisit this earlier moment of change. The following pages address these concerns in Mississippi by suggesting that one way to understand the racial transformations is to follow the daily racial routines of African Americans and whites across time.

1

INTIMATE SPACES

Performance and the Making of Jim Crow

H. A. Scott Sr. was born in the mid-1920s in the Mississippi Delta town of Yazoo City. His father worked in a sawmill six days a week; his mother was employed at a steam factory for dry cleaning. Scott has vivid memories of growing up in the Jim Crow South. Like many other Mississippians on both sides of the racial line, he remembers black and white children playing together. He remembers too that white people addressed him as "boy," and that this moniker stayed with him even after he reached adulthood. Some of Scott's most intriguing memories, however, relate to physical space. He recalls that some places had a double-sided door, two entrances side by side, "one for white and one for black." The doors then opened into a larger area divided only by a row of stools separating the space for whites and the space for blacks. As Scott explains, "You could see each other but there was a space between you."[1]

Scott may be thinking about one place in particular or perhaps a composite of many places. Regardless, his description captures a compelling visual image of the geography of segregation. On the one hand, the stools hint at the significance of lines, important enough that in the absence of a full wall, something tangible was deemed necessary to divide these two spaces. On the other hand, one might wonder about a line of stools' qualifications for being a barrier. One can imagine that these stools could have been easily moved or knocked over, and that individuals on either side could have accidentally or intentionally nudged these stools, adding space to one side as space was subtracted from the other. But even if no one moved the stools, even if those stools had been bolted down, they still could not have fully separated black people from white people. Lines of vision and presumably voices would have effortlessly crossed the space between. Thus, if the stools split the larger area, they nonetheless preserved a black presence and a white presence within that area; the stools allowed for a separated togetherness. Ultimately, then, Scott's description spotlights two intertwined components of segregation. Explicitly, he directs our attention to the physicality of this racial system and has us wondering, like Richard Wright in the elevator with his hat and his packages, about the props and the other material things of this segregation stage. Implicitly, he also pushes us to think about these black people and white people looking across the stools and seeing each other.

The space that Scott looked out upon was part of a racial geography that had been forged a generation earlier. In the 1880s and 1890s, new laws firmed up racial lines and in the process made segregation more official and more permanent. Tied to customs of racial separation that extended back into the period of enslavement and to the black codes of the postemancipation period, the earliest legislation targeted physical spaces. In 1881, Tennessee passed the first state segregation law pertaining to travel, a measure applied to railcars and which was in part a response to discrimination and the mistreatment of first-class black passengers. The law required railroad companies to provide "separate cars, or portions of cars cut off by partition wall" for black passengers with first-class tickets.[2] Seven years later, Mississippi passed legislation requiring separate accommodations in sleeping cars and railroad rooms. White legislators believed that this measure was simply reflecting what was already being practiced.[3] Nonetheless, in the last two decades of the nineteenth century and extending into the new century, states and municipalities across the region enacted scores of laws and ordinances that mandated racialized public spaces with racial boundaries on trains, in waiting rooms, on streetcars, in places of leisure such as movie theaters and ballparks, in restaurants, and in countless other places. Legal measures served as a blueprint that altered the physical landscape of the region. White Southerners erected walls and other types of partitions, they put up curtains and constructed dual entrances, and an entire industry sprang up to mass-produce racial signage for "whites only" and "colored" spaces.[4]

It was no coincidence that white Southerners pushed through legal measures targeting physical spaces during this period. Following generations of enslavement, African Americans occupied new spaces, and they also occupied familiar spaces in new ways. During the Reconstruction years, African Americans populated polling booths and the legislative halls of state government. Some of them rode on trains as first-class passengers alongside white males and females. And some walked the sidewalks ignoring the custom from the period of enslavement to step aside for approaching whites.[5] As Leon Litwack observes, by the 1870s, many white Southerners worried especially about the presence of a "New Negro" who had never been enslaved and who was perceived as more aggressive.[6] They compared this less-deferential individual to what they remembered as a faithful slave who, in contrast to this New Negro, had always—at least in their memories—looked and acted the part of a social and racial inferior.[7] In the nineteenth century, many whites increasingly found themselves in public spaces where African Americans insisted on playing the part of social equals.

Other factors also fueled white Southerners' concerns about race and space. Across the South, the growth of towns, the expansion of railroads, and a more mobile population meant that blacks and whites were ever more frequently meeting in public spaces as strangers.[8] And even if the African American stranger did not take on the role of the assertive New Negro, interracial interactions in shared space blurred the lines of difference and potentially undermined a racial hierarchy that positioned "white" as superior to and above "black." In the past, notes historian Grace Hale, slavery informed social interactions between blacks and whites and preserved the hierarchy. As long as slavery existed and was limited to one group, it marked everyone in that group as inferior. The abolition of slavery removed the defining racial distinction between black and white, and for many whites this circumstance was most unsettling where people interacted as strangers, such as on trains and in cities. Accordingly, laws served to mark space not only in response to a New Negro but also as a means to solidify racial difference. As Hale contends, segregation created and labeled spaces as inferior or superior, and by extension it then marked the people occupying these spaces.[9] Furthermore, the first segregated spaces tended to be those that allowed for especially intimate forms of physical contact, such as places for eating or sleeping, including restaurants, hotels, and homes.[10] Thus, as segregation affirmed racial hierarchies, it also created distinctions where boundaries were most fluid.

Segregation, then, can be understood as an answer to a racial question, an answer that involved the use of space to reestablish difference and hierarchy and to thwart black assertiveness. Certainly, the passage of new laws and the physical manipulation of the landscape, as well as an unprecedented wave of violence in the 1880s and 1890s, transformed these spaces and made racial lines more rigid. At the same time, Scott's recollection of two entrances and a row of stools highlights two other critical components in the making of racial space. First, even within a segregated system, African Americans and whites regularly interacted in public spaces such as in bars and on buses and in the private spaces of the home. Black Southerners and white Southerners, observes historian George Frederickson, "were too much involved with each other" to ever be sharply divided by racial boundaries.[11] Thus, an investigation of segregated space is necessarily an investigation of interracial space. Second, Scott's memory of black people and white people looking out across each other suggests that the meanings and boundaries of these spaces depended not only on the stools and the doors but also on the people themselves, and on how these people moved, interacted, gestured, and looked at each other. It is an indication, too, that segregated space had to be made daily.

Cultural geographer Doreen Massey contends that any given space is the product of interactions among people and is "formed through a myriad of practices of quotidian negotiation and contestation." Massey also makes a case for understanding spaces as unstable, in which the regular negotiations among individuals mean that spaces are "always in the process of being made."[12] Applying this notion to segregation in the U.S. South, it suggests that even as the blueprints of laws and customs and the physical materials of signs and barriers combined to form a Jim Crow stage, the meanings of that space still depended on how people daily navigated this stage. These performative components of Jim Crow indicate too, as historian Thomas C. Holt argues, that race had to be made and remade in the "'ordinary' events of everyday life . . . perpetrated by 'ordinary' people."[13] Meanings of Jim Crow—of what it meant to be white and what it meant to be black—were made by what blacks and whites did and did not do as they looked at each other across a row of stools. The central point in these observations about making space and about making Jim Crow is that we can understand both blacks and whites as actors on this stage. While it is generally well known that African Americans regularly "wore the mask," pretending at deference in the interest of survival, they were not the only ones playing a part. Indeed, as Ralph Ellison noted in the 1950s, donning a mask was something white Americans had been doing at least since masquerading as Indians at the Boston Tea Party.[14]

In 1930s and 1940s Mississippi, blacks and whites performed on a Jim Crow stage that had been largely constructed decades earlier from the laws and practices of the 1880s and 1890s. This stage, however, featured daily showings. In their interactions with each other and with "props," blacks and whites remade Jim Crow with each daily performance. Focusing on Jim Crow as a series of enactments reveals one of the central features of this racial system. Many white Southerners imagined a world not of separation or isolation but rather of a particular form of racial intimacy and harmony. In that world, which was reflected in laws, customs, barriers, and expectations, they imagined whites as superior masters, as paternalists with privileges who cared for and protected black people. Meanwhile, they imagined blacks as inferior, as lazy, and as prone to mischief or crime, but also as loyal servants who loved white people and preferred segregation. These white Southerners thus tried to make real a world of white paternalists and black servants that would depend on both blacks and whites playing their respective parts.

Although we might think of a singular Jim Crow stage—one where whites and blacks were always expected to enact a particular role—the physicality of racial spaces varied widely. Across the South, the laws and customs of the late nineteenth and early twentieth centuries created and allowed for spaces formed from a range of physical materials that ultimately sustained different levels of interaction between the races. In Mississippi in the 1930s, 1940s, and 1950s, black actors and white actors entered these spaces with scripts—with expectations—for how to move, to wait, and to interact. Often these actors followed the script but sometimes they did not, and these unexpected performances by blacks and by whites served to disrupt and redefine the racial meanings of these Jim Crow spaces.

CONSTRUCTION: THE JIM CROW STAGE

In the early 1940s, noted sociologist Charles S. Johnson, an African American originally from Virginia, conducted research on segregation throughout the nation for Gunnar Myrdal's monumental exploration of race relations in the United States, *An American Dilemma*. Johnson's findings, published in 1943 as *Patterns of Negro Segregation*, included an incident about three white men who took a fishing trip with a black guide. After fishing all morning within the confines of a small boat, at lunchtime the white men placed a stick between themselves and the black guide in an effort to maintain segregated eating practices.[15] Johnson included the story as an example of how strictly Southerners adhered to segregation rules. Yet, similar to H. A. Scott's row of stools, it also represents another example of the importance of pretense in establishing a physical separation that preserved interracial togetherness. Indeed, Johnson noted that with the stick in place conversation between the black guide and the white men "took place without strain."[16] Scott's stools and Johnson's boat were necessarily about the geography and the materiality of Jim Crow, about how black Southerners and white Southerners interacted with physical space and objects and with each other.

The racial geography of the 1930s and 1940s had been largely formed in the late nineteenth century during a period of swift changes. Customs, laws, and evolving practices served as blueprints, and bricks, lumber, and paint served as the raw materials for the physical construction of barriers.[17] It was a particularly volatile and violent moment in which white Southerners and black Southerners were working out racial meanings.[18] The legacy of these early Jim Crow years—the legislation and ordinances, as well as the physical construction of signs, walls, and buildings—bequeathed a legacy to the later Jim Crow period experienced by Scott and by Johnson's fishermen. That is, they navigated a landscape that from their perspective had long ago been established. In numerous ways, however, the later Jim Crow period was quite distinct from the earlier one.[19] For instance, by the 1930s, the frequency of lynchings had declined dramatically since the 1890s and early 1900s.[20] In addition, the later generation of black Southerners and white Southerners were born into a world in which at least the broad features of Jim Crow, one that included extensive racial rules and racially marked spaces, would have seemed more or less settled or even permanent.[21] Accordingly, in examining the racial geography of the 1930s and 1940s, it is necessary to consider the legal and physical parameters that grew out of the early Jim Crow period and the particular ways in which a later generation of black Southerners and white Southerners imposed their own meanings on the landscape, which hosted widely varying levels of separation between the races.

At one end of the spectrum were the spaces of near-complete racial separation, where blacks and whites encountered each other only sporadically. Schools, churches, and the homes of African Americans, for example, tended to be racially exclusive. Some of this separation developed in the aftermath of emancipation, as African Americans, whose daily lives had been closely monitored by white masters, were eager to create their own clubs, churches, institutions, and private spaces free from white control.[22] In addition, some of the earliest laws, beginning in 1866 in Tennessee, required white students and black students to attend separate schools.[23] Still, even as segregation became more formalized in the Jim Crow era and the racial lines around these spaces more rigid, separation was often incomplete. In Mississippi, for example, white superintendents regularly monitored the activity in "colored" schools in their districts. In addition, schools for white children might employ black janitors. In the case of restaurants, many black employees worked in restaurants that were off-limits to them as customers. The extent of interaction within these spaces depended on the location. Interactions were more frequent in the Deep South, where the percentage of African American residents was much higher than in other regions. Within Mississippi, interactions were especially common in the Delta, where in some counties African Americans made up a majority.

Toward the middle of this spectrum were spaces with partial physical barriers that would have involved some level of regular interaction between blacks and whites. These were the spaces of separated togetherness, such as H. A. Scott's room bisected by a line of stools or the interior of a boat divided by a stick. Other examples of these types of spaces included buses, waiting rooms, and theaters. In these locales, blacks and whites were likely to occupy distinct but separate areas. Theater sections might be separated by a rope or with a balcony; buses and waiting rooms could be carved up with signs and curtains. These spaces often had dual entrances or separate pathways into an area. A tangible or imaginary line separated blacks from whites, but the divisions were incomplete. If, for example, blacks and whites occupied separate sections of a bus or theater, they could still hear and see each other. The level of engagement varied, but interracial interaction was a regular feature of these spaces.

At the far end of the spectrum were the spaces with few or no physical barriers, where no signs or structures marked off racially separate sections. These sites included many stores, post offices, the homes of whites, and sidewalks. Absent signs, or lines or other physical markers, these locations were the sites of interracial interactions marked by physical closeness, where white bodies and black bodies intermingled in common spaces. Thus, even if a black domestic worker ate in a separate room after whites had eaten, that worker and her employer were regularly together, next to each other, and conversing as she served them dinner, cleaned their house, and nurtured their children. In public spaces too, blacks and whites might regularly find themselves occupying the same sidewalks and the same lines in stores. In these spaces lacking a physical marker of race—such as a sign—the meaning of Jim Crow depended wholly on the behavior of the individuals. The Southern landscape was a hodgepodge of spaces across this spectrum, and many considerations played a role in limiting the extent of racial separation and thus allowing for regular interactions between blacks and whites.

Throughout the Jim Crow era, a primary consideration in creating and maintaining racial separation related to expense. In the 1880s, for example, with the passage of laws requiring railway cars for blacks and whites, legislators expected transportation companies to comply with the mandate for separate cars, adding a significant cost for these companies.[24] To accommodate the relatively small number of first-class black passengers, companies turned to a less-expensive alternative than a completely separate car. They often added partitions to a single car, which would separate black passengers and white passengers somewhat less fully than having different cars. In the 1930s, chain restaurants, which were emerging across the region, faced a similar challenge. In most locations, laws and ordinances required restaurant owners to erect walls that could create completely separate rooms. This arrangement would have replicated the eating patterns in white homes, where the white family and their black employees ate in separate rooms. However, as the Depression deepened, floor-to-ceiling walls became cost prohibitive. In response, notes Elizabeth Abel, restaurants tried creative alternatives, such as a U-shaped counter with a screen that came down inside the "U" to block customers on each side—whites on one side, blacks on the other—from seeing each other. The customers would still have been able to hear each other, and in some cases they could still partially see each other.[25] As these solutions imply, many businesses depended on support from both races and could not afford to exclude one group of customers. In these situations, the expense of total separation was impractical.[26]

In other circumstances, the lack of total separation was likely related not only to cost but also to other sources of impracticality. At Grand

Central Station in Houston, Texas, for example, blacks and whites had their own waiting rooms, but there was only one bag check service and one newsstand. Both were in the white waiting room, and while blacks were not allowed to "wait" in the white area, they were permitted to move through it to check their bags or make a purchase from the newsstand.[27] In many smaller towns, segregation practices were even more relaxed. In towns without a freestanding bus terminal, passengers purchased tickets and waited for buses at "terminals" inside other establishments, such as an auto garage, a drugstore, or some other business. Many of these buildings contained no separate sections, and black passengers bought tickets inside the building and then waited outside. In a station in Johnson County, North Carolina, whites and blacks both waited outside in a common area unmarked by any signs.[28] In smaller towns, as evidenced by the various businesses that doubled as bus stations, local officials likely balked at the extra expense involved in separating these facilities. At the same time, it is clear that individuals in these towns did not desire separate spaces enough to require it or pay for it.

The courtroom was another site that in its physical features allowed for various forms of interracial interactions. In the courts in Nashville, for example, blacks and whites could sit in the same row—blacks on one side, whites on the other—as long as they maintained an extra space between the races. Birmingham courts, meanwhile, had no racially designated sections, although blacks and whites were not allowed to sit in the same row.[29] In these places, then, the operating principle was guided by preventing intermingling among blacks and whites, and that allowed for spaces of separated togetherness. Another space likely to be a racially interactive one was the rural country store. In the interest of financial success, many stores depended on black customers and white customers and catered to both.[30] Sometimes interracial clientage was accomplished by dividing the space temporally. For instance, in a country store in the Mississippi Delta that doubled as a juke joint, whites used the space early in the evening and blacks later in the evening. At any given time, however, whites and blacks could be in the store at the same time. In each of these spaces, creating and maintaining totally or even mostly separate spaces was cost prohibitive and not deemed important enough to warrant the cost.[31] Similarly, throughout much of the rural South, whites and blacks patronized the same country stores, commissaries, and many other places.[32]

Patrons dancing at a juke joint in Clarksdale, Mississippi, November 1939. Library of Congress, Prints and Photographs Division, Washington, D.C. (LC-USF34-052596-D [P&P]).

In other situations, the convenience of white people trumped the rules of racial separation. In fact, white Southerners regularly violated segregation laws. The courthouse in Birmingham, for instance, contained separate elevators for blacks and for whites, as required by law. Nonetheless, whites sometimes used the "negro" elevators, presumably because they were more convenient than the "white" ones.[33] Blacks, however, were not allowed to ride the "white" elevators. In some theaters, the balcony could be occupied by whites and by blacks, with the two sections being separated by a chain. If the white section filled, white customers could move into the black section.[34] Presumably, black customers could not overfill their section and spill into the white one. These exceptions to separation illustrate that, as Grace Hale argues, "whites made modern racial meanings not just by creating boundaries but also by crossing them."[35] Throughout the South, legal measures generally allowed whites to have access to any space they wanted, even if that space was technically reserved for blacks. While these practices then reinforced white privilege, they also increased the instances in which blacks and whites would be together. The irony of these exceptions was not lost on African Americans. As Ellie Dahmer recalled about blacks and whites sharing an elevator, "We could stand together on the elevator and . . . you could be pretty close to a person, much closer than you would be sitting on a stool. . . . It was all silly."[36] Silly or not, and whether the motivations were cost or convenience, the effect was that throughout the South, even in segregated spaces, blacks and whites interacted with each other daily. Sometimes, such as in the more convenient elevator, whites allowed for a black presence, or more accurately, they allowed for a white presence in a "colored" space. In other situations, however, they also desired a black presence, including in the legally most segregated spaces.

Whereas some exceptions allowed whites to cross into "colored" space—such as in theaters—others allowed some African Americans into "white" space. For instance, the 1881 Tennessee law that required blacks to ride in a separate railcar contained one key qualifier: It excluded black domestic servants, who could accompany the white family into any car.[37] This exception was consistent with a policy that had been adopted in Nashville the previous year.[38] In clarifying the meaning in the 1881 law, Tennessee federal judge David Key explained that "as long as a colored passenger occupies a servile position, he may ride anywhere. . . . Let a woman black as midnight be the nurse of a white child, or a man equally as dark be the servant of a white man [and] there is never the slightest objection to their having seats in the ladies car or any other."[39]

The Tennessee law, then, might more accurately be described as a measure intended to ban only some African Americans from the first-class car.[40] It excluded members of the black elite and middle class, black professionals, and blacks who were neither dependent on nor employed by whites. It, however, would not apply to black servants present with their employers. In this case, African Americans who were in a position of servitude could cross boundaries into a space of both racial and class privilege. Ultimately, this measure legally created a space for white masters and black servants.[41]

Many other laws, ordinances, and policies made similar exceptions. A 1912 Virginia law established racially separate residential districts, but blacks employed by whites were allowed to live on the premises of the white homes.[42] A decade later, with the rise of the automobile industry, Mississippi became the first state to pass a law regulating travel in taxicabs.[43] Black drivers could carry only black passengers, and white drivers only white passengers, but with this exception: Blacks employed by whites could ride in the taxi with their white employers.[44] In addition to these formal legal exceptions tied to white employers, there were other ways in which blacks might be present in a "whites only" space. On trains, black porters could attend to white travelers, and some establishments had black employees working behind a whites-only counter.[45] In each of these circumstances, the black presence revolved around service, and specifically, these legal measures preserved an "integrated" space in which blacks waited on or worked for whites. One can read these accommodations at least in part as another exception tied to convenience for whites. In the case of rail travel, for example, it would have been inconvenient for a white passenger to be separated from a servant. Thus, just as whites could cross racial lines to use the much closer "colored" elevator, blacks too could cross a racial boundary when it benefited whites. Yet something more than white convenience is at work here. Consider, for example, the Tennessee law on railcars. That measure could have stipulated other rules for black servants who accompanied their employers, such as confining servants to the back of the car or perhaps requiring them to occupy separate rows. But it did not, and the reason, as Judge Key explained, was that any black passenger in that car would be in a "servile position." On the one hand, the exception that allowed blacks into the car illustrates the critical importance of racial performance in which racial boundaries would be marked by blacks publicly playing the part of servants to whites. At the same time, this exception also preserved a public space for a form of interracial intimacy. It established the first-class train car as a stage for white masters and black servants. In effect, the only individuals legally banished from this car were African Americans unattached to whites. This recognition of a world populated by white masters and their black servants of course reflected an idealized Jim Crow world of intimacy, where, as Key suggested, blacks nursed white children and serviced white families. Legal measures were central to legitimating a vision of masters and servants, and the physical props tangibly supported this vision.

Within shared spaces, a third element—customs—also played a role in constructing racial spaces, particularly because laws and insufficient barriers allowed for daily interracial interactions. In general, the customs that governed interactions predated the laws, and in many cases, the legal measures emerged from the customs that defined race relations in the slavery period, in which whites expected blacks to show deference.[46] Legally, the black codes of the 1860s also served as a model for Jim Crow measures.[47] In the Jim Crow era, various customs guided behavior in shared spaces. Stetson Kennedy, in his research on segregation in the late 1950s, chronicled many of these practices. He observed, for instance, that African Americans were generally not supposed to light a cigarette for a white smoker, that whites and blacks did not shake hands, and that a black person should not call a white person a liar. Blacks, he noticed, removed their hats for an approaching white person, but whites did not have to remove their hats for an approaching black person.[48] Given the desire for an interracial intimacy, these customs were especially crucial for defining acceptable and unacceptable forms of interaction. The customs guiding hats, for example, became visual performances of the hierarchy, with only the person in the subordinate position expected to remove his hat. Customs also defined the nature of Jim Crow intimacy. It was an intimacy in which the black person could not challenge the authority of the white person (whites could not be labeled liars) and one in which blacks had to physically acknowledge white authority (the removal of the hat). The intimacy could not convey status as equals (no shaking hands), and at least in public it had to be absent any hint of sexual or romantic intimacy, which would have been performed in lighting a cigarette with white hands or mouths in close proximity to black hands or mouths.

In private spaces, too, customs established the nature of intimacy between the races. Many African Americans worked as maids and servants for white families, and the wages were so paltry that middle-class families could afford to hire a maid.[49] The presence of a black maid signaled the employer's social status as middle class and white. Domestics cleaned, cooked meals, and often assumed the primary responsibility for raising the children. In turn, many whites imagined and later remembered their "mammies" as members of the family whom they loved dearly and who loved them back.[50] That relationship, which was a distinctively Southern one, was enacted over and over again within popular culture and advertising, and it was at the heart of a romanticized Jim Crow world of masters and servants.[51] Given the physical closeness of blacks and whites in these spaces, the customs were particularly important for defining the enactments of intimacy in these spaces. African Americans were in close physical contact with white children, with the food consumed by whites, and with the spaces and things in the white home, and in each of these endeavors it allowed many whites to imagine blacks as members of their family. At the same time, African Americans could not enter through the front door, they were not allowed to eat with whites, and they could not sit in the parlor of white homes.[52] Each of these actions would have suggested equality with the employer and a presence as an equal member of the family. Instead, the expectations of intimate contact combined with the rules for navigating these spaces left African Americans in white homes in a complicated position.[53] They were imagined at once as servants and inferiors and also as loved members of the larger white family.

Of course, if Jim Crow represented a larger project to replicate an earlier form of interracial intimacy, not everyone shared that vision. In the 1880s and 1890s, the fear of a black threat and the perpetuation of this myth as a threat to white women and to civilization led some whites to seek a more complete racial isolation between blacks and whites.[54] Some legal measures reflected these intentions. Texas train coaches, for example, were required to have a "good and substantial wooden partition" to separate white passengers from black ones. Alabama had a similarly themed law pertaining to transportation companies, requiring separate waiting rooms for black travelers and white travelers in which the partition was to be "constructed of metal, wood, strong cloth, or other material so as to obstruct the vision between the sections."[55] The wording of each of these measures suggested a desire for a rather complete separation of space so that blacks and whites could not see or hear each other. In a similar fashion, the impetus to establish separate schools for white students and black students indicated an attempt at an isolation of the races, and so too did the bans on integrated neighborhoods in Louisville, Richmond, and Atlanta, even if these bans sometimes came with exceptions.[56] Each one of these efforts seemed to reflect a desire for maintaining spaces exclusively white and exclusively black, to create Jim Crow stages where blacks and whites would never interact.

Similarly, an image of a larger family of paternalistic whites and loyal blacks did not inform every response to African Americans in shared spaces, such as on roadways. In part because automobiles often obscured the racial identities of the passengers inside, the racial rules were somewhat murky, although, in general, black drivers were not allowed to pass cars driven by whites.[57] Alma Ward, an African American who was born and raised in Itta Bena, learned about these roadway expectations following an incident involving her father. Her father passed a white man in his car, and afterward the man informed his father's boss and added that he would "kill that nigger if he ever pass me again." The warning left Ward's father in tears.[58] It also suggested a complicated form of racial paternalism, with the white man going to the white boss and threatening violence. For many whites, the goal was not intimacy but instead a desire to exercise privilege and power over black people. Yet, despite the varying racial ideas within the white community, the laws, props, and customs conspired together to create a stage that would also allow for regular performances of intimacy and racial difference.

Overall, laws, customs, and props transformed the racial geography to promote two roles in particular—white masters and black servants—and at least two groups occupied a precarious position on that stage. Neither independent African Americans nor poor whites quite fit within this racial fiction. Indeed, a rather explicit goal in the hardening of segregation and the accompanying violence was the attempt to permanently exclude African Americans who were not dependent on whites. Accordingly, this group in particular had to play the servile role convincingly in public spaces.

The role for poor whites in a Jim Crow world was somewhat more complicated. In many circumstances, the geography and rules of segregation allowed them to play the role of masters. They had access to privileged spaces that were symbolically and usually physically superior, such as the "white" water fountain, the "white" school, and the "white" section of restaurants. On a bus, if the white section filled, they could expect black passengers to get up and give them a seat, and they could expect black individuals to address them with a title. In public spaces then, every white person had numerous opportunities on a daily basis to experience their privileged position over blacks. Yet even as they could play the part of masters, they could not necessarily play the role of the paternalist. Poor whites generally had no political weight, for example, to assist a black individual who was in trouble with the law. Nor could poor whites afford to hire domestics to work in their homes; and in fact in some cases they were sharecropping alongside African Americans.[59] In addition, poor whites did not have the financial means to enter some "whites only" spaces where middle-class and elite whites could bring black servants.

For poor whites, an inability to embody the idealized white role of the paternalist may also have fueled conflicts within the white community and with African Americans. One ethnographic study of the Delta in the 1930s found a great deal of tension between poor whites and middle- and upper-class whites. The research juxtaposed this intra-racial animosity with the love expressed between upper-class whites and many black people.[60] Similarly, David L. Cohn, a Delta native and member of the intellectual elite, also depicted his Delta of the 1930s as a place of mutual affection between the planter class and blacks, contrasted with the hatred and violence that poor whites unleashed on blacks.[61] Both of these assessments closely mirrored the Jim Crow world imagined in laws and customs. And as poor whites became the scapegoats for racial violence, this also served to push them to the margins of this imagined world. They could not fully play the part of masters, nor were they dependent servants. Accordingly, on the Jim Crow stage, race and class often combined to inform performances of blackness and whiteness.

If class complicated racial roles, by the 1930s white Mississippians and black Mississippians interacted on a physical landscape that would have seemed fixed and familiar. An architectural style characterized by dual entrances and lines of stools, as H. A. Scott experienced, had been formed decades earlier through a combination of new laws, old customs, and physical construction. The efforts of this previous generation left behind a range of segregated spaces that allowed for and often reflected a desire for much interaction between blacks and whites. Yet if the landscape conveyed permanence and predictability, it nonetheless still depended on black Mississippians and white Mississippians always knowing where to move and how to move, and it then depended on them actually moving in these expected ways.

EXPECTATION: THE JIM CROW SCRIPT

In 1934, psychologist John Dollard, then a researcher at Yale University, traveled to the Delta town of Indianola, the county seat of Sunflower County. He would spend five months observing and interviewing local blacks and whites for his book, *Caste and Class in a Southern Town* (1937). He initially rented a room in a boardinghouse, and soon after his arrival, Dollard, a white man who considered himself a "Yankee" outsider in the South, found himself in an awkward position over racial customs. It began when "a Negro friend came to [the] boarding house and knocked on the *front* door" (Dollard's emphasis). Because the man had not gone to the back of the house as custom dictated for black visitors, it created, according to Dollard, "a crisis for him, for the family, and for me." Dollard worried that he "had unwittingly aided in imposing a humiliation on [his white] hosts." And then the moment became even more awkward for the researcher. Another black man arrived, and Dollard's friend proceeded to introduce them. Dollard faced a dilemma, asking himself, "Should we shake hands? Would he be insulted if I did not, or would he accept the situation?" In order to signal to the visitor his intentions and hoping to minimize embarrassment and insult, Dollard kept his hands in his pockets, indicating that a handshake would not be forthcoming.[62] Dollard's decision—using his body to find an alternative between a handshake and a blatant refusal—was not so different from Richard Wright's juggling of boxes in an elevator to avoid acknowledging a white man. The image of Dollard standing awkwardly on the porch points to the complexities of interracial interactions, even in the most basic of engagements. It illustrates too that Jim Crow carried performative expectations for both blacks and whites whenever they were in close proximity.

Given the regularity of interracial interactions, Jim Crow had to be re-created every day. Remaining faithful to Jim Crow meant acting—performing with the body and the voice—in a predictable way on this racial stage.[63] Meanings of whiteness and blackness, then, were attached not only to the space itself but also to how individuals occupied these spaces, and more specifically to how individuals moved and waited.[64] Literature scholar Hortense Spillers argues that "a powerful stillness" of the black body has been a central characteristic of racial domination within a New World context. For Spillers, this stillness is interconnected with the sociopolitical order beginning with enslavement, in which those in power impose meaning on the black body.[65] For African Americans, Jim Crow expectations regularly imposed a stillness on the body, and this stillness also allowed for the greater and easier movement of white bodies. More than a metaphor, the stillness of blacks and the movements of whites materialized in physically measurable ways in the daily lives of Mississippians, especially in the spaces where blacks and whites found themselves together, including in customer lines, on sidewalks, on buses, and in the homes of whites.

Prior to the hardening of racial lines in the late nineteenth century, black Southerners already had much experience with segregation, but that experience did not necessarily prepare them for "the thoroughness of Jim Crow," which extended into virtually every public and private space, from homes, to courthouses, to theaters, to ballparks, to hospitals, to prisons.[66] Visually one of the more persistent examples of this thoroughness, in which Jim Crow was dramatized in stillness and movement, was in the politics of customer lines at stores, banks, post offices, and other businesses. In the places that lacked racially separate sections, black patrons and white patrons waited in the same lines to make a purchase, pick up mail, or conduct bank business. The prevailing Jim Crow custom called for white customers to be waited on first. If black people were standing in line, a white person could cut in front of them, including to interrupt an exchange already in process. Pinkey Hall, who was from Meridian, recalls, "You could be standing there, and a white woman or a white man would just come up to the counter and just get right on in front of you, you know, and they [sales clerks] would just go right on and wait on them. You'd just have to stand and wait and get waited on whenever you could, you know, paying the same price and everything and holding the money in your hand and the garment, too."[67] As a racial performance, the encounter Hall describes involved three actors: the black customer, the white customer, and the sales clerk.[68] The scene began when the white customer took the initiative to move to the front of the line and to step in front of the black customer. The next part belonged to the clerk, who would have to acknowledge this move by turning his or her attention, and possibly his or her body, away from the black customer and toward the white one. If that happened, the third person in this drama, the black patron, was then forced to wait to complete her or his purchase.

The collusion between the clerk and the white customer was especially important if, as in the case of Hall, the black customer was already in the process of paying. That was likewise the case for Hettie Love, who grew up in the Delta in the 1930s and 1940s. Love recalls an episode at a store when she was already paying for her purchase and a white person stepped in front of her. Love had to wait.[69] For both Hall and Love, their role was one of inaction, of simply standing still until the white customer's transaction had been concluded. In these spaces, whiteness was defined by moving forward and blackness by waiting, and these two enactments were correlated. The gain of the white customer—a better physical position, a faster checkout—came at the expense of the black customer. The politics of lines accrued material benefits to white customers, and these privileges were necessarily tied to a black sacrifice.

The customer line, then, existed not only in space but also in time. As black patrons stood behind their white counterparts, their own purchases would take more time. In ways similar and parallel to Spillers's notion of a powerful stillness—of the black individual fixed in space as others moved—Michael Hanchard argues that in a society defined by a racial hierarchy, time itself becomes racialized. Temporal experiences, he notes, become a signifier of racial difference, with black people waiting longer for access to goods and services and with white people gaining access to these goods and services first. For example, when black schools used the discarded textbooks from white schools—as was the case in Mississippi—black children's access to the most up-to-date knowledge was delayed, and in this cycle of handed-down textbooks, they never would get the books with the latest information.[70] White students always had newer textbooks and accordingly had access to newer, or the most current, information.

In numerous ways, a temporal stillness informed the daily experiences of African Americans. Eva Gates, an African American who grew up on the Gulf Coast in the 1950s, remembered times when she waited "at least thirty minutes or longer" to buy groceries because white customers were cutting in front of her.[71] A more structured form of racial time also governed eating practices on trains. Most trains passing through the South had only one dining car, and while some of these cars had separate sections, many of them did not. In the 1940s, sociologist Charles Johnson found that on these trains, segregation was achieved through the dining schedule, as African American passengers had to wait until the end of the dinner service to eat, when white customers had finished eating.[72] Their access to food was delayed, and perhaps too they would have had fewer options if some items had been sold out. Whether on trains or in grocery stores or elsewhere, black patrons were ever waiting for white patrons, and each stoppage slowed time down for African Americans while speeding time up for white patrons. Both temporally and spatially, many Jim Crow practices that called on blacks to stand still in time and space made daily routines easier and more convenient for whites as it made those routines less convenient and less comfortable for blacks. Beyond emerging from functional concerns about white convenience, these practices often did other work for Jim Crow.

In standard practice, a line of customers would have been informed by democratic principles—first come, first served, regardless of social rank. A line in which a white customer waited behind a black customer was a demonstration of racial equality. But when a white person moved to the front, he or she replaced a democratic principle with a Jim Crow principle. The practice of white people cutting in line not only racialized time and space; it was also a performative reinforcement of the social hierarchy. As Charlie Parker, an African American who was born in the 1890s near Laurel, remembered about the lines at banks and post offices, when a white customer came in, blacks "would always get back and let him [the white person] go first, you come last."[73] Parker's word choice here is important. From his perspective, it was not simply that he came *after*, but that he came *last*. That construction suggests a function beyond white convenience.[74] If the customs around lines were meant to benefit whites, they also sent a message to blacks about their place in this society.

Just as the line in its least complicated form was potentially a democratic one, the relationship between the buyer and the seller also raised possible complications for a racial hierarchy. Many establishments owned by white individuals depended on both a white and a black clientele. Even if white storeowners had wanted to exclude black customers, many could not have afforded to do so, and thus white clerks and black customers regularly engaged in a one-to-one relationship.[75] Within the marketplace, the individual with money—the customer— generally assumes a privileged position. The money allows the customer to expect the clerk to provide goods or service, and in many cases that would have meant that a white clerk was in the position of waiting on and serving a black customer, an arrangement that potentially disrupted the master-servant construction. Just as the practice of cutting in line demonstrated that not all customers were equal, many clerks found other ways to reestablish white authority in the presence of a black patron. Alma Ward, for instance, recalls a postal worker always dropping black people's mail on the floor instead of handing it to them.[76] Unlike cutting in line, dropping the mail provided no material benefit for the white postal worker. It did, however, mark blackness through an additional movement and an inconvenience experienced by the black patron. The performance was an unmistakable signifier of difference.

A worker purchases goods at a plantation store in the Mississippi Delta, November 1939. Library of Congress, Prints and Photographs Division, Washington, D.C. (LC-USF34-052452-D [P&P] LOT 1648).

Similar practices in stores also allowed whites to assert their racial role over their market role. Researcher Stetson Kennedy found that white clerks and owners routinely insulted black customers and ejected them from their shops.[77] As well, in many clothing stores, black customers were not allowed to try on clothes before buying them.[78] This performance of trying on clothes (whites) versus not trying on clothes (blacks) connected race to physical comfort. Whites had the opportunity to confirm that their clothes fit and were comfortable, while for black customers, as Eva Gates recalls, "most of the time we would get the wrong size."[79] Visually, race was marked in the fit of clothing, and race was experienced in how comfortable or uncomfortable those clothes were. In addition, the clothing practice had a temporal dimension. White bodies were deemed cleaner and at a more advanced stage of civilization compared to the black body, which was marked as too dirty to be allowed to try on clothes.[80] Each of these routines remade the marketplace into a site where African Americans moved differently and experienced inconvenience. Significantly, unlike the practices of cutting in line, where black inconvenience allowed for white convenience, the

rules for trying on clothes were not directly correlated with white convenience. These measures did not allow whites to try on clothes more
quickly; it only made this a privilege that was reserved for whites. Like
other expectations, though, it drew a performative line of difference
where blacks, relative to whites, would experience inconvenience and
discomfort. In the process, these enactments negated a marketplace
performance of a white person waiting on and serving a black person.

The notion of stillness—of waiting in time and space—is a useful
one for understanding how spaces were racially reconstituted on a
daily basis. It does not, however, capture the full dynamism of these
spaces. Indeed, many spaces required blacks not to remain still but to
move. On sidewalks, in restaurants, and on buses, for example, segregation was defined by African Americans taking excessive action, such
as stepping aside, taking a longer route, or being forced to move suddenly from a position of rest. Like the scenarios that called for waiting,
some of these additional movements were attached to white comfort
and convenience. For example, in many theaters open to both blacks
and whites, white patrons were accorded a relatively direct and short
route from the ticket window to their seats. In theaters with balconies
for black patrons, the entrance to the balcony often meant walking
outside and up an additional flight of stairs, and at least some black
patrons recalled being out of breath once they arrived at their seats.
In the balcony of a segregated theater, black moviegoers found themselves in a section far away from the speakers, close to the noise of the
projector, and often facing the screen at an odd angle.[81] Visually and
aurally, the movie experience could be less enjoyable for those sitting
in the balcony. Sending blacks to the balcony allowed whites to have a
more comfortable viewing experience. The process that produced this
white convenience was somewhat different from the performances of
lines. Whereas with a line the white person made the initial move to
claim his privilege, spaces such as segregated theaters depended on
African Americans taking the initiative and moving themselves to the
inferior space. A similar process defined restaurants that would serve
black customers only from a back window, defining their experience by
an additional physical effort. Even when these episodes involved only a
few extra steps, symbolically they reminded African Americans that an
interracial world required them to segregate themselves. Trips to the
movies or to restaurants might only be occasional, but on a much more
regular basis, sidewalks called for similar performances.

Unlike water fountains, restrooms, or many restaurants, sidewalks did not have signs or barriers. Similar to interracial places of business, sidewalks functioned as amorphous, racially ambiguous spaces. Accordingly, the racialization of these areas depended entirely on the interaction between blacks and whites. Customs that guided interactions on sidewalks predated the Jim Crow era and extended beyond Mississippi. An 1857 Richmond, Virginia, ordinance that required black walkers to step aside indicates that even before emancipation, whites were concerned about the behavior of blacks in public spaces. Yet, as historian Jane Dailey demonstrates for Virginia, in the time between enslavement and Jim Crow, the sidewalks became especially contentious sites. Whites registered numerous complaints of being forced off the sidewalk and into the street by passing black men and women.[82] Sidewalks became a battleground over what black freedom would mean, and in Danville, in 1883, a sidewalk altercation between a black man and a white man led to a riot, leaving four people dead. As Dailey contends, one of the central issues around sidewalks in the early Jim Crow years revolved around uncertainty. When black walkers bumped into whites, the whites were left to wonder if the bump was intentional or accidental.[83] In the Jim Crow era, the racial expectations for moving in public space would resolve that uncertainty; and in Mississippi, black walkers were always expected to step aside for approaching white walkers.

Recollections of life in Mississippi from African Americans contain numerous references to the politics of sidewalks. In her memoir, Unita Blackwell, who lived in the Delta, notes that "if a white person was walking toward me on the road, I would get over on the grass and let him or her go by."[84] Franzetta W. Sanders provides a similar but more detailed response. Sanders, who grew up on the Gulf Coast in the 1940s, explains: "I would notice sometimes if we were on the walkway meeting [whites], . . . we would be the ones to have to either stop or step in the street or step wherever so they could pass through. Be it young or old, lame or sick, or whatever. Age, it didn't matter. . . . If you were white, you know, you came first. The blacks just stepped back, and seemed like it was automatic. We knew to do that and that's the way it was."[85] Sanders and Blackwell each describe the expectations for them: They stepped aside when meeting whites on the sidewalk. The physical processes involved in this performance differed from the stillness of waiting in a line. Unlike the line, in which a black patron simply waited for the white customer to finish, the sidewalk enactment was a multi-step physical disruption. The black walker stopped, stepped out of the way, waited for the white walker or walkers to pass, and then returned to the path and again moved forward. For African Americans, then, the time it took to get from point A to point B was extended. As African Americans experienced the sidewalk as a series of physical and temporal disruptions, white walkers moved along the sidewalk with the privilege to continue in one fluid motion from point A to point B. In creating a space of white convenience, black people altered their movements—changing direction, stepping aside, and breaking the cadence of their gait—so that the flow of white people could continue unabated.[86] As racial spaces, then, sidewalks were first and foremost "white" spaces, whereas the "black" space shifted, moving to the side when necessary. Unlike separate schools or water fountains, as spaces of segregation, sidewalks were unpredictable and could become whites-only spaces at any point, adding another component—anticipation—to the performance.

Anticipation coupled the physical dynamic with a mental one. To stay in the appropriate "place," African Americans always had to be ready to move; they had to be looking ahead, watching out for approaching whites, and perhaps also thinking about the optimal place to step aside to avoid cars or puddles of water or other hazards. Accordingly, as their physical movements were disrupted, so too were their thoughts. The black walker playing his or her part for approaching whites removed an obstacle from the white person's path, freeing the white walker not to think about how to maneuver and perhaps not even to notice the black person on the sidewalk. The repetitiveness of these mental and physical exercises was key. As Charlie Parker noted about getting back on the sidewalk, if more were "coming we got to get back off."[87] These mental preparations also distinguished the sidewalk custom from the cutting-in-line performance. With lines, the racial performance depended on a white person claiming the space at the front. The role of the African American was to react by remaining in place. On sidewalks, however, the initial Jim Crow move fell to the black walker. Rather than a performance of stillness, it was one of action, of self-segregation in the presence of whites. Sidewalks, then, required blacks to actively participate in and physically acknowledge their subordinate status.

Sidewalk practices did other Jim Crow work, which was revealed in the nature of white spaces and black spaces at the moment of passing. At the point at which the white walker and the black walker were side by side, the white person was on the path and the black walker would have been to the side, perhaps veering into dirt, mud, a ditch, or a roadway. The sidewalk was thus not only a more direct and more convenient path; it was also a cleaner and more refined one. By way of contrast, Blackwell recalls moving to "the grass," while Sanders first refers to stepping in the street or "wherever" and then describes it as blacks stepping "back." Whatever the nature of the space that ran along the sidewalk, it was by definition less ideal for walking, and if circumstances required stepping in the street, that space could also be more dangerous. Thus, just as textbook policies limited black access to outdated knowledge, sidewalk encounters limited them to a rougher and wilder space at the very moment that the white walker was enjoying the better path. Each performance on the sidewalk signaled that the modern, civilized space of the sidewalk was foremost a "white" one and that there was no room for any African Americans to share that space with whites. By the 1940s, a similar message would be expressed with school buses, as most white students rode to school on buses and most black children walked. Racial difference was marked and was experienced not only through technology (the bus) but also through how blacks and whites moved to and from school.[88] If in quantifiable terms it meant that it took African Americans longer to get from point A to point B, in a symbolic sense it also meant that they were to remain in a less modern space.

In many of these scenarios, when African Americans played their role and moved out of a path that had suddenly become a whites-only one, they could be practically invisible to the whites who passed them. Indeed, that often seemed to be the case when the goal of this practice was white convenience. But on other occasions, the sidewalks required a different performance from African Americans. Sometimes on sidewalks African Americans were hyper-visible; they were the objects of whites and they were expected to entertain them.[89] In addition to stepping off then, blacks also had to be ready for capricious variations. For example, in Clarksdale, Bennie Gooden often heard a policeman yelling at blacks to get off the sidewalk nearest the swimming pool for whites and to walk on the other side.[90] Herman Leach recalls that the police arrested blacks for walking on the sidewalk if they had not paid the "street tax." It did not matter whether such a law actually existed, because, as Leach realized, "whatever [the police officer] said, that was the law."[91] In these two examples, the unspoken, unwritten rule of moving away from white people was eclipsed by a spoken, improvised command to move for white people. There is a substantive difference between these two expected actions. In the first scenario—moving away from whites—the motions of black bodies vanquished black people from the path, sight, and consciousness of white people. In the second scenario—moving for white people in response to verbal commands— black people became hyper-visible vessels of Jim Crow blackness. These two performances were variations on the servant role, one in which black sacrifice made life easier for whites and another in which black sacrifice functioned as white amusement.[92] In some imaginings of sidewalks and public space, the role of the black individual was tied even more explicitly to entertainment for whites.

In his 1946 book about life in the Mississippi Delta, David L. Cohn included a story of a black man named Joe Moss. Cohn describes Moss, a harmonica player, as "a rambling, rolling, train-riding, harp-blowing man."[93] Without a steady job to tie him to a white employer, Moss could have been perceived as a threat to the social order, which was the case for many black men in the Jim Crow South. Indeed, Moss had numerous run-ins with the law. According to Cohn, however, this "black troubadour" always escaped harsh punishment by entertaining authorities with his harmonica.[94] For example, Moss avoided one arrest by agreeing to play a lively tune for a police officer, and on another occasion a judge dropped charges against him and instead kept Moss and his harmonica in the courtroom "playing all morning long."[95] Cohn told the story as a true one. Whether mostly true, partially true, or completely fictional, though, the story reveals one of the ways in which black Mississippians were expected to move in public space. If those movements were not evasive, they were often about amusement, moving for and to the delight of whites. At least in the retelling by Cohn, Joe Moss is a willing participant, eager to entertain white authorities. Whatever the scenario, blacks always had to be ready to move. And if encounters on sidewalks sometimes ended with a song, they could also be quite dangerous places, especially for black women and uniformed black men.

On Constance Baker's daily walks to school, approaching white boys would sometimes spread out across the width of the sidewalk, forcing her to step off and let them pass.[96] Just as Gooden and Leach had to be prepared to react to the verbal cues of police officers, Baker had to adjust to the physical cues of the white boys. Similar to Gooden and

Leach, Baker had to perform her subordinate status on demand for a white audience. However, as a female, Baker's regular ordeal added another potential layer of fear. Baker's female body was all too visible to the white boys, and her expected performance on the sidewalk was backed by the ever-present fear of sexual assault. As Winson Hudson explains about her childhood in Mississippi, "White boys would rape you and then come and destroy the family if you said anything. . . . I couldn't walk the roads at anytime alone for fear I might meet a white man or boy."[97] Baker and Hudson are describing an additional variation on the hyper-visibility of the black body on sidewalks. For Leach and Gooden and Joe Moss, hyper-visibility on a sidewalk meant performing to the delight of white audiences, while for many black women and girls, it meant being consumed by the eyes and aggressive actions of white males. Accordingly, in part because sidewalks lacked fixed racial barriers, they could be disruptive and dangerous spaces. Racial meanings and boundaries depended entirely on the ways in which blacks and whites moved in these spaces. Related processes governed interactions on buses, where the racial boundaries were visible and movable.

The policies regulating spaces on buses were drawn from measures dictating other modes of transportation, beginning with new laws for railcars in the 1880s and continuing with streetcars across the South in the first decade of the new century.[98] In Mississippi, most buses separated white passengers and black passengers with a curtain or a sign, either of which the bus driver could move toward the front or the back. For African Americans, buses entailed several different enactments. As with lines in stores, if blacks and whites were waiting to board, African Americans could expect to board only after all white customers had boarded.[99] Once on board, black customers first paid up front and then moved to the "colored" section toward the back of the bus. On some buses, that meant walking past whites in the front section, which, similar to stepping off the sidewalk, entailed an act of self-segregation in front of whites. On other buses, after paying up front, black passengers were expected to exit the bus and then reenter toward the back. Sometimes bus drivers departed before a black passenger had reboarded. Even if the driver waited for the passenger, bus travel involved numerous disruptive physical movements—including turning around and stepping off—or waiting for whites to board.[100] As well, each of these disruptions facilitated the comfort and convenience of the white travelers, who could move first and unimpeded to their seats. And, of course, each of these racial enactments was carried out before an interracial audience. Segregated buses then depended on passengers moving in tightly scripted ways.

In terms of expected movements, what distinguished the bus from sidewalks and store lines was that the racial boundaries could change at every stop. If more whites boarded and filled their section, blacks were expected to move farther back, and if the "colored" section filled, then blacks had to stand. Accordingly, the racial performance did not necessarily end once black passengers had made it to their place in the "colored" section. They always had to be paying attention to this shifting line, often marked by a movable sign. As E. Hammond Smith, a black man born in Hattiesburg in 1894, explained, "You would stand up and let the white folks sit. They had a mover thing."[101] Similarly, Johnny Barbour, who came of age half a century later, noted about the sign marked "colored" that "it was moveable. They'd move it when they got ready. And just move you on back. And you paid the same money everybody else paid."[102] Like Pinkey Hall and Eva Gates waiting in store lines, implicit in Barbour's comments is the injustice of paying full price for less service. Accordingly, the racially differentiated movements of blacks and whites on buses was a performative reminder, like that of store lines, that black and white customers were different, that even if they paid the same money—and perhaps especially if that were the case—it did not grant them the usual marketplace rights of the consumer. As well, in Smith's and Barbour's assessments, one should note the use of the word "move." Smith uses it as an adjective emphasizing its function as a thing that moved black people. Barbour uses derivations of "move" three times—the sign moved, they moved the sign, and they moved you on back. Significantly while conjuring an image of signs and bodies in motion, Smith and Barbour are also deflecting the action from themselves. From their perspective, they did not choose to move, but rather someone—or something, such as the sign—moved them. If these recollections hint at some nuanced ways in which blacks could imagine the process of self-segregation as one where they had little choice, the effect was that, on a regular basis on buses, black passengers were expected to always be watching and ready to move and to give up their seats for whites.

Structurally, too, the space inside the bus was a unique one. Within a confined area, the physical dimensions of white space and black space were mutually constituted. An increasing white space came at the expense of a decreasing black space, and by extension the crowdedness and relative discomfort of black passengers made possible the comfort and convenience of white passengers. Likewise, black riders were the only ones on the bus who had to think about moving. A white rider could board the bus and get lost in thought, knowing that he or she would not have to move. In a tangible way, racial difference was marked on black bodies in motion and on black bodies being disrupted, in contrast to the white bodies at rest. As well, even with a dividing line, this physical space was one of separated togetherness in which the driver and the passengers could still see and hear each other from their seats. Thus, the segregated space of the bus called for a continual racial performance. While the white rider could relax, these circumstances could generate much tension for the black rider.

Constance Baker, who grew up in Hattiesburg in the 1910s and 1920s, once rode on a bus in the middle of a rainstorm in which all the windows in the back of the bus—in the "colored" section—were broken out. The back of the bus was wet, so Baker sat closer to the front. However, soon after she was in her seat, several white girls boarded the bus, and as Baker recalled, the driver said, "Girl, get up and let them white women sit down." Baker explains: "You see how humiliating that kind of thing can be—and I was a grown woman at the time."[103] For Baker, part of the degradation came from having to move from her original seat. However, it was also intertwined with issues of race, gender, and age. She was humiliated not only by moving but also by how the driver interacted with her. Baker specifically notes the bus driver's choice of words—"girl" and "white women"—versus her own characterization as "a grown woman." Her Jim Crow role, as described by the bus driver, stripped her of her femininity and of any privileges of womanhood or age. In spite of her status as the adult and as a woman, she had been forced to sit in the wet seats. In moving, her space of dryness and relative comfort became available for the white girls.

In Baker's case, the bus driver told her to move. Yet in most situations, as with the sidewalks, white people expected black people to know the rules and to follow them—to segregate themselves—without being told by whites. For example, in 1946, Elport Chess, a World War II veteran, was arrested and beaten for not giving up his seat as more whites boarded a Jackson bus. According to the *Jackson Advocate*, Chess claimed that he had never been asked to move and that no other seats where available.[104] For this veteran, however, the expectation was that he would know to move, that he would not have to be told by others. Both Baker and Chess had been expected to police themselves—to move to the appropriate spot. If Baker's bus driver had been more tolerant in reminding her of how she had to move, on a full bus with presumably substantial numbers of black and white passengers, Chess was given less leniency. Accordingly, Jim Crow buses were spaces where, even when African Americans rested, they could never afford to completely rest, and the continual moving of black passengers for white passengers defined these spaces. Many of these buses also transported domestic workers to and from the homes of whites, another complicated, shifting space of segregation.

Perhaps no space better personified the efforts to create a Jim Crow world of masters and servants than that of white homes. As previously noted, homes were spaces of partial physical barriers, and African Americans, as workers, could move throughout the house so long as they played the part of a servant—cleaning rooms, serving dinner, or taking care of the children. Blacks and whites, however, occupied and experienced these rooms in distinct ways. For example, the dining room was generally off-limits to blacks except when they were serving a meal to the white family.[105] Punctuating this difference, as Charles Johnson observed, blacks and whites almost never ate together. Similarly, the parlor room, a space intended for relaxation and entertainment, was off-limits to African Americans unless they were waiting on whites.[106] In addition, African Americans were expected to stand in these rooms, and thus the parlor room and the dining room each connected whiteness to comfort, relaxation, and privilege and blackness to always being on guard and ready to serve whites.[107] By comparison, while the entire home was a white-controlled space, the kitchen became a space of relative comfort for the African American cook. Here she could exercise some authority over what happened in that space.[108]

On the surface, these dynamics might appear to be little different from any employer-worker relationship, particularly within a home, in which work expectations dictated how servants moved in this space. The Jim Crow distinction, however, that linked domestic work to the movements in lines, on sidewalks, and on buses was that these interactions were also an enactment of an interracial intimacy, and in this way they differed from domestic service in other parts of the country.[109] Many white families wanted not only to be waited on by a black domestic worker; they wanted to love and be loved by this "mammy" figure, who watched over and nurtured her adopted family as if it were her own. Domestic workers, then, were imagined not only as employees but also as members of a larger white family. The expected movements in the home thus had to carry out two complicated, almost contradictory tasks in expressing a familial closeness while also maintaining racial difference. This dual mission could be conveyed in African Americans standing and waiting in spaces of leisure, such as the parlor room and the dining room, juxtaposed with more casual and isolated movements in nurturing children or cooking in the kitchen.

Another critical component in this dual performance of intimacy and difference related to black workers' relationship with white children. While African Americans were generally expected to address whites with titles, they could call white children by their first names. For white children, this practice suggested a more intimate and personal relationship than what they would have seen in how black adults and white adults communicated with each other. This exchange early in childhood as well as the nurturing duties of domestic workers would likely have led many white children to form a close relationship with these women who raised them, and indeed many of the expressions from whites of their love for domestic workers begin with memories from childhood.[110] At the same time, this intimacy also had to preserve difference and reinforce racial boundaries. Accordingly, the custom of calling white children by their first names would be disrupted later, usually during the teenage years, when whites were to be addressed with titles. For Rosie Bynum, when Billy, a white child she helped raise, turned twelve, she was told that for her he was now "Mr. Billy."[111] This transition also occurred in relationships outside the home. H. J. Williams recalls that when a white boy turned sixteen, the boss would tell all his black employees that it was time to call the boy "Mr."[112] This verbal performance, much like the bodily enactments of standing and waiting, carved out a unique position for African Americans in white homes, allowing them to be at once servants and family members and reinforcing the Jim Crow notion of a segregated world where blacks and whites loved each other.

The reality was often something different. Historian Rebecca Sharpless, for instance, argues that generally black women who cooked in white homes understood their work as employment rather than as an act of familial love.[113] That contention would seem to be supported by how rapidly and extensively black domestic workers during World

War II fled white homes for emerging war industry jobs, where they received better pay and had more control over their work space.[114] In addition, if for some African Americans love for a white family was genuine, for others there were practical reasons to perform intimacy. Performance studies scholar E. Patrick Johnson notes, for example, that if black domestic workers delivered a convincing performance of racial deference, they could acquire some authority, control, and power within white households.[115]

Regardless of the physical space, whether it was marked by nearly complete separation or partial separation or no separation, public and private spaces carried expectations for how whites and blacks moved through these spaces. If the rules allowed whites to play the part of masters and of a relatively privileged group, for African Americans the rules established variations on a servant role. Those expectations ranged from waiting for whites to waiting on whites. They included moving out of the way of whites to facilitate white convenience and moving for whites for the sake of amusement. On a regular basis, the performative aspects of Jim Crow provided for white comfort and advancement at the expense of black discomfort and sacrifice. Most important, regular adherence to those rules allowed whites to imagine this racialized world as natural and normal, as one equally desired by blacks and whites, and as one of both interracial intimacy and racial difference. Nonetheless, if geography, customs, laws, and experiences created expectations for racial performances, it is worth remembering Doreen Massey's contention that spaces are always in the process of being made. In Jim Crow Mississippi, spaces were also always in the process of being unmade, especially when white actors and black actors deviated from the script and delivered an unexpected performance.

REVISION: THE UNEXPECTED PERFORMANCES

Gladys Austin grew up in the 1920s and 1930s in Laurel, a county seat in the pinelands. From her childhood she recalls, "We just went to the colored fountain and didn't think anything about it. We knew [we] couldn't sit at a lunch counter and we didn't go there. . . . We went in the back door, and this was no big deal. . . . We just didn't even think about it. I guess we thought that was the way it was supposed to be."[116] Austin had been born into a world where the weight of repetition and the seeming fixedness of this racial landscape took many of the decisions away from her. For her, the movements appear to have become automatic. It seems likely, too, that most of the time many other blacks and whites in Mississippi would have followed suit, moving where and how they were expected to move. After all, to do otherwise was to risk a violent reprisal. Still, each day provided new opportunities for interracial encounters, from domestic servants working in the homes of whites, to walkers and passengers meeting on sidewalks and buses, to customers in cafés staring out across a line of stools. Every one of those encounters became a test of Jim Crow, a moment in which each individual on this stage could deliver the expected performance—could, for example, go to the appropriate water fountain without thinking about it—or could do something unexpected. And when a white person or black person delivered an unexpected role, that performance altered the meanings of a given space, and accordingly it altered the meanings of whiteness and blackness.

The record of oppressed groups doing unexpected things to undermine the rules established by the oppressor is well documented, and scholars have generally situated these actions within the dialectic of domination and resistance. In this construct, the acts of resistance to domination range from dramatic moments, such as an armed revolt by enslaved people, to other, subtler, and more mundane activities. During the slavery era, for instance, enslaved individuals sometimes improved their living and work conditions by breaking tools, stealing food from the kitchen, or abusing work animals.[117] Likewise, James C. Scott demonstrates that in everyday life, forms of resistance are often concealed within songs, jokes, and gestures and that these "hidden transcripts" can form a foundation for open defiance and social movements.[118] While some of the unexpected actions of African Americans constituted resistance that contributed to a larger black freedom struggle, the performance framework provides other ways to analyze these moments.[119] Attention to the unexpected movements of the body and utterances of the voice reveals the ways in which both blacks and whites sometimes broke from the script and delivered performances that carried the potential to redefine racialized spaces and even to redraw boundaries. On a stage of carefully scripted racial roles, the "wrong" line or movement could be quite disruptive, and thus the performative necessities of Jim Crow produced an ever-present tension that belied the myth of racial harmony.

Across the South, African Americans often rejected the role that had been prescribed for them in customs and laws. In Virginia, in the 1880s, as previously noted, the sidewalks became a place where blacks enacted their status as social equals in part by refusing to move aside for whites, much to the dismay of many white walkers. In the process, as Jane Dailey contends, "African Americans denied white privilege and struck at both the boundaries of whiteness and the assumptions and purposes of racial categorization."[120] Meanwhile, when state and local authorities introduced segregation measures for train travel in the early 1880s, black passengers countered with numerous challenges and lawsuits.[121] As officials applied similar laws and ordinances to streetcars at the turn of the century, African Americans turned to protests and boycotts in every Southern state, including in Natchez, Jackson, Pasca-goula, and Vicksburg in Mississippi.[122] Journalist Ray Stannard Baker's 1908 study of race relations in the United States, *Following the Color Line*, also commented on the continuing racial tensions on streetcars and trains.[123] In this first generation of legal segregation, many African Americans challenged new legislation and, more broadly, the expecta-tions that they were to move in specific ways or that their movements would be confined to certain areas. If additional laws, Supreme Court decisions, physical barriers, and the passage of time settled some of these issues for the next generation, interracial interactions would nonetheless continue to produce unexpected performances into the 1930s and 1940s in Mississippi.

The most likely spaces for unexpected performances were those that required African Americans to move in order to remain segregated, such as on sidewalks and buses. In 1943, for instance, Elwood Cook, a black army sergeant, was walking along a sidewalk in Flora, a small town twenty-five miles northwest of Jackson, when he brushed up against a white police officer. The incident attracted media coverage from the black-owned newspaper, the *Jackson Advocate*. Cook claimed that his contact with the officer was accidental, and according to the newspa-per, the sergeant attempted to apologize to the officer. Nonetheless, the police officer assaulted and arrested Cook.[124] Fortunately for the ser-geant, military officials intervened to obtain his release. Cook's contact with the white man, whether or not it was intentional, was an unex-pected racial performance. In physical terms, his actions altered the movements of the officer and in the process suggested that the black walker had as much right to the sidewalk as the white walker did. In the short term, the sidewalk beating and arrest of Cook reestablished the sidewalk as a space of white privilege. The intervention of the military officials, however, suggested a more complicated negotiation over the meanings of this space.

One of the key factors in this incident related to Cook's uniform. During the World War II years across the South, numerous local conflicts stemmed from the public presence of uniformed black men.[125] In many cases, white individuals demanded that a black soldier remove his uniform, and if he refused, a fight and an arrest often ensued. One way to read these episodes is to recognize that many African Americans returned from fighting abroad emboldened and with greater expectations for being treated as equals, and these veterans, including Cook, may have been more aggressive in asserting their rights.[126] Another possibility shifts the attention to the white citizens, who may have interpreted the uniform as a visual challenge to Jim Crow.[127] As Robin D. G. Kelley observes, the black man in uniform "signified an antifascist, pro-democratic message" derived from a federal authority.[128] Extending that analysis within the context of expected performances of servitude, the uniformed man no longer looked the part of the servant. Indeed, concerns that African Americans were no longer willing to play the appropriate Jim Crow role were also articulated in rumors spreading across the South during the war. As sociologist Howard W. Odum documented at the time, stories circulated that black soldiers were refusing to sit in colored sections of buses, that black men were assaulting white women, that domestic workers were refusing to work in white women's homes, that black women were forming "Eleanor Clubs"—named for Eleanor Roosevelt—to challenge racial norms, and that blacks were stockpiling ice picks and guns to lead an attack against whites.[129] If these over-the-top rumors were, as historian Bryant Simon suggests, a way for white Southerners to come to terms with racial tensions, they also were an indication that white Southerners were closely and nervously watching how African Americans performed blackness. That watchfulness was especially true for those individuals such as Elwood Cook who were in uniform.[130]

A related issue surrounding Cook and other black soldiers in Mississippi was the changing and very real presence of the federal government in the South. If, as others have argued, New Deal programs tied the South more closely to the federal government, World War II made those connections even more explicit. The war brought troops, expanded military bases, and defense industry jobs to the South, and with these changes came greater federal authority over local communities in the region.[131] The presence of a relatively large number of black troops also unsettled many local whites. For example, in a town near a military base in Georgia, white residents registered numerous complaints about black soldiers from the base directing local traffic.[132] In an inversion of expected racial movements, these black men were literally controlling white movements, commanding them to stop or to turn. In this case, the presence of the military allowed—required, in fact—black men to play a different role. Similarly, in the incident involving Cook, the military presence introduced new actors to the Jim Crow stage. Federal officials intervened in the interaction between a white man and a black man, and if the officer was not punished for the assault, his authority over the black man was nonetheless undermined by the actions of military officials.

The military intervention on Cook's behalf also points to another way in which the racial role of whites was being disrupted. The idealized white role of the paternalist protector had always coexisted with the reality of much racial violence. In an earlier era, violence had often been justified publicly as a necessary response to black aggression, fueled especially by the myth of the black savage beast as a threat to white women. By the World War II era, however, the evidence of white violence was increasingly a problematic one. Not only, as Grace Hale notes, were white Southerners seeing their acts of violence as potentially destroying white civilization, showing themselves to be the savages, but, as we shall see, by the 1950s, activists and the media would be barraging a national public with images of white Southerners as violent racists.[133] The public actions of the police officer potentially fueled growing tensions within the white community between paternalistic ideas and violent practices, while the involvement of a federal official signaled the arrival of a new player on the stage. This federal actor delivered a different and, from the perspective of many local whites, disruptive performance of whiteness.

Sometimes the expectations of playing the paternalist led to complicated interactions. Ellie J. Dahmer, whose husband, Vernon, was killed in 1966 for his civil rights activities, recalls an encounter related to the custom of whites cutting to the front of the line. As Dahmer recounts, she was waiting in line at a grocery store in Hattiesburg when a white woman "just pushed on in front of" her. A white man in line behind

Dahmer touched the woman's shoulder and, as Dahmer remembers, said, "Hey, you get in line just like everybody else. You don't push your way in front of nobody like this."[134] This encounter raises a number of questions, including Why was the white man standing behind Dahmer? At the very least, it indicates that not all whites followed the customs of cutting in line. Meanwhile, his response may have been one intended to protect or defend Dahmer or it may simply have been that the white woman was cutting in front of him too. We also do not know if the class status of the two white individuals factored into the confrontation. Still, if the white man's physical position behind Dahmer was an unexpected performance, so too was his rebuke of the white woman, carried out in Dahmer's presence. That is, in this instance and in front of a black woman, the white woman was denied the opportunity to exercise her racial claim to the front of the line. Her attempt to play that role had been undermined by a white man.

Many of the most intense encounters and unexpected performances occurred on buses.[135] In Mississippi, as in other Southern states, buses were particularly contentious spaces where within a confined interracial space black passengers always had to be ready to move. As noted previously, for example, Elport Chess's unexpected non-movement in 1946, when he failed to give up his seat for a white passenger, led to his beating and arrest. When Chess claimed that no one had told him to move, he challenged the expectation that he should always be watching and listening and preparing to vacate his seat and thus to prevent any potential disruption or waiting on the part of white passengers. Accordingly, Chess's challenge was essentially one of passivity, of not being aggressive enough in staying in his place. In his case, similar to Cook's, the white response was to reestablish the boundaries of racial space through force. It would have served as a reminder to Chess and to other passengers that he did not know his role well enough.

Another bus incident involving a soldier in 1946 illustrates the extent to which these spaces depended on a nonstop performance while on board. According to the *Jackson Advocate*, a black soldier recently returned from the war was sitting in the colored section and complaining about the Jim Crow buses. Those sentiments were not uncommon. Many veterans were increasingly reluctant to accept second-class status after returning home. On this occasion, white passengers overheard the soldier. Even though he was sitting in the racially appropriate place, the police arrived, beat the man, and then jailed and fined him.[136] The unexpected movement here was a verbal one, which was a public display of dissent. The soldier voiced a racial critique in an integrated verbal space, and those comments deviated from the script, which called for an acquiescent, contented black man. Especially in the climate of the World War II years, it is likely that bus drivers and white passengers visually and aurally scrutinized black men in uniform even more closely. Similar to ordeals involving Chess and Cook, the response of force was one intended to reestablish appropriate black behavior in these spaces. At the same time, even as these unexpected performances resulted in violence, on the surface they would seem to have done little to redefine these spaces. However, regardless of how the event ended, the performance disrupted the imagined Jim Crow world in at least two ways. First, it represented an alternative performance of blackness, one that publicly and before an interracial audience—on the bus and in the newspaper—rejected the role of contented servitude. For the black audience, such an enactment may have been inspirational.[137] For a white audience, that performance undercut the notion that blacks preferred segregation. If that happened once, it might be dismissed as an anomaly; but each time it happened it could raise doubts about the fundamental fictions that justified Jim Crow. Second, as was the case with Cook, Chess forced whites to play the part of violent aggressors. Accordingly, even as Chess's arrest and beating reestablished racial boundaries and norms of behavior, the unexpected performance had introduced other enactments of blackness and whiteness. While these reactions often produced a violent response, sometimes the white response could be equally unexpected.

John Peoples grew up in Starkville, served in the U.S. Marine Corps in World War II, and then attended Jackson College (later renamed Jackson State University). He recalls numerous incidents on buses, including a trip to Memphis in which a black man was beaten and arrested for refusing to move behind the curtain that separated the sections and another on a bus near Starkville in which a bus driver used the backside of a hatchet to beat a black soldier sitting in the front of the bus. That beating left the soldier paralyzed from the neck down.[138] Peoples also recounts another incident that did not end in violence. In Jackson, Peoples boarded a bus with no white passengers. He notes that in the absence of whites, black passengers generally observed an unwritten rule that the front two seats were off-limits. On this occasion, however, Peoples sat in one of these seats. The white bus driver, according to Peoples, asked him to move farther back. Peoples refused, reasoning to the driver, "The sign says from the rear to the front and this is the front." Peoples also noted that because it was dark the driver could not see if more seats were available farther back, and, according to Peoples, there was nothing the driver could do.[139]

Peoples's unexpected performance was both physical and verbal. In addition to not moving, like Elport Chess, Peoples verbally defended his actions before a white man. Here, however, the white response differs from others that ended in bloodshed. While Peoples notes that the driver could do nothing, the driver in fact had several options. He could have stopped the bus and called the police. He could have taken matters into his own hands and tried to forcibly move Peoples. But the driver did nothing. The driver initially followed the expected role when he told Peoples to move back, but he did not then follow through. We can only speculate regarding the driver's actions. Perhaps he considered it less of an issue given the absence of white passengers/witnesses, or maybe he did not feel comfortable standing up to Peoples in a space that contained only black passengers.[140] Whatever the reason, Peoples had altered the meaning of the space, and he had, even in the absence of white passengers, integrated a whites-only space and stood up to a white man. Especially emphasized in Peoples's retelling, the black man was the aggressor and the white man became passive and helpless, as "there was nothing he could do." Meanwhile, this unexpected performance played out before an audience of black passengers. If the actual performance was staged only once, it could nonetheless be performed multiple times as those in the audience told it to others. And as such, it may have been told or interpreted as a model for others or simply as a point of pride. Either way, moments like these—seemingly minor events without violence—could take on a life of their own in the witnessing and the retelling. In another bus ordeal, the audience is central to the story.

Mamie Phillips recalls an incident from the 1950s when she was a passenger on a bus heading toward Mendenhall, about thirty miles southwest of Jackson. The bus contained a number of black passengers and white passengers, and the sections were separated by a curtain that prevented black passengers from seeing out the front of the bus. At one point, Phillips notes, a black passenger stood up, pulled out a knife, and cut through the curtain. Several black soldiers were also on the bus, and, according to Phillips, the bus driver did nothing because he did not want to be challenged by the soldiers. The episode also included a black preacher who, after the man with the knife disembarked, said, as Phillips recalls, "I'll tell you what, the black and the white would be better off if all you and your kind was dead." While it is unclear in the retelling to whom the preacher was speaking, both black passengers and white passengers began to laugh. The next time Phillips rode on this bus, the curtain was gone.[141]

This bus scene is a complicated one. It includes an aggressive challenge from a black passenger with a knife and the latent challenge represented by black soldiers. The response, meanwhile, included a silent white driver and presumably silent white passengers, a critique of the action from a black preacher, and some sense of collective relief from both black and white passengers. The reaction of the passengers underscores the intensity of the unexpected performance. The slashing of the curtain created a tense moment and an uncertainty on the part of both blacks and whites about what would happen next. The ultimate result was a tangible, if limited, change in the physicality of this racial space. Still, the slashing of the curtain had modified this space, not only mitigating some of the inconvenience for black passengers—they could now see out of the front more easily—but also making the inside of this bus a more integrated one where now blacks and whites could see each other throughout the ride. Significantly, this modified space remained, as bus authorities decided not to put up a new curtain. In the case of Phillips and of Peoples, it is difficult to know why these disruptions, unlike those of Chess and Cook, did not lead to violence. It may have depended on the presence of a white person—particularly the driver—committed to enforcing racial expectations. It may also have depended on the ratio of white passengers to black passengers.

Another unexpected performance, one that in many respects carried fewer risks, was the act of avoidance in which blacks minimized encounters with whites in particular spaces. For example, many African Americans, in order to avoid the indignity of going to a back door at a home or place of business when they needed to speak with a white person, would simply wait until they could encounter the person on the street.[142] In a similar fashion, when H. A. Scott was about twelve years old, a white storeowner wanted Scott to address his son, who was about Scott's age, as "Mr." To avoid that verbal performance, Scott walked two blocks farther to another store. In each of these cases, African Americans were exercising some control over the racial dynamics of their encounters with whites. Curiously, to avoid some of the humiliations of Jim Crow, their enactments meant moving more—such as going to the next store—or waiting longer—such as waiting for someone to come outside. These efforts, then, like Jim Crow expectations, could be defined by waiting or by making extra movements. Still, it also meant avoiding the more humiliating performance and, like Richard Wright in the elevator choosing to juggle packages over giving a demeaning grin or a coerced thank-you to a white man, it was a compromise, a third solution between degradation and rebellion. It may not have been a great choice, but it provided some sense of control over the situation. In addition, it did in fact alter these racial spaces. For example, in refusing to play the part of the deferential servant using the back door, the space inside the home became less interracial. In these brief moments, whites were denied the chance to see the world as one of interracial intimacy and acquiescence.

For black Mississippians and white Mississippians in the final decades of Jim Crow, every day presented opportunities to move or not move, to act or not act, as expected. Each opportunity affirmed or altered meanings of racial space. Making this point is not to say that Jim Crow rule was in danger of being overthrown with every disruption on a sidewalk. In fact, white people had an extensive material advantage in economic and political power and generally the support of the federal government throughout the Jim Crow era. In these daily battles, though, at stake was what it meant to be living within this racial system. And in that sense, every encounter served to define what that meant for whites and what it meant for blacks, and each unexpected performance posed a challenge to the normative racial roles of a Jim Crow world.

IN THE 1930s, as H. A. Scott Sr. looked out across segregated spaces, he saw a Jim Crow stage where blacks and whites were separated but also very much together. Members of an earlier generation had created that stage. They erected barriers and passed new laws to remove from public spaces African Americans with political or economic leverage. In its place, the racial project of Jim Crow imagined a world where whites were in complete control in a paternalistic position, and it imagined blacks contentedly playing a role as servants. Importantly, it imagined blacks and whites loving each other as family members. The geography of Jim Crow, its signs and barriers, served to emphasize and make real that story. So too did the bodily physicality of Jim Crow, with the expectations for whites and blacks to move in ways consistent with their imagined roles. Nonetheless, dependent on these daily enactments, these interactions were charged with energy in which, in subtle and dramatic ways, whites and blacks gave unexpected performances. Thus, an imagined Jim Crow world daily vied for significance with the world that blacks and whites made, unmade, and remade together.

The bodily performances of whiteness and blackness were critically important to shaping the everyday realm and to defining for individuals what it meant to be, in the words of Richard Wright, "living Jim Crow." Physical space, however, was not the only arena where blacks and whites worked out the meanings of race and Jim Crow. Another key performative stage was a narrative one formed by the stories blacks and whites told about Jim Crow. And from these written and oral accounts, it would seem that multiple Jim Crow worlds existed at once.

2

BENEVOLENCE, VIOLENCE, AND MILITANCY

Competing Narratives of Race and Aggression

On a Sunday morning in May 1959 in the Delta town of Clarksdale, the Coahoma County sheriff's office responded to a report that Jonas Causey, a black man, had shot two white men outside his house. One of the men, Orville Bailey, died at the scene; the other man, B. W. Knight, survived with only minor injuries, and he called the sheriff's office from a nearby house. Shortly, at least fifteen county and city law enforcement officials converged outside Causey's house, with Jonas and his wife, Elnora, inside. Jonas was armed, and the police fired teargas cartridges into the house as they implored him to surrender. The teargas drew out Elnora but not Jonas. Approximately two hours after surrounding the house, officers opened fire with shotguns and machine guns, and the barrage of bullets killed Jonas. Also, at some point during the morning, someone shot Elnora in the leg.[1] Jonas's death brought the standoff to a close, but the stories about what had happened were just beginning to be told. Over the next several days, competing narratives of these events emerged in local and even national newspapers, with much of the attention focused on who Jonas Causey was.

The initial coverage from the local white-owned newspaper, the *Clarksdale Press Register*, described Jonas as a "crazed 70-year-old Negro." Supporting this assessment, the article noted that, according to the sheriff, Causey shot the white men for no reason. A more peculiar claim, coming from other officers at the scene, was that Jonas shot his wife in the leg because "she didn't fix his breakfast for him."[2] Similar accounts appeared in other white-owned newspapers and the wire services. The *Greenville Delta Democrat Times*, for example, carried the Associated Press story with the assertion from the officers that Causey shot his wife.[3] A reference to a dispute over breakfast also made its way into the pages of a national black publication. The *Chicago Defender* carried the story from the United Press International wire service and ran the article under the subheading, "Says Man Upset When His Wife Didn't Cook."[4] Each of these accounts painted an image of a mentally unstable man who was physically and verbally abusive to his wife and who had gone on a shooting rampage.

A somewhat different version of Jonas Causey was being discussed within the local black community. The black-owned *Jackson Advocate*, a weekly publication, had its first opportunity to publish an article on the events almost a week after the shootings. Similar to the other newspapers, the *Jackson Advocate* noted that Causey allegedly killed Bailey and that he had gone "berserk" when his wife had not fixed his breakfast. The most intriguing claim—one that diverged from mainstream coverage and that, if true, altered the fundamental meaning of the shootings—was related to the two white men who were shot. According to the *Jackson Advocate*, Causey knew Bailey and Knight; they "had previously threatened [the Causeys] in their home and [according to Elnora] 'fired the first shots.'"[5] This reference to a provocation by the two white men also appeared in a request by local NAACP president Aaron Henry for an FBI investigation.[6] As for the shooting of Elnora, the *Jackson Advocate* published a statement from her in which she declared that one of the white men, not her husband, shot her in the leg, and that it was this shot and an "advancing" Bailey that "enraged" Jonas and led him to shoot Bailey in the face.[7] Whereas the *Press Register* narrative characterized Jonas as the aggressor, endangering random strangers and his wife, the stories coming from the local black community framed Causey's actions as defensive and purposeful, as a reaction to violence initiated by white men, while also presenting multiple possibilities for Elnora's injury.

These characterizations by African Americans in the community had staying power. Nearly a year later, in front of a Civil Rights Advisory Committee, Aaron Henry referred to the incident as an example of police brutality against blacks.[8] Eight years later, Myrlie Evers, in a memoir of her life with slain civil rights leader Medgar Evers, connected Causey's death to the larger civil rights struggle, remembering him as one of the "victims" of 1959.[9] In each of these narratives from the local black community, the police and the white men were the attackers and the aggressors, while Causey was portrayed as a victim who had died defending his family and his home.

If both of these accounts agreed on some basic facts—the deaths of Jonas Causey and Orville Bailey and the injuries to Elnora Causey and B. W. Knight—the discrepancies point to two very different racial events. Depending on which facts we accept as true, these shootings relate a story of black criminality, of domestic abuse, of white vigilantism, or of police brutality. The real-life Jonas Causey may have been a criminal, a madman, an abusive husband, a victim, or a hero—or perhaps some combination of these. In this case, the surviving historical record is unclear about what happened and why. Nonetheless, the conflicting stories about Jonas Causey reveal a narrative clash over the representations of black aggression and white aggression.[10] This clash tapped into a much longer battle between blacks and whites over the meanings of race and violence, over the labeling of aggressors, criminals, protectors, victims, and heroes. Just as Jim Crow depended on the daily physical and verbal performances of race in everyday space, it also depended on the narrative performances of race where blacks and whites told stories about aggression.

Characterizing the telling and retelling of acts of aggression as performances allows us to examine the narratives on their own terms, as distinct cultural artifacts separate from the events being described. As such, we can consider how blacks and whites made sense of these moments. Within a Jim Crow context, we can chart the extent to which the characters in these accounts of violence resembled the expected racial roles of superior paternalistic whites and subservient loyal blacks discussed in the previous chapter. As performances we can also read these stories not simply as reflections of a particular racial view or as competing perspectives but rather as attempts to name the world and to narrate into existence conflicting versions of a Jim Crow world. That is, for both blacks and whites, the telling and retelling of an event was an opportunity for scripting it, for conforming the event to a particular worldview, for writing blacks and whites into specific roles, and, ultimately, for telling a story about Jim Crow. Words and subtle variations in the selection of verbs and adjectives served as key tools in these scripts. Facts were important, but no more so than exaggerations and understatements or the choices made in including some facts while excluding others. As the Causey shootings illustrate, episodes of aggression generated numerous writers-narrators. That group included the reporters and editors from the black press, white-owned newspapers, and wire services. It could also include law enforcement officials, civil rights activists, witnesses, and countless others sharing and passing on these stories in their daily interactions. In addition, the narrative performances emerged from a number of genres, from straight news stories to editorials to firsthand accounts to memories, and the audiences might include local whites and local blacks, as well as, at times, a national and international public. As narrative performances then, these accounts of white aggression and black aggression became another opportunity, similar to the daily battles over physical space, for staging and upstaging Jim Crow.

The narratives around race and aggression had a long, complicated history in the South and throughout the nation. Stories about black violence had been central to the creation of Jim Crow. In the 1880s and 1890s, for example, whites across the South used stories of black savage rapists to justify an explosion of racial violence against blacks.[11] Within these narratives, black violence made white violence necessary.[12] Beyond this defense of lynchings, the stories of a black criminal threat necessitated white domination, and both segregation and disfranchisement were closely tied to these racial fictions. Yet stories about black criminals were not confined to the South. During these formative years of Jim Crow, reformers in the urban North and social scientists were also talking about a black criminal threat. They rooted their stories in science and statistics to identify blacks with criminality. Ignoring social conditions, municipal policies, and other inequities that produced higher crime rates in black neighborhoods, reformers and intellectuals instead blamed blacks themselves.[13] As Southerners turned to a violent black threat to defend lynching, urban Northerners turned to tales of black crime to gloss over their own Jim Crow policies, which allowed for residential segregation, discrimination, police brutality, and occasionally vigilante violence.[14] Across the country, then, in the early twentieth century, the stories that white Americans told about black aggression became the basis for instituting and preserving racialized practices.

African Americans also tapped into a long tradition of talking about aggression. For African Americans, narratives of violence emerged in part from challenging the stories whites told about black criminality. For instance, in the 1890s, as tales of the black savage rapists accompanied lynchings, Ida B. Wells began documenting these incidents.[15] She countered that the charges of the rape threat were grossly exaggerated and often functioned as a cover story for white fears of black mobility.[16]

Her efforts represented the first of several national campaigns by black activists and white activists to debunk the myths surrounding lynchings and to narrate alternative versions of white aggression.[17] Meanwhile, stories of black aggression among African Americans also had a complicated history. Some African Americans distanced themselves from discussions of black crime as they embraced an ideology of racial uplift and tried to show through the performance of middle-class respectability that they were equal to whites.[18] Others, however, such W. E. B. DuBois and Monroe Work, challenged the notion of blacks as innately criminal and pointed to the racism and social conditions as key factors in crime in the urban North.[19] In other forms, too, narratives of black aggression produced alternative models to mainstream constructions of black criminality. For example, folktales and, later, blues music featured images of a trickster or badman skirting the law and outsmarting authorities and white people.[20] These stories framed black aggression as heroic and white aggression as immoral and oppressive. It was a tradition that glorified a violent or aggressive response to abuse and injustice, and often did so through a coded language that hid the racialized meanings from some audiences.[21]Accordingly, in 1959, both black Mississippians and white Mississippians drew on extensive legacies of talking about aggression that were part of the everyday culture of race and that fit within how blacks and whites understood Jim Crow.

This chapter charts the narratives of race and violence from blacks and whites in the three decades that preceded the Jonas Causey incident in 1959. Like the daily interactions in shared space, the narrative performances around racial aggression regularly served to affirm, question, and redefine the meanings of whiteness and blackness. For many white Mississippians, stories about aggression reinforced the myth of a Jim Crow world populated by white paternalists and loyal black servants. That vision appears within their accounts of white aggression in the form of lynchings and state executions. Stories around white benevolence are also present in the letters and petitions from white citizens related to paroles, pardons, and suspended sentences for black convicts. Conversely, many black Mississippians created their own narratives that portrayed whites as violent aggressors and blacks as heroic and brave. Circulating within the black community and revealed in black-owned newspapers and oral histories, these narratives jointly emphasized white injustice and black militancy. Finally, some events, like the Causey ordeal, inspired conflicting and complicated narratives from whites and from blacks, including the stories of Eddie Noel, a black man who in 1954 shot and killed three white men. Amid these varying accounts of violence, perhaps no tales evoked racial meanings in the Jim Crow South quite like those surrounding lynchings and their less-heralded "legal" cousins, state executions.

NARRATIVES OF LYNCHINGS AND EXECUTIONS
IN THE WHITE COMMUNITY

From 1882 to 1960, more than 3,400 African Americans were lynched in the United States, with the overwhelming majority of these episodes carried out in the South. Mississippi led the way, with 539 of those lynchings. Broken down by decade, the highest number of lynchings of African Americans occurred in the 1890s, with 1,132 such incidents; every decade after that witnessed a drop from the previous one, from 752 in the 1900s, to 555 in the 1910s, to 248 in the 1920s, to 123 in the 1930s, to 33 in the combined decades of the 1940s and 1950s.[22] Statistically, then, the history of lynching during this period is one of steady decline. Formative changes also marked this time period. Lynchings from the 1890s to the 1910s regularly took the form of a spectacle attended by hundreds or even thousands and were presented as dramas of "popular justice"; by the 1920s, these massively attended community events were gradually giving way to smaller, more secretive killings, even as the next decade witnessed a few spectacle lynchings.[23] Some of these transformations are reflected in the ways white Southerners narrated these events, indicating that if dramatic displays of violence were a central feature of Jim Crow, so too were the shifting stories whites created to explain these acts.[24]

The rapid increase in lynchings in the 1880s and 1890s came partly in response to fears of African American economic and political advancement that had accelerated in the Reconstruction era.[25] While some white Southerners expressed concern about the rise in the number of lynchings, many others wholeheartedly endorsed these practices as necessary in stifling a particular black threat.[26] At the center of this justification for lynching was a story of black aggression, and especially of black male sexual aggression toward white women.[27] This narrative theme was present not only in accounts of actual lynchings but also within the hypothetical realm of possible ones. As national journalist Ray Stannard Baker explained in *Following the Color Line* (1908),

"Every argument on lynching in the South gets back sooner or later to the question of rape. Ask any high-class citizen—the very highest—if he believes in lynching, and he will tell you roundly, 'No.' Ask him about lynching for rape, and in ninety-nine cases out of a hundred he will instantly weaken."[28] Baker's observation suggested that many white Southerners—and he assumed in particular that this was true for the elite—generally opposed lynchings. But he used this point to set up the exception related to an accusation of rape. Thus, the uneasiness among whites about lynching could only be assuaged by the presence of a black male sexual aggressor, a character that would be regularly deployed in the retelling of these violent acts.[29]

The other central character in these early narratives was the white victim. Indeed, Baker's remarks also implied the narrative necessity for a white female victim of sexual assault. That character routinely appeared in hypothetical stories about lynching—such as Baker's reference—and it appeared within popular culture artifacts. One of the best-known examples from this early Jim Crow period comes from Thomas Dixon's 1905 novel *The Clansman*, which D. W. Griffith adapted into the national blockbuster film *Birth of a Nation* (1915).[30] The novel and the film depicted the story of black advancement during Reconstruction as a sexual threat to white women. Fictional accounts strengthened the public perception that associated lynching with black men sexual assaulting white females. In reality, only about 25 percent of lynchings were related to the accusation of rape or attempted rape.[31]

Beyond the hypothetical circumstances referenced by Baker and in literature and film, accounts of actual lynchings also included altered details in order to narrate an event featuring the characters of a black male aggressor and a white female victim. Such was the case in the lynching of Sam Hose in 1898 outside Atlanta. Hose killed his white employer and fled. After Hose was apprehended, a mob seized him, tied him to a tree, and cut off various body parts before burning him alive.[32] Beyond these basic facts, accounts of the initial encounter varied. A hired detective concluded that during an argument between Hose and his white employer, the white man pulled out a gun. Hose responded by grabbing an ax, throwing it at the white man and killing him. In this account, the white man had been the aggressor and Hose had acted in self-defense. But that version did not appear in local newspapers. Instead, the local press omitted details of a white aggressor and situated Hose as the initial attacker.[33] In addition, within the community, rumors circulated that Hose had also raped his white employer's wife, and thus in the retelling, the black man became a murderer and a rapist. The framing of these events hints at the ways in which a Jim Crow ideology set narrative rules for framing acts of white aggression. To exist alongside white paternalism, stories about lynchings depended on black villains and white victims, regularly depicted as the black savage rapist and the innocent white female.

By the 1930s, the stories white Southerners told about lynchings were changing. Nationally, the NAACP continued to push for antilynching legislation and to publicize its own accounts revealing the motivations and the brutality of lynching and building on the early efforts of Ida B. Wells. Other narratives emerged from antilynching researchers, such as Jessie Daniel Ames and Arthur Raper, who likewise noted the lawlessness and savagery of these incidents.[34] In addition, the national media occasionally publicized acts of violence and racial injustice in the South, such as with the case of nine Scottsboro, Alabama, African American teenagers falsely accused of raping two white women in 1931.[35] Within the context of this intensified scrutiny, many white Southerners increasingly expressed concern that lynchings, as Grace Elizabeth Hale contends, showed whites to be lawless savages.[36] More to the point, this image of white violence threatened the narrative of white paternalists and black servants that Jim Crow supposedly preserved. Nationally, it also competed with a nostalgic rendering of the South, embodied in the 1930s and 1940s in films such as *Gone with the Wind* and *Song of the South*, which imagined a simpler, bucolic South of plantations and laidback, carefree blacks.[37] Meanwhile, even as the yearly rate for lynching steadily dropped, the practice had become almost exclusively a Southern one. Within this dynamic, Mississippi continued to outpace other states in the region as a site for these racialized killings. Accordingly, the stories that white Southerners, and white Mississippians in particular, told about lynchings were especially important in explaining and justifying Jim Crow to themselves and to a national public. And if these narratives contained some familiar elements from an earlier generation—the black aggressor and the white, usually female, victim—they also revealed developing divisions within the white community. Ultimately, these stories shifted responsibilities for lynchings away from the white community in an effort to disassociate racial violence from Jim Crow rule.

In Mississippi in the 1930s and 1940s, the stories about lynching drew on the earlier accounts as well as growing concerns as to what this vigilantism potentially suggested about white people.[38] Accordingly, narrating lynchings in particular ways would continue to be important within the white community, as was the case involving African American Elwood Higginbotham. The lynching of Higginbotham in 1935, like that of Sam Hose, was related to a dispute between a black man and a white man. Higginbotham rented and farmed land in the northern hill country near Oxford. Glen Roberts, a white neighbor, was upset that Higginbotham had driven cattle across his property. According to an investigation of the incident that appears in the records of the Association of Southern Women for the Prevention of Lynching (ASWPL), Roberts went to Higginbotham's house intending to whip Higginbotham. Roberts approached the front door and demanded to be let inside. Higginbotham refused, prompting Roberts to go around the house and then to use an ax to break down the back door and an interior one. As Roberts hacked at the doors, Higginbotham waited inside and warned Roberts not to come in "or I will hurt you." Roberts ignored him, though, and as he charged forward, Higginbotham gunned him down at close range.[39] Higginbotham fled the scene but was soon apprehended. He was indicted for murder and claimed self-defense. As the jury deliberated, a rumor spread "about town that two of the jurors were holding out for acquittal." A mob of about one hundred individuals formed and took Higginbotham from the jail and lynched him.[40] In this version of the story, from the ASWPL investigation, the white man was the aggressor. He had come to Higginbotham's home and torn down the doors. Presumably, he was still holding the ax as he charged toward the black man. In contrast, the report characterized Higginbotham's actions as defensive, which even included a warning to Roberts. In this account, although the black man had not been passive or submissive, he was also not the initiator or the aggressor.

A different version of these events appeared in the local newspaper, the *Oxford Eagle*. This article did not mention that the fight occurred at Higginbotham's house, nor did it mention that Roberts burst through the door with an ax. It also omitted the details about a possible whipping. Instead, through its vagueness about the location and the initial cause, the *Oxford Eagle* coverage suggested that the two men had been involved in a random, spontaneous encounter in some public space. In this narrative, the white man was not the aggressor but the victim. Higginbotham's role was also rewritten, as he became a criminal who killed a white man and who thus got what he deserved. It was the omissions that altered the story, and those omissions were intentional. When asked about his version of the story, the editor explained to the investigator "that he had to live in Oxford and that he wanted to get along with the people there, and that the race situation made it practically impossible to carry the facts about the killing."[41]

In noting a desire to "get along with the people," it is not clear precisely to which people the editor is referring. He may have meant all of his white readers or members of the lynch mob or local authorities. It is equally unclear what he meant by the "race situation." That might have been a reference to the reaction of local blacks or even to the reaction of a national public. Nonetheless, it is clear that in telling a story about a lynching, the editor believed that he had to tell the story in a particular way for his audience.

In narrating accounts of lynchings, it was not only that white people could not be the aggressors but also that the acts of aggression could not be framed as the collective will of the white community, as had been the case in an earlier generation. Collective violence in the name of the community contradicted the regionally and nationally circulating image of a racially harmonious South. To account for this contradiction—to preserve the narrative of white benevolence amid the continuance of white vigilantism—lynching narratives steadily shifted responsibility away from the white community and toward the isolated actions of working-class and poor whites, or in some cases, to particular towns or regions deemed out of step with the rest of the state.[42] This shift occurred even as mob violence continued in some locales. For example, in Scooba, Mississippi, in 1930, near the Alabama border, a white mob seized two African Americans from the police and carried out a spectacle lynching. The mob hanged the two men as, according to the *New York Times*, the officers, who had been tied to trees, looked on helplessly.[43] Similar in format to the lynchings of an earlier period, this one would seem to suggest a unified white community acting under the guise of popular justice. However, many white individuals in the state and across the South roundly condemned it. The nearby *Meridian Star* criticized it for fostering "social, business, and civic ruin."[44] A Norfolk, Virginia, newspaper called it a "disgrace" and an "indictment against southern civilization," while the *New Orleans Times-Picayune* labeled it an "exhibition of savage lawlessness" that "decent" Mississippians had abandoned long ago.[45] As these critiques expressed some concern for the larger consequences or for what the actions might reflect about white Southerners, they also separated the lynchings from Jim Crow. That is, instead of framing these events as defenses of white civilization, they framed them as actions in which "decent" white people would not engage.

Within Mississippi circles, references to "decent" people juxtaposed with lynch mobs could evoke not only class divisions but also overlapping geographic ones. As V. O. Key Jr. observed in 1949, throughout the twentieth century, political contests in the state often played out as a battle that pitted the wealthy Delta planters and their industrial and commercial allies against the "rednecks" and small farmers from northern and eastern counties in the hills and the piney woods.[46] Indeed, these assessments mirrored the perceptions of Delta elites, such as David Cohn, who, as noted in Chapter 1, placed nearly all of the blame for racism and violence on poor whites and their "blind hatred" of blacks.[47] In similar fashion, the Scooba killings, occurring in the eastern hill country, could have been imagined not only in class terms but in sectional ones. In this imagining, it was not the Jim Crow system that was the problem, but rather it was the actions of a few unenlightened whites.

Similar concerns informed the response to a pair of 1942 lynchings, which also occurred on the east side of the state. In Shubuta, Charles Lang and Ernest Green, fourteen-year-old African American boys, had been playing outside with a thirteen-year-old white girl. A passing white motorist saw them, and soon the two boys were arrested and charged with attempted rape. While in custody, a mob seized them and hanged them from a bridge. The governor condemned the lynching, saying that he "wanted the public to know" that "the better class of people [in Mississippi] condemn this wrong."[48] The governor's reference to a better class sought to situate blame with a less respectable segment of the community. A *Meridian Star* editorial extended that assessment by comparing the lynchers to Adolf Hitler and suggesting that the mob should have left the case for a "civilized court."[49] Similar then to the Scooba lynching, this killing also sparked concerns that it potentially reflected badly on the entire white community, and authorities throughout the state acted quickly to distance themselves from the incident.

Less than a week later, and just thirty miles down the road in Laurel, African American Howard Wash was convicted of murdering his white boss. The jury found him guilty of manslaughter and delivered a life sentence. Upset that Wash had not been sentenced to die, a mob stormed the jail, took Wash, and killed him. Echoing the *Meridian Star*'s critique of the previous week's lynching, a *Laurel Leader-Call* editorial referred to the situation as a "crisis" and reminded its readers that "violence is not the remedy for lawlessness."[50] A *Jackson Clarion-Ledger* editorial also condemned the lynching, calling it "deliberate murder" and noting that the mob had attacked not only the victim but also "the State, the courts, and the government."[51] Confirming the fears of many individuals throughout the state, these two lynchings attracted national attention, and for the first time in the Jim Crow era in Mississippi, they also drew a federal investigation.[52] The *Meridian Star* responded to this federal presence by criticizing the intrusion and arguing that it threatened "the mutually happy inter-racial unity and cooperation in the South."[53] In some respects, these condemnations of both the lynchings and the federal involvement emerged from the same ideological position, in which poor whites and outside investigators could be jointly blamed for jeopardizing the racial harmony between the "better class" of whites and black Mississippians.

Meanwhile, in other cases, concerns about possible lynchings also exposed tensions within the white population between local and state authority. In 1940, for instance, in the town of Prentiss, between Jackson and Hattiesburg, African American Hilton Fortenberry was sentenced to die in the shooting death of a white man, J. C. Sanford. Another African American, James Franklin, who, according to Fortenberry, had fired the shots that killed Sanford, had his death sentence commuted to life in prison by Governor Paul Johnson Sr.[54] Concerned that Fortenberry might be lynched, the governor dispatched thirty state guard troops, four officers, four highway patrolmen, and a major general to guard Fortenberry until his execution.[55] The local newspaper, the *Prentiss Headlight*, remarked that the sheriff had advised the governor that he did not need assistance. In an editorial, the newspaper referred to the intervention as "another insult to the people by the man in the governor's office," arguing that "the people of Jefferson Davis County are not a horde of blood-thirsty, uncivilized brutes."[56] Along with this direct response, the news story on the front page also suggested that the guard presence was excessive and unappreciated by locals. According to the story, as Fortenberry approached the scaffolding moments before being hanged, the local minister accompanying him called off the guard, explaining that "the people here are law abiding citizens."[57] Embodied in the governor's reaction was a general concern among many whites about the appearance of savagery in lynchings, related either to their own sense of white civilization or to national perceptions of the South. Those sentiments, however, directed attention away from the larger Jim Crow system that allowed for continuing acts of racial violence, and imagined lynching as an isolated and unfortunate response from a select few, or in this case, from a particular community. In response, the editor, the minister, and perhaps other whites in Prentiss took exception to being thought of as potential lynchers capable of such savagery. It is also likely that in countering the assumption of barbarism with civilized orderliness, the Prentiss newspaper emphasized Fortenberry's calm demeanor and mentioned that officials had given him a narcotic before the hanging.

While locals were insulted by the presence of troops in their town, that tone was absent from the media coverage of the execution outside Prentiss. The *Jackson Clarion-Ledger*, for example, contained no direct or indirect criticism of the governor, noting instead that the presence of the guard would preserve "the South's extended no-lynching record."[58] In a few respects, these various papers found common ground. None of them questioned the decision to put Fortenberry to death. And in carrying out that sentence, they all suggested that vigilantism and dramatic, unpredictable displays of a white mob should not be part of it. Prentiss whites simply claimed that they would never resort to such tactics. Accordingly, the effect of telling a lynching story as an isolated event or as the actions of poor whites was to expose a class or sectional division within the white community. If the narratives of lynchings became ever more important in explaining violence and race relations in the 1930s and 1940s, they were not the only stories of white aggression circulating within the white community. Executions produced their own accounts of race and Jim Crow. As explained below, those narratives engaged with dialogues around lynching and benevolence while also revealing tensions within the white community over paternalism and white authority.

From 1930 to 1950, the State of Mississippi put to death 104 individuals, including 86 African Americans. Thus, similar to lynchings, the death penalty was overwhelmingly applied to black individuals.[59] Executions and lynchings had even more in common, including a shared history. The spectacle lynching that became prevalent in the late nineteenth century emulated the model of the public hanging, featuring, for example, a highly ritualized performance of community justice, an expected confession from the condemned, and a large crowd. As others have demonstrated, lynchings and executions both performed the work of racial discipline, delivering a message to the black community about the reach of white authority and the dispensability of black life.[60] Yet despite these similarities, in Jim Crow Mississippi executions generated far less angst within the white community than did lynchings. In fact, politicians and others regularly trumpeted the successful administering of the death penalty as a display of justice and law and order. In numerous cases, judges and other officials pushed for a speedy trial and execution as a means of preventing a lynching.[61] Accordingly, executions provided additional opportunities for white Southerners to tell stories about race, aggression, and benevolence.

Regardless of the race of the condemned, the accounts of executions, which regularly appeared in newspapers, consistently contained several elements. The standard narrative included a religious reference, noting for example that the condemned had undergone a religious conversion or made peace with God or simply that a minister had been present in the final moments before the execution. These narratives often featured a performance of contrition in which the condemned admitted guilt and remorse and then issued a warning to others not to follow in the same path. Collectively, these thematic components reinforced the solemnity of the event and affirmed that the death sentence had been correctly applied.[62] The account in the *Meridian Star* of the 1941 execution of African American Booker T. Childress, who had been convicted of murdering a black female, contained these narrative elements.[63] While executions for crimes within the black community were unusual, and might appear to exist outside a Jim Crow racial framework, the story about this execution was very much a Jim Crow one.

The *Meridian Star* noted that shortly before the execution, Childress had confessed and that as he walked to his death, other prisoners sang a "religious song." The reporter focused on two items in particular: the portable electric chair and Childress's body. Childress was only the fifth person in the state to be put to death in the state's portable electric chair (its first use had come seventeen months earlier), and probably because of the novelty of this new technology the reporter provided information about the electrocution process, including extensive technical and aesthetic details about the skull cap, the electric chair, and the electrodes attached to the condemned's legs.[64] Mississippi's move to electrocution reflected national changes in the twentieth century, as states shifted from hangings to firing squads to electrocutions to gas chambers to lethal injections. Each successive measure suggested a more civilized, less painful method of causing death. Thus, as the practice of lynching continued to revolve around torture or at least to be associated with torture, the execution narrative was notable for regularly emphasizing the absence of torture or even discomfort.[65] In the Childress story, for example, the reporter noted that Jimmy Thompson, the man who operated the electric chair, asked the condemned "if he was comfortable" and then added, "You are not going to be hurt a bit!"[66] At a moment when many whites were concerned about the potential barbarity of lynchings, executions were narrated as civilized, orderly, and humane.[67] Within a racial context, executions and the narratives about them set the stage for white Mississippians to more easily perpetuate a myth of white benevolence, in which, unlike for lynchings, officials could comfort a man about to die. Yet if the emphasis on comfort seemed to distinguish this execution from a lynching, the discussion of the body reconnected the narratives in these two practices.

The performance of the lynching regularly featured mutilations of the body. Lynch mobs often tortured the victim before death by burning the body or by cutting off body parts, especially the genitals. Witnesses in some cases left with body parts as souvenirs or had their picture taken with the body.[68] Similarly, in the article on Childress's death, a narrative suggesting orderliness and solemnity, themes of body mutilation slipped into the story. The reader learned from the *Meridian Star* story that the switch was thrown and that two minutes later Childress was pronounced dead. But rather than ending the story there, the reporter directed the reader's attention to Childress's lifeless body. Childress's left leg was crippled, which had prevented officials from sufficiently separating his heels. As a result, when the current passed through his body it also jumped across his heels. The reporter painted a vivid picture of burning socks as the "body jerked backward."[69] Thus, while the reader did not witness firsthand a black body being disfigured and ultimately put to death, he or she was nonetheless able to read about it. In this way, the execution narrative could still contain a familiar theme of a black body being mutilated and destroyed by whites but without whites getting their hands dirty. The execution narrative, like the lynching, continued to tell a story of white power and white superiority, while at the same time civilizing white aggression. Like lynching, it also left in place an element of voyeurism and sadism, experienced here in the retelling. If the execution can be read as a contained and lawful killing of a black man, the story about it could turn that execution into a demonstration of compassionate white benevolence, where even death could now be delivered with comfort.

In executions involving a condemned African American and a white victim, newspaper stories emphasized a process that appeared to be much different from the vigilantism of lynchings. On the Gulf Coast in 1941, the *Port Gibson Reveille* covered the execution of Roosevelt Green, an African American convicted of raping a white woman. Uncharacteristic of many other execution articles during this period, this one was only four sentences long. But, similar to lengthier articles, it focused on the nature of the proceedings. The last sentence, for example, remarked that "the electrocution was as orderly and quiet as the trial, all of which attested the law-abiding spirit of our community."[70] Two years later, the *McComb Enterprise* struck a similar tone in noting that the execution of African American Sam Porter had been "carried out very quietly, legally."[71] These terms—"legally" and "quietly"—hinted at a sense of civic pride that Porter had not been lynched and that the larger community had shown restraint. At the same time, this language to describe how justice had been dispensed drew on a much longer discursive history. In both the South and the nation, earlier explanations for executions and lynchings had also often emphasized the orderliness and restraint of those who carried out a formal or informal sentence of death.[72] By the 1940s, however, with growing national and federal scrutiny and with concerns about how lynchings in particular reflected on white people, narratives characterizing the response as a civilized one became even more important in Mississippi.

Yet, while white Mississippians often seized upon the successful execution as an occasion to suggest that vigilantism was in the past, at times the dialogues about how to punish black aggression revealed rifts within the white community. These tensions, for example, surfaced in 1946 in discussions about the sentencing of three black men found guilty of robbery with a deadly weapon of a white man. Two of the men, John Augustine and Howard White, received the death sentence, while the third, Virgil Smith, was given a twenty-year prison term.[73] Numerous white individuals wrote to Governor Fielding Wright.[74] Some were upset that Smith was not sentenced to death; others argued that none of them should have been given the death penalty for robbery. Echoing some of the concerns over lynching, one of the letter writers criticized the statute that allowed robbery to be punishable by death, calling it "a most savage and barbarous statute—the most savage of any state . . . a disgrace to Mississippi."[75] Maurice Gatlin, a New Orleans attorney and native of Mississippi, asked the governor to reduce Howard White's sentence. Gatlin's request was made public, and in response a district attorney suggested that the New Orleans attorney worked for a "negro organization." Gatlin refuted this accusation in his letter to the governor, remarking that Mississippi did "not need the assistance of any negro, communist or subversive organization."[76] If the personal attack was relatively minor, it was nonetheless a reminder that advocating for leniency carried risks for the Jim Crow reputations of whites. In a broader sense, the criticism leveled at Gatlin illustrated that within the white community there sometimes existed a thin line between performing benevolence and advocating racial equality, as well as an implicit question as to who should deliver the act of benevolence. Accordingly, many white individuals who argued for a less severe response to black aggression against whites also clearly stated their white supremacy credentials.

Concerns over the appropriate Jim Crow response emerged in a case involving fifteen-year-old Charles Trudell and fourteen-year-old James Lewis. In February 1946, these two black teenagers were found guilty of murdering their white employer.[77] Following the trial, letters poured into Governor Wright's office from individuals from Mississippi and across the country. Few disputed the charges, but a significant number argued against the death sentence, related primarily to the age of the condemned. One of these letters came from a woman in Alabama who was a native of Mississippi. She explained that she shared the governor's "views and all other white Mississippian's views about the blacks—they take to crime like fish to water." She also believed "in keeping them in their place," but she could not "swallow the idea of executing children." She concluded by noting that the "troublemakers in the north" would make the boys into martyrs.[78] This writer, in arguing against execution, solidified her beliefs in white supremacy through a reference to black inferiority and the criminal threat, while also noting how a national public might respond to an execution. Another letter, from a white man in Canton, framed his argument similarly. He first noted his general support for white aggression against blacks, remarking that some blacks "should be thrown in the river with hands and feet tied behind them." But he then declared that children should not be executed and concluded with a public opinion concern by noting that Mississippi was already in the "limelight enough."[79] At least one writer tapped directly into the ideology of white supremacy to argue against the execution by claiming that blacks at the age of fifteen were less intelligent, less mature, and mentally less developed than whites of the same age.[80] In each of these cases, the concerns about executing Trudell and Lewis were quite similar to concerns about lynchings. Many whites worried that some executions risked attracting negative national publicity, which would ultimately lead to federal involvement in the South. In addition, each expressed a concern about the larger implications of executing children. Indeed, each of these letters reflected a view of the world where blacks were inferior and whites had a duty to advocate for and protect them. These writers distinguished themselves from the vigilantes and lynchers without renouncing Jim Crow.[81]

By the 1930s, the ways in which white Mississippians talked publicly about racial aggression had changed since the early days of the Jim Crow era. If in an earlier period lynchings were staged as acts of community justice, a later generation framed lynchings as isolated incidents unrepresentative of the larger community. Poor whites continued to take much of the blame for vigilante violence. Meanwhile, many white Mississippians positioned executions as a more civilized response to black aggression. In the process, they could continue to imagine Jim Crow as a system defined by benevolence and white protection rather than by violence. The persistence of dramatic, public displays of violence undermined the claims of benevolence, making the stories about white aggression that much more important. Conversely, if the narratives of white aggression sometimes exposed intraracial tensions, advocates for white supremacy found it much easier to talk about crime within the black community in ways that justified Jim Crow and reinforced a belief in white benevolence.

NARRATIVES OF BLACK CRIMINALITY

Criminal justice in Mississippi reflected other Jim Crow practices. In cases involving white victims, alleged African American perpetrators could expect to be punished more severely than white perpetrators. Meanwhile, cases in which both parties were African American were often characterized by leniency and neglect.[82] Some crimes among blacks were virtually ignored, including adultery, bigamy, prostitution, and the rape of black women.[83] On plantations, landowners often handled criminal incidents among their laborers, and within the legal system many landowners could get charges waived against their black workers. All of these factors contributed to a high rate of aggression within the black community. In the first three decades of the 1900s, African Americans were three times more likely than whites to be murdered.[84] Accordingly, in its inattention to black-on-black crime, the criminal justice system articulated Jim Crow values that privileged white life over black life.

In the narratives about black crime in the South, a few individuals, similar to reformers in the urban North, expressed concern about aggression within the black community. In the 1930s, a number of intellectuals made a connection between Jim Crow and black aggression. Scholars John Dollard and Hortense Powdermaker each commented on a proclivity among black Mississippians toward violence.[85] Similarly, Mississippian David L. Cohn remarked that "crime among Negroes is one of the gravest problems against which the Delta struggles."[86] Despite these observations, however, crime within the black community in the South drew relatively little critical discussion from white Mississippians prior to the 1950s.[87] Yet, if white officials devoted scant attention to alleviating black crime, the narratives they constructed around it did important work for Jim Crow, serving to extend the performative roles that positioned blacks as servants and whites as merciful paternalists.

From the 1930s to the 1950s, narratives about black crime appeared within the thousands of letters that white Mississippians wrote to the governor about black convicts.[88] Some letter writers argued for commuting a death sentence to a life term or for keeping a death sentence in place. Some made requests for a lighter sentence, a suspended sentence, or a pardon. Some wrote to the governor in the hope of securing the release of a laborer, especially during the World War II years, when labor was in high demand. Each of them ultimately made a case for or against leniency for an African American.[89] The letters themselves were performative on multiple levels. To achieve a specific aim, such as a pardon for a convict needed on a farm, a writer may have disguised his true intentions or he may have worded the letter to achieve a desired result. Still, even in accounting for these calculated efforts, the letters consistently tapped into a discernible narrative about black criminality and white expectations.

Regardless of the position taken for or against leniency, the central character in the letter, the black convict, nearly always fell into one of two categories: the "good Negro" or the "bad Negro."[90] The "good Negro" was an individual who was loyal and deferential to whites. The "good Negro" was someone who knew his or her racial "place," and most important for eligibility for leniency, she or he was someone who represented no threat to the white community. The "bad Negro" was his or her opposite. These individuals were likely to be surly and insubordinate around whites, and they likely considered themselves the intellectual and social equal of whites. The "bad Negro" may or may not have been a physical threat to white people. Relative to expected racial performances in daily life, this individual moved in unexpected ways, such as refusing to step off the sidewalk for whites or refusing to give up a seat on a bus. Within this system, the black individual's performance around white people, as a "good" or as a "bad" Negro, was at least as important as other factors, such as demonstrating repentance or that one had been rehabilitated.

Many of the requests explicitly used this good Negro/bad Negro discourse. In 1935, M. L. Aldridge, the superintendent at Parchman Farm, the state penitentiary, wrote to the governor about one of his inmates, Eddie Barrett, who was serving a sentence for murder. Barrett, Aldridge noted, was "one of the best 'white folks negroes' in the whole county."[91] A 1941 letter supporting the suspension of Louberta Thompson's sentence for manslaughter remarked that she was a "splendid servant, humble negro."[92] A letter seeking a release for Willie Price, who in 1949 was sentenced to death for the murder of a black child, went a step further, explaining, "Unlike many educated Negroes, he was humble and groveling around white people, like many white people expect Negroes to be."[93] Price's sentence was commuted. In describing the "good Negro," "humble" was a particularly popular word choice, and this descriptor aligned closely with the performative expectation that all blacks should be humble, deferential servants.

If having a reputation for being a "good Negro" could help an individual, having a reputation as a "bad Negro" could be detrimental. In 1952, Alfred Carter was serving a sentence of more than twenty years for manslaughter and assault and battery with intent. He also had five previous arrests for assault and battery. Carter requested clemency, and in response, Carl H. Everett, Carter's employer, argued against clemency, referring to Carter as a "bad negro" and a "trouble maker."[94]

Four years later, a prison report on Allen Golden noted that he was "a very bad negro," without going into detail.[95] Neither of these references explained what was meant by "bad," indicating that the writer assumed the reader would know the meaning.

Occasionally, an individual up for parole or seeking a reduced sentence received mixed character reviews from those writing to the governor. In 1955, Lucious Evans, a World War II veteran, pled guilty to manslaughter for what he referred to as the accidental shooting death of his wife.[96] He was sentenced to a four-year prison term with a recommendation for parole after eighteen months. In October 1956, a penitentiary report summarizing his case noted that Evans's employer, Mrs. W. T. Rogers, supported his parole and that she had called him "the most dependable, intelligent, and humble darkey she has ever employed."[97] Rogers's characterization was unusual in that it combined the two characterizations. "Dependable" and "humble," along with the derogatory term "darkey," referenced the image of a "good Negro," a minstrel-like character loyal to whites. The word "intelligent" however was not normally associated with the "good Negro." Perhaps Rogers recognized and appreciated his intelligence without realizing that this characterization might work against his release. In fact, another letter implied that Evans was not a "good Negro." A police officer believed that Evans "considered himself above most of the negroes for he had worked with white people so long he considered himself their equal."[98] In these letters, the variations on "good" and "bad" Negroes reflected a Jim Crow worldview in which the writers imagined idealized roles for blacks, meek and subservient to whites. In another regard, these letters—or at least the sentiments in these letters—could inform the racial performances of African Americans. We do not know if Lucious Evans or Willie Price played a particular role to aid their early release, but we can assume that many black convicts recognized that if they played the part of the humble servant, they might be rewarded with a lighter sentence.

As the letters pointed to expected racial performances for African Americans, the clemency process also had important consequences for the racial roles played by whites, and in particular for allowing white citizens to play the part of paternalists. In requesting clemency, authorities encouraged individuals to submit a petition signed by "some reputable citizens of the county and as many of the county officers as are willing to sign."[99] While it seems likely that letters from attorneys, judges, law enforcement officials, and others connected to the criminal justice process carried much weight, governors also wanted an assurance that local whites supported the decision on clemency. Tom Allen Draughn's pardon request, for example, included separate petitions of support signed by the "Citizens of Yazoo County" and "Citizens of Covington County."[100] Draughn's attorney informed the governor that "every white citizen" in the community had signed it.[101] The opportunity to sign or not sign a petition extended some authority to white citizens in deciding the extent of punishment for African Americans, just as spectacle lynchings had represented an act of judgment by the white community. In these cases though, the petition was not to authorize an act of violence but instead to endorse an act of mercy.[102] Even if the decision rested with the governor, the role of white citizens in this process was one that not only reinforced racial hierarchies but also let white citizens play the part of paternalists making decisions about black lives.

As petitions and letters allowed whites to demonstrate benevolence, this process also led some to question whether or not whites were living up to that expectation. For example, in a 1946 incident in which a black man killed a white man, Daisy Cochran argued for commuting a death sentence to life imprisonment, observing that "we, as a people, have probably neglected our duty to the negro race by failing to develope [sic] them into more intelligent and better educated citizens who, with these developments, might be more able to control their passions, moods and tempers."[103] In her letter, Cochran tapped into assumptions about blacks as overly emotional and less intelligent than whites, but she also took to heart the idea of paternalism, concluding that whites had not fulfilled their obligations to blacks. In this case, that sentiment is even more striking, given that the condemned man in question had been found guilty of killing a white man.

Related to this paternalistic strand in the letters were characterizations of blackness that linked childlike behavior and black injury to white amusement. Indeed, variations on this image appeared within the national popular culture, such as in postcards that depicted cartoon black children injuring or killing each other or recklessly climbing into the mouth of an alligator.[104] White Mississippians also told stories in which black people injuring and killing each other served comic purposes. In David L. Cohn's *God Shakes Creation* (1937), an extended essay about the Delta Negro, the Delta native tells the story of a black woman who has been charged with shooting a black man. In court, her lawyer cautions her to say as little as possible. She ignores his advice, however, and once on the stand she launches into a long-winded story that ends with her explaining that the gun accidently went off in her hands. She is acquitted, and afterward her landlord tells her not to let a gun go off again or she would be locked up. Cohn then delivers the story's punch line: The widow assures the landlord that it will not happen again because the next time she would take some cocaine and cut the man's neck off with a razor.[105] In Cohn's narrative, told as a true account, blacks occupy a stage as entertainers who mutilate and kill each other in comic fashion, to the delight of a white audience. Thus, when blacks killed whites, it was likely to end in an execution or a lynching; when they killed each other, it could become the punch line to a joke.

One also sees variations of this narrative of black aggression within the letters to the governor. In 1935, for example, an attorney argued for a pardon because "the offense . . . was a simple assault and what might be classed as a 'negro fight,'" which he further explained was a case of "friends fighting and [then] friends again."[106] Similarly, in 1949, another attorney requested a suspended sentence for a black convict, reasoning, "The case was the usual Saturday night cutting between two negroes."[107] In each of these letters, the writers tied their arguments for leniency to the notion that there was such a thing as a "negro fight" or a "Saturday night cutting." Each argued that such acts were excusable because that was what black people did, and the underlying tone conveyed a playfulness in black people injuring each other.

The stories about black aggression within the black community— appearing in letters to the governor and in other more polished accounts—embodied Jim Crow imaginings of the world. They provided an opportunity for whites to affirm their beliefs in black inferiority. In addition, through these narrative exercises, whites could show mercy and play the part of the paternalist for blacks, specifically for the "good Negroes," who through a performance of racial humility demonstrated that they deserved leniency. For others though, stories of black crime became an opportunity to imagine the world as a minstrel stage where fun-loving, heavy-drinking blacks mutilated and killed each other for the pleasure of a white audience. These stories of black aggression were particularly significant because they could further convince white Mississippians that their Jim Crow world of masters and servants was a reality. Whites, however, were not the only ones telling stories about aggression.

In the 1959 incident in Clarksdale in which Jonas Causey shot and killed a white man and the police shot and killed Causey and someone shot Elnora, the local black community—including the press and civil rights activists—could draw on a long history of discussing violence within a Jim Crow context. As African Americans interpreted the parts played by the two white men and the police, they could turn to earlier stories that featured white aggression against African Americans. They could also make sense of Jonas Causey's aggressive actions by tapping into earlier stories about black aggression toward whites. Indeed, many black Mississippians who grew up between 1920 and the 1950s—at least a generation removed from the especially violent, early Jim Crow period—heard stories about atrocities committed by whites and about African Americans taking up arms against white people and law enforcement officials.

Within the black community, stories featuring white aggression directed at blacks were regularly conveyed to children at a young age, and many of these accounts were of experiences from the period of enslavement. In some cases, individuals who had been born enslaved shared their experiences, and more commonly by the 1930s, a generation born after slavery continued to pass these stories on to their children. These narratives often related the harshness and brutality of slavery.[108] For example, some children heard that white masters prohibited their ancestors from praying.[109] Georgia Bay's grandmother explained that she put a bucket over her head to disguise her praying.[110] Many of the tales recounted extreme violence. Eura Bowie, who was born in 1911, remembers her mother telling numerous gruesome stories about enslavement, including enslaved people being forced to eat from a trough and a black man being "burnt up."[111] Similarly, Minnie Weston, born just a few years earlier than Bowie, recalls her father telling stories of slavery he had heard from the previous generation. One of these stories involved enslaved people being made to stand on top of bricks that had just been pulled from a fire. Her father heard that his mother had been forced to stand on these hot bricks, and, according to Weston, "that made him hate" white people.[112]

Some of these stories of violence and mistreatment were set after enslavement in the Jim Crow era. Herman Leach's grandparents told him about blacks being hung from a bridge, while both Hettie Love and Minnie Weston heard from grandparents about relatives who had been lynched.[113] Unita Blackwell's grandmother told her that her grandfather was killed in a sugarcane field in Louisiana after the owner accused him of something he had not done.[114] For others, the more contemporary tales were also more personal. John Johnson, who grew up in the 1940s and 1950s, remembers his mother telling him about how the police treated his father. If his father had been consuming alcohol, they followed him until he had walked almost home, and then they arrested him.[115] Meanwhile, Cora Fleming's mother told her that a white man had raped Cora's grandmother. As a young girl, Cora decided that an old white man in town was the one who had raped her grandmother. She threw bricks at him, at which point her mother explained that he was not the one.[116] These stories from a slavery past and from a Jim Crow present could serve multiple purposes. Accounts that included horrific details—especially in incidents from the recent past—were likely intended as cautionary tales, meant to educate children about the dangers of the Jim Crow world and to remind them to be careful around white people.[117] There are certainly numerous examples of parents using fear to protect their children. One can also understand these stories, coming primarily from grandparents, as a means of passing on a personal and communal legacy. These storytelling projects, however, have additional implications that distinguish them from standard genealogical motivations.

Trudier Harris observes that violence, and in particular lynching, is a persistent theme in the work of black writers. As she notes about this literary tradition, scenes of violence portray "whites as inherently violent and brutal." At the same time, these stories allow for different characterizations of African Americans. Even as the scenes most often end in death, the focus on black characters in these moments allows them to realize a different meaning of manhood and womanhood.[118] Adam Gussow makes a similar point about blues music in arguing that it was in part a response to lynching. Blues became a "mode of resistance: a way of bearing coded and overt witness to terror . . . a way of bringing oneself and one's community back to life by getting loud, fierce, and *down.*"[119] Alongside these stories of aggression from musicians and writers were the stories about violence that African Americans shared in their everyday lives. The stories that Cora Fleming told about her grandmother being raped and that John Johnson heard about his father being arrested not only served to explain racial violence; they also provided alternative explanations of Jim Crow. Counter to the standard narrative that represented blacks as content to be subordinate and whites as loving masters, these stories told of whites brutally and senselessly abusing African Americans.[120] Accounts of racial horrors, whether about slavery or a recent nearby lynching, underscored the injustice and tragedy that defined the status quo for blacks. Thus, these stories not only contradicted the mainstream Southern narratives of lynching by having the role of instigator and victim change racial places; they also imagined a very different Jim Crow world.[121]

As African Americans regularly narrated accounts of white aggression, they likewise told their own stories about black aggression. In the Jim Crow South, actual episodes of African Americans taking up guns against whites were relatively rare. In Mississippi, these incidents were few, because as Neil McMillen observes, whites "enjoyed a clear preponderance of firepower and could virtually always count on the support of police and militias."[122] Still, on a number of occasions throughout the South, African Americans fought back aggressively and in large numbers, including most notably in Elaine, Arkansas, in 1919 and Tulsa in 1921.[123] In addition, the turbulent World War II years produced numerous armed conflicts between blacks and whites.[124] Many black veterans returned home from the war with expectations of better treatment, and equally important, the presence of black men in military uniforms—connoting an authority that circumvented Jim Crow hierarchies—made many whites nervous.[125] Those circumstances fueled confrontations between blacks and whites across the South, including a riot in Columbia, Tennessee, in 1946.[126] In Mississippi, too, the historical record is littered with run-ins between black veterans and whites in the early to mid-1940s.[127]

Alongside the actual moments when blacks aggressively challenged whites were the stories African Americans told about these events. In the retelling, a particular incident took on a performative life of its own, circulating within the black community and in some cases surviving for decades as these stories were handed down from one generation to the next. In these narrative performances, then, the account of a black person standing up to whites happened over and over again with each retelling. In addition, as performances, whether the events described in the story were mostly true, partially true, or even completely fictional is not particularly relevant. Regardless of their veracity, African Americans regularly heard and told stories about a black militancy that defied the Jim Crow constructions of protective whites and meek, happy blacks.

One of these stories came from Lou Allen, a Greenwood native who grew up hearing about an incident from the 1920s involving a white landowner and a black sharecropper. Early in the morning, the white man went to the sharecropper's house and demanded that he go to the field immediately. The black man refused and went back to his breakfast. According to Allen, the white man pulled out a gun, but before he could use it, the farmer had drawn his gun and fired, killing the white man.[128] Allen did not include names, and perhaps over time she forgot the names, or maybe she never heard the story with names. But the structure of this story mirrored many others. It featured a white character as the initial aggressor, who overreacted with violence or threatened to kill a black individual. It also featured a black individual who was armed and ready and who defended himself by killing his white attacker. In Lou Allen's story, we do not know what happened to the black farmer. He could have been lynched or arrested and tried, or, although less likely, perhaps he got away with it. Without a known conclusion, however, this story functioned simply as a black man emerging victorious in a battle with a white aggressor.

Even as these stories often revolved around a violent white attacker and a black man fighting back, they nonetheless could convey a range of messages. In some cases, in fact, the same incident produced varying accounts within the black community. Consider, for example, an incident involving an African American preacher that occurred in the early 1950s in Itta Bena. In separate interviews, Booker Frederick and Hettie Love, both African American and both from Itta Bena, recalled what happened. According to each of their accounts, the preacher purchased furniture on credit and then lost his job and could not make the payments. White men then went to the preacher's house and found him waiting for them with a shotgun. It is less clear what happened after that. According to Frederick, the sheriff came to the house, several shots were fired, and the police discussed burning down the house. They then convinced the preacher to give up, promising that something could be worked out. The preacher was taken to the county farm, where prisoners were forced to work, and he was beaten, which, Frederick noted, upset many people in the black community.[129]

Hettie Love, however, remembered an outcome that diverged from Frederick's story at the point that the white men were waiting outside with the armed preacher inside. In her version, the preacher escaped during the night, eventually making his way to California.[130] We have no way of knowing which outcome was real, or even if it was something else. For these individuals, however, both stories functioned as truth, and their significance lay in the messages they conveyed. Both of them also tapped into themes present in other narratives of African American militancy. As was the case with Lou Allen's story, each variation of this story was an example of a black individual under attack and fighting back. Frederick's rendition ultimately became a story about injustice winning out, with white people inflicting violence on a man who had lost his job. That story directly undermined the image of the white paternalist. In Love's version, the black man was vaulted to a heroic position because he escaped punishment by outsmarting white officials. Each of these narratives contained important counter–Jim Crow narratives, one challenging white paternalism and the other serving as a story of racial pride and inspiration.

While many of the stories revolved around encounters with land-owners, employers, and creditors, some related to civil rights activism. Nathaniel Lewis, who was born in McComb early in the twentieth century, recalled an episode involving Frank Hurd, a schoolteacher in Amite County. Hurd had been advocating equal pay for black teachers. One day while Hurd was at the school teaching, he was told that a group of whites were coming there to kill him. According to Lewis, Hurd sent the students home, pulled out a Winchester rifle he kept with him, went into the woods, and waited. As the group of white men attacked, Hurd fired back. Hurd was eventually gunned down, but as Lewis recalled, "I think this black man killed sixteen ones that day, before they killed him. He ran out of ammunition."[131] In the retelling, Hurd was a hero and a martyr who fought for a just cause and paid with his life. It is worth noting, too, that Hurd went down fighting. He sent the students home—acting as their protector—but he did not himself run, instead accepting his fate. He also did not wait to be killed, but instead he was determined to shoot and kill as many of his attackers as he could. Those actions, real or not, made him into a sort of badman hero, unafraid of death and fighting to the end.[132] In the world depicted in Lewis's narration, there existed no white paternalists, only white villains. In this world, whites still held the balance of power and blacks still died, but they did so bravely and selflessly. Compared to the mainstream narratives within the white community, this account and others from the black community reframed both the acts of white aggression and the acts of black aggression.

One of the curious features of the narratives cited above is that in all of them the individual fighting back was male, including the stories coming from female narrators, such as Hettie Love, Franzetta Sanders, and Lou Allen. One might wonder if this gender discrepancy reflected reality, that is, if black men aggressively challenged whites significantly more often than did black women. That conclusion, however, is called into question by other findings in Mississippi. Charles Payne discovered that many black women in the 1960s took up guns in response to white threats, and Akinyele Umoja references communities in the state with long traditions of armed self-defense that included black men and black women.[133] At the same time, occasionally in these stories a black female appears in the lead role. For example, Alma Ward recalled from her childhood in the 1930s and 1940s an episode in which her grandmother, wielding an ax, chased off a white city official who had accused her of "stealing" city water.[134] Still, within the oral histories of this period, the protagonists in these aggressive challenges to white people were overwhelmingly represented by black males, leaving one to wonder how to explain the gender imbalance.

One might suspect that because black men represented a direct threat to the authority and position of white men, black men were much more likely to be lynched and much more likely to be confronted by white men, leading to more situations for them to challenge whites physically. Still, black women regularly faced the threat of sexual assault, so they too would have had many opportunities to be confronted and to challenge whites. A more likely answer for why black male protagonists are featured more regularly in these tales resides in how and why particular stories circulated.[135] These tales, whether based on facts or rumors, were narratives that responded to Jim Crow narratives in which, in multiple ways, black males were prevented from fulfilling the normative patriarchal role of provider and protector. In economic terms, black men usually had less stable jobs than black women, who could nearly always find domestic work in the homes of whites. Black men were often the last hired and the first fired. Those who worked as sharecroppers meanwhile were likely to be financially indebted to white landowners and merchants. In these circumstances, black husbands could rarely be the breadwinners in their families.[136] Perhaps more important, black men were regularly denied the role of protector. Black women who worked in white homes were especially vulnerable to sexual assault or other abuses, and black husbands and fathers had few viable options in trying to prevent or respond to these incidents.[137] As well, the black male's authority was undercut in public by expectations of submissiveness to whites. The routine interactions of black males stepping aside for whites, using titles for whites, and generally deferring to whites were regular reminders that, unlike white males, black husbands and fathers could not play the part of protective patriarchs.

In the narratives of black aggression, however, black males functioned as protectors, and accordingly many of these aggressive acts are told as a husband, father, or teacher defending the home, the family, and the children. In that light, one can understand why the 1959 shooting of Elnora Causey became a crucial point of contention, marking a line between a man crazy enough to shoot his wife and a man trying in vain to protect his wife from white attackers. Within these stories was an important masculinist rhetoric, and as historian Steve Estes notes, these gendered understandings of Jim Crow led some black men to join the civil rights and Black Power movements, at least in part to defend their manhood and claim the role of protecting women and children.[138] They may have then drawn on these earlier narratives of African American militancy that featured brave and fearless black male protagonists. At the very least, these stories functioned as a counterbalance that challenged mainstream constructions of black masculinity.

If the gender dynamics of these aforementioned stories were clear but somewhat hidden, in other stories those issues were in the forefront. Johnny Jones, who served in the military during World War II, told a story about an encounter with whites sometime after he had returned home from the military, perhaps in the late 1940s. Jones discovered that several young white men were going to a local ballpark with a group of black women and having sex with them. He explained that this situation was particularly frustrating to him because he knew that if he only so much as looked at a white woman, he could be lynched. Less clear in his account were the motivations of the black women. We do not know, for example, if they were willingly accompanying these white men or if they asked Jones to intervene. In Jones's account, the women were passive and almost confined to the background of a story that featured black men versus white men.[139] As Jones explained, he and several of his friends decided to end these late-night rendezvous. On a night that the white men were at the ballpark with the black women, Jones and his friends confronted the men, leaving one person stationed nearby with a shotgun. According to Jones, the white men did not challenge them, and the black women left. The following night, the black men were arrested and jailed and then released after each paid a twelve-dollar fine.[140]

Even if we are missing some key details about this incident, as a story it is a forceful message about black male power, and in particular of black men successfully challenging white men. It is consistent with a normative masculinist rhetoric in which, in Jones's telling, the black men are protectors who come to the rescue of the black women. Even as they pay a penalty—an arrest and fine—the black men emerge victorious over white men. We do not know for sure why the black men did not face a harsher punishment, although Jones noted that one of the white men was married and was worried about his wife finding out.[141] That possibility is another indication of the sometimes tenuous nature of Jim Crow rule, a moment in which Jones and his friends could challenge white males with less risk of serious reprisal.

Other stories told by blacks could convey similarly complicated gender and racial dynamics. Rosie Sanders recalled hearing about an incident, likely from the 1920s, in which a white man stepped into an argument between Bee Anderson and his wife. According to Sanders, Anderson told the man that he had no right to interfere. The white man pulled out a pistol and shot Anderson in the hand. The two men then struggled for the gun, and Anderson shot and killed the white man. When a group of whites came looking for Anderson, he hid behind a creek bank and, according to Sanders, shot his pursuers as they came over the bank. After the group finally apprehended Anderson, they castrated him, pulled his eyes out, and tied him to a car. They then dragged his body along the highway for other blacks to see. Anderson was finally hung from a tree and shot until there was little left of his body.[142]

This story echoes elements of many other accounts of militancy— an initial white attack, the black man protecting his home, the black man taking down as many whites as possible even as his own death is inevitable, and a final act of white violence. Like many other stories in this period, Anderson is both a hero and a victim. This narrative is also a domestic story about black masculinity and white male access to black women. At the beginning of the encounter, the white man had intruded not only into the black home but also into the private realm of marriage. Sanders's retelling, it should be emphasized, began with the argument between a husband and wife and with a white man challenging Anderson's authority as husband. Anderson was thus defending his position as the patriarch of the household. Anderson eventually died, but not before an aggressive display of masculinity, cutting down his attackers and seemingly dying without fear. That scene is consistent with the stories of Frank Hurd and Jonas Causey, with each dying while shooting back at the attackers.

As African Americans told their own stories about these moments of black aggression, the strands of militancy extended beyond the realm of actual events. They also created hypothetical situations, imagining and talking about how they *might* respond in a particular situation. For example, Tommie Lee Williams Sr. explained that he always carried a pistol, and he was prepared to shoot to kill if he realized he was going to be lynched.[143] Hobert Kornegay kept a rifle near his garage and vowed that if any white person ever hit him or shot at him, he would fire back at the attacker, and "that was going to be the end of him."[144] Likewise, Franzetta W. Sanders's father kept a gun on the premises, and he explained to his daughter that he would kill anyone trying to force his way into the house, even if he was killed in the process.[145] Beyond guns, others simply noted a willingness to respond to a white attack, such as George Bailey, who explained that if a white person hit him, he would hit back.[146]

As far as we know, none of these moments ever materialized for these individuals, and it is impossible to know if any of them would have followed through on their stated intentions. Nonetheless, each of these hypothetical moments was also a narrative of black aggression that may have been told many times or in which possible scenarios may have been regularly imagined. Leaving a gun in the garage, for instance, suggested planning on the part of Kornegay. For the others, too, the mental preparations for what they might do indicated that they had thought it through, that they had gone over it again and again in their minds. They had perhaps regularly imagined these scenes in which they fought back. Likewise, when they shared these episodes, as Franzetta Sanders's father did, it became a story about militancy, in which others too could envision an aggressive response to whites.

These hypothetical encounters contain a number of elements found in the stories of actual events. Each imagined a white person or a mob as the initial aggressor, making the black response a defensive one. As well, two of these situations were set at home, making the armed response an effort to protect the family. As these narratives recast the heroes and villains, they also expressed bravado and fatalism. Williams, for example, imagined himself standing up to a lynch mob, while Kornegay confidently predicted killing his attacker. They almost certainly knew that hitting or shooting at a white person would put their own lives in danger. Yet each expressed a readiness to fight back in order to protect his family or as a matter of self-respect. Significantly, the emphasis in these hypotheticals was not on what *might* happen to the black person but on what *would* happen to the white attacker. These imagined moments were framed as African Americans bravely taking down their attackers.

Throughout the Jim Crow era, African Americans were telling stories about aggressively and often violently standing up to whites, stories that replaced a world of white paternalists and black servants with violent white aggressors and heroic blacks. Sometimes these stories took the form of imagined possibilities in their minds; sometimes they were based on actual events. In each instance, though, there was a significance not only in what happened but also in what the storyteller said happened, in much the same way that a lynching or an execution was often told in ways to preserve particular racial myths. Without a doubt, very different narrative performances of aggression circulated within the white community and the black community. Indeed, one way to understand the creation and implications of conflicting stories is to consider how distinct traditions of storytelling converged in the narratives about Eddie Noel.

MADMAN, BADMAN, AND CRIMINAL: THE NARRATIVES OF EDDIE NOEL

On January 13, 1954, near Lexington in Holmes County, Mississippi, Eddie Noel, a twenty-eight-year-old African American, shot and killed Willie Dickard outside a juke joint/country store. Dickard owned the business, which catered to both a black clientele and a white clientele at different times in the evening. Prior to the shooting, Dickard and Percy Cobbins, Noel's cousin, had been engaged in an argument in the store. When their dispute spilled outside, Noel opened fire on Dickard. Noel then fled to his house, and when a group of white men arrived, he shot his way out, killing two more white men, including a deputy sheriff, and wounding two others. Noel escaped, and a hastily organized and armed group of local whites continued the pursuit. But even with the offer of a $1,000 reward, Noel continued to elude his pursuers. Two weeks later, with authorities seemingly no closer to locating him, Noel turned himself in. The trial process stretched into the spring and late May as a board of physicians from the state mental institution in Whitfield examined Noel. Only a few days after the U.S. Supreme Court issued its *Brown v. Board of Education* decision, the board found Noel mentally insane, and he remained in the state hospital at Whitfield. By November, the case had been effectively closed. In 1972, Noel was released from the state hospital, and he left the state, settling in Fort Wayne, Indiana, where he lived until his death in 1994.[147]

As these events unfolded, a number of narratives about Eddie Noel emerged, and forty years after the shooting, locals were still talking about what happened. In narrating Noel, the shootings, and the white response, black Mississippians and white Mississippians tapped into distinct traditions of telling stories about aggression. Out of these traditions, Noel was variously constructed as a dangerous criminal, a mentally unstable man, a hero, a victim, and a war veteran defending his civil rights. Some stories ignored any racial motivations in the shooting and manhunt, while others put race and white aggression at the center. In the many narrative performances of Eddie Noel, black and white Mississippians struggled over how to make sense of him, and in the process, their narratives reflected competing visions of the Jim Crow world.

The first published account of what happened appeared in the white-owned *Lexington Advertiser*. Its outspoken editor and owner, Hazel Brannon Smith, proved countless times in her career that she was not afraid to challenge the local elite on racial issues, and in 1964 she would win a Pulitzer Prize for her reporting on the Citizens' Council. Compared to other editors in the state, she could be expected to provide relatively fair coverage of these events. That said, in 1954, her newspaper was not openly critical of segregation.[148] The *Lexington Advertiser*'s initial coverage came the day after the shooting, when, we can assume, reporters would have still been scrambling to separate facts from conjecture and nail down the basic details about what happened. This was likely the most dramatic event to have occurred in Holmes County in nearly a decade, and the newspaper's report on the incident covered much of the front page above and below the fold. The story explained that Noel had shot Dickard and fled, shot two more individuals on the highway, and then later shot his way out of his home. The newspaper laid out a likely motive in the headline—"Three Holmes Men Dead, Two Seriously Injured by Negro Man Following Argument over Whiskey"—and repeated in the article that Noel "committed the crimes as the result of an argument that began over whiskey." The whiskey motive was probably a reference to the dispute between Cobbins and Dickard and was also an allusion to the illegal distribution of liquor in the county.[149] The coverage was quite straightforward. Other than labeling Noel a "Negro man," the article avoided overtly racial language and downplayed the racial angle of a black man shooting white men. This issue contained no calls for vengeance against Noel or the black community. Instead, Smith appeared to go out of her way to tell the story as an unfortunate series of crimes related to liquor. Nonetheless, alongside this seemingly objective account, a different story about Noel and the shootings was being told by the black press.

The *Mississippi Enterprise* was one of the more conservative black press publications in the state, and for that reason it was an unlikely source for Jim Crow critiques. Launched in 1939 from Jackson, this weekly newspaper espoused a Booker T. Washington philosophy of racial politics, emphasizing, as historian Julius Thompson noted, "the better side of Negro life" without being critical of "our good white friends" whom the paper depended on for financial backing.[150] Its first coverage of the Noel shooting came in its January 29 issue, and it provided another explanation for what sparked the shooting. The *Enterprise* reported that the shooting occurred after the white man, Dickard, "slapped another Negro, Percy [Cobbins]."[151] The *Advertiser* had not mentioned a slap, and likewise the *Enterprise* made no mention of whiskey. It is unclear which of these versions is more accurate, and it is possible that both were precursors to the shootings. As stories, however, these two explanations created separate trajectories—one revolving around criminal activities and the other around a white man slapping a black man. We do not know who the source was for the slap, but if that story was not circulating within the black community before January 29, it most certainly was after.

In considering how blacks might have received a story about the slap, the larger context is important. Perhaps it dredged up thoughts about the daily humiliations African Americans faced. Or perhaps locals linked it to the extensive history of blatant racial violence within their own county. That history in Holmes County included a white man killing a black youth in 1946 in what blacks and whites considered "the most cold-blooded murder in the town's history." From the same year, it also included the lynching of Leon McTatie, who was falsely accused of stealing a horse saddle. As well, in 1954, the Holmes county sheriff, Richard F. Byrd, had a history of abuse directed at African Americans, including, just a few months after the Noel incident, shooting an unarmed African American man in the back.[152] Within that context, the inclusion of a motive justified and legitimized Noel's response as one of direct retaliation, even if that response was extreme. At the very least, the *Enterprise* inserted an instance of racial abuse into the storyline. Similarly, while the *Lexington Advertiser* referred to Noel's shooting as a "crime," the *Mississippi Enterprise* did not use that word. That omission, along with the reference to the slap, reserved judgment on Noel's actions and left open the possibility that he was responding to racial abuse.

In the ensuing weeks and months, much of the coverage would arise from these two basic narrative frameworks. Yet it would be misleading to suggest that all whites adopted one version and all blacks adopted another version. In fact, the evidence reveals some variations in both communities, which further illustrated the desire by various constituencies to control this narrative of aggression. For example, appearing alongside the first article on the shooting in the white-owned *Lexington Advertiser* was a letter to the editor signed by four local black citizens. They expressed grief and shame "that one of our number [has become] a desperado and [committed] what is almost mass murder."[153] One of the signers was Dr. Arenia C. Mallory, president of a local industrial college and a friend of Hazel Brannon Smith. This group may have been drawing on racial uplift ideologies, and accordingly they may have worried that the shooting would reflect badly on the black community. They may also have been trying to stave off a violent white response, which would be consistent with Smith's attempt to downplay the racial implications.

Within the white community, too, the reactions were mixed. About a week after the shooting, while Noel was still at large, a column in the white-owned *Jackson Daily News*, which was later reprinted in the *Lexington Advertiser*, observed that some people in Jackson felt sorry for Noel. The journalist did not provide additional details about this sentiment, but he was almost assuredly referring to white people, given that the racial status of blacks (as "negroes") was always designated in mainstream newspapers. Even if we do not know why some people felt sorry for him, it was an indication that the white community was at least somewhat divided.[154] Without any of these explanations, however, the journalist responded to the sympathy for Noel by noting only, "He killed." The writer then fortified this image of Noel as a killer and a criminal by referring to him as a "lead-splattering Negro" who had "entered the fracas [between Cobbins and Dickard] by blasting young Dickard with his rifle."[155] Thus this journalist reacted to sympathy toward Noel by embracing the criminal narrative and repositioning the "young" white man as an innocent victim.

After the initial shooting, the manhunt provided another opportunity for the press to narrate aggression and to tell additional stories about Noel. The local black press continued its positive portrayals of Noel. For example, both the *Mississippi Enterprise* and the *Jackson Advocate* consistently referred to Noel's service in the military during World War II. In the 1940s and 1950s, black newspapers throughout the United States regularly highlighted the military service of African Americans in their stories. This practice can be read in part as a response to mainstream newspapers, which used titles of respect when referring to whites but not when referring to blacks. The military connection also contained other meanings in which noting the veteran status of an African American became an important narrative performance of authority, a subtle way to challenge Jim Crow monikers such as "boy" and "uncle." Military service conferred respect and sacrifice upon the subject. The consistent reference to Noel as a veteran lent him credibility and even suggested that he might have had a legitimate reason for shooting the white men. In short, it left wide open the possibility that Eddie Noel was a hero, not a criminal.

The black press also devoted much attention to those who were searching for Noel. The *Jackson Advocate* called it "one of the biggest, if not actually the biggest manhunt in the history of the state," and described the group as involving "up to 500 armed men, bloodhounds, and a spotter plane."[156] The *Mississippi Enterprise* put the figure at "nearly 800 men" who were searching for "the sharp-shooting veteran." In the meantime, the black press had learned more about Noel. The *Mississippi Enterprise* included this statement: "Noel has a reputation for being able to shoot combs from his wife's hair, to light matches held between her teeth."[157] Both the emphasis on this massive mobilization of white men—all of them searching for one man—and the seemingly hyperbolic reference to Noel's shooting skills suggested admiration for Noel and for his ability to unsettle whites. By this point, Noel was beginning to sound like the trickster of an earlier folk tradition, a black character who skirted the law and took advantage of whites by outwitting them.[158]

In addition, within the black press, the story expanded beyond the shooting, and it increasingly became a story about white aggression. The *Jackson Advocate* reported that the manhunt had "spread terror among Negro citizens." The newspaper explained that an armed posse was searching the homes of blacks without first securing search warrants. The same article also recounted the attack on Noel's house, which had been set on fire "with a rain of rifle, shotgun, pistol, and tear gas bombs."[159] At the same moment in which the black press spoke glowingly of Noel's abilities, they were also calling attention to violence committed by whites. An incident that began with a black man shooting a white man was becoming a story about whites terrorizing the black community. The Eddie Noel who appeared in the black press was a respected veteran and a skilled sharpshooter, while those who pursued him had become the vigilantes and the criminals.

The coverage of the manhunt in the mainstream press included references to a large posse of law enforcement officials and civilians with numerous photos appearing in the Jackson newspapers. The *Jackson Clarion-Ledger* put the size of the manhunt at 400 men. In addition, as authorities and others searched for Noel, they attached various descriptors to him in article titles and captions, including "the Negro killer," "the trigger happy Negro," and "killer Noel." The *Jackson Daily News* showed pictures of Eddie Noel's burned house after authorities opened fire on it, thinking Noel was inside. The newspaper also noted that Eddie's wife and "other relatives" were being held in jail "temporarily." Beyond these images, however, there was no mention of the raids within the black community such as those reported by the *Jackson Advocate*. The mainstream press omitted details that imparted any current or past hero status on Noel while also leaving out any descriptors that might have portrayed the search party as vigilantes. Reports about a large group of armed white men raiding houses in black neighborhoods in search of Noel would have posed a challenge to the myth of white benevolence. Instead, the mainstream press told stories consistent with idealized roles of racial harmony. As authorities and a large group of white men searched in vain for Noel, a narrative of a black hero/trickster and white vigilantes competed against the mainstream narrative about a black criminal.

After Noel turned himself in, the mainstream story about a black criminal evolved into a story about a crazy black man. In custody, the mainstream press began to pay more attention to the state of his mental health. Hazel Brannon Smith investigated Noel's past and reported that, according to state records, he had been "insane" since childhood, including his time spent in the military.[160] The black press also addressed Noel's mental status but offered a different interpretation. The *Jackson Advocate* noted the questions about Noel's sanity and reported that, according to a friend, Noel had recently "discussed with increasing bitterness the things that he was told that he was fighting for while in the army only to find upon his return that Negroes in Holmes County were still being denied the most elemental rights of an American citizen."[161] Thus, as the mainstream press told a story that moved from Noel the criminal to Noel the insane, the black press continued to situate Noel's actions within the racial politics of Jim Crow. From the earlier report of a slap by a white man to references to military sacrifice to details about a white posse invading black homes, the black press was telling a civil rights story. As the black press connected the shootings to a larger framework of racial injustices, the mainstream press, first through a discourse of crime and then later through one of mental health, consistently made the shootings an individual, isolated incident.

Press coverage faded quickly following the decision to leave Noel in the state hospital, but the memory of the events lived on. The black community kept alive the story of Eddie Noel, and in these memories Noel was clearly a hero. Booker Frederick was in his early twenties in 1954. Recalling the episode more than forty years later, he said he heard that after Noel surrendered, "he [Noel] told [officials] he could have killed about all of them if he had wanted to, but he didn't want to."[162] T. C. Johnson meanwhile echoed the decades-earlier accounts of the manhunt from the black press in remembering with a note of pride that "just one man, a black man, made five hundred whites move."[163] It is worth emphasizing the point that forty years after the event Johnson recalled a specific detail symbolizing how a black man with a gun had unnerved whites. For both Frederick and Johnson, Noel was a variation on the "badman," cleverer and more dangerous than his white pursuers. Or, as another local African American recalled about Noel, blacks "who would go crazy, kill up a whole lot of white folks . . . were respected."[164] Within the local black community in the 1990s, the characterization of Eddie Noel as a black man feared by whites was remarkably similar to the 1954 version that appeared in the black press.[165] Indeed, the endurance of this story may say something about the importance of this narrative for African Americans as well as for white officials, whose actions in 1954 suggested that they wanted the memory of these events to fade as quickly as possible.

FOUR YEARS AFTER Eddie Noel was sent to the state mental hospital, reports of another "crazed" black man—Jonas Causey—appeared in local newspapers. While the outcome for Causey was different, the various narratives seeking to make sense of him were quite familiar. On one side was a tradition rooted in stories about lynching, executions, and black criminality. Those accounts tried to preserve an image of white benevolence, sometimes by blaming lynchings on poor whites or particular communities, and even more often by scripting blacks as prone to violence and criminal behavior. On the other side was a tradition within the black community in which brave African Americans aggressively defended themselves and their families against unwarranted attacks from whites.

The Eddie Noel shootings, the hypothetical and actual acts of black aggression, the letters to the governor about black criminality, and the letters and articles about executions and lynchings reflected something more than differing racial perspectives about aggression. Within these narrative performances, the meaning of Jim Crow was at stake. In these stories, blacks and whites sought to name the world. In this regard, the narratives paralleled the performative roles of laws, customs, and props. Those elements, as noted in Chapter 1, defined the movements of blacks and whites. They set up the expected Jim Crow scene. The stories about aggression, meanwhile, came after the scene was over, and for advocates of white supremacy the retelling became an opportunity to rewrite the scene according to expectations and to make what happened fit within the appropriate racial framework—a larger narrative about racial harmony between benevolent masters and loyal servants. By the same token, in the retelling, African Americans could narrate a very different world through cautionary tales and through inspiring accounts of militancy and sacrifice. In the various Jim Crow narratives, the subtleties of language, exaggerations, and omissions were significant for particular audiences.

By the mid-1950s, the efforts of white Mississippians to narrate stories of white benevolence were becoming more difficult. In 1955, as Eddie Noel languished in a state hospital, about twenty miles from where he shot the owner of a juke joint, another African American— Emmett Till—was kidnapped and killed. This violent event, though, would attract international attention and a range of stories about violence and justice in Mississippi, contributing to a reconsideration of the everyday performances of race.

3

JIM CROW AUDIENCES

*Southerners, the Nation, and the Centralization
of Racial Surveillance*

Perhaps no racial episode of the 1950s is better known than the kidnapping and death of Emmett Till. On August 24, 1955, in a country store in Money, Mississippi, the fourteen-year-old from Chicago may have grabbed the wrist of Carolyn Bryant, a white woman, may have said something "obscene" to her, and may have let out a wolf whistle as he left the store and joined his cousins waiting outside. On August 28, in the middle of the night, Carolyn's husband, Roy Bryant, his half-brother, J. W. Milam, and possibly others kidnapped Till. Three days later, Till's body was found in the Tallahatchie River with a cotton gin fan tied around his neck. He had been beaten and shot in the head, his eyes had been gouged out, and his body was bloated and disfigured. Three weeks after that, Bryant and Milam stood trial for the murder. On September 23, just under a month after the incident at the grocery store, an all-white jury deliberated for about an hour before acquitting the two men. Four months later, Bryant and Milam confessed to committing the crime in an interview with a journalist for *Look* magazine.[1]

As a performance, the initial event at the country store shared much in common with Richard Wright's aforementioned encounter on an elevator. Recall that in this earlier moment, a white man had removed Wright's hat, and instead of a risky "thank-you" or a demeaning grin, Wright pretended the packages in his arms were falling. Neither Wright nor Till delivered the expected enactment of blackness, which would have called for some version of humility and deference to whites. For each one, the outcome depended on how others—specifically a white audience—perceived the performance. Wright assumed that his audience was watching, and that assumption influenced his actions. Till, however, likely was unaware of the extent of the audience watching him.

That audience included Carolyn Bryant in the store and perhaps Till's cousin and other friends standing outside the store, and it also had at least two more members, Carolyn's husband and his half-brother and perhaps others, who witnessed this scene in her retelling. Through her eyes and her narration, they saw Till deliver the wrong performance, and after seeing it, they responded with violence. If the scene involving Till in the country store and the one with Wright in the elevator seem radically different, it is in part because they ended differently. The initial interactions in these encounters, however, shared a fundamental performative component that guided daily life in Jim Crow Mississippi: the localized, informal, and yet seemingly ever-present surveillance of a white audience.

In exploring the audiences that watched and responded to daily performances of race and how these processes of watching changed in the 1950s, I define "surveillance" broadly. This term refers not only to the formalized, regimented forms of observation, such as with undercover agents and cameras, but also to the ways in which people are regularly monitored and disciplined in their everyday routines. This surveillance could entail ordinary citizens watching, such as Carolyn Bryant and Wright's elevator passengers. Beyond physical observations and retellings, surveillance could also take more bureaucratic forms, such as tracking individuals through reports in files and data collection. Ways of watching and listening could be carried out by individuals that included police officers, informants, journalists, employers, and citizens, or by groups such as government agencies, community organizations, and vigilante organizations.[2] This conceptualization of surveillance also applies to forms of observation that operated on a larger scale, somewhat more abstractly than one-to-one interactions. I am thinking in particular of the ways in which the nation "watched" the South, in which, for example, reporters and photojournalists became the eyes and ears for a national public. Those observations, like the ones involving secret agents or local citizens, represented a type of eavesdropping with their own consequences. In 1950s Mississippi, two audiences engaging in two distinct forms of surveillance were on a collision course. One involved a local audience watching daily performances of race, and the other encompassed a national public watching the South via the media.

The surveillance of a local audience had been a critical component at least since Jim Crow first emerged in the late nineteenth century.[3]

White Southerners, notes Leon Litwack, expressed concern that black people "be rigidly monitored and regulated."[4] While new laws and an emphasis on older racial customs were intended to regulate that behavior, whites found that black Southerners nonetheless regularly failed to follow the increasingly more stringent racial rules. Monitoring racial lines then required an active and daily vigilance, and that vigilance was backed up by the authority of white citizens to accuse, judge, and punish racial transgressions outside the courts. In that regard, Robyn Wiegman argues that the spectacle lynching became the primary engine that drove racial surveillance. The spectacle lynching was a highly ritualistic, public affair, often attended by hundreds or thousands, including families, and it frequently involved the castration or other forms of bodily mutilation of the lynching victim. Its power, contends Wiegman, extended beyond the death scene: "Because the terror of the white lynch mob arises from both its function as a panoptic mode of surveillance and its materialization of violence in public displays of torture and castration, the black subject is disciplined in two powerful ways: by the threat of always being seen *and* by the specular scene."[5] In other words, the black community was meant to witness both this spectacular act of torture and the collective participation of the white community. These events could then function as a form of panoptic surveillance, in which, from the perspective of the black individual, an unseen agent was potentially always watching and prepared to discipline the subject. Wiegman's analysis is compelling in linking violence to daily observations, although, as we shall see below, other forms of violence, such as sexual assault, contributed to other forms of a seemingly ever-present surveillance.[6]

While the dramatic display of the spectacle lynching suggests far-reaching white authority, other sources hint at the hard work involved in monitoring racial lines every day and everywhere.[7] At the turn of the century, for example, journalist Ray Stannard Baker noted the frequent encounters on streetcars in which white passengers and drivers became involved in keeping or moving black passengers to the appropriate section. Similarly, four decades later, Birmingham buses were also frequent scenes of conflict between black passengers and white passengers and drivers.[8] While Robin D. G. Kelley references these encounters as evidence of black resistance, they also reveal the workings of a form of surveillance by white people on the bus.[9] That is, these incidents made it into the city records because white passengers and drivers were watching and listening and then trying to enforce the racial rules that black passengers violated. This local means of watching black people had deep roots in the Jim Crow system, and in the 1950s it would run up against another form of surveillance involving the national media and a national public.

Throughout the Jim Crow era, the national media had covered racial incidents in the South—such as the 1931 Scottsboro, Alabama, trial involving nine African Americans charged with rape. This coverage often depicted a South stuck in the past and behind the rest of the nation. These accounts of the South appeared sporadically. In the 1950s, a related but much more sustained narrative about the South took shape around an emerging civil rights movement. That story featured angry, violent, racist, working-class whites versus peaceful, innocent, middle-class blacks. As Elizabeth Abel contends, photojournalists, who with an image could freeze the action, played a key role in finding, cropping, and even at times staging the action to capture this scene.[10] Civil rights activists took advantage of these circumstances and regularly performed nonviolent protest and dressed in their "Sunday best" to gain sympathy and support from a national public.[11] Television's influence over the movement narrative came somewhat later, but these officials, in the interest of capturing a national audience, also narrated the movement as a national story that marginalized whites in the South.[12] If activists understood the power of the media, so too did their opponents. Police officers often confiscated cameras and film, and Mississippi television viewers became accustomed to their local television stations experiencing "technical difficulties" when the national networks reported on major movement events.[13] Accordingly, the South was under a somewhat selective form of surveillance, one that sought out particular images and themes for its audience. The problem for many white Southerners in the 1950s, then, was that their own localized form of surveillance, one that empowered local white citizens to act on their own, fed into this national narrative about the South as a violent, racist place, out of step with the nation and in need of federal intervention.

In response to steadily increasing national scrutiny, Mississippi officials adjusted their own processes for tracking civil rights activity and, more broadly, for monitoring blacks within the everyday realm. The earlier system had been localized and informal and had charged white citizens with the authority to watch and respond. The new system was more centralized. It relied much more on official agents of the state and on a hierarchical structure. Two new organizations, the Mississippi State Sovereignty Commission and the Citizens' Council, as well as a network of state police, high-level politicians, and other prominent segregationists, took the lead in creating and defining this emerging surveillance network. These transformations represented an attempt to continue the daily policing of racial performances while concealing images of violence from public view, including the kinds of vigilante violence that had long marked racial interactions in the South.

LYNCHING, SEXUAL ASSAULT, AND EVERYDAY SURVEILLANCE

Throughout the Jim Crow era, local audiences occupied a central position in the policing of racial lines. As historian C. Vann Woodward noted, Jim Crow gave the authority of enforcement to the "streetcar conductor, the railway brakeman, the bus-driver, the theater-usher, and also . . . the hoodlums of the public parks and playgrounds."[14] Indeed, that authority to enforce extended to virtually any white person. On a daily basis, white audiences watched and reacted to the routine performances of race, and thus every interracial encounter functioned as a form of surveillance. Two types of threats imposed a seriousness on this watchfulness and informed how African Americans occupied interracial spaces. First, African Americans moved through daily spaces aware that the wrong performance could be met with a beating or even death.[15] The threat of lynching hovered over each interaction. Second, many African Americans also had to be wary of being sexually assaulted. If the possibility of a lynching served to compel blacks to deliver an appropriate performance, the surveillance attached to the threat of sexual assault had little to do with whether or not the black individual was playing the expected role. Instead, these assaults represented the ultimate demonstration of white male authority and domination. Together, these two forms of violence informed a surveillance that potentially made every interracial encounter a tense one.[16]

Into the 1930s, lynching remained connected to surveillance even as these acts occurred less frequently and were more likely to be carried out by a few individuals.[17] Alongside these changes, many white Southerners were expressing an uncertainty about these violent acts outside the law, concerned that they might be evidence of white barbarity.[18]

Accordingly, in the 1930s, lynchings were increasingly accompanied by two messages. One was the traditional reminder that African Americans could be assaulted and killed for any reason or no reason, while the other was an attempt to justify each lynching, to explain these vigilante acts in ways that did not contradict the Jim Crow narratives of intimacy and paternalism.

Consider, for example, a case from 1933 in Louisville, Mississippi, in the eastern part of the state. According to an investigation by anti-lynching researcher Jessie Daniel Ames, Lee McDowell, a white man, was upset that the hogs owned by Rueben Micou, a black man, were in his cornfield.[19] The two men argued about it, and, according to Ames's findings, the argument was about more than hogs. McDowell wanted Micou's farm, and Micou apparently refused to sell it to him. Later that night, a carload of men kidnapped Micou, and a larger group of white men beat him and shot him to death.[20] The local newspaper, the *Winston County Journal*, putting the episode into context for its readers, explained, "Negroes must learn and most of them do know—that they occupy a peculiar place in this land, and must keep it. . . . The colored person in this country still has one consolation. It matters not what his brother may do, if he walks aright, he will receive just as strenuous protection as his unruly brother may receive condemnation."[21] In effect, the newspaper blamed Micou for his own death for failing to "keep" his place, and in the process it shifted responsibility for the death away from the mob. But the message in this article was directed especially at other black citizens in the community. This message held out the threat of violence, but at the same time it also suggested that the lines were clearly drawn, that blacks who stayed in their Jim Crow place would not only avoid being lynched but would even enjoy the protection of whites. Thus, local white people were watching and prepared to reward black people with the benefits of paternalism or to punish those who failed to keep their "peculiar place."

Tied to the community and deeply localized, the surveillance of lynching was characterized by the familiarity and high visibility of the watchers. Those who watched tended to be the individuals African Americans encountered in their daily lives, such as employers, bus drivers, and storeowners. In the case of Micou, it was a neighbor. African Americans then were likely to know and even to be intimately familiar with the people who were watching. Alongside this familiarity between parties was a direct and immediate relationship between the process of watching and the subsequent response. It would have been clear to everyone in the community why Micou had been murdered. Ironically, while in the legal arena lynchings were often defined as being conducted "at the hands of persons unknown," the black community would have likely known who the lynchers were and why the lynching had occurred. At the very least, African Americans would know that the lynchers were white people in their community. Significantly, while the act itself was carried out in seclusion—making it different from the spectacle lynching—the narration of the event was intentionally public and visible. In the death of Micou, for example, the newspaper became a tool of surveillance, indicating that the white community was watching and that members of that community were watching closely those individuals who did not remain in their place.

To say that this surveillance depended heavily on the participation of white citizens does not mean that the law and the police were irrelevant. Law enforcement officials were watching, too, and on numerous occasions they successfully prevented lynchings by safely securing prisoners and refusing to turn them over to a mob. At the same time, many other lynchings were possible only with the complicity or acquiescence of these officials.[22] More broadly, the courts also were important in ensuring that vigilante violence would continue. By the 1940s, even as lynchings were steadily followed by the arrests of the alleged lynchers, all-white juries consistently reached not-guilty verdicts. In some cases, even African Americans were part of this network. In 1930, for example, a mob of more than 150 whites witnessed the shooting death of Dave Harris for killing a white man, after a black man turned him in.[23] Yet even as this system involved police, juries, and others, at the point of contact along the daily boundaries that separated black from white, local citizens represented the first line of defense. Much of the policing of Jim Crow was initiated in these regular encounters in daily life, in ordinary white people observing black people and acting.

For those being watched, this informal, localized system generated particular responses. Because those watching were familiar and highly visible, African Americans often knew that they were being watched and who was watching.[24] Yet alongside these knowns, what filled every interaction with latent energy and tension was one major unknown: how white people might react. Observing this uncertainty in the 1930s, ethnographer John Dollard remarked, "Every Negro in the South knows that he is under a kind of sentence of death; he does not know when his turn will come, it may never come, but it may also be at any time."[25] Everyday surveillance was rooted in things at once familiar and unknown, and together these features produced particular types of fears from those being watched, as both Unita Blackwell and Aaron Henry understood.

Blackwell, who would become a key activist in the civil rights movement in the 1960s, was born into a sharecropping family in 1933 in the Delta and spent most of her early life in Lula and across the river in West Helena, Arkansas.[26] Recalling her childhood, she notes, "You did not do certain things because you were black, and because the white people would kill you, beat you, hang you or whatever, and it was just set up on fear."[27] Blackwell was remembering a system in which the fear of violence hung in the air and influenced her decisions. She explains elsewhere, "Obedience to white people was a custom based on the simple fear of what might happen to me if I incurred their wrath."[28] It is worth emphasizing Blackwell's word choice here. She could have focused her attention on particular groups, such as the police, or even on specific individuals. But instead she mentions "white people" and "their wrath." Her fears were of an entire, undifferentiated audience. Fearful of white people, Blackwell would have likely been on constant alert. In addition, her fears were tied to uncertainty, knowing that she might be killed or beaten and always fearing "what might happen." Getting African Americans to focus on the seemingly limitless possibilities of terror had a bearing on their behavior—"you did not do certain things." Likewise, a few examples of lynchings or stories about lynchings went a long way in perpetuating African American fears and reminding blacks to move cautiously around white people.

Aaron Henry, who, like Blackwell, became a leader in the Mississippi movement, related similar concerns from his childhood.[29] Born in 1922 in Clarksdale, Henry, in his memoir, recalls his Jim Crow education: "No rules were ever written, and there was no need to explain them. We were never told we couldn't come in a front door, and we didn't know what would happen if we tried to violate the customs. This fear of the unknown kept the Negro community in its place. We did know, however, that Negroes were lynched for more flagrant violations of the code, such as speaking an alleged obscenity to a white lady or even looking at her the wrong way."[30] Henry emphasizes customs and unwritten rules rather than laws, and, like Blackwell, he notes the importance of fear and hints at the possibility of violence. For both Blackwell and Henry, their fears were connected in part to the unpredictability of the white response. Would a racial transgression be met with a lynching or just a beating? The ambiguity of punishments could inspire fears among black people that they could be punished for any violation. Henry's observation is also more specific than Blackwell's. He refers, for example, to the extremeness of the white response in noting that looking at a white female "the wrong way" could lead to a lynching. This concern was also a gendered one. Black men worried especially about their actions around white women, and as we will see below, black women worried about white men. Nonetheless, Blackwell and Henry describe a racial system in which whites were presumably always watching, in which the expected behavior of blacks was somewhat unclear, and in which part of the terror was tied to the uncertainty of how whites might respond.

A rather different form of surveillance accompanied the threat of sexual assault. While black females were occasionally the victims of a lynching, they were much more likely to be raped. Unlike the documentation of lynchings, which began in 1882, we have no reliable figures for sexual assaults against black women by white men.[31] These incidents rarely appear in the legal record because the legal system protected white men and rarely recognized such assaults as criminal. Meanwhile, cultural images of the hyper-sexualized black temptress perpetuated the myth that black women were incapable of being raped, portraying them as seducers. Yet if evidence of sexual assaults rarely shows up in official state documents or in newspapers, and if these acts have garnered much less scholarly attention than lynching, references to sexual assault frequently appear in the memoirs of black women.[32] And those sources indicate that sexual assaults were quite common and that, like lynching, they contributed to a system in which whites were daily watching blacks.

In the surveillance that emerged from sexual assault, the watchers were primarily white men and the watched were primarily black girls and women. Like lynching, watching and acting were coupled with men knowing they could violate black bodies without fear of legal consequences. Accordingly, many African American girls learned early on to be especially careful around white males. Winson Hudson, for example, knew that she could be raped by white boys, and she thus avoided walking alone.[33] We do not know if she learned that lesson from her parents, from other family members, or from her friends. Regardless, her cautiousness suggests these concerns were circulating within the black community. While Hudson sought protection in numbers, for many black women and girls, regular contact alone with white men was unavoidable, especially for those females who worked in the homes of whites.

Endesha Ida Mae Holland, who was born in 1944 in Greenwood in the Delta, began working as a domestic when she was a young girl. When she was eleven years old, the wife of her employer sent her upstairs to her husband's room, where the man proceeded to rape her. In Holland's case, the white wife was complicit, indicating that the watchfulness of the white male sometimes even came from the white female. Holland surmises that as many as three-fourths of the black girls who worked in white homes were sexually assaulted by white men.[34] The homes of whites represented an especially dangerous place for black females where on a daily basis they could find themselves alone with a white man. These circumstances point to an important distinction between the surveillance of lynching and that of rape. Whereas lynchings were often intentionally public, or at least publicized, sending a clear message to the black community, rapes were intentionally private. In many cases, white husbands would not have wanted their wives or the community to know that they had had a sexual interaction with a black female. Sexual assaults, then, were much more likely to be secluded, individualized attacks, perhaps comprising an audience of one and lacking the publicity that came with lynchings.

Still, as a means of surveillance, the white gaze attached to sexual assault extended outside the privacy of the home and into virtually every space where blacks and whites might interact. The risks were everywhere. As Holland explains, black females "could just as easily be picking cotton or walking to the store or spending money in the white man's store when the mood would take him and he'd take us—just like that, like lightning striking."[35] In addition to the homes of whites, Holland suggests, no place was safe; there was virtually no escape from the white man's gaze. Like the fears of being lynched, the fears around sexual assault pervaded everyday life, reminding the black woman to be careful around white people and particularly around white men. At the same time, cautiousness might not be enough, and the white woman might still send her upstairs.

But what then was the message that went out to the black community, and what was the larger effect of these acts? At least one message cut across both of these practices: white people had the authority to damage and destroy the black body. In other ways, however, rape and lynching produced distinct types of surveillance. Lynching was tied, if ostensibly, to a performance of justice. The public narrative presented the lynching as addressing a wrong, and lynchers often went to great lengths to elicit a confession from the victim, to demonstrate that the person deserved the punishment. In the aftermath, the lynching was framed publicly as a legally and morally justified act. Conversely, rape had no pretense of law or fairness, and the assault required no claim of a racial violation. It was instead a performance of white male domination, and more than that, it was an enactment of the very social system that whites had tried to create with signs and laws and customs. That is, the sexual assault was a performance that made white men masters and black women servants. It was also another instance in which in daily life African Americans were expected to entertain and perform for whites. Sexual assaults were reminiscent of an earlier period when slave owners had unchecked sexual access to the slaves they owned.[36] As Holland explained, in ways that linked slave ownership to sexual assault, "No longer any one man's property, now we belonged to everyone."[37] In a Jim Crow world, virtually every white person, whether in the cotton field, the store, the street, or the white man's home, was a potential master. As a form of surveillance, the threat of sexual assault was made more potent by the realization that any white man might want to play the role of master.

The interracial intimacy of Jim Crow, then, produced a surveillance network closely tied to the possibilities of violence and to a white audience daily watching. Accordingly, within this system, some spaces— homes of whites and public ones—were more dangerous than others. While some whites gained information from black informants, white eyes and ears did not extend so pervasively or easily into the private realm of black homes or to the public places occupied almost exclusively by blacks, such as churches, barber and beauty shops, and juke joints. Within these enclaves, blacks could more safely express their discontent and their true feelings about whites through sermons, speeches, blues lyrics, jokes, and casual conversation.[38] Consequently, as the fears raised by Blackwell, Henry, and Hudson indicate, the spaces of greatest tension were interracial ones, and for much of the Jim Crow era, whites generally ignored black-only spaces. Perhaps believing that most black Mississippians were satisfied with segregation, many felt little need to infiltrate these spaces.

Throughout the first half of the twentieth century, an informal surveillance network coalesced around the power of whites to inflict physical harm on blacks, represented most poignantly by lynching and rape. The fears around those possibilities shaped a surveillance that was local and personal. It was a system based on high visibility in which those being watched could often see those who were doing the watching. The unknowns related to how those watching might respond. As well, the acts of violence that accompanied this surveillance were likely to be direct and immediate. The watchers were often the attackers and that made the connection between surveillance and violence transparent. This community-based system of surveillance, dependent on a local audience, proved an effective tool for much of the Jim Crow period. In the 1950s, however, this surveillance would be undermined by another audience, a national one, that was increasingly seeing white Southerners commit acts of violence against black Southerners.

EMMETT TILL, RACIAL VIOLENCE, AND THE NATIONAL SURVEILLANCE OF THE SOUTH

National public opinion and the media played a role in the development of the civil rights movement in the South in the 1950s and 1960s. Through the pen of the journalist and the lens of the photographer—and later through the lens of the television camera—Americans across the country saw, heard, and read about racial atrocities in the South. And Mississippi regularly appeared in the headlines and captions of these events, including Till's death in 1955, the assassination of civil rights leader Medgar Evers in 1963, and in the following year, the murders of civil rights workers James Chaney, Michael Schwerner, and Andrew Goodman in Neshoba County. As historian Joseph Crespino observes, during the civil rights era, Mississippi became a metaphor for racial violence.[39] Furthermore, photographers and reporters did not simply open their shutters and capture random shots. Rather, they framed a particular narrative for the nation and even in some cases moved props and people or in other ways set up a scene to capture the desired effect.[40] Civil rights activists also took advantage of these opportunities through their appearance and their actions to convey an image of middle-class respectability in front of the cameras.[41] If this media coverage was not exactly scripted, it nonetheless sought out and told a movement story that revolved around white Southerners violently attacking peaceful black victims.[42] Those images outraged a national audience, which at times pushed a reluctant federal government to intervene.

The role of the media in the civil rights movement has garnered much attention from scholars.[43] Less well known are the ways in which a national audience watching the South and seeing regular performances of racial violence also provoked changes among those individuals who were fighting to save Jim Crow practices. Even as a few vocal white Southern leaders advocated defiance and even as violence continued, quietly a fundamental racial transformation was under way in the mid- to late 1950s. In Mississippi, in response to the images of racist violence that appeared on a national stage, a number of segregationists targeted the nature of racial surveillance in the state. A system that had previously emerged from informal, local interactions and that was tethered to public, overt displays of violence, such as lynchings, was being replaced by a much more centralized and formal surveillance. That system would preserve violence while also functioning to conceal acts of violence from journalists and photographers. For many white Mississippians, the coverage of the Till murder and trial represented a critical moment in this transition, even as this shift was connected to longer-term changes in the relationship between the South—especially Mississippi—and the nation.

The relationship between the nation and the South had a long, complicated history. If sectional divisions had contributed to the Civil War, the late nineteenth century became a period of reconciliation in which a shared sense of whiteness and of white supremacy patched over regional differences.[44] With the emergence of Jim Crow—a racial system marked by hundreds of lynchings, the disfranchisement of most black voters, and the passage of segregation laws—the federal government as well as the national public showed little interest in the racial developments in the South. As late as the 1940s, in fact, Gunnar Myrdal observed that the Northern public preferred "to hear as little as possible about the Negroes, both in the South and in the North."[45] Within this climate of indifference and a shared belief in white supremacy, much of the nation nonetheless imagined the South as different, and as pre-modern. Karen Cox notes that before World War II national popular culture portrayed the region as "the land of happy-go-lucky blacks, southern belles, rural landscapes, and life lived at a leisurely pace."[46] In its most positive connotation, such as in the 1939 film *Gone with the*

Wind, the region became a bygone world of honor and paternalism.[47] Occasionally, more negative forms of this South emerged, such as the mockery directed at the region following the 1925 Scopes trial over the teaching of evolution in Tennessee, in which the South was conceived as backward and out of step with the rest of the modern nation.[48] It was, however, only sporadically that a national public expressed a pronounced interest in Southern racial politics.[49]

By the World War II years, however, differences between the South and the nation were increasingly being expressed in racial terms. Some of these distinctions related to steady pressure from African Americans and civil rights groups and subsequent actions by the federal government. For instance, in response to A. Philip Randolph's threatened March on Washington, Franklin D. Roosevelt ordered the integration of defense industries. A few years later, Harry S. Truman called for integration in the armed forces. Even if neither of these initiatives fully integrated the defense industries and the military, they nonetheless signaled a new national discourse around racial integration. Likewise, even as discrimination and segregated residential patterns characterized urban areas throughout the North and the West, it was the racial practices in the South that increasingly attracted national attention. Thus, in 1944 the U.S. Supreme Court's decision in *Smith v. Allwright* outlawed "whites only" primaries, a practice that in the South had prevented blacks from voting in Democratic Party primaries, which in the one-party South were the only ones that mattered.[50] Likewise, as World War II gave way to the Cold War, evidence of racism and discrimination in the South—but not in other parts of the country—undermined the State Department's claims that the United States represented freedom.[51] Accordingly, in 1957, as audiences around the world witnessed an Arkansas governor refusing to allow nine students to enter a Little Rock high school, few Americans heard about white homeowners in Levittown, Pennsylvania, who two weeks earlier had violently resisted the efforts of an African American family to integrate their neighborhood.[52] Cold War politics, then, solidified the discursive link between racism and the South. Thus, into the 1950s, an emerging national narrative of racial liberalism, one that often ignored racist practices in the North and the West, cemented the South's status as antimodern and as a problem.

White Southerners, of course, were not oblivious to this changing relationship. After all, Truman's endorsement of civil rights in 1948 produced a momentary break with the Democratic Party when some Southern Democrats created a States' Rights party and endorsed their own presidential candidate in opposition to Truman.[53] Within Mississippi in particular there were other indications of a growing national concern about their racial practices.[54] In November 1945, authorities in Laurel charged Willie McGee, an African American, with raping Willette Hawkins, a white woman.[55] The following month, the jury deliberated for less than three minutes before rendering a guilty verdict, and McGee was scheduled to be executed in January.[56] The Civil Rights Congress (CRC) then took on the case, and McGee's new attorney, Bella Abzug, engineered several appeals, arguing that McGee had been denied his civil liberties, including the suppression of evidence, a coerced confession, and the exclusion of key witnesses from the trial.[57] In addition to legal support, the CRC helped to publicize the case and to present it as another example of racial violence and injustice.[58] In 1950, a rally for McGee in New York City at Madison Square Garden attracted 18,000 people.[59] Support for McGee's case came from a number of well-known individuals in the black community, including Josephine Baker, Ossie Davis, and Julian Mayfield. Meanwhile, William Faulkner weighed in, arguing that McGee's guilt had never been proven, and Jean-Paul Sartre and Albert Einstein signed petitions sent to Governor Fielding Wright.[60] Nonetheless, on May 7, 1951, the State of Mississippi executed McGee.[61]

The McGee case brought a great deal of scrutiny to Mississippi, and in this regard it might have signaled to segregationists that the national and international landscape had shifted. It might have indicated to them that opposition to Jim Crow practices in the South was growing. At least outwardly, however, the case did not lead state officials to reconsider how they talked about or defended Jim Crow before national and international audiences.[62] Perhaps because the CRC was connected to the Communist Party, Mississippi leaders could more easily dismiss international interest in the case. Regardless, state officials did not read the reaction to McGee's conviction and execution as a warning. Accordingly, four years later, even though white Mississippians were no strangers to outside attention and criticism, they were nonetheless unprepared for the ways in which the Till murder would shape perceptions of the state and the region.

In the fall of 1955, reporters from across the country descended on the state and provided detailed accounts of the proceedings.[63]

Photographs in particular became central to the Till story. In Chicago, Mamie Till Bradley included in the lining of the casket, just above the disfigured body, three photographs of her son.[64] One was of Till in a hat and tie, another showed Till with his mother, and a third one, from Christmas Day 1954, was of Till in a tie and leaning against a television. As Maurice Berger notes, the photographs conveyed a middle-class respectability and provided a stark contrast to the grotesqueness of the violence revealed on the body in the coffin.[65] Throughout the civil rights era, this juxtaposition between white violence or the effects of that violence and peaceful, respectable-looking blacks would be a mainstay of media coverage of the Southern movement. Photographs in particular often froze the violence and hatred at its visually dramatic peak: angry whites yelling at quiet, peaceful blacks, police clubs or baseball bats in midair about to descend on an individual on the ground, a police dog lunging at a black man. Beyond the violence itself, the photographs also captured class, regularly showcasing working-class–looking whites as violent actors and educated, middle-class–looking African Americans as victims.[66] Television news was still in its infancy in the late 1950s, but similar images also appeared there. Thus, when the nation "watched" the South, via the media, they saw violence and backwardness.[67] For defenders of segregation in Mississippi, an awareness of this dynamic—and what it meant for Jim Crow practices—would become clear only as the coverage of the murder and trial unfolded.

Journalism scholars Davis W. Houck and Matthew A. Grindy analyzed the day-by-day newspaper coverage of scores of Mississippi dailies and weeklies, charting the tone and language of articles, editorials, and letters to the editor during the Till murder investigation and trial. From that coverage, as well as comments from various officials, the response of white Mississippians, beginning with the kidnapping and concluding with the acquittals of Milam and Bryant, can be divided into four stages.[68] In the first stage, the initial five days of coverage, virtually every newspaper in the state portrayed Till as the innocent victim of a terrible tragedy. The killers, the press collectively maintained, deserved to be punished to the full extent of the law.[69] This response was not so different from how many white Mississippians had narrated racial violence in the state at least since the 1930s. The intellectual and economic elites regularly divorced themselves from lynchings, positioning these acts as the isolated workings of a few rednecks and as unrepresentative of the good relations enjoyed by white paternalists and blacks. Indeed, as noted in Chapter 2, that narrative was at the heart of David Cohn's discussion of the "Delta Negro" in the 1930s and 1940s. In 1955, elements of this narrative theme appeared within the comments of both Governor Hugh White and the arresting sheriff—each regretted the killing and expressed confidence that the state would get a conviction.[70] Likewise, Robert Patterson of the newly formed Citizens' Council called the death regrettable. Local newspapers published the 1954 Christmas Day photo of Till and also expressed sympathy for him and his family. A letter to the editor of a white-owned newspaper, the *McComb Enterprise-Journal*, called out the "hoodlum white trash" who committed the act.[71] In this first five days after the murder, then, politicians, leading proponents of segregation, and the press downplayed the racial angle, as the event became an unfortunate tragedy perpetrated by poor whites.

The first rupture in this interpretation came five days later, and it came in the wake of a response from the national NAACP office. On September 1, a national figure pointed a finger at all of Mississippi. The NAACP's executive secretary, Roy Wilkins, issued a statement reasoning that "the killers of the boy felt free to lynch him because there is in the entire state no restraining influence, not in the state Capitol, among the daily newspapers, the clergy, nor any segment of the so-called better citizens."[72] Wilkins shifted the focus away from "white trash" and held responsible politicians, the media, religious leaders, and "better citizens," which was probably a reference to the political and economic elites, including the Citizens' Council. In calling out the state, Wilkins was likely thinking of other recent murders in the state, including the deaths of Lamar Smith, who was shot and killed on the courthouse lawn in Brookhaven for his involvement in voting efforts, and the Reverend George Lee, who was also involved in civil rights activities.

Wilkins's comments led to a second discursive stage in which the media and various officials reacted angrily and became more defensive. As Houck and Grindy note, the Mississippi press changed its tone overnight. The media and state officials criticized the NAACP for interfering in the case. Perhaps most notable, having previously paid little attention to the two men charged with the murder or having reduced them to "white trash," the media began to rally around them. Various newspapers in the state now began to identify Milam and Bryant as "World War II veterans" and ran photographs of the two men in their military uniforms. Gradually, officials came to question the evidence against the men, with the presiding sheriff, H. C. Strider, suggesting that the entire case might have been a plot orchestrated by the NAACP and that the body might not even be Till's. After previously ignoring Carolyn Bryant, the local media now cast her as an attractive wife and mother, which served as a first crucial step toward humanizing her and reconfiguring her as a victim.[73] Indeed, it was a step toward transforming her into a white female victim fighting off a black beast rapist. What began as a local murder case had now become a much bigger fight between Mississippi officials and the NAACP over the state's reputation. Still, white Mississippians seemed to be generally unaware that not only the NAACP but a much larger national audience was reading the reports and seeing the photographs.[74]

The third crucial shift came after the acquittals of Milam and Bryant. Immediately following the verdict, many white Mississippians across the state expressed much relief for having averted a crisis. They mistakenly believed that the fight had been between the state and the NAACP, and that the trial itself, regardless of the verdict, had shown the world that justice prevailed in Mississippi. They believed that because they had followed due process with a jury (an all-white one), this had been a fair trial. At this moment, they also believed that they had defeated the NAACP's charges of racism and injustice.[75] While they knew that a national audience was watching, they had little idea what the national audience had expected or hoped for in the trial. This third stage was a short one and it ended abruptly.

In the fourth stage, coming almost immediately after the expressions of relief, Mississippi politicians and the media began to realize their mistake. They had, they now understood, grossly miscalculated how closely the nation was watching the trial. Many white Mississippians especially underestimated national sympathy for Till and the extent to which a national public believed that the evidence against the two men had been overwhelming. Up until that moment, members of the Mississippi press had paid little attention to the reaction of the American public, so focused had they been on the NAACP and the national media. Now, in hindsight, some of them began to consider the damage that had been done to the national perceptions of the state. These perceptions would be summed up two months later by Oliver Emmerich, a racial moderate and editor of the *McComb Enterprise-Journal*. The editor observed that white Mississippians had believed that a not-guilty verdict would give the NAACP a "kick in the teeth" but that instead it had only fueled the integrationist cause by showing the South to be antiblack. He further explained: "Outsiders accuse us of being unjust to the Negroes of Mississippi. They seek to drive a wedge between the good Negroes and good white people of Mississippi. . . . We manifest an attitude that is contrary to law and order."[76] Even as staunchly segregationist newspapers such as the *Jackson Daily News* maintained that the Northern press lied about Mississippi, they also concurred with Emmerich's assessment that much of the nation saw Mississippi as a violent, racist place, rather than one where blacks and whites lived in peace and harmony.[77] The national response to Till, which was strongly influenced by the photographs of a respectable Till and of a grotesque corpse, showed not only that the nation was watching Mississippi and the South but also that what they saw was an entire region of backward, racist, violent whites.

For many white Mississippians, the aftermath of the Till trial became a moment of reflection. The response to the murder and the trial revealed that the image of the South as a place of contented, loyal blacks and paternalistic whites was competing with an image of the region as one of angry, aggressive whites and peaceful black victims. It was not a moment in which segregationists reconsidered their own ideas about race relations—and many continued to believe and to tell themselves that most African Americans preferred Jim Crow—but it was a moment in which they reconsidered the relationship between the informal, local-centered surveillance that had led to Till's murder and the state's national reputation. In these reflections, segregationists imagined new ways of monitoring racial lines.

THE CENTRALIZATION OF EVERYDAY SURVEILLANCE

In response to a national audience watching the South and seeing violence, Mississippi officials adapted their racial practices, seeking especially to create a centralized and more carefully managed system of racial surveillance.[78] Two new organizations were instrumental in this transformation. One of these groups, the Citizens' Council, had been born in the shadow of the *Brown* decision. In July 1954, Robert Patterson, a plantation manager, brought together local political and business leaders in Indianola, and the group dedicated itself to preventing racial integration in schools. By its second year in existence, the Citizens' Council claimed to have more than 80,000 members in the state, with other chapters springing up across the South.[79] Local chapters tended to be populated by the most prominent community leaders, including businessmen, professionals, politicians, attorneys, and judges. High-ranking supporters of the organization included Mississippi Supreme Court Justice Tom P. Brady, Senator James Eastland, Representative John Bell Williams, and Ross Barnett, who would become governor in 1960. Its supporters also included perhaps the two most powerful members of the media in the state, the brothers Thomas and Robert Hederman, who owned Jackson's two daily newspapers, the *Clarion-Ledger* and the *Jackson Daily News*.[80]

The Citizens' Council tapped into a class-based discourse that, as noted in Chapter 2, had previously led David Cohn and other white elites to associate acts of racial violence with the white working class. In similar fashion, spokespersons for this new organization contrasted their efforts with the vigilantism of the Ku Klux Klan by claiming to represent "the 'better class' of southern whites," to seek "law-abiding" strategies to preserve segregation, and never to advocate violence.[81] These proclamations had deep roots in the older racial paternalism narrative, which depicted a special familial bond between white elites and the black population. In addition, the Citizens' Council's allusions to race relations, class, and violence were also responding to the national media's image of the South as violent and backward. As Tom Brady explained, "Unless we keep and pitch our battle on a high plane, and unless we keep our ranks free from the demagogue, the renegade, the lawless and the violent, we will be branded, as we should be branded, a fearful, underground, lawless organization."[82] Senator Eastland, in a December 1955 speech in Jackson, made a similar appeal, warning his audience that "violence hurts the cause of the South" and proposing instead that supporters of segregation engage in a "just and legal fight."[83] Publicly, Citizens' Council leaders and their supporters advocated a move away from violent tactics and from the groups who used them. In practice, however, this organization was part of a larger effort not to end violence but rather to move it beyond public view. And that approach embraced new forms of surveillance and intimidation.[84]

The second group critical to the centralization of surveillance was the Mississippi State Sovereignty Commission.[85] In January 1956, roughly three months after the acquittals of Milam and Bryant in the Emmett Till trial, the Mississippi state legislature created the agency to carry out a dual strategy of public relations and investigations in the interest of preserving segregation. Both arms of the agency's work represented responses to the negative image of the South nationally. Initially, the Sovereignty Commission devoted most of its attention to public relations, which will be explored in Chapter 5 as part of the transformation in racial discourses during this era.[86] While the agency's investigative agenda developed more slowly, its efforts were a product of broader changes in surveillance already under way within the state, as various individuals and groups sought a more hierarchical and professional network designed to hide the most repressive racial practices from public view. This network would still depend on local observations such as in elevators and country stores, but now locals, including police officers, would be encouraged to watch and report, rather than watch and act. As the earlier surveillance system had depended on directness, immediacy, and the high visibility of the watcher, this developing system would be marked by documentation, planning, secrecy, and hidden watchers.

Compared to the Citizens' Council and its 80,000 members across the state, the Sovereignty Commission was tiny. With its mission "to maintain segregation," the agency was initially made up of nine elected officials—the governor, lieutenant governor, attorney general, speaker of the house, three state senators, and two state house members—and three citizens appointed by the governor.[87] A small staff—never more than three agents were employed at any one time—carried out the day-to-day operations. Even with a small staff, over the course of eighteen years, the agency accumulated and produced more than 132,000 reports, clippings, letters, and other documents, which contained the names of approximately 87,000 individuals.[88] In the early years of the surveillance work, one of the primary investigators was Zack Van Landingham, who had twenty-seven years of experience as an agent for the FBI.[89] Additionally, by the end of 1959, the group claimed to have "eyes and ears" in every county in the state.[90] That claim was tied in part to having agents visit each county. These trips served several purposes in the development of a statewide surveillance network. They allowed agents to build relationships with local officials and other citizens and to establish a hierarchy in which the state agency, not locals, would take the lead in orchestrating responses to Jim Crow transgressions. Agents could also learn if particular groups or individuals in the community needed to be tracked, and this tracking often proved useful in future investigations. Thus, despite their small numbers, the Sovereignty Commission, with a presence in every county, presided over the growth of an extensive and hierarchical surveillance network. In the process it helped create a system designed not only to uncover civil rights activism but more broadly to police the everyday racial routines between blacks and whites.

Beyond the Citizens' Council and the Sovereignty Commission, many other individuals were directly and indirectly involved in surveillance. Local citizens reported their own observations, law enforcement officials conducted investigations and communicated regularly with state agents, and high-ranking political figures frequently initiated investigations or participated in planning with agents.[91] Indeed, the birth of an organization dedicated to surveillance did not mean the end of the forms of watching that Richard Wright experienced in the elevator. Instead, these groups sought to organize the observations, to create a much more hierarchical and structured system out of a web of surveillance that seemingly stretched across and through every community in the state.

An example from 1961 will help to illustrate how this network operated. At an NAACP meeting in Greenwood, someone—perhaps a local police officer or citizen—copied down the license tag numbers on the cars parked outside the meeting place and then sent the list to the Sovereignty Commission. Albert Jones, the Sovereignty Commission director, assigned agent Tom Scarbrough to investigate. Scarbrough traveled to Leflore and Bolivar counties, where he met with law enforcement officials, a circuit clerk, a superintendent, a car dealer, a local banker, and another local business owner. Some of the visits focused on finding out who owned particular cars at the meeting. Other visits targeted employers of those individuals known to have attended the meeting. One of the cars, Scarbrough learned, belonged to Lois Ware, a black teacher in Leflore County. The agent informed Otis Allen, the white superintendent of the county schools, that one of his teachers had been at the meeting. Allen promised to handle the situation. For another license tag belonging to an unknown owner, Scarbrough met with a local car dealer. The dealer did not know who had purchased the car but offered to look into it and pass any additional information on to Robert Patterson of the Citizens' Council. Before returning to Jackson, Scarbrough visited the Bolivar County sheriff and gave him a list of the license tags and names from the meeting.[92]

TITLE: Yazoo County
* ** * * * * * * * * * * * *

INVESTIGATIVE PERIOD: March 15, 1961
* *

DATE REPORTED: March 29, 1961
* *

REPORTED BY: Tom Scarbrough, Investigator
* *Y * * * * * * * *

APPROVED BY: _____
* * * * * *.* * * * * * * * * * * * * ** ** *** * * * * * * * *** *

TYPED BY: Marie Rayfield
* *

On March 9, 1961, I received an order from Director Albert
Jones to proceed to Yazoo and three other counties to check with
Public Officials and Civic Leaders as to NAACP and subversive
activities, and to especially appraise the Circuit Clerks about
Civil Rights Investigators being in Mississippi and to appraise
the Clerk of the investigators methods of operation.

On March 15, 1961, I checked with officials and civic
leaders in Yazoo County. Upon my arrival in Yazoo City I checked
with officials in the Court House; namely Sheriff, W. T. Stubblefield,
Red Sleigh, Billy Woodle, his two Deputies, Tax Assessor A. P. Kelly,
Circuit Clerk Mrs. C. A. Fisher, W. C. Martin, his two office assist-
ants and T. A. Norris, former Representative. Senator Herman Decell
was out of town. Dr. R. J. Moorehead was operating on a patient.
I was not able to see him. I talked to Derwood Teaster, one of the
Directors of the Yazoo County Citizens Council and Art Russell, Chief
of Police of Yazoo City.

Chief Russell told me the night before about 8 p.m, March 14,
1961, two men drove up to the front of Soloman T. Nichols home, with
their brief cases in hand came upon Mr. Nichols front porch and knocked on Nichols front door. Mr. Nichols said the men introduced
themselves. He said he did not remember their names. Mr. Nichols
said the men asked him if they could talk to him about the school
situation in Yazoo County.

Mr. Nichols said he told the men he did not care to discuss
with them or anyone else the school situation in Yazoo County. He
said so far as he knew everyone in the County was satisfied with
their schools and he felt there was nothing to discuss. Mr. Nichols
said the men went back to their car and left. He said he did not
notice the kind of car they were driving or from what state the
tag indicated.

Mr. Nichols is a Catholic and does not send his children to
the Public school. His children go to a private Catholic school.

2-13-19

The first page of an investigative report from the Mississippi State Sovereignty
Commission's Tom Scarbrough. The report details the agent's visit to Yazoo
County to investigate possible NAACP and civil rights activities. Scarbrough met
with a sheriff, a chief of police, city and county officials, a local Citizens' Council
member, and others. SCRID# 2-13-0-20-1-1-1, MSSCR; courtesy of the Archives
and Record Services Division, Mississippi Department of Archives and History.

For the Sovereignty Commission, the investigation set in motion additional efforts to both silence and track individuals who attended the meeting. In the case of Ware, a presumed conversation with her employer and perhaps the threat of being fired functioned as intimidation. Scarbrough's visit and report also initiated a bureaucratic trail. Ware's name and her license tags went into a Sovereignty Commission file and name index that linked investigations, letters, newspaper clippings, and other documents. With this filing system, the agency could follow Ware's activities.[93] In addition, any time a local official or the FBI wanted information about an activist, the Sovereignty Commission could easily provide a rundown from its previous work. In fact, the agency regularly provided local and state police officers with license tag information of suspected activists, making it possible for these individuals to be tracked more easily. In Ware's case, it is unclear what happened after the initial investigation. We do not know, for example, how the superintendent addressed the issue. Perhaps he warned Ware, perhaps he threatened her, or perhaps something else. Her name, though, does not appear elsewhere in the organization's files. Likewise, we do not know specifically how the sheriff's office used the tag information. We know from other cases that local law enforcement officials used information obtained from the state agency to follow activists in their cars and even to harass those drivers.[94]

Even without knowledge of the follow-up efforts, one can identify a change from previous forms of surveillance. That is, a different type of audience was watching Ware's performance than the one that had watched Richard Wright in the elevator. Unlike the white people around Wright, many of these audience members remained unseen. Also, unlike Wright's audience, Ware's watchers came not from a random encounter in daily life but from a targeted and coordinated effort. That coordination was extended to draw in her employer so that Ware could continue to be watched and so that she would know that someone had seen her and that presumably she was still being watched. Another distinction from the Wright episode was that the response to Ware's actions—attending a meeting—came much later and it disconnected the initial watcher from the employer. Instead of an immediate and direct confrontation, this NAACP meeting generated much documentation and behind-the-scenes activity. It led to paperwork, meetings, and presumably discussions about how to proceed. All along, the goal had been to intimidate Ware—to correct her performance of blackness and return her to her Jim Crow place—but unlike earlier forms, the means were carried out quietly and hidden from the public.

In Ware's case, the report and the lack of additional information about her suggest that the operation went smoothly. For the Sovereignty Commission, success in thwarting every challenge to Jim Crow depended on building a network and training an audience to watch and report on the daily performances of African Americans. For agents, that objective meant establishing and maintaining strong relationships with local officials and citizens. Agents frequently visited communities, sharing and seeking information about civil rights activities. Meeting with various officials, agents asked about the mood among local blacks, if the NAACP was currently active in the community, and if there were any individuals who might cause trouble in the future. Details about particular activities or individuals, including local activists such as Lois Ware, flowed back and forth, linking state agents, politicians, local officials, and local citizens.[95] These meetings produced much documentation useful for longer-term monitoring of citizens. In addition, it also cemented the hierarchical lines of communication and action, with regular reminders that state-level officials were in charge.

With the emergence of this new surveillance agency, though, one should be careful not to overstate its influence. It would be inaccurate to imagine late 1950s Mississippi as a setting for a John le Carré spy novel teeming with secret agents lurking around every corner. None of the groups engaged in surveillance had adequate resources to watch the entire population. In fact, the Sovereignty Commission at times employed only one full-time investigator. In addition, throughout its history, politicians regularly debated the purpose, existence, and funding of the group. As these realities limited the group's power, the agency very much needed the participation of local citizens, who represented an extension—albeit an imperfect one—of its surveillance. In this regard, then, state agents—in the guise of local citizens and law enforcement officials—were potentially lurking around every corner. It was the hope of the Sovereignty Commission that all of these informal agents in the field would remember to play a supporting a role and defer to the agency.

Beyond the pursuit of known activists, then, the agency also sought out the random regular observations by white citizens. The Sovereignty Commission files are filled with information from local whites reporting on individuals in their communities, with citizens encouraged to note anything that looked like "suspicious behavior." In their observations, white citizens went way beyond the realm of organized protest and civil rights, reporting seemingly anything that looked like a Jim Crow transgression. For instance, the observations from local citizens included a black man opening a business in a "white" section of town, blacks talking back to whites, and blacks in Gulfport laughing at a white bus driver for trying to enforce segregated seating.[96] The new surveillance, then, as with the community-based surveillance, was a tool for maintaining much more than segregation; it was a means for watching all the daily performances of race and then reporting any enactment that seemed out of place in a Jim Crow world. Those performances would come to include E. M. Gregory's nightly beer purchases.

Gregory lived in Shaw, a small town along the border between Bolivar and Sunflower counties in the Delta. The Sovereignty Commission learned about Gregory, an African American, from a white storeowner. The storeowner thought he overheard Gregory making positive remarks about Fidel Castro and Russia, and the white man further believed that Gregory was passing out "subversive literature" and holding meetings of an "unknown nature" in his home. In addition to possible comments about communist leaders and communist countries, something else made the merchant suspicious.[97] He explained to the agent that Gregory bought several quarts of beer every night for parties and always paid in cash. Thus, in building a case, three elements made the black man suspicious to the storeowner—possible references to communism, buying beer every night, and paying with cash. In the eyes of the storeowner, these actions by Gregory indicated that he was not performing the expected role of the obedient, meek, subservient Jim Crow black man. The storeowner's suspicions that his customer was involved in civil rights activities, however, were unfounded. A Sovereignty Commission agent investigated Gregory and learned that he had been handing out religious pamphlets and concluded that he was neither a communist sympathizer nor a threat to segregation; he was a Jehovah's Witness.[98] Still, the case illustrates how carefully white citizens were watching African Americans and, equally important, how seriously the agency treated these observations. In this one, the agent carried out a full investigation before dismissing it.

The Citizens' Council also utilized the surveillance carried out by local citizens. With relatively autonomous chapters, these efforts were less structured than those of the state agency. One of the clearest illustrations of this process came in response to petitions demanding integrated schools in the summer of 1956. A full two years after the *Brown* decision, the NAACP-prepared petitions called for integrated schools beginning in the fall term. Chapters in Vicksburg, Natchez, Jackson, Clarksdale, and Yazoo City accumulated signatures from black parents and submitted the petitions to the local school boards. The state attorney general, J. P. Coleman, who would be elected governor a few months later, officially advised school boards to ignore the petitions on the basis that they were not in the form of a legal document.[99] Coleman's suggestion was meant to avoid direct confrontation and to find a way to undermine the petition drive based on a legal technicality.[100] The Citizens' Council, meanwhile, did not ignore the petitions but rather used them as an opportunity to turn its gaze on black people in these locales.

In each of the communities where petitions circulated, the Citizens' Council scheduled meetings open to all white citizens. The organization's leaders used the meetings as an opportunity to increase the group's membership and its financial base through membership dues, but they also served as warnings to local black citizens—who were excluded from the meetings—that whites were mobilizing and watching. In Clarksdale, the local newspaper noted that 1,000 people attended the Citizens' Council's organizing event.[101] The Citizens' Council also worked with the media to take steps to ensure that African Americans knew that whites were not only organizing but were specifically watching those who signed the petitions. The *Clarksdale Press Register* published the approximately 300 names on the petition. In Yazoo City, the local newspaper published the names and addresses of those signing the petition, and a week later the Citizens' Council in Yazoo City took out a full-page ad, "as a public service," again listing the name and address of each signer.[102] In some locales, these names were posted in storefronts, at banks, and in cotton fields.[103] Some signers withdrew their names, and many others faced economic and physical reprisals. In the days after the names were publicized, local newspapers reported that many of those who had signed now wanted their names removed. Some of the reports claimed that black parents misunderstood the request being made or that the NAACP had intentionally misled them.[104] The steadily decreasing number of petitioners became a focal point in the coverage. In Clarksdale, the number of signers dropped from over 300 to 288.[105] In Yazoo City, in the span of three weeks the original number of 53 signers dwindled to 3.[106]

The entire operation was carried off without reports of violence appearing in the national press. At the same time, in these communities the Citizens' Council and the media had conveyed a powerful message to African Americans. Not only were white people watching, but they could target particular individuals so that every white person in an individual's life, including employers, bank officials, and storeowners, would know to watch out for this person and to make his or her life more difficult. Indeed, in signing up new members, Tom P. Brady encouraged whites to use economic pressure to put down the threat.[107] The NAACP records in these cases reveal that the surveillance that came with having one's name published in the newspaper or posted in public places included a range of reprisals. A local merchant informed one signer that a loaf of bread would now cost him one dollar, about five times the regular price; the Delta National Bank forced some signers to withdraw their funds; distributers refused to make deliveries to a grocery store owner; Jasper Mims received threatening phone calls and reported that a hearse had been sent to his house; Willie Wallace and several others were fired from their jobs; some were driven off the plantations where they worked.[108]

The surveillance mobilized by the Citizens' Council was more direct than an agent copying license tags at a civil rights meeting. In these situations, the watchers and the enforcers were the same individuals, similar to the surveillance that had been attached to lynching and rape. This surveillance disrupted the daily lives of the signers and attracted little national media attention. Furthermore, even if the Citizens' Council avoided the use of violent tactics, or publicly claimed to do so, African Americans could not afford to assume that all white citizens would comply. Certainly the effectiveness of the surveillance against Jasper Mims was the possibility that the hearse was a warning that he would be killed. The response to the petitions, then, contained some of the elements of traditional Jim Crow surveillance—such as a threat of violence and the possibility of always being seen—but it also pointed to new ways of watching. While many of the Sovereignty Commission efforts embraced secrecy and behind-the-scenes maneuverings, the media's and the Citizens' Council's utilization of the white community relied on publicity and visibility, on alerting whites to whom to watch and where to watch.

Ultimately, these two organizations organized and directed surveillance in local communities.

Yet even as the process became more centralized, neither group was completely successful. For all the times in which they quietly prevented protests or other challenges to Jim Crow, numerous other incidents perpetuated the image of the state as a place of racial violence. One of those moments came from the Gulf Coast in 1959 after authorities arrested African American Mack Charles Parker for the rape of a white woman. Before he could be brought to trial, a mob seized him from the jail, shot and killed him, and dumped his body in the Pearl River.[109] The Parker lynching again drew the national media to the state. It also brought the NAACP's Roy Wilkins to Jackson to address the local chapter. Some officials within the Citizens' Council set up a plan for Wilkins to be arrested, but, as a Sovereignty Commission report noted, the agency helped to prevent the arrest and thus to avoid bad publicity and further attempts "to smear and discredit the State of Mississippi on the part of the northern and eastern press."[110] If the claim of this report was in part meant to justify the Sovereignty Commission's work, it also showed an awareness of a new media landscape in which the arrest of a national civil rights leader would further damage the state's image. Similarly, the Parker case revealed that even as behind-the-scenes efforts could prevent some bad publicity, officials could never fully seize control of a long-standing surveillance network tied to public and highly publicized displays of violence.

For segregationists, another important pool of watchers in this network came from the black community. These efforts, in fact, drew on earlier traditions. During the period of enslavement, some white masters turned to trusted enslaved individuals for information about the enslaved population. Later, under Jim Crow rule, prison officials in the state relied on black trusties to watch and discipline black prisoners. While many segregationists in the 1950s continued to argue that black Mississippians preferred segregation, the steadily increasing public protests suggested otherwise. Officials thus became much more interested in eavesdropping on conversations within the black community and especially in penetrating the spaces that had been mostly inaccessible to white people, such as black churches, community organizations, and civil rights meetings. For entry into these spaces, the Sovereignty Commission and numerous local law enforcement agencies employed black informants.[111]

An individual became an informant for a variety of reasons—financial or political gain, jealousy of a particular activist, or even a belief in segregation. Or as Unita Blackwell recalls, "You always had black folks . . . who did what the white men told them to. Some of them were scared not to. Others just wanted to pick up a dollar or two."[112] Informants sometimes provided agents with the names of individuals they believed to be NAACP members or to be otherwise active in civil rights efforts. Officials asked informants to attend meetings of local civil rights organizations, and when Martin Luther King Jr. visited Clarksdale, the Sovereignty Commission tried unsuccessfully to put a hidden microphone on an informant who attended King's speech.[113] Upon the suggestion of one informant, the Sovereignty Commission considered creating an anti-NAACP organization of Mississippi blacks that would work to protect segregation.[114] That proposal, however, was never developed, partly because in addition to organizational expenses the informant requested $5,000 to $6,000 per year to run it.[115]

Beyond the information gathering requested by the Sovereignty Commission, other state officials sought various favors from black informants. Curiously, as many segregationists positioned their own public efforts as legal, some officials asked black informants to handle the "extralegal" work. For example, in Clarksdale, a city official tried to get an informant to kill prominent activist Aaron Henry. On a separate occasion, the same official offered this informant ten dollars to "beat the hell" out of a group of white college students from Iowa who were active in the movement in Clarksdale.[116] The informant rejected both offers. Similarly, in the 1960s, as civil rights demonstrators filled the jails, it was often other black prisoners who were paid or in other ways compelled to beat activist inmates.[117] On the one hand, these acts were not so different from those performed by trusties at Parchman Farm. On the other hand, in this new climate, paying or in other ways persuading an African American to inflict physical violence on an activist denied the national media an image of white brutality.

As surveillance became more secretive and as agents sought to maintain their invisibility, the work of black informants could be especially valuable. However, for a variety of reasons, the information from these sources was often unreliable. For example, one informant reported that activists in Shaw planned to poison the water in the swimming pool for whites.[118] On another occasion, an informant (perhaps the same one) reported that activists planned to bomb the white school in Shaw.[119]

Another informant, prior to Martin Luther King Jr.'s visit to Clarksdale, reported that a black female was going to frame the mayor on a rape charge.[120] None of these scenarios played out, and no corroborating evidence exists in these records to suggest that anyone ever discussed these tactics. In the cases of faulty information, it is not clear whether the informants knowingly gave erroneous reports or if local activists, aware that someone was watching and listening, intentionally misled informants. Likely, both of these situations occurred with some regularity. Agents also seemed to be aware that information derived from informants might be faulty. One agent remarked that a particular informant was "a liar and an opportunist" who had made up numerous stories simply to get money from law enforcement officials.[121] Thus, as with the participation of local whites, state officials remained cautious in how they used black informants.

A final component of the new surveillance network was the use of technology. It seems likely that Mississippi officials looked to the FBI for a model. Not only did the Sovereignty Commission include a former FBI agent, but J. Edgar Hoover had, since the 1930s, professionalized the federal agency and extended its surveillance efforts, including contemporaneous campaigns targeting Martin Luther King Jr., Fannie Lou Hamer, and other civil rights leaders. The Sovereignty Commission also turned over some of its own findings to the FBI.[122] Under Hoover, the federal agents used informants, wiretapped telephones, and installed bugs.[123] Compared to the FBI, the Sovereignty Commission had limited resources, and there is no evidence in the early years that the agency tried to tap telephone lines. However, on a small scale and with limited success, it began to experiment with some of these technologies to infiltrate previously hidden spaces. For example, the Sovereignty Commission attempted to record King's speech in Clarksdale in 1962 (a black informant was also in attendance) by placing a recorder in an adjoining room. Agents, however, could not get the machine to record.[124] While these new technologies produced few results, they nonetheless signaled an important transition in how white people watched and listened to black people.

In the mid- to late 1950s, the nature of surveillance and the role of the audience monitoring racial performances in the daily realm were changing. The use of new technologies, the reliance on informants and citizens, and the covert operations of official agents of the state constituted a network in which surveillance was intentionally hidden from those being watched. Official agents of the state were increasingly present and increasingly invisible. These efforts also relied more on other types of enforcement that developed from watching and listening, then documenting, then conferring, then planning, and finally acting. Compared to the informal and intimate schemes that had previously defined surveillance, these new forms were more centralized, more professional, and more impersonal. Of course, if the tools and techniques of watching were changing, then we might also suspect that those who were being watched would be among the first to notice the changes.

For those being watched—African Americans and their allies—a number of uncertainties marked this evolving system of surveillance. With a lynching-based system, the great unknown revolved around how whites might react at any given moment. With the more centralized system, however, the unknowns expanded to encompass who might be watching and how. For instance, when—that is, if—the superintendent confronted Lois Ware, he may not have told her how he knew she was at an NAACP meeting. He may not even have known who had copied down license tags. Thus, we can imagine Ware realizing well after the fact that someone—and by this point several people—knew she had attended that meeting. She may have worried about losing her job, but she may also now have worried about being watched every time she was in her car. E. M. Gregory, the Jehovah's Witness, was also being watched, first by the merchant and then via an investigation by a Sovereignty Commission agent. Given that the investigation turned up nothing suspicious, he never had to be threatened, and he may have had less reason to be concerned about being watched subsequently.

Whereas the surveillance of the Sovereignty Commission regularly perpetuated an image of hidden eyes and ears, Citizens' Council efforts found ways to hide surveillance in plain sight. Similar to the surveillance around lynching, they delivered a message that potentially everyone was watching. The difference, however, is that the Citizens' Council efforts were often more focused around a particular moment of organized activity. For example, the response to the school petitions in 1956 was to let a specific group of African Americans—petition signers—know that white people were watching them and that in some cases it was known where they lived. Similarly, about a year after the petition efforts, the Regional Council of Negro Leadership—a statewide civil rights group—scheduled a meeting in Clarksdale to discuss voting rights. The Citizens' Council paid for advertisements in numerous

Mississippi newspapers with the expressed purpose of acquainting the "white citizens of the Delta with the plans for the meeting and its announced objective." The *Clarksdale Press Register* also published a story on the upcoming meeting, noting both the location of it and the names of those individuals scheduled to speak.[125] The media coverage functioned as both surveillance and intimidation. Even before the meeting date arrived, participants knew that whites would be watching. At the meeting, they would have to worry about the police or vigilantes attacking them. Before and after the meeting, they would also have to worry about other forms of intimidation, with their names now public knowledge.

In most of these situations, we are left only to speculate how those being watched responded to these dynamics. In a few instances, however, we have individuals speaking directly about how they reacted to this surveillance and the types of fears it inspired. Sheila Michaels, an activist from St. Louis, came to Mississippi and participated in the movement in Jackson and, later, in Hattiesburg. In 1962, she worked for the *Mississippi Free Press*, a Jackson-based newspaper known as the voice of the movement, and during that time she kept a diary. Here are excerpts from her entries for September 1962:

> The police car parks outside the house nightly with the lights off, watching our comings & goings, so they know where to find us when they want us. . . . I say we should send the [telephone] bill to them because they use it whenever we do.

> Tonight Hollis [Watkins] & I were sitting around after dinner when someone knocked at the kitchen door & wouldn't answer us. Hollis made me get behind the Frigidaire. . . . Hollis picked up the bread knife on the way to the door; which is something because Hollis is absolutely non-violent. It was Dewey Greene [a fellow activist].

> The other night Lavaughn came in around 2 am. I was reading & when I heard a noise I blew out the candle.[126]

It is helpful to compare Michael's discussion of her fears to the racial fears from childhood of an earlier period expressed by Unita Blackwell and Aaron Henry. Michaels, like Blackwell and Henry, spoke of the fears of violence that always seemed to be lurking. None of them mention an actual attack but rather a fear that violence was possible.

For Blackwell and Henry, that fear was of not following customs when white people were around. For both of them, the watchfulness of white people meant being cautious in the presence of white people, and it meant, when possible, avoiding white people.

Michaels, however, is describing a surveillance that is more intrusive and seemingly inescapable. In Michaels's case, it is less about the everyday interactions with locals than it is about targeted and official surveillance by the police. She worries about being attacked, not only when she is in public spaces, or around Mississippi whites, but also when she is behind a locked door in her house. Based on the number of attacks on the homes of activists, including a firebomb thrown into Martin Luther King Jr.'s house in Montgomery, Alabama, and Medgar Evers being gunned down outside his house, Michaels's fears would seem to have been justified. While it appears that she could see who was watching—the police across the street—she also described unseen and unknown listening via the telephone line. It is possible that officials tapped telephones, although that seems unlikely, given their otherwise limited and unsuccessful use of the latest technology. But what is relevant here is not whether the police were eavesdropping but rather that Michaels believed they were. From Michaels's perspective, that possibility—expressed here as a joke—conveys a fear of a much different type of surveillance, one that was professional and secretive and one that could be anywhere, inside the house and even inside the telephone. The fear that the State of Mississippi/white people/police could be anywhere contrasts with earlier ideas of safe spaces, such as juke joints, black schools, and churches. Paid black informants, new technologies, and the coordination of the police and other state officials fostered the perception that whites had potentially infiltrated every space, public and private. Michaels was an active participant in the movement, and it is less clear how African Americans in their everyday lives, including those not involved in movement activities, may have experienced fears about being watched.

The differences in these fears also reveal distinctions in who ultimately took charge of watching black people and their civil rights allies. Aaron Henry, growing up in the 1920s and 1930s, spoke of following the unwritten rules to avoid a possible lynching—positioning the community as the enforcers of the status quo—while Michaels in the 1960s identified the police as the source of a seemingly imminent threat. Michaels's entries contain an implied fear that the police could take action at any moment or that any knock at the door might be an attacker. Certainly, in both time periods the police contributed to the daily fears experienced by African Americans and those who challenged Jim Crow. In the earlier period, however, regular citizens exercised proportionately greater authority over daily surveillance than they would by the late 1950s. At the same time, these distinctions in fears do not mean that those expressed by Blackwell or Henry were less real or less serious than the fears of Michaels. The contrasts in these experiences, though, illuminate a critical shift in racial repression, from fears of an informal surveillance to fears of a more professionalized system of watching by law enforcement officials, other agents of the state, and others in the community. It represented a shift from a fear of the visible and the unknown to a fear of the unseen and the unknown. In the transition from a system anchored to the threats of lynching and sexual assault to one featuring secret agents and extensive files, much had changed in how both the watched and the watchers experienced surveillance in daily life. Richard Wright knew, or at least could see, everyone who was watching him, and he knew that if he made a racial mistake, they were the ones who would punish him and punishment would come immediately. Emmett Till's surveillance was also localized, and the response came soon after the transgression. Compare those two moments to that of E. M. Gregory, the Jehovah's Witness, who may not have known that people were monitoring his beer purchases and conversations. The experience of those being watched was changing, and so too was the responsibility of those doing the watching. At the local level, ordinary citizens were still encouraged to observe, but instead of responding, they were now expected to report. The new surveillance, supported by a larger network, added layers of officials and created a much more formal system in which those who watched were likely to be invisible strangers to those who were being watched.

These transformations in surveillance also altered the racial performances and daily interactions between blacks and whites, undercutting the imagined intimacy of interracial spaces. Enactments of whiteness and of blackness now included an unseen audience, and the audience's response might not be known immediately or ever. This lag altered the relationship between blacks and whites in shared space. While white citizens were still charged with monitoring black behavior, their role had been reduced. In the earlier system, as noted in Chapter 1, having the authority to respond to any black transgression empowered the ordinary white citizen and allowed him or her to play the role of master. That was the nature of white privilege in an informal, localized racial system. But the emerging surveillance network, which called on white citizens to report rather than act, changed their performance from one of master to one of messenger. In a more centralized racial system, then, the ordinary white citizen had been demoted.

Shifts in surveillance came not only because various political leaders were trying to save segregation, but specifically because the South, and in particular Mississippi, was also being watched, both differently and more intently than before, by a national audience, via the media. If in local communities the old performances of an interracial intimacy allowed white citizens to act as masters before black servants, the media captured a performance of injustice with white people attacking peaceful black victims. Civil rights activists took advantage of this opportunity, dressing the part and enacting nonviolence. Segregationist leaders in Mississippi understood it too, and to a great extent the changes to surveillance in the 1950s were a response to how the nation was watching the South.

Regardless of the effectiveness of these developments for saving segregation, a more centralized form of surveillance contributed to fundamental racial transformations in the late 1950s and early 1960s. Increasingly, official agents of the state would take the lead in monitoring racial lines, and in the process they began to replace a system of relations tied to ideas of intimacy with one associated with distance and the coldness and invisibility of the state. Surveillance, however, was only one step in this process. Indeed, the processes of monitoring and regulating racial lines and black behavior in the everyday realm often led to arrests and other responses within the legal arena, which were similarly undergoing a dramatic transformation.

4

BREACHING THE PEACE
Arrests and the Regulation of Racial Space

On Mother's Day, May 14, 1961, at the bus station in Anniston, Alabama, a group of local whites led by the Ku Klux Klan attacked a Greyhound bus carrying black and white Freedom Riders who were traveling across the South in an attempt to desegregate interstate travel. The bus then left the station with a late-arriving police escort, followed by thirty to forty cars loaded with white people. Soon after the police abandoned the bus, the other cars caught up with it. Klansmen slashed the bus tires and forced it to the side of the road. The group then firebombed the bus and initially blocked the exits. Passengers fled the burning bus only to be met and attacked by a mob. A second bus of Freedom Riders made it to the bus depot in Birmingham, where more Klansmen materialized as the bus pulled into the station. This time the first two Freedom Riders off the bus, a black man and a white man, came under attack as they attempted to get to the waiting rooms. Other passengers left the bus, fleeing in every direction as the mob moved out of the station and onto the sidewalks and streets. It was a gruesome, chaotic scene. The police arrived only after the violence had subsided and the Klan members had left.[1]

In the next state—Mississippi—the Freedom Riders would receive a much different greeting. Governor Ross Barnett promised Attorney General Robert F. Kennedy that no similar acts of violence would occur in his state.[2] Numerous officials, including the governor, the Jackson mayor, the Jackson police chief, and the state attorney general, issued public statements imploring citizens to let the authorities handle the situation. "We cannot afford," Barnett cautioned, "an unlawful incident or violence."[3] On May 24, when a busload of Freedom Riders pulled into the depot in Jackson, there were no firebombs, Klan members, or violence. Instead, a group of police officers met them and arrested all twenty-seven riders, charging them with a breach of the peace. Over the next few months, more than 300 Freedom Riders entered Mississippi, and authorities arrested and charged them with breach of the peace, and at least one individual, James Bevel, with contributing to the delinquency of a minor.[4] For Mississippi officials, the carefully planned response could not have gone better, and local officials applauded themselves for controlling the situation and for avoiding the displays of violence that had transpired in Alabama and had been seen on televisions and in newspapers throughout the country.

The responses to the Freedom Riders in Alabama and Mississippi represented two very different types of performances. The overtly violent scene in Alabama could draw a direct line from the localized reactions that had long been a hallmark of Jim Crow, with individuals acting immediately and forcefully to discipline the wrong racial enactment. In 1961, this display of white Southerners attacking peaceful activists was precisely what the national media and a national audience expected to see in the South. By way of contrast, the Mississippi performance was notable for its lack of public violence. It was different from the Alabama response in that the police and local politicians took the lead role in preventing violence at the scene. With the nation watching, law enforcement officials oversaw an orderly and peaceful performance. It was still a display of authority rooted in white supremacy, but that authority was articulated through a legal measure rather than public displays involving bodily injury. The Alabama performance cast hooded white people as defenders of segregation, while the Mississippi performance cast uniformed white people as defenders of law and order.

To be sure, if Mississippi avoided violence in this instance, on other occasions in the late 1950s and early 1960s the state was the scene of horrific violence where numerous activists were beaten or killed.[5] Within this context, University of Mississippi professor James W. Silver in 1964 likened the state to a totalitarian society with leaders relying on violence and intimidation to stifle dissent.[6] A subsequent generation of scholars has similarly shown that during these years the frequency and intensity of violence in Mississippi served as a deterrent to civil rights activism.[7] Yet not to be overshadowed by the dramatic displays of white authority was the steady shift to the quieter performance witnessed in the response to the Freedom Rides. This performance revolved around police officers, arrests, and laws and, at least in the legal language of the charges invoked, appeared unrelated to segregation or race.

Historically, policing throughout the South was interconnected with racial concerns. Southerners established the earliest police forces in urban areas with large concentrations of enslaved people.[8] Slavery also often blurred the line between law enforcement and vigilantism, as slave patrols assumed police powers in the search for runaway slaves.[9] Meanwhile, in the Jim Crow era, as police forces expanded in Southern cities and as the number of spectacle lynchings climbed, policing in rural areas varied widely by location. In some instances, law enforcement officials prevented lynchings—most often by refusing to turn over a prisoner to a mob—and in other cases mobs "overpowered" law officers, or those mobs could count on police agents to be willing participants.[10] In Mississippi, policing, similar to the informal racial interactions that governed daily life, was decentralized. A law that allowed sheriffs to be recalled by popular vote enhanced the localized nature of law enforcement. In addition, a statewide police force did not exist until 1938, and until the 1950s the authority of this state patrol was largely limited to highways and traffic laws. Accordingly, state-level officials had little control over policing, and whether officers of the law aided or prevented vigilantism varied by the individual and the community. In the mid-1950s, Governor J. P. Coleman, frustrated by the relative independence of local law enforcement, oversaw two especially important developments designed to give the state greater authority in local matters. First, he put in place a popular recall procedure in which a chancery court chosen by the governor could remove a police officer from his position. Second, as he curbed the autonomy of local law enforcement, he also greatly expanded the state highway patrol.[11] These two steps not only helped to transform the nature of local law enforcement but they also contributed to a more centralized response to civil rights activism and other racial transgressions. By the late 1950s, in Mississippi and throughout the South, the police, and in particular the state police, were positioned to play a significant role in the defense of segregation.

In the decade following the *Brown* decision in Mississippi, the police arrested thousands of activists in the state. These included two women who tried to integrate a Jackson train depot in December 1956, the "Tougaloo 9" in 1960 for trying to integrate a public library, the Freedom Riders in 1961, and many others.[12] Following the murder of civil rights leader Medgar Evers in Jackson in June 1963, officials apprehended so many demonstrators that they converted stockades at the state fairgrounds into holding pens.[13] Away from sites of public protest, Mississippi authorities also arrested many other suspected activists in their homes, on the roads, and in their businesses. By the late 1950s, the arrest had become a standard response to public protests. As well, the turn to arrests was not exclusive to Mississippi. In April 1960, for example, as a wave of sit-ins rolled across the Southern states, police arrested more than 2,000 demonstrators. In the summer of 1963, with hundreds of sit-ins, marches, and other public demonstrations being staged throughout the region, authorities arrested and incarcerated more than 20,000 activists.[14]

Law enforcement officials and the arrest of activists make regular appearances in the narratives of the civil rights movement. They are sometimes referenced as examples of activists using arrests strategically to mobilize local communities, such as in the arrest of Rosa Parks in Montgomery, Alabama, in 1955 for refusing to move from her bus seat, or in Birmingham in 1963 when Martin Luther King Jr.'s arrest and jailing captured the attention of the nation. Meanwhile, on the other side of the racial line, with few exceptions, images of angry police officials—such as Birmingham police commissioner Bull Connor—or of police officers brutally beating and arresting demonstrators have served as examples of white Southern intransigence, and vigilantes and law enforcement officials have been lumped together in this depiction of racism and violence. Arrests and prisons, then, have become iconic symbols for both the sacrifices of movement participants and the injustice and hatred of their opponents. Lost in this narrative is a consideration of why segregationists used arrests, what laws they used and why, and how those tactics were related to other performances of white authority, such as the violent one that greeted the Freedom Riders in Alabama. Indeed, if the attempt to avoid violence against the Freedom Riders in Jackson in 1961 was the result of negotiations with federal officials, the choice of arrests and the breach of the peace charge reflected other recent changes in how local and state officials addressed Jim Crow challenges.

More than a narrow tactical response to public protests and civil rights activists, the use of arrests was part of a fundamental transformation in the racial routines of the everyday realm. While Mississippi officials regularly targeted organizations and reacted to demonstrations, they also extended their reach into local communities to address virtually any real or imagined Jim Crow transgression. Thus, officials sought to use the legal system to do the work that had previously been carried out at the local level by citizens and local officials. Similar to the changes in surveillance, arrests were part of a more centralized, professionalized, and hierarchical approach to the daily policing of racial lines. The first significant legal thrust came in response to the *Brown* decision with the passage of new segregation laws. Those measures were largely ineffective, and soon officials turned to other laws and other policing practices. The revised approach regularly involved using investigations to intimidate and incriminate activists and anyone who challenged Jim Crow norms. As well, new legal measures and the creative use of other laws—from theft to littering—became the centerpiece of arrests for racial transgressions in the late 1950s and early 1960s.

NEW SEGREGATION LAWS

Following the 1954 *Brown* decision deeming segregated schools unconstitutional, legislatures across the South passed more than 450 laws related to race and segregation, including measures to prevent or limit school integration, as well as more extreme efforts.[15] Similar to the rest of the region, Mississippi experienced a wave of legislative activity. Anticipating the *Brown* ruling in the spring of 1954, the legislature passed a pupil placement law that would allow students to be placed in schools based on factors other than race. It was an effort to forestall desegregation plans.[16] During the same session, they also passed a stricter voter registration law.[17] In 1956, Mississippi legislators approved at least eighteen resolutions and laws dealing directly or indirectly with integration and civil rights issues, including the measure that created the Sovereignty Commission. Beyond new legislation, politicians in Mississippi and throughout the South pursued other avenues related to the legal arena, such as constitutional claims for states' rights over federal power.

Historians have generally associated the various legal efforts with "massive resistance," a term coined by Virginia senator Harry Byrd that initially referred to the legal strategy of interposition to challenge the *Brown* ruling. Citing this legal position, officials claimed the right of states to "interpose" themselves between the federal government and the citizenry. Interposition advocates hoped to use this doctrine to refuse legally to desegregate public schools.[18] While the label "massive resistance" was thus attached to a narrow legal response to the *Brown* decision, in time it came to refer to the entirety of the segregationist response to integration efforts. The phrase itself has suggested a unified white Southern reaction of bold defiance, glossing over ideological divisions and the more subtle responses to desegregation.[19] Similarly, the passage of new laws generally is overlooked or treated as another example of an unsophisticated and uncompromising response, lumped together with the birth of the Citizens' Councils, acts of vigilante violence, and bellicose public rhetoric.[20] Without a doubt, the legislative efforts in these first two years after *Brown* could be read in part as a reactionary response to a sweeping court challenge to Jim Crow. This legal turn, however, also was a step—albeit a halting and uncertain one—in a different direction. If the new laws themselves were mostly inconsequential, as few of them were ever invoked in practice, the approach of creating and revising laws and transferring more authority to the police and the courts signaled a departure from how race had functioned in the daily lives of African Americans and whites for most of the Jim Crow era.

Prior to the 1950s, the last time the South had witnessed a sustained flurry of legislative activity around racial issues had been in Jim Crow's early days in the late nineteenth and early twentieth centuries. These measures detailed racial restrictions in travel, leisure, education, business, employment, and numerous other arenas where blacks and whites might interact. If these laws helped to formalize the emerging racial system, they were nonetheless largely symbolic. Of these initial Jim Crow laws, most of them, notes Michael Klarman, "merely described white supremacy; they did not produce it."[21] The laws substantiated and made more uniform the racial practices that were already in place. Indeed, as an indication of the role of the law in this initial phase, legislators abandoned the project before it was completed, and Southern states, Mississippi included, never fully codified segregation into state law.[22] Similarly, while segregation measures were important in imbuing the Jim Crow worldview with legitimacy, in the regular functioning of this racial system it was, as noted in Chapter 1, the daily interactions that regulated and gave meaning to racial spaces and actions.

In the decades leading up to the *Brown* verdict, Southern officials were acutely aware of Jim Crow challenges coming within the legal arena. For much of the twentieth century, the NAACP and other civil rights organizations pursued federal legislation to prevent lynching. They later found more success in other legal efforts, including key court victories in *Gaines v. Canada* (1938), which required states to provide equal graduate school facilities for black students or to integrate them into existing schools, and in *Smith v. Allwright* (1944), which outlawed whites-only primaries. A few years later, the *Sweatt v. Painter* (1950) ruling deemed segregated state-supported law schools to be unequal and thus unconstitutional.[23] As civil rights organizations challenged Jim Crow in the legal arena, a number of politicians anticipated future legal decisions threatening segregation, and in the late 1940s and early 1950s, before *Brown*, some were pursuing measures such as an equalization plan to increase funding and improve facilities for black students in order to bring the state in line with the notion of "separate but equal."[24] Accordingly, for many Southern political leaders, the *Brown* decision was not unexpected. Having seen other court rulings against Jim Crow practices, they responded in kind with new legal measures. Not surprisingly, then, Mississippi officials also responded in similar fashion—at least initially—to a different kind of challenge that came outside the courtroom: the public demonstration.

In January 1956, two black women, Susie Ramsey of Yazoo City and LaVerne Ephraim of Detroit, Michigan, tried to enter the white waiting room at the railroad depot in Jackson. Their integration attempt came in the wake of an International Commerce Commission (ICC) ruling that banned railroad companies from posting segregated signs in the station. Ephraim and Ramsey may have wanted to test the ICC decision. They may also have drawn inspiration from the Montgomery Bus Boycott launched in the previous month.[25] That boycott, initially spearheaded by the Women's Political Council, protested unfair treatment on the buses, and the well-organized campaign had succeeded in keeping virtually the entire African American community in Montgomery off the buses.[26] Whatever the motivations for Ephraim and Ramsey, their demonstration challenged not only the division of physical space but also the expected performance of blackness in Jim Crow space. And in this regard, it represented a much different kind of racial transgression than those white Mississippians usually encountered. By way of contrast, consider, for example, Richard Wright's refusal to grin on the elevator and Emmett Till's interaction with a white woman in a country store. Wright's and Till's transgressions occurred within the flow of daily routines. The interactions had been random, and the tension had escalated suddenly and unexpectedly. The 1956 performance of these two women, meanwhile, had been planned. In stepping into the white space—in moving the wrong way according to Jim Crow norms—their performance was intentional, collective, and premeditated. Visually and physically, their actions brazenly redefined these spaces and rejected the expected role for where and how black individuals could move. In time, various supporters of segregation would counter these enactments with their own planning, looking for ways to prevent these protests or, when that failed, searching for the most appropriate response.[27] In this early demonstration, Mississippi officials reacted in much the same way as they responded to the *Brown* decision—by turning to the law and by passing new laws.

Local police arrested the two women and charged them with violating the state's "Jim Crow law."[28] It is unclear which law that was, although it likely was a reference to the state's conspiracy law, passed in 1942, which defined conspiracy in part as an attempt to overthrow segregation. The next move came from legislators. In the following two months, Mississippi lawmakers passed several new laws targeting integration efforts. Some of these laws directly contradicted the ICC's mandate and effectively made it illegal for any business to follow that federal body's policy. One bill, for example, required railroad and bus companies to have separate waiting rooms marked with signs for "White" and "Colored," and a second bill required separate restroom facilities "for the races" designated with similar signs. These two laws made it the responsibility of businesses to create segregated spaces. They also suggested an expanded role for the state legislature. In much more specific detail than had occurred in the previous seventy years, these laws described how to make and maintain racial spaces, including, for example, instructions for the placement of signs.[29] In the process, legislators were taking over aspects of boundary making that had been dictated previously by custom and daily interactions. A third measure focused on the patrons by prohibiting persons from entering and using the wrong waiting room.[30] All three violations carried fines of up to $1,000, and two of the bills included a possible jail sentence.

An additional measure passed during this period—just three weeks after the Ephraim and Ramsey arrests—prohibited individuals from creating a "disturbance" in a public place of business and carried a maximum penalty of up to $500 and up to six months in jail.[31] That law was clearly aimed at demonstrators who might attempt to demand service in businesses or sections of businesses reserved for whites. The day after passing that measure, the legislature approved a bill conferring the right of a business or business owner to choose its customers.[32] Each of these bills, which appeared to be directly or indirectly a reaction to the integration attempt at the Jackson railroad station, came during a period in which the Mississippi legislature was passing a number of other segregation measures, including laws that prohibited whites and blacks from attending the same schools, limited the influence of the NAACP in the state, and prevented blacks from registering and voting.[33]

Despite the zeal with which politicians passed these laws, few of these measures were subsequently invoked in making arrests. In this regard, this legislation was akin to the dramatic public statements in which politicians publicly pledged to fight desegregation at every turn but then privately negotiated with federal officials. The legislation, in other words, was important in demonstrating a commitment to segregation for local constituents.[34] In addition, on the rare occasions when these laws were applied, they created complications. Such was the case around the legal response to three cases involving white individuals and black individuals living together in 1958.

In August, near Jackson, J. W. and Stella Vaughn, a white couple, held a revival at a black church, and during the revival they stayed at the home of the black pastor, Phillip Coleman. Rumors of this arrangement spread throughout the community, and soon police officers, accompanied by a group of reporters, came and arrested all three of them. Initially, authorities charged each one of them with vagrancy but then changed the charge. In the absence of a specific law about "house guests of another race," officials turned to a vague catch-all law about enforcing segregation customs.[35] Unsure about how to proceed in the case, however, local authorities contacted the Sovereignty Commission. Director Hal DeCell believed local officials had handled the situation poorly. He worried about the media presence at the arrest and questioned the decision by local authorities to alert them. DeCell's first action, then, was to personally contact every reporter who witnessed the arrest and to win assurances from each one not to play up the story.[36] Subsequently, all three defendants were found guilty and sentenced to thirty days in jail and fined fifty dollars.[37] The sentence itself was relatively minor. It seems likely, given that the infraction was not part of a coordinated civil rights campaign, that the punishment was intended as a token demonstration by officials of their determination to protect segregation. The penalty served as a warning to local blacks and their supporters that Jim Crow violations would not be tolerated.

The ordeal would have likely ended with the sentencing except that Coleman, the black minister, decided to appeal the decision on the grounds that the segregation law was unconstitutional. Officials backed down immediately and sought a compromise with the minister. The judge suspended Coleman's sentence, and in turn Coleman agreed to drop his appeal.[38] This case and its outcome underscore two issues related to the policing of everyday spaces in the 1950s. First, officials attempted to use the law in response to a violation of a custom. In Jim Crow terms, Coleman and the Vaughns had been guilty of occupying a shared space as social equals. It was, in other words, the wrong performance of blackness and the wrong performance of whiteness. Yet when officials tried to use the law and the arrest to correct this performance and in effect send a message about appropriate racial behavior, the legal approach created obstacles for them, potentially providing countless opportunities to challenge segregation in the courts. Accordingly, officials recognized that they would have to be more careful in how they used the law and in what measures they could apply to a particular case. Second, officials would also have to take into account the potential presence of a national audience. The Sovereignty Commission initially succeeded by working behind the scenes with the media to keep the arrests quiet. But the threat of appeal would have risked attracting national attention to the case, creating a test of not only the law but also public opinion.

Two similar cases involved a newly revised law from 1956 that had established harsher penalties for interracial marriage.[39] The amended section applied to persons who were in a marriage that was "prohibited by law by reason of race or blood." Such a marriage would be "declared to be incestuous and void," and persons could be sentenced up to ten years in prison.[40] The phrase "incestuous and void" would pose a legal dilemma for the courts. In the fall of 1958, Daisy Ratcliff, a sixty-six-year-old black woman, and Elsie Arrington, a white man, were arrested and charged under this revised law. According to one report, the relationship was well known in the community and only became a concern when the sheriff learned of it.[41] Arrington, who had spent time at the state mental hospital, was sent back to this institution, and authorities found Ratcliff guilty and sentenced her to the maximum ten-year sentence. Her lawyer appealed the case, noting that this law, because it referred to marriages that were declared both incestuous *and* void, could not be applied to Arrington and Ratcliff or, for that matter, to any interracial relationship.[42] While a person defined as legally white and a person defined as legally black could certainly have been related, the lawyer, like many others in the state, assumed—or at least preferred to assume—that a black person and a white person would not be related, and thus an interracial marriage could not also be an incestuous one. The Mississippi Supreme Court noted the awkward wording and agreed with Ratcliff's attorney and overturned her conviction. On the basis of this decision, the convictions of another interracial couple, a white woman, Mary Rose, and a black man, Joe Scott, were also overturned.[43] The amendment had been poorly worded, but more than that, the case illustrated that the law required a precision of language that had been unnecessary in the more informal policing of daily spaces. The legal approach necessitated different types of performances. Laws existed in print and could be read, debated, and interpreted, and court cases created trails of evidence and dialogue to be studied. Such precision had not been necessary in a system governed by encounters and reprisals occurring outside the law. As the legal arena became more important, officials would increasingly pay attention to the language in new legislation. In fact, while most of the mid-1950s laws were too direct or too poorly worded to be useful to defenders of segregation, at least one measure from this period utilized a linguistic approach that would foreshadow a more sophisticated use of the law to come.

Senate Bill 1954, passed in 1956, outlawed common-law marriage. For a marriage to be legally valid, this new measure stipulated that a couple would need a state license and a marriage ceremony performed by a state-authorized official. In effect, the bill meant that common-law marriages, which were especially prevalent in the black community, would no longer be valid. This measure further stated that failure to comply with both requirements would render a "purported marriage absolutely void and any children born as a result thereof illegitimate."[44] The bill, which seemed on the surface to be about marriage, was in fact tied to the battle over segregation. As legal historian Anders Walker notes, Governor J. P. Coleman, a racial moderate, was considering a school placement plan that would not be tied to race but rather to issues of morality and health. Accordingly, illegitimate black children could be kept out of some schools on moral rather than racial grounds. Even though Coleman's school plan was never instituted, this legal step in that effort nonetheless provides an early example of a new strategy in which white privilege would be preserved in laws that appeared in their subject and legal wording to be unrelated to race.[45] In fact, after the flurry of bills passed in 1956, very few new Mississippi laws made direct reference to segregation. In 1958, for example, no legislation used the words "integration" or "segregation," and only one measure—a resolution calling for an investigation of the NAACP and its communist ties—alluded to race, reasoning that the organization was not "dedicated to the best interests of either the white or negro race."[46] Instead in the post-1956 years, new bills adopted a veiled language. For example, two separate measures in 1958—one that gave the governor the authority to close public schools and another that authorized the governor to close state parks—explained that such action might be necessary "to promote or preserve the public peace, order or tranquility."[47] In effect, that phrase meant that if either space was desegregated, the governor could close it, and references to "public peace," "order," and "tranquility" linguistically stood in for the defense of segregation.

The coded language in Mississippi laws has gone mostly unnoticed by historians, probably in part because officials and the media continued to speak openly about what these laws were intended to do. In 1956, for example, the *Jackson Clarion-Ledger*'s front-page article on the bill banning common-law marriages ran under the headline "House Passes New Segregation Bill," and Associated Press journalist Douglas Starr explained to readers that the measure was "another barrier to keep Negroes out of white society."[48] In the following years, even as the legal language mirrored the racial opacity of this law, Mississippi politicians nonetheless continued to vow to preserve segregation. Thus, publicly, segregationist leaders in the state embraced an overt racial language of defiance, but within the legal arena an important shift was under way, one that would become more pronounced as both public protests and a media presence increased.

Overall, in the four years following *Brown*, the segregationist response to Jim Crow transgressions was relatively straightforward. Legislators passed numerous segregation measures to cover gaps in the law and to use against individuals who challenged racial norms. While these measures represented a more centralized response to the policing of racial lines, they also proved ineffective and inconsequential in practice. Even worse for segregationists, they provided an opportunity for activists to test segregation in the courts with every arrest. The new laws, then, were rarely used, and this step toward a reliance on arrests and laws turned out to be a small one. It was also, however, a significant one in that it altered the performative aspects of everyday interracial encounters. In regulating racial spaces, official agents of the state—politicians, lawyers, and police officers—assumed an expanded role, with lawmakers more involved in defining racial spaces and officers of the law more involved in regulating those spaces. Necessarily, the part played by local citizens became a more limited, supporting role. Steadily, too, state officials made adjustments to the types of laws they passed, and, they also discovered new ways to police racial lines by working behind the scenes before racial transgressions became public.

INVESTIGATIONS, INTIMIDATION, AND INCRIMINATION

In the mid-1950s, because the *Brown v. Board of Education* decision was immediately interpreted as a significant blow to segregation— more so than local protests or other forms of activism—the initial response from Southern officials revolved around constitutional arguments and the law. *Brown*, in other words, signaled that the battle over Jim Crow would be fought in the courtroom. Increasingly, however, the public demonstration presented new challenges for segregationists. Mississippi officials thwarted the attempt to integrate the Jackson railroad station in 1956, but they witnessed successful integration attempts outside the state, including the boycott that led to the end of segregated public busing in Montgomery and, in the fall of 1957, the enrollment of nine black students into previously segregated Central High School in Little Rock, which was aided by the presence of national guard troops. Especially in the example set by Little Rock, it was the publicness of these demonstrations that complicated segregationist strategies. African Americans and their allies used the media as an ally, and they gained national support through a peaceful performance that, compared to the angry, violent white protesters, allowed them to claim the moral high ground. Many white Mississippians hoped to avoid such scenes in their own state by preventing public protest altogether. Accordingly, as nine black students endured their first semester at Central High School, Mississippi officials stepped up investigative work to find would-be public protesters before they became public. The Sovereignty Commission took the lead in these investigations and used them to centralize the old Jim Crow tactic of intimidation, and sometimes to employ a new one, incrimination.

The investigations of the Sovereignty Commission, as noted in the previous chapter, contributed to a more hierarchical form of daily surveillance intended to get local officials, citizens, and informants to report rather than act on suspicious behavior.[49] As well, the routine visits to communities throughout the state helped to establish a network of contacts, and that network became especially important when agents responded to a report of a possible Jim Crow infraction. In dealing with a local incident, information gathering served as a critical first step that could then lead to either intimidation or incrimination. Frequently, both options revolved around crime.

In 1960, the investigation of the Reverend P. R. Watkins began after local white citizens complained to their state senator, W. B. Alexander, about Watkins, a black minister, who had opened a secondhand dry goods store in Pace, a small town in Bolivar County in the Delta. The store sat on Main Street in a section of town recognized informally as an area for white-owned businesses only. The senator notified the Sovereignty Commission. Given previous concerns about vigilante violence and media attention, the agency must have been pleased with the local response. Agent Tom Scarbrough traveled to Pace and met with Watkins and his wife, as well as numerous other locals, including the chief of police, a city clerk, the circuit clerk, and the mayor. According to a police officer, Watkins had a "hatred for white people." From the perspective of the Sovereignty Commission, that character assessment meant that not only had Watkins occupied the "wrong" space—a black man in the white section of town—but he had also delivered a "wrong" performance by displaying hatred rather than deference toward whites. During the visit, one of the agent's central concerns was whether or not the minister was involved in organized civil rights activities. Scarbrough met with the circuit clerk to inquire if Watkins had registered to vote. He had not. The bulk of Scarbrough's visit targeted Watkins's moral character. From the chief of police, two other local officers, and a black man who owned a service station, the agent learned that Watkins had been arrested several times on various charges in Mississippi and Chicago. When Scarbrough confronted Watkins, the minister admitted to being arrested in Chicago for "dope peddling" and shoplifting but countered that he had been exonerated. In addition to inquiring about a criminal past, the agent also asked Watkins about his past marriages and extramarital affairs. Scarbrough met separately with Watkins's wife, and the agent subsequently characterized her as "a low caliber class of Negro, ignorant and inclined to be on the smart insolent order."[50]

The critical turning point in the investigation revolved around whether Watkins was part of a civil rights organization or was simply acting on his own. Once Scarbrough determined that Watkins was not connected to an organization, he set out on a course of intimidation. In a second confrontation with the minister, the agent informed Watkins that "he was not even a fourth class Negro, much less a first-class citizen." The agent then told Watkins that he was unwelcome in the town. Scarbrough concluded by warning the minister that he would be returning to the town soon and that Watkins should be gone by then. The minister agreed to comply.[51]

It is worth focusing for a moment on the role that the agent assumed in this encounter. In a previous era, local citizens or officials would likely have handled an isolated incident such as this one. In this case, however, a state agency extended its reach beyond civil rights activities and intervened in the realm of daily racial practices. Even once the agent realized that the case was not part of a larger organized effort and that Watkins had no connections with civil rights groups, he still followed through rather than handing it over to a local official. The agent thus wielded the traditional Jim Crow tools of intimidation and threats but did so in a quieter way that was visible to his African American target and yet unseen by a larger public. The agent's response could also be considered alongside the Citizens' Council efforts to intimidate local African Americans who signed the NAACP school petitions in 1956. As noted in the previous chapter, the publishing of names in the local newspaper functioned as intimidation that avoided a public display of violence. Both circumstances allowed for intimidation and threats that would be visible to the individuals guilty of a Jim Crow transgression (Watkins, NAACP school petition signers) but invisible to the national media's audience of readers.

Scarbrough's report also sheds light on how he interpreted this performance of blackness. Watkins's unexpected performance—setting up on Main Street and his "hatred" of whites—violated Jim Crow norms. More than that, Scarbrough seemed to view this behavior as indicative of a moral failing, in which Watkins's criminal past and possible improprieties with women supported his belief that Watkins and his wife were of low character who were acting "smart" and "insolent."

Both the racial performance and the moral evidence contributed to a portrayal of the couple as deceptive and opportunistic. In other words, the spheres of racial transgressions and criminal transgressions overlapped. For many other white Southerners, the linkage between immorality and civil rights was one way to explain why local blacks—believed to be contented—would be involved in the civil rights movement.[52] In the Watkins case, criminal activity helped the agent explain to himself why a black man had violated the Jim Crow code.

The search for criminal activity factored into many other investigations by the Sovereignty Commission. In another case carried out by Scarbrough in 1961, the agent investigated several students who had been involved in a public demonstration in Jackson. One of those students was Opal Anderson, a student at Jackson State College. The agent journeyed to Anderson's hometown of Carrollton and met first with her principal. He learned from the principal that Anderson was a good student who had received a scholarship from Jackson State. She was also, according to several teachers interviewed by the agent, likely to be "involved in a racial controversy." Then, just as he had done with Watkins, Scarbrough checked out the criminal record of Anderson and, soon after, the record of her entire family. No one in her immediate family had been in trouble with the law, but the inquiry turned up a grandfather who had been a bootlegger and an uncle who was serving a prison term. In his report, Scarbrough concluded that on the basis of the records of the grandfather and the uncle, the Andersons were not "good law abiding Negroes" and they should "be listed as possible trouble makers." For the agent, the Andersons warranted watching based on character descriptions from school officials and on the criminal record of two family members.[53] Similar to the case with Watkins, Scarbrough assumed that an African American dissatisfied with segregation was morally flawed. In Anderson's case, the investigation did not lead to a response of intimidation or incrimination, only a flag for further observations. But for many others in the civil rights era, real or manufactured reports of criminal activity were central to incriminating activists.

The well-documented case of Clyde Kennard is a good example of how various state officials used incrimination to preserve segregation.[54] In 1959, Kennard, a native of Forrest County, attempted to register at all-white Mississippi Southern College (now the University of Southern Mississippi). Discussions about how to respond to Kennard involved Sovereignty Commission officials, college president William D. McCain, Governor Coleman, local officials, and a few local black individuals who were at least somewhat supportive of segregation.[55] An attorney offered to have Kennard's car "hit by a train," but state officials rejected that option, preferring a method that would minimize the risk of attracting publicity.[56] The Sovereignty Commission dug up information on Kennard but found little they could use. They uncovered what appeared to be a false medical certificate and an incomplete academic record at the University of Chicago, and on that basis the college rejected Kennard because of a "lack of good character." Kennard met with the president and accepted the decision. However, upon leaving the campus building, two local police officers—apparently acting on their own—arrested Kennard and charged him with reckless driving and possession of whiskey.[57] The arrest had not been part of the plan, and in fact, the Sovereignty Commission agent, Zack Van Landingham, suspected that a couple of renegade local officers had taken matters into their own hands. The agent immediately contacted the governor's office and explained that it "appeared to be a frame-up with the planting of the evidence in Kennard's car."[58] Nonetheless, once the criminal initiative was set in motion, rather than deny it and expose a cover-up or divisions in the state, the Sovereignty Commission aided the criminal prosecution.[59]

At trial, Kennard was found guilty and fined $600. The judge—who had privately consulted with the Sovereignty Commission throughout the trial—announced to the press that "of all the cases I have ever heard, the state has proved more in this one the guilt of the defendant."[60] The trial and the statements about the trial, then, extended beyond the scope of criminal punishment and into a more expansive campaign of publicly discrediting Kennard by portraying him as a common criminal. The judge was likely trying to assure the public that Kennard's guilt was tied to the possession of whiskey, not to an integration attempt. The trial reframed Kennard's activism, and for the moment it silenced an activist. Kennard, however, was not easily deterred. A year later, he again tried to enroll at Mississippi Southern. This time he was arrested away from the college, allegedly for having a teenage boy steal twenty-five-dollars-worth of chicken feed. The case hinged on what the *Mississippi Free Press* referred to as the confused, contradictory testimony of the supposed thief.[61] Nonetheless, the all-white jury deliberated ten minutes before finding Kennard guilty. For this alleged twenty-five-dollar theft, he was given the maximum sentence, seven years in the state penitentiary.[62]

If the Sovereignty Commission and other state officials belatedly joined a poorly planned local effort to incriminate Clyde Kennard, on other occasions, they aggressively tried to find or invent information that would show an activist to be a criminal. An especially prominent target of these efforts was Aaron Henry. Few African Americans in the state were as vocal or as active as Henry. The World War II veteran registered to vote in 1946 and became president of the state NAACP in 1959.[63] He was one of the most visible civil rights leaders in the state, and he was actively involved in voter registration efforts, boycotts, and the writing of letters to the governor seeking redress for individuals who had been the victims of racial violence.[64] Given his open activism, Henry attracted much attention from segregationists, and the behind-the-scenes discussions about Henry reveal some of the tensions and differences of opinion among segregationists, ranging from local citizens to a local police chief to top-level state officials, all of them interested in thwarting Henry's civil rights efforts.

There were numerous ways authorities could have tried to silence Henry. As noted in the previous chapter, a city official tried to get an informant to kill Henry. No doubt murdering him would have sent a powerful message to civil rights activists in the state. However, it also would have drawn negative national publicity and possibly would have transformed Henry into a martyr for the civil rights movement. Top-level state officials instead tried to publicly discredit him through criminal activity. Henry owned a drugstore in Clarksdale, and Sovereignty Commission agents, law enforcement officials, and informants closely monitored it. While some of these observations may have been intended to gather news about civil rights activities, the primary objective was to uncover evidence of criminal activity by Henry. Early in the campaign, Sovereignty Commission agent Tom Scarbrough pursued the possibility of having Henry arrested for selling pep pills, only to learn from an FBI agent that selling pep pills was not illegal.[65] Too impatient to wait for Henry to do something illegal, local officials hired an informant and used him to try and get Henry to sell illegal drugs. That did not work either, and agents continued to watch for a legal misstep. Following years of surveillance, local law enforcement officials arrested Henry in 1962, allegedly for making "unnatural [sexual] advances toward a white [male] hitchhiker."[66] Henry had been arrested for molesting a

Aaron Henry (on the right) standing in front of his drugstore
in Clarksdale, Mississippi, date unknown. Courtesy of the Tougaloo
College Archive, Tougaloo, Mississippi.

white man, and the charge represented a dual assault on Henry's character, in which he could potentially be castigated publicly as a criminal and as a homosexual. Henry, in noting that officials had previously
tried other labels such as branding activists as communists, surmised
that they had turned to the new charge of homosexuality, which would
be "detested equally by whites and Negroes."[67] Thus, even if the criminal charge was overturned—and eventually it was—officials may have
hoped that the allegation of homosexuality would turn the local black
community against him. Before a larger local and national audience,
these officials tried to expose Henry in a performance of immorality
tied to crime or to sexuality.

While attempts at publicly discrediting activists came most commonly through criminal involvement, the charge of homosexuality, as
Henry recognized, served a similar purpose. A year after Henry's arrest,
for instance, another African American male from the Delta became
the target of a similar effort. The individual had publicly announced
that he would attempt to enroll at all-white Mississippi Southern College in Hattiesburg. Following an extensive investigation, Erle Johnston Jr., the Sovereignty Commission director, sent a letter to William
D. McCain, president of the college, explaining how to handle this

integration threat. Johnston instructed McCain to inform the applicant that "we have information that you are a homosexual" and that if he persisted the information would be released to the press. The potential applicant did not persist.[68] We have no way of knowing if officials would have followed through on their threat to expose this activist or if going public would have had a bearing on the integration attempt. Nonetheless, through this behind-the-scenes intimidation, the threat served its purpose; it prevented a civil rights event without attracting publicity. Discussions about homosexuality arose in other episodes as well. In 1964, a highway patrolman sought incriminating evidence about a black college president, who had recently signed a petition supporting the Civil Rights Act of 1964. The patrolman met with an informant, a professor at the college, who claimed that the president had engaged in homosexual activity. It is not clear whether this information was ever used.[69]

Along with crime and homosexuality, the other major focus of incrimination was communism. Linking civil rights and communism was not new in the 1950s, and it was not unique to the South. Nationally, federal officials used charges of communist infiltration and arrests during the early years of the Cold War to target activists such as Paul Robeson and Alphaeus Hunton, who were linking U.S. racism to European colonialism in other parts of the world.[70] In the 1940s and 1950s, one of the central figures in the anticommunism efforts was Mississippi senator James Eastland, who regularly claimed that integration efforts were part of a communist plot. In 1945, Eastland attacked the Fair Employment Practices Commission (FEPC), which had been created in 1941 to end racial discrimination in government jobs and the defense industry. He accused the FEPC of being staffed by communists.[71] As Sovereignty Commission agents would do in the following decade, Eastland laced his defense of segregation with references to a communist threat. Other Mississippi officials had also readily responded to criticism about the state's racial practices with references to communism. In 1950, for instance, when the Willie McGee case attracted international attention, the Civil Rights Congress (CRC) planned a demonstration in Jackson. Mississippi governor Field Wright responded by refusing to meet with CRC leaders and explained that he would not "tolerate a wild-eyed, howling mob of communists and sympathizers."[72] Mississippi officials would draw on this tradition of merging civil rights and communism, even as the Red Scare faded and as claims of communist infiltration no longer held the same potency as it once had.[73]

From the mid-1950s and extending into the early 1960s, Sovereignty Commission agents, Citizens' Council leaders, and other supporters of segregation searched for communist connections among integrationists. In 1955, William J. Simmons of the Citizens' Council contacted J. B. Matthews, a well-known national "red hunter" who accumulated thousands of files on individuals and organizations suspected of having communist ties. Simmons explained to Matthews that they were "hampered by the lack of expert knowledge on the personal backgrounds of many of the radical leaders [of the integration movement]." Simmons then inquired about gaining access to Matthews's files on communist-front organizations working in the South.[74] It is unclear how much information Matthews supplied to the Citizens' Council. However, four years later he was in Jackson testifying at a state senate hearing on whether the legislature should ban the NAACP. At the hearing, Matthews claimed that the Communist Party had infiltrated the NAACP and that the party was dedicated to overthrowing Mississippi's state government. Matthews also provided the committee with the names of various individuals with ties to Mississippi who were, according to him, linked to the Communist Party. This group included Ruby Hurley, Martin Luther King Jr., Carl and Anne Braden, and even Hodding Carter Jr., the editor of the Greenville newspaper and a racial moderate who frequently criticized the Citizens' Council and its tactics. At the same hearing, Sovereignty Commission agent Zack Van Landingham testified that the NAACP should be outlawed in the state because black Mississippians were inviting speakers from communist-influenced organizations to come and speak. The legislature ultimately decided not to pass a law banning the NAACP.[75]

As various officials continued publicly to conflate communism and civil rights, more quietly and covertly they also used anticommunism accusations to undermine integrationists. In 1959, Meady Pierce, the chief of detectives in Jackson, contacted the Sovereignty Commission about a new black newspaper, the *Gulf Coast World*, which allegedly had direct ties to the NAACP and was being managed by Medgar Evers. Van Landingham investigated, and in the most recent issue he found a front-page article authored by Evers that was critical of a speech Ross Barnett had made at a Citizens' Council meeting in

Jackson. Similar to the agency's response to Aaron Henry, Van Land-ingham recommended a form of behind-the-scenes intimidation. The agent noted that some of the advertisements in the newspaper were for white-owned businesses, and he suggested contacting these business owners to inform them that they were "advertising in a negro communist newspaper."[76] Van Landingham's use of the communist tag here is interesting. He could have, for example, as easily have suggested that white advertisers be alerted that it was an "NAACP" or a "civil rights" newspaper. However, like other intimidation tactics around crime and homosexuality, the communism charge was also on the surface tied to immorality rather than race. Also, not to be lost in this response is that these white men would be made aware that state officials were monitoring their involvement with a "communist" newspaper.

On some occasions, in searching for information, segregation supporters linked activists to both communism and crime. In 1961, for example, numerous agencies were involved in investigating each of the Freedom Riders arrested in Jackson. The *Jackson Clarion-Ledger* reported that most of the riders had prior police records, and the newspaper also provided the names, hometowns, and previous criminal charges for each rider.[77] While most of those charges were related to other civil rights activities, such as being arrested for a breach of the peace, other charges included a violation of the Selective Service Act and a traffic violation. The references to communism were even more extensive. Approximately one month after the first Freedom Riders had been arrested, T. B. Birdsong, head of the state highway patrol, announced that after a thorough investigation he had learned that the Freedom Rides were linked to communist leaders in the Soviet Union. Birdsong explained that the Freedom Rides had been planned in Havana, Cuba, by Soviet officials. He further noted that the Soviets taught the riders "how to make sit-ins, walk-ins, kneel-ins and Freedom Rides."[78] Senator James Eastland similarly connected the Freedom Rides to "high level meetings in Europe" and contended that communists had planned these demonstrations to embarrass the United States internationally.[79] These public claims worked in conjunction with the initial arrests of the Freedom Riders. Whereas the arrests were intended to present state officials as peaceful and orderly, the subsequent attempts at discrediting the Riders were intended to reframe the activists as communists and criminals.

In the late 1950s and early 1960s, as officials avoided the use of segregation laws, investigations became a popular response to activism and to any form of racial transgression. Their usage positioned state officials such as Sovereignty Commission agents and officers of the law in the role of intimidators, a role that had previously been a product of daily interactions at the local level. This more organized form of intimidation, however, depended on information and planning. It was a slower, more cautious process because, more so than in a previous era, a larger audience was watching the state, and watching with the assumption that state officials, not activists, were the immoral ones. Indeed, it was the watching of a larger audience that made the tactic of incrimination so appealing. Many segregationists recognized that they were engaged in a battle of perceptions and that the key to preserving segregation was to transform the national narrative about the South. Through incrimination, officials sought to transform activists/ victims into criminals, communists, and homosexuals. Investigations became a first step when officials needed more information before acting. In other circumstances—and especially when a public demonstration was in progress—officials had no time to gather information. They then turned to arrests and utilized legal strategies in new and more sophisticated ways.

ARRESTS AND THE CONCEALMENT OF RACIAL INTENT

In trying to thwart a growing civil rights movement in the late 1950s, Mississippi officials quickly realized that their response to public protests had to be considered carefully. While investigative work could be done quietly behind the scenes, demonstrations were highly visible, not only to local people, but through the media to a larger audience too. As well, protesters, in embracing the tactics of nonviolence and often in donning the clothing and the demeanor that conveyed middle-class respectability, performed a role that won support and sympathy from a national public. These enactments heightened perceptions that the battle in the South was between violent working-class whites and peaceful, respectable black citizens. Within that context, officials had to consider ways to stifle a protest while also considering how their own performance might appear in front of cameras. Additionally, they had to keep in check other white citizens ready to turn to vigilantism in response to a demonstration. For all of these reasons, arrests became a viable option. At the same time, as previously noted, by the late 1950s, officials had abandoned using charges directly related to segregation, fearful that they would be challenged in court. They instead relied on new and newly revised laws, as well as deploying old laws in creative ways. Those choices varied based on the location, the situation, and the presence or absence of an audience.

Arrests at the scenes of public protest often came at the end of much planning and consultation among politicians, local law enforcement officials, and other state agents. Legislators passed new measures designed to be used to prevent civil rights protest, but the language of many of these laws was so cryptic—at least in relation to segregation—that it would not have necessarily been clear to local law enforcement officials that a particular law should be used or how it should be used. State officials thus attempted to keep local officials informed. The Sovereignty Commission sent out lists of new measures to law enforcement officials across the state, and agents met in person with local law enforcement officials to explain what a new law meant and how it could be applied to specific situations.[80] In some cases, law enforcement officials made an arrest on one charge and then, after consulting with other officers or contacting the Sovereignty Commission, changed or added charges. Similar to the processes that led to investigations, arrests of protesters emerged from a long, fluid process that depended on communication between state and local officials and that sometimes produced confusion or conflicting strategies, as was the case with the first arrest of Clyde Kennard. Nonetheless, coordination related to legislative changes was another indication of the centralization of policing, and it produced some consistency in how segregationists used the law during this period.[81]

The most regularly invoked charges included breach of the peace, disorderly conduct, and resisting arrest, and by a wide margin the breach of the peace measure was the one used most often against civil rights activists.[82] The version of this law that passed less than a month after the integration attempt at the Jackson railroad station defined a "breach" as a disturbance that could include "offensive talk, the making of threats or attempting to intimidate, or any other conduct which causes a disturbance," and it allowed for a maximum penalty of $500 and up to six months in jail.[83] Four years later, Mississippi legislators revised this law, and the most significant change was in the extensive details about public space. Whereas the 1956 measure referred only to businesses and "any other public place," the 1960 version referred to public streets,

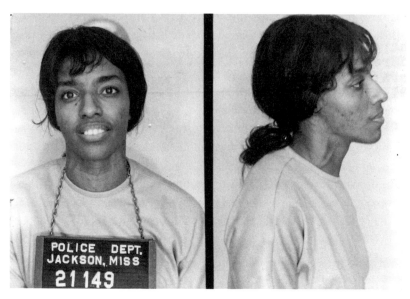

Roena Rand, after her arrest in Jackson, Mississippi, during the
Freedom Rides, July 9, 1961. Courtesy of the Archives and Record Services
Division, Mississippi Department of Archives and History.

highways, and sidewalks; public buses, taxicabs, and other vehicles;
businesses, such as in a "hotel, motel, store, restaurant, lunch counter,
cafeteria, sandwich shop, motion picture theatre, drive-in, beauty parlor,
swimming pool area, or any sports or recreational area or place."[84] The
revised law seemed to spell out every conceivable place a protest could
be staged—that is, any place where segregation might exist. For segregationists, the vagueness of this measure was both its strength and its
weakness. On one hand, it made no reference to race or segregation, and
the ambiguity of the language meant that it could be applied to virtually
any situation, including making a case that any individual's actions had
the potential to cause a disturbance. On the other hand, in the courtroom, this vagueness placed a greater burden on the interpretation of the
actions at a particular scene, such as how one might define "offensive" in
offensive talk. It also left open a question about who caused the breach.
Was it the person sitting calmly at the counter or the individuals behind
them who were taunting them? The revisions to the 1960 law likely came
from the belief that the earlier law was so general that it was of little use.
Yet even with more detail, the revised version still depended on officials
being able to prove that a protest was a disturbance.

Leaving aside for the moment its application, the breach of the peace law, and in particular its labeling of specific spaces, reveals key features in a developing legal defense of segregation. First, even without mentioning segregation, the law represented a legal blueprint marking off segregated space. Any attempt at integration in these places could be understood by authorities as a disturbance. Thus, this law did the work that the earliest segregation measures in the late nineteenth century had left incomplete; it defined precisely where segregation applied. Without using the word "segregation" and without referring even indirectly to race, this measure had fixed segregation and segregated space within the law. Second, in creating a map for where disturbances might occur, it shifted the focus to the spaces themselves and the responsibility for the disturbance to the people who entered and disrupted those spaces. In essence, it meant that law enforcement officials were protecting particular spaces rather than targeting individuals. Third, and related, the law itself and the references to spaces represented a direct inversion of the developing media narrative around black victims and white attackers. Before a national audience, this law would be used to suggest that the (nonviolent) protesters risked inciting violence and that, therefore, they were the violent, disruptive ones.[85] In short, officials hoped to use this law not only to avoid using a "segregation" measure but also to revise their own image and reclaim the moral high ground nationally.

Among those charged with breach of the peace were the nine students from Tougaloo College who tried to integrate a Jackson public library in 1960, a black woman in Biloxi who sat in the white section of the public bus in 1961, four students who tried to integrate a lunch counter in Jackson in 1961, and the Freedom Riders in 1961 who were attempting to integrate interstate bus travel.[86] In each of these cases, the most obvious violation—which demonstrators were testing—was the state segregation law. Once officials decided that a segregation charge was off-limits, the high visibility of these incidents—that is, the presence of witnesses and the media—left them with few choices. If officials were not willing to claim legally that demonstrators were violating a segregation law, then what else could they claim? With few options, the breach of peace law and its inherent ambiguity often won out by default.

Other charges used at scenes of public protest—that is, places with an audience—were similarly vague. In October 1961, law enforcement officials in McComb arrested a group of adults who were leading a student protest and charged them with contributing to the delinquency of minors.[87] In Clarksdale, in August 1963, local police arrested and charged six civil rights workers with littering, and ten days later authorities arrested eighty-one demonstrators on the charge of "parading without a permit."[88] Two months later, in Jackson, a group of African Americans who tried to attend white churches were found guilty of trespassing and disturbing public worship.[89] With the exception of littering, all of these charges, like a breach of the peace, were both ambiguous and subjective. That is, these charges hinged more on the interpretation of various behaviors, such as "disturbing" and "contributing to delinquency" than on the burden of producing tangible evidence. At first glance, these charges may seem almost arbitrary, with activists being charged with virtually anything at the discretion of the arresting officer. Indeed, officers sometimes made arrests based on every charge imaginable in the hope that at least one might apply. They had to think quickly, if not creatively, to justify an arrest. Yet despite the sometimes improvisational nature of protest scenes, several patterns emerged in law enforcement officials' use of particular laws.

First, and most obvious, local officials steadfastly avoided segregation laws even if they found it difficult to explain why they had used other charges. Consider, for example, the arrest of Johnny Frazier in August 1960. Frazier refused to move from the "white" section of a bus in Winona. Police officers arrived on the scene and beat him before taking him into custody. In this instance, one sees elements of the old system—an immediate, forceful response—carried out by official agents of the state. In custody, Frazier was then charged with "resisting arrest," and in essence his refusal to move from the seat became an aggressive act of violence. Within the official public record of the arrest, Frazier was beaten not because he violated a Jim Crow regulation but because he attacked a police officer. For good measure, authorities also charged Frazier with disturbing the peace. The novelty of an approach that relied on non-segregation charges meant that local officials at times had difficulty explaining an arrest to the public without reverting to racial terms. In speaking to the press about Frazier's arrest, for example, Sheriff Earl Patridge first remarked that Frazier had not been arrested for sitting in the white section but, rather, for using "abusive language" and resisting arrest. The arrest, according to Patridge's public statement, had nothing to do with race. Nonetheless, the sheriff was forced to concede, when questioned, that he did not know specifically how Frazier was disturbing the peace, although according to a Jackson newspaper, the sheriff noted that Frazier had "talked mighty big."[90] The sheriff's comments to the press reveal a local official straddling the line between two discursive systems. Some of his public statements veer from legal definitions of disturbance and instead hint at a Jim Crow system of racial discipline in which Frazier's arrest came from his "mighty big" talk, almost certainly a euphemism for a black man verbally challenging white people. The sheriff's comments make it clear that unofficially Frazier was arrested for stepping out of his expected performance, for refusing to move, and then for not following the verbal script of Jim Crow. Officially, though, in legal terms, he had simply resisted arrest and disturbed the peace. For local officials, the transition to this emerging form of enforcement was an uneven one. Patridge and many others were adjusting to how Jim Crow was coded into new laws and a new language, and they were still learning their own roles in these daily racial performances. Once again, the legal language was ahead of the public discourse in its concealment of racial intentions.

Another pattern in the arrests relates to public space. Group demonstrations or other protests in public—such as Frazier's refusal to move on the bus—attracted witnesses, potentially including the media and its national and international audiences. Officials worried about images of police officers beating demonstrators appearing on TV or in the press. Along with the actions of law enforcement officials, they were also cautious about the charges used in public spaces with witnesses present. Officials were hesitant to invent charges or manufacture evidence against activists and, in the process, transform activists into public martyrs and expose the undemocratic practices of the state. Thus, when the public was watching, Mississippi officials applied laws that would indicate that the police were acting not in the interest of segregation but in the interest of public safety. In public spaces, compared to ones concealed from public view, officials were cautious and much more likely to use vague, objective allegations, such as disturbing the peace and resisting arrest.[91] As well, in responding to public challenges, local officials were generally much more likely to communicate with state officials and devise a particular course of action.

By contrast, when the media and other witnesses were absent, law enforcement officials exercised many more options in making arrests. In particular, they abandoned vague charges such as breach of the peace

April 7, 1960

MEMO TO: File

FROM: Zack J. Van Landingham

SUBJECT: Marcell Gordon
         Agitator

On April 1, 1960, Mr. John Poole, an attorney, FL 3-6672, Jackson, Mississippi, telephoned to advise that he had a connection with a bonding company here that was interested in making a bond for a negro. According to Attorney Poole, the negro had attempted to integrate a train at Batesville, Mississippi, and had subsequently been arrested at McComb, Mississippi, charged with disorderly conduct and possession of whiskey, and had been returned to the jail at Batesville. The negro attorney Jess Brown of Vicksburg is attorney for the negro. Attorney Poole stated that the bonding company was rather hesitant in making bond for the negro unless they felt it would be o.k. with the authorities. I told Mr. Poole that certainly if the negro was entitled to bond, I shouldn't think there would be anyone who would object to him making the bond. Mr. Poole said he intended to call the Sheriff at Batesville and get his opinion on this matter. When I inquired for more information, he referred me to Mr. Robert Graham, an attorney in the Barnett Building, FL 3-5670, who had more complete information.

I telephonically contacted Mr. Graham on April 5 and he advised that the negro's name is Marcell Gordon. He is 36 years of age, having been born in 1923. His address is 4607 Calumet Street, Chicago, Illinois. His parents and grandparents live at Kentwood, Louisiana. According to Mr. Graham, the negro had been tried in Panola County and fined $150. It has been appealed by his attorney Jess Brown and bond set at $500. Mr. Graham says that he had the parents and grandparents come to Jackson from Kentwood, Louisiana, to sign the bond. He stated that the charges against the negro were possession of whiskey and disorderly conduct. He advised that he understood that there was something with reference to racial trouble on the train at Batesville involving the negro. He did not have the facts. He said he would attempt to secure these facts from Jess Brown, the negro attorney, and advise the writer.

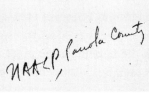

STATE SOVEREIGNTY COMMISSION

APR 7 1960

INDEXED
SERIALIZED
FILED

2 - 106 - 6

The first page of an investigative report from the Mississippi State Sovereignty Commission's Zack J. Van Landingham. Mississippi authorities arrested Marcell Gordon during an integration attempt on a train. McComb officials charged Gordon with disorderly conduct and possession of whiskey. SCRID# 2-106-0-6-1-1-1, MSSCR; courtesy of the Archives and Record Services Division, Mississippi Department of Archives and History.

in favor of more specific ones. On the roads, authorities arrested various activists on charges of drunken driving, having an improper license tag or driver's license, failing to yield the right of way, failing to signal, running a red light, and illegally transporting narcotics.[92] In 1962, in Coahoma County, police officers arrested several individuals involved in voter registration efforts and charged them with reckless driving.[93] Away from roadways, officers of the law arrested others who challenged Jim Crow and charged them with armed robbery, public drunkenness, theft, shoplifting, disobeying an officer, possession of whiskey, possession of untaxed whiskey, sexual molestation, and assault.[94] Other arrests were the products of coordinated efforts between local and state officials. Most of these minor charges can be read as tactics of intimidation similar to the ways in which a Sovereignty Commission agent had threatened the Reverend P. R. Watkins. As targets of intimidation, activists were likely to be arrested or ticketed many times on a range of charges. A highway patrol officer pulled over Bob Moses, a prominent civil rights leader, for a "routine" driver's license check and subsequently charged him with resisting arrest.[95] In Sunflower County, local police officers arrested a black minister who had helped other blacks register to vote, and the authorities charged him with writing bad checks.[96] Officials in Humphreys County indicted a "Negro agitator" for selling insurance without a license.[97] Samuel Eckles publicly complained of racial discrimination after he had attempted to vote, and soon after that complaint local officials found untaxed whiskey on his property.[98] Each one of these examples of arrests beyond public view suggests an aggressive response compared to the more defensive posture of a breach of the peace charge at a public protest.

As with public demonstrations, segregation charges were not used. However, in these situations where there were no witnesses, officials had much more freedom. Away from an audience and removed from a protest in progress, law enforcement officials were more creative. Officials could rely on violations that were tied to concrete evidence, such as bad checks or whiskey bottles, even if, as sometimes happened, they planted the evidence. Arrests hidden from the public provided officials with much more control over the arrest scene, including control over the evidence of wrongdoing. Accordingly, the burden of proof in these cases rested on something tangible and seemingly incontrovertible rather than on an interpretation of what, for example, constitutes a disturbance. As well, charges tied to criminal activity rather than political activity had the potential to discredit the activist within the local community and to undercut the image of protesters as middle class and respectable. Through these arrests, segregationists hoped to characterize the activist as a common criminal, such as a thief, a drunk, or a bootlegger, rather than as someone who wanted to sit at the lunch counter or ride in the front of the bus. These charges, in other words, were intended to undercut the nonviolent protesters' performance of dignity that was being captured in media coverage of the movement.[99] It should be emphasized, too, that many white Southerners believed that activists were immoral. After all, their discontent challenged the Jim Crow worldview, and in this respect the bridge from activism to criminality could seem logical to many individuals. For state officials, the arrests that occurred in seclusion were meant not only to silence activists but also to reveal to local and national audiences that activists were criminals. These arrests were also intended to reverse the growing negative national perceptions of white Southerners.

As the legal turn centralized responses to public protests and provided tactics for arrests beyond public view, it also provided a means for moving racial violence behind closed doors. In fact, in terms of its connection to violence, the reliance on arrests was part of a longer-term transformation. As noted in Chapter 3, public displays of violence, such as that of the spectacle lynching, had gradually become more hidden from public view, at least since the 1920s. In the late 1950s, with national attention focused on the state, the centralization of racial practices and the increased role of the police facilitated that process. In custody, activists were often physically beaten. At a moment in which politicians and others dismissed the publicized incidents of racial violence as the isolated acts of poor whites and vigilante groups such as the Ku Klux Klan, these beatings in custody went largely unnoticed by the public.

In many situations, arrests were a pretense for physically intimidating African Americans. In 1961, for instance, Bessie Turner, a nineteen-year-old black woman from Clarksdale, attempted to register to vote. Soon after that attempt, local police officers arrested her for allegedly stealing seventy-eight dollars. While in custody, she later testified, officials took her to a room, forced her to raise her dress, and proceeded to beat her with a strap across her buttocks and chest. Authorities then dropped the charge against her and released her.[100] Likewise, well-known activist Fannie Lou Hamer recounted her own beating in a

Winona jail cell, in which a state highway patrolman ordered two black prisoners to beat her with a blackjack.[101] In these instances, the act of violence functioned as a form of intimidation that could send a warning to one audience—activists and others who likely heard about the beatings from Hamer and Turner—while remaining hidden from the media and the larger public outside the state. The beating in custody, in other words, allowed white Mississippians to continue a performance of physical intimidation without drawing public attention.[102]

Authorities applied these practices of intimidation to both black and white activists. In June 1962, William Higgs, a white attorney working with other civil rights activists, attended a political rally in Clarksdale. Afterward, Higgs left in a car with three others (two whites and one African American), and soon after, law enforcement officials pulled them over, arrested them, and took them to the county sheriff's office. According to the *Jackson Daily News*, the group was held "on suspicion." Higgs claimed that the only response they received as to why they had been arrested was that it was "illegal to ride in a car interracially." In custody, officials questioned members of the group about whether they dated or had sex with members of the other race. At least one of the individuals in custody was beaten. Twenty hours later, still not officially charged with breaking a law, Higgs and the others were released.[103] In this case, the only result of the arrest was a beating. It is also worth noting that authorities made the arrest only after the group had left the rally and all its potential witnesses.

Many other activists have recounted being beaten while in custody, indicating that the use of arrests as a means of intimidation was a widespread practice. Indeed, it would be difficult to overestimate the extent of physical abuse directed at civil rights workers. Peter Stoner's experience—although coming a little later, in the spring of 1964— underscores the continuing relationship between arrests and violence. Stoner, a white University of Chicago student from Pennsylvania, first came to the state in 1961 with the Freedom Riders. Still active in the movement three years later, Stoner compiled a report of his experiences as a Student Nonviolent Coordinating Committee (SNCC) worker, which included a continuous record of harassment, arrests, and beatings by law enforcement officials. In January, two Hattiesburg police officers arrested Stoner for obstructing traffic, parking illegally, possession of narcotics, and not having a Selective Service card. The day after being released from jail, the same officers arrested him for

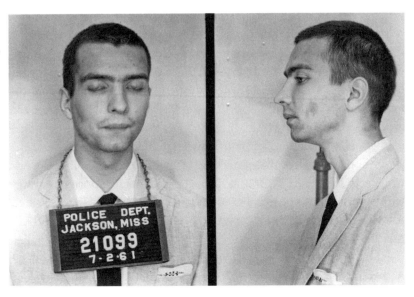

(Harry) Peter Stoner, after his arrest in Jackson, Mississippi, during the
Freedom Rides, July 2, 1961. Authorities also arrested Stoner numerous times
in the spring of 1964. Courtesy of the Archives and Record Services Division,
Mississippi Department of Archives and History.

having improper tags on his car, having no driver's license, interfering
with an officer, and using profanity. Eight days later, an officer arrested
Stoner for "improper passing" in his car. That was January. In the following month, upon trying to visit activist Lawrence Guyot in a county
jail, county law enforcement officers at the jail arrested Stoner and
found him guilty of disturbing the peace, resisting arrest, using profanity, and contempt of court. He was imprisoned and then beaten by a
fellow prisoner while a guard watched. On two other occasions during
his time in jail, a constable struck Stoner across the face, and he was
again beaten in his cell. Authorities released Stoner from jail on May
21. Within the span of five months, he had been arrested four times
and beaten at least three times and had spent more than three months
in jail.[104] As Stoner's experience reveals, arrests, rather than replacing
violence, served to conceal it. Stoner's arrests and beatings functioned
as harassment. For Stoner and for others in Mississippi during the
movement, the reliance on arrests was part of a larger effort to move
the processes of racial policing from local citizens and vigilantes to
official agents of the state.[105] Controlled and hidden from view, acts
of racial violence could continue to serve as warnings to others, just

as lynchings had done. Even though Stoner and others were beaten in private, officials probably assumed that they would report these episodes to other activists.

Arrests regularly targeted known activists connected to civil rights organizations, but they also had a much broader application, extending into the daily realm as a response to racial transgressions in general. Sometimes officials turned to arrests when they were not sure how else to respond to an uncertain threat. In these situations, an arrest and detainment of suspicious individuals provided time and information about how to proceed. In 1961, in Clarksdale, for instance, two white men from California, David Mangurian and Donald Hill, had been staying with a local black man, Wade Walker. While obviously a violation of a ban on interracial cohabitation (similar to the 1958 incident involving the Vaughns and Phillip Coleman), the sheriff knew nothing else about the men or their intentions. He jailed them "under suspicion of burglary" and then contacted the district attorney and the Sovereignty Commission. The two men spent the night in jail, and the following morning, agent Tom Scarbrough came to Clarksdale to question locals about the Californians and Walker. In the meantime, the sheriff interrogated Mangurian and Hill. He did not ask them about a burglary but instead focused on their reasons for being in the state and their thoughts on integration. Mangurian and Hill explained that they had come to Mississippi to find and record "hidden" blues talent. Among those on their list to record were Fred McDowell, Johnny Temple, Big Boy Crudup, Boozie (likely Bozie) Sturdivant, Jasper Love, and Sam Chatman (likely Chatmon)—a rather impressive group of blues musicians. Mangurian and Hill were connected to British blues scholar Paul Oliver and were also working for two record companies, one in Newark, New Jersey, and one in London. When asked about civil rights activities, both men denied involvement in any organized effort but also acknowledged that they believed in integration and believed that blacks and whites were equal. The agent also questioned Walker and characterized him as "an ignorant Negro who believes himself much smarter than he is." The sheriff and the district attorney believed that the best course of action was to release the men and tell them to leave the state. Scarbrough agreed.[106]

Although this case was in many respects similar to the 1958 Coleman-Vaughn incident of interracial cohabitation, the official response was much different. For starters, the media were never alerted. As well, even though the Californians and Walker had violated a segregation law, officials never considered bringing that charge against them. And ultimately they opted not to prosecute anyone, likely because they determined that the threat was too minimal to be worth risking the publicity. However, they arrived at that conclusion only after they had considered their options and questioned the men. The arrest on burglary charges—apparently two burglaries had in fact been reported that night—provided enough of an excuse for them to bring them into custody. Both the district attorney and the sheriff believed that handling the situation differently might have attracted "other agitators" to the area. The arrest served as a key tool in a cautious and measured approach.

If a reliance on criminal charges often seemed the safest response to a possible racial transgression, on some occasions the law became an obstacle, and the move to a centralized, law-based approach exposed tensions between state authorities and local communities. In the fall of 1960, Louvenia Knight attempted to send her two sons to a public school for white students in Jasper County on the eastern side of the state, just north of Laurel.[107] The school board denied her application because the local white community considered the Knights to be "negroes." Sovereignty Commission agents A. L. Hopkins and Tom Scarbrough investigated the case and initially focused on the birth certificates of Knight and her sons. Louvenia's birth certificate listed her as "negro" while both her sons were listed as "white." Their father, whom Louvenia had never married, was also listed as white. The agents met with local school officials and the local sheriff, and they discussed it with the state attorney general, Joe Patterson. They then visited Knight. She explained that her family did not consider themselves to be "negro," and she claimed that the "negro" designation had been a mistake. She agreed not to try to enroll either of her children until she had her birth certificate corrected to identify her legally as "white." The agents were satisfied with this response, and they seemingly had succeeded in taking care of the potential problem without drawing public attention to the case.[108]

However, three years later, Louvenia Knight again tried to enroll her sons in the white public school. The county superintendent requested that the Sovereignty Commission reinvestigate. This time the agents conducted a much more thorough inquiry, and they learned that Louvenia's brother, Davis Knight, had been involved in a legal case in

1948 related to his racial identity. After marrying a white woman, Davis had been charged with violating the state's "miscegenation" law. The case hinged on whether Davis was at least "one-eighth negro," which would legally define him as "negro." The trial involved an extensive reconstruction of his family tree and testimony from witnesses regarding the extent of his great-grandmother's "negroid" features. He was convicted, but the Mississippi State Supreme Court overturned the decision on the basis that it could not be proven beyond a reasonable doubt that Davis Knight was at least "one-eighth negro."[109] Fifteen years later, the Sovereignty Commission returned to this case and realized similarly that under the law Davis Knight's sister Louvenia could not be more than "one-eighth Negro," and that her children could be no more than "one-sixteenth negro."[110] Thus, under the laws of Mississippi, they were "white." In the eyes of the school officials and local whites, however, they were "negroes." The school board refused to admit them and further noted that if the boys were enrolled there, it would lead to violence.[111] As one agent observed, they had reached an impasse.[112] The two boys could not be enrolled in a white school without creating a great deal of public attention and possibly violence. Nor could they be enrolled in a black school, because as "white" students they would be violating the segregation laws and "would possibly throw the white schools . . . open to integration attempts by Negroes."[113] The agents tried to persuade Louvenia to move to another district and send her sons to a white school where no one knew the family, but she refused. The Sovereignty Commission even considered having the local school pay for private instructors to teach the Knight boys in their home, but this was deemed to be impractical.[114]

As the case continued with no resolution in sight, Sovereignty Commission officials worried that the story would attract national media attention. In January 1964, the Sovereignty Commission director, Erle Johnston Jr., expressed relief that even though Jackson journalists were aware of the case, they had agreed not to cover the story.[115] But Johnston was not convinced that the press would continue to sit on the story, explaining to Governor Paul Johnson in a letter the following month that he was "afraid the news media will begin to publicize this case as two white boys who cannot go to school in Mississippi."[116] Concluding that the situation was at a stalemate, the Sovereignty Commission closed the case. The following year, after a district judge ordered the immediate desegregation of three school districts in the state, Louvenia Knight enrolled her two sons in the white school in Jasper County.[117] Meanwhile, the Jackson press never covered the case, revealing the extent to which the local media sometimes silenced itself regarding racial issues. Spread out over five years, the ordeal involving Louvenia Knight's sons revealed one of the difficulties in the transition to a centralized, law-based approach. In this situation, local white sentiment was at odds with the law, and it left the agency uncertain how to handle it. The law and the local community observed different definitions of race, and as a result they embraced conflicting understandings of what constituted a racial transgression.

Beyond this complex case, in other ways too, the use of arrests and laws to respond to violations of racial customs crept into daily life. In 1960, for example, Earline Tucker, a black woman, allegedly used profane language in speaking on a pay phone to a white telephone operator. Nothing else is known about the nature of the comments, but the operator contacted the police. According to a Sovereignty Commission report, Tucker also "cussed" to the police, and they arrested her for using profane language.[118] Meanwhile, in 1963, Andrew J. Bradley, a sixty-seven-year-old black man, flagged down a white postal carrier to ask about an overdue package. According to Bradley, the carrier responded, "A nigger has no business stopping a postman." Shortly after that, a police officer came to Bradley's house, beat him, and charged him with disorderly conduct and resisting arrest.[119] In these two cases, police officers arrested a black individual who had delivered a racial performance that violated Jim Crow norms. We can only speculate about how these two encounters might have unfolded a decade or two earlier, and certainly, in a previous era, officers of the law often participated in and initiated acts of violence against African Americans. Yet by the late 1950s the presence of the police and the law had taken on much more significance within the everyday realm. In this context, the arrest became a common response not only for participating in a public demonstration against segregation but also for refusing to show deference to a white person.

The expanded authority of the law and of the individuals who enforced it also altered the nature of the daily interactions between blacks and whites. Whites continued to assume the part of masters and to demand a submissive role from African Americans, but the unexpected performance—whether it was a civil rights protest or not—was handled differently. Witnesses were expected to report these enactments to the authorities, and local law enforcement officials were expected to consult with state-level officials. The ultimate response might still include physical intimidation and violence, yet increasingly these actions were carried out in seclusion and under the cover of arrests. Ultimately, whether the performance that challenged Jim Crow norms came from a white activist, a black activist, or a black citizen in general, the attempt to correct that performance had steadily become a matter for the law.

THE GROWING RELIANCE on laws and arrests in the late 1950s and early 1960s by Mississippi officials was a response to both the performative nature of the public protest and the presence of new audiences watching that performance. A national public tuned into the South and expected to see angry racist whites attacking peaceful blacks. The performance of protesters, meanwhile, as a blatant rejection of the expected racial role, confounded state officials and compelled them to reconsider how they policed racial space. If some individuals continued to preach defiance and massive resistance and if some individuals continued to take matters into their own hands, in responding to protest activities and more broadly to racial transgressions in the everyday realm, a number of segregationists were quietly instituting a more centralized system to silence dissent and regulate racial behavior. Initially, within the context of the *Brown* decision and the Montgomery Bus Boycott, Mississippi politicians, like their counterparts throughout the South, solidified segregation in state law with a number of new legislative measures in 1956. In practice, however, they turned to other tactics within the legal arena. The first option was always investigations in the hope that, beyond the view of the public, agents could dig up information linking activists to crime, communism, or homosexuality. When those attempts failed or when officials responded to an actual public protest, they relied on arrests, avoiding segregation laws, and hoping, like the investigations, to transform political actors into common criminals and deviants.

These efforts failed to preserve segregation in part because activists continued to organize and protest and to perform the role of peaceful, respectable citizens before a larger audience and in part because evidence of violence continued to undermine these quieter efforts. Yet if these new state practices were unsuccessful, they nonetheless transformed daily life, too. Police and arrests would play a greater role in the everyday lives of citizens. This more centralized system coded white privilege in seemingly race-neutral laws, transferred the role of intimidation to official agents of the state, and concealed racial violence from public view. Thus, in the late 1950s, as state-sanctioned segregation was coming to an end, the ways in which Mississippians monitored and policed racial spaces were being replaced by more centralized and more sophisticated tactics. Supporters of segregation were in the process of revising racial roles on the Jim Crow stage. And beyond these changes in physical performances and spaces, they were also in search of new ways to talk about race and the South to the nation.

5

INTIMACY, BLACK CRIMINALITY, AND WHITENESS

The Evolving Public Narratives of Race

In the fall of 1956, Mississippi governor J. P. Coleman asked the Sovereignty Commission director Ney M. Gore Jr. to compile a county-by-county list of all homicides in the state during the previous year. A similar study had been conducted for 1954, and like that one, Coleman was interested in the total number of murders, with the victim and the perpetrator identified by race. The governor also asked Gore to include state executions and deaths at the hands of an officer of the law. After learning from the Bureau of Vital Statistics that the state officially recorded 235 homicides in 1955, Gore contacted every county sheriff for more details about each killing.[1] The final report for 1955 showed that 184 blacks and 51 whites died by homicide. For the African American deaths, five had been killed by white citizens, six by officers of the law, four by execution, and one by suicide. Four were listed as unsolved.[2] In a majority of the cases—163—the homicide had been committed by another black individual.[3] The numbers closely paralleled the results from 1954.[4] The agency would later carry out at least two similar homicide reports for 1963 and 1965.

In the decade following the 1955 report, the findings from these studies appeared in a range of materials defending segregation, including in newspaper articles, mailings from segregationist organizations, and public and political speeches. Segregationists especially referenced the number of murders within the black community as proof of black inferiority. The allusions to black crime represented one of a number of approaches white Mississippians and other white Southerners embraced to justify their racial practices. Their defense also included constitutional arguments for states' rights over federal authority, religious justifications rooted in the Judeo-Christian tradition, and Cold War claims of a communist infiltration.[5] The rhetoric around black criminality, however, stood apart from these other arguments because, more than simply a last-ditch effort to save segregation, it represented a critical transformation in Southern racial discourses that would continue beyond the Jim Crow era. In particular, the statistic-laden stories of black criminality signaled a shift by segregationists to bring their own racial narratives in line with those that informed national racial discourses.

The rhetoric of segregationists in the late 1950s and early 1960s is best known not for adjustment and convergence but for defiance and belligerence. This popular perception is often linked to the strong public stances of a few prominent political figures, such as Mississippi's Ross Barnett, Georgia's Lester Maddox, and Alabama's George Wallace, each of whom at least outwardly conveyed a determination to fight to the death for segregation. Meanwhile, a number of scholars have attributed a more complex, coded racial discourse to Southern political moderates or to white populations outside the rural Deep South. In Atlanta, for example, white residents framed their objections to desegregation not in a negative attack on the black population but rather in positive terms as their right to choose their own neighbors, employees, and classmates.[6] And in suburban areas around Atlanta and Charlotte, white citizens embraced a class-based discourse of racial innocence in which they denied responsibility for larger forces that had produced residential segregation.[7] Within the Deep South, a few segregationists, including J. P. Coleman, have similarly been credited with adopting a less overtly racist and racialized language in defense of segregation. Coleman, not unlike white elites in Atlanta, expressed a willingness for compromise, and he used a less bombastic rhetoric than his successor, Ross Barnett.[8] This discursive sophistication, however, was embraced not only by moderates and populations on the margins, but also by many other white Mississippians, including staunch, hard-line segregationists. And narratives of black crime figured prominently in this public discourse.

Of course, as noted in Chapter 2, stories of black aggression had a long history in the South, from providing a justification for lynching, segregation, and disfranchisement in the late nineteenth century, to defining expected racial roles in which blacks killing each other functioned as white entertainment.[9] In the 1950s, as white Mississippians drew on this heritage, they also looked to national narratives of race and black criminality. These stories similarly had a lengthy history, stretching back into the antebellum and colonial periods and wedding racial discourses to ideas about crime, disease, intelligence, cleanliness, and other assumed markers of civilization. A complicated matrix of signifiers informed racial hierarchies that always positioned white/ northern European–based groups at the top. Accordingly, the narratives of deviance and civilization informed and justified discriminatory policies and laws against nonwhites at home and sustained imperialism projects abroad.[10] In the Progressive era, white liberals rejected the biological determinism that had positioned black people as inferior, and yet, as historian Khalil Muhammad observes, the link between blackness and criminality remained. White reformers, secure in their faith in the infallibility and objectivity of statistics and social scientific methods—which indicated higher crime rates among black populations—continued to assume that blacks were prone to criminal behavior.[11] Statistical work, then, was instrumental not only in creating the idea of black criminality but also in obscuring racist criminal justice practices that existed within a climate of racial liberalism.[12] In the 1950s, Mississippi segregationists, long proficient in talking about a black criminal threat, would also incorporate the statistical and social scientific features that defined national discourses of race and black criminality in the post–World War II era.

For white Mississippians, this transformation in public racial discourses represented a reaction to the national media's version of a Southern exceptionalism defined by extreme racism and violence. These accounts, which revolved around images of white citizens and police officers attacking African Americans, fueled public support for the civil rights movement and, significantly, also had the potential to undermine support among white Southerners. In response, Mississippi segregationists put forward two quite distinct narratives of Southern race relations. In one, they told a version of Southern exceptionalism that revolved around the familiar story line of paternalism and racial harmony, with white Southerners playing the role of benevolent, caring masters for contented, loyal black servants. The other account of race relations revolved around black crime and deviance. In these stories, segregationists downplayed Southern exceptionalism altogether and instead emphasized a shared national identity around whiteness and Americanness across regional lines. These performances imagined nonwhites in the South, throughout the nation, and even beyond national boundaries as deviants and criminals. Significantly, in identifying a nonwhite threat, segregationists eschewed emotional appeals in favor of accounts laced with data, hard science, and rational claims. Neither narrative could save segregation, and yet, by the early 1960s, many white Mississippians and many white Americans everywhere else were talking about race and black criminality in remarkably similar ways. Indeed, as many segregationists had long recognized, their racial attitudes were not so different from the attitudes held by the majority of the white population throughout the nation.

NARRATIVES OF HARMONY AND INTERRACIAL INTIMACY

On an especially rainy night in Jackson in early December 1955, Mississippi senator James Eastland spoke at a Citizens' Council meeting. It had been just over two months since the conclusion of the Emmett Till trial, which had cemented the state's status as a symbol of racial violence. Within that context, Eastland sought to rally the segregationist troops: "We must take the offense. We must carry the message to every section of the United States. . . . The great majority of the rank and file of the people of the North believe exactly as we do. . . . After all, the average American is not a racial pervert. We must place our case at the bar of public opinion."[13] By the end of 1955, the senator and many other segregationists in Mississippi and throughout the South were realizing that the battle over desegregation involved not only lawyers, judges, and activists but also "the average American."[14] And while Eastland spoke here specifically of (white) Northerners, many segregation proponents increasingly worried too about losing the support of white Southerners.

A particularly daunting challenge for Eastland and other segregationists was related to the stories and images of Southern race relations being circulated nationally by the media. In the mid-1950s, as journalists and photojournalists descended on the South to report on racial events—the murder of Emmett Till, the Montgomery Bus Boycott, the desegregation attempt at Central High School in Little Rock—they narrated the civil rights movement as a distinctly Southern story, as another example of how the region was different from and out of step with the rest of the nation.[15] Media accounts in news articles, photographs, and television footage expressed this regional difference through portrayals of extreme racism and violence against black

Southerners.[16] Many segregationists recognized that these depictions of race relations were eroding public support for segregation, and, as Eastland suggested, they set out to carry their own message about the South to every region with the hope of swaying public opinion.

One of the narratives embraced by segregationists emphasized inter-racial intimacy and racial harmony. That version of the South would likely have been a familiar one to non-Southern audiences. Stories of black Southerners and white Southerners living in harmony, as noted in Chapter 2, had long characterized national representations of the region, even as those stories competed with reports of racial violence, including lynchings.[17] From the minstrel stage, to the minstrel-like roles in radio, film, and television, to the images of mammies and uncles and servants on food boxes and in the form of salt and pepper shakers, the South was nationally imagined as a place where happy, simple, and jolly blacks served paternalistic whites.[18] These stories of the South came from a range of divergent sources, including the propaganda campaigns of the Citizens' Council and the Sovereignty Commission, as well as the press coverage from the mainstream press in Mississippi.

The Citizens' Council, which formed after the 1954 *Brown* decision to fight desegregation, embarked on numerous efforts to distribute its message both regionally and nationally. The organization had, according to founder Robert Patterson, mailed an estimated 2 million pieces of literature by the end of its second year, and Citizens' Council leaders regularly delivered speeches to groups throughout the country. In October 1955, the group began publishing a four-page newspaper, the *Citizens' Council*, which, with an average monthly circulation of 40,000, was widely distributed throughout the South.[19] The organization also delved into film and radio production. A fifteen-minute weekly broadcast called the *Citizens' Council Forum* featured interviews with U.S. representatives and senators and others who regularly discussed integration and communism as threats to the nation. The program aired on radio and television stations across the South and in numerous markets outside the region.[20]

Meanwhile, in the month following Eastland's speech to the Jackson Citizens' Council, state legislators passed a measure creating the Mississippi State Sovereignty Commission, whose stated mission was to tell the nation the "true story of race relations in Mississippi."[21] Similar to Citizens' Council efforts, the Sovereignty Commission created brochures, sent leading segregationists to speak to audiences outside the

South, and attempted—with some success—to influence TV and film productions about segregation and the South. By the end of its second year, the agency had mailed out more than 200,000 pamphlets to groups, individuals, and media outlets throughout the nation.[22] The third entity, the mainstream press in Mississippi, was led by the *Jackson Clarion-Ledger* and the *Jackson Daily News*, the largest circulating newspapers in the state. The Hederman brothers, who were ardent supporters of the Citizens' Council, owned both publications. Many other newspapers throughout the state would also cover local and regional events related to the civil rights movement. Despite the differences in these sources—the Citizens' Council message was more defiant and more overtly racial, the Sovereignty Commission adopted a more moderate tone, and local newspapers varied widely—each also embraced a similar racial language and tapped into related themes in discussing the South and segregation. Especially in the mid-1950s, segregationists talked about race by turning to a familiar narrative of racial harmony.

Emphasizing racial harmony, the Citizens' Council and the Sovereignty Commission devoted much attention to explaining to a non-Southern audience the relationship between blacks and whites in the South. That relationship closely mirrored the performative characteristics of the daily interactions, with these segregationists imagining a world of white paternalists aiding less fortunate, grateful black people. Many segregationists believed that the national media had misled the public and fostered misunderstandings about the relationship between black Southerners and white Southerners. As Judge Tom P. Brady, a fierce critic of the *Brown* decision, informed a southern California audience in 1957—seemingly in response to an unstated misconception of the region—the "South doesn't hate the Negro." Meaning the "white" South, Brady replaced the media image of violent whites with one of white people who had "nurtured the Negro, taught him, provided for him, educated him, and endeavored to make him a worthwhile citizen."[23] The speech later became a pamphlet for the Citizens' Council. While Brady explained the attitudes of the white Southerner to his audience, William D. McCain, the president of Mississippi Southern College who formerly denied admission to Clyde Kennard, focused on what black Southerners thought. Speaking on behalf of the Sovereignty Commission, McCain informed a Chicago audience that Mississippi blacks "prefer the paternalism and understanding and consideration of the southern white man to the attitudes of men in other states and even the northern members of their own race."[24] In foregrounding black affection for whites, the college president suggested that Southerners had achieved a closeness across racial lines that differed from the rest of the nation and that exceeded even the racial ties among African Americans across regional lines. These stories of an intimacy between the races also came from African Americans. The Reverend J. W. Jones, of New Albany, prepared a statement for the Sovereignty Commission in which he wrote: "White citizens are interested in our welfare and are glad to give advise [sic] and help." He also explained that "the colored people of Mississippi trust the judgment of the white people more than we do members of our own race."[25] Similar to the statements from McCain and Brady, Jones's remarks went well beyond a refutation of hostility between the races and claimed instead a relationship rooted in a love and intimacy felt by both blacks and whites.

These narratives of racial harmony also highlighted evidence of material progress among African Americans in the South and correlated these advances with Jim Crow practices. For example, in 1958 William J. Simmons, a founding member of the Citizens' Council and the editor of its newspaper, explained to an Iowa audience that because of the system of segregation, "the Negro in the South made more rapid strides in economic and educational progress than any ethnic group in the history of the world."[26] Segregationists also sought ways to quantify these assertions of black Southern progress. In 1959, the Sovereignty Commission carried out a study of black economic conditions in the state. Hal C. DeCell, the public relations director, mailed a questionnaire to county officials throughout the state. For each city or town, the survey inquired about the number of black businesses, the value of those businesses, the number of black professionals, the estimated income of those professionals, the number of black landowners, and the acreage and value of these landowners' property.[27] The categories suggested an interest in the financial successes of the black middle and upper classes. Note, for example, that the survey did not ask about sharecroppers. Information obtained from the survey was later included in a brochure illustrating the prosperity of black Mississippians. When the study was released to the public, United Press International wire-service reporter John Herbers wrote on the findings. Herbers's lead summarized the report by noting that "Mississippi Negroes . . . are making progress in their economic status." He then followed with a few details, such as the number of black farm owners (27,746), the total value of their land ($95 million), and the number of black professional and technical workers (12,061). None of these statistics were compared to any other data, such as earlier figures or related statistics in other states, so presumably the expectation was that the numbers spoke for themselves in indicating black economic progress.[28]

Statistics intended to illustrate that African Americans in the state were not "poverty-stricken" were directly addressed in another Sovereignty Commission pamphlet. That document noted that 26 percent of the adult black population in the state owned automobiles. It also compared the number of blacks with incomes under $500 (73,230) to the number of whites with incomes under $500 (114,810).[29] In presenting data that showed some African Americans as landowners, as professionals, and as automobile owners, each of these references used quantifiable evidence to replace an image of blacks living in fear with one of blacks prospering.

Some stories of racial harmony emphasized white assistance, others focused on black progress, and a few combined these two themes. This was especially true in the discussions of schools. National stories about schools in the South regularly positioned them as sites of racial inequality where black students were denied the right to an equal education or as sites of white anger and aggression, such as in 1957 in Little Rock, where a photographer famously captured angry white men and women encircling young Elizabeth Eckford, one of the black students trying to integrate Central High School. Mississippi segregationists countered with statistics and narrative threads that featured white people supporting black education. These accounts, often heavily reliant on statistics, served as another version of whites performing the role of paternalists who took care of black people. For example, the Citizens' Council produced a pamphlet entitled *Racial Facts*, in which the "facts" were intended to contest claims made by supporters of desegregation. Included in these facts was that the state had spent $36,048,396.45 on classrooms for white students compared to $62,362,848.72 on classrooms for black students.[30] Although unstated in the pamphlet, those numbers reflected an effort to improve black facilities and to build new black schools in the hope of preventing desegregation. Other facts in this document referred to state support for black colleges, black hospitals, and dependent black children. Ultimately, the reliance on statistics was relatively basic, but each of these references was part of a larger narrative of cooperation linked to white paternalism.

As segregationists told stories of racial harmony, they also tried to convince national journalists to depict this version of the South. Toward this end, the Sovereignty Commission was sending materials to roughly 10,000 newspapers outside the South.[31] Hal DeCell, the public relations director, met with numerous reporters and film crews who came to the state, including journalists from *Jet*, *Ebony*, the *Christian Science Monitor*, the *Boston Herald*, the *Washington Post*, the *San Francisco Call Bulletin*, and *Newsweek* magazine.[32] DeCell was also in contact with officials from all three national television networks, who at different times were involved in producing television documentaries about segregation and Mississippi. In these circumstances, DeCell was focused as much on limiting the negative portrayals of white Southerners as he was on trying to introduce a positive representation. In 1957, for example, DeCell convinced a filmmaker to delete references to Emmett Till, change the title of a documentary from *Crisis in the South* to *Segregation and the South*, and add interviews with two African Americans speaking in favor of segregation.[33] The public relations director believed that he had successfully "toned down the entire implication of the film" by the time it aired nationally in June 1957.[34] Three years later, the state agency commissioned its own documentary, paying nearly $30,000 for the making of *The Message from Mississippi*. A report likely produced for the state legislature to justify the expenditure included proposals for distribution and a suggested advertising budget for television markets outside the South. According to the report, the film told "the true story of Mississippi's segregated way of life, and how it benefits both races." It also included "scenes of racial harmony . . . Negro success stories . . . proof of the advantages available to Negro students . . . [and] interviews with Negroes and state officials."[35] The film was shown to various groups around the country.[36]

One of the more unusual attempts to alter national narratives about the state involved bringing journalists from New England newspapers to visit Mississippi. Hal DeCell arranged the tour, and in October 1957, twenty-one editors and publishers spent a week and a half touring towns from the Delta to the Gulf Coast and meeting with state and local officials, businessmen, and some African Americans. They visited newly constructed schools for blacks, and, while the visitors met with some black leaders who had been selected by the agency, they also had opportunities to meet with local African Americans on their own. At least a few of these individuals expressed their dissatisfaction with seg-regation. DeCell knew that such conversations were risky and might challenge the message about black contentment, but he also believed it was crucial that the journalists believe they had access to anyone in the state.[37]

Despite the opportunities to search out and speak with local black leaders, the trip was also carefully planned and designed especially to emphasize earlier representations of the South. The tour included a trip on a steamboat down the Mississippi River and ended in Vicksburg, where the group visited a national cemetery where some of the Civil War's Union and Confederate dead had been interred. They also vis-ited antebellum mansions, and, as a local journalist explained, at one stop, "pretty girls in the long, hooped skirts of antebellum days pased [sic] out Confederate money."[38] Alongside the references to the state's past, the group heard from local whites commenting on current race relations. In Kosciusko, for example, a native New Yorker now living in Mississippi informed the group that the South handled the "race problem" better than the North and added that he "had yet to find an unhappy Negro in the South."[39]

When the group returned to New England, Governor Coleman publicly endorsed the trip, believing that the journalists had been "enlightened" about the state.[40] DeCell hoped that these newspaper editors and reporters would begin to write more favorably about seg-regation in Mississippi. Certainly some of them did. An editor from Foxboro, Massachusetts, remarked that as a result of the trip he now believed that the national stories he had read about the state "are distorted."[41] The same editor commented on being "served in hotels and restaurants by cheerful Negroes." He also found "no signs of racial tension," as he had observed in Northern cities. Similarly, an editor from Maine noted after his return home that "the Southern Negro is not anxious for integration to come."[42]

Ultimately, in trying to win over these members of the media, the Sovereignty Commission attempted to present a positive image of the state—one that, in contrast to media depictions of unrest and violence, painted Mississippi as a peaceful place of racial harmony. To make this point, officials drew on other national imaginings of a Southern past that included antebellum plantations and "cheerful Negroes" waiting on whites. It also attempted to merge that narrative with a present where white people built new schools for black students and black people expressed a preference for segregation. In this regard, these non-Southern editors were brought to Mississippi to see a familiar racial performance set in the South. The enactments borrowed from the rustic, easygoing, plantation image of black servants happily serving white people, an image that had, in an earlier generation, been embraced and even co-created by non-Southerners. Accordingly, officials had good reason to believe that they could alter the perceptions of the South as a place of violence and racism with more positive images of mutual support and affection between the races. At the same time, segregationists were presenting a similar message to local white audiences.

According to a 1957 Gallup poll, nine out of ten white people in the Deep South disagreed with the *Brown* decision. Other data from this era suggested that a majority of white Southerners believed that black people were inferior to white people.[43] Yet if these figures suggested uniformity among white Southerners, the levels of devotion varied widely, even beyond white liberals and those individuals who participated in the movement. Support for efforts to save segregation often depended not only on racial attitudes but also on how it affected individuals personally. Southern businesspersons, for example, at various moments endorsed concessions when they realized that resistance to desegregation spawned vigilante violence and threatened business interests in the region.[44] Meanwhile, in Atlanta, white citizens living in upper-class and racially homogeneous areas accepted some aspects of desegregation that would have little bearing on their neighborhoods.[45] As well, some white citizens who initially supported closing public schools to avoid integration later sought to reopen schools, even if integrated, because they wanted their children in school.[46] Even the most powerful and vocal defenders of segregation often disagreed over how to proceed, including whether the state should make some concessions to the calls for desegregation.[47] Varying opinions also extended into the black community. Even as Mississippi officials grossly misread African Americans in the state as content, at least some individuals, for a range of reasons, advocated for continuing segregation or at least for not getting involved with civil rights activists. Ida Mae Holland's mother, for example, worried about her daughter's safety and warned her not to hang around with civil rights activists.[48] Confronting this diversity of opinions and wary especially of the white population's level of commitment, segregationists regularly presented narratives to local audiences designed to strengthen their resolve. Similar to the propaganda targeting non-Southerners—mailings, documentaries, and speaking tours—within the state, Mississippians encountered a theme of racial harmony in their local newspapers.

In the late 1950s, Mississippi newspaper readers would have found a steady stream of articles discussing racial issues in the South.[49] Many of these stories directly disputed national stories about Southern racial violence while also offering their own accounts of race relations in the region. In October 1957, for example, the *Daily Times Leader*, a newspaper from West Point in the eastern part of the state, set out to explain in an editorial why Mississippi had "less racial conflict" than elsewhere. The reason, according to the newspaper, was the friendship between blacks and whites, in spite of the recent "unfavorable national publicity." The editorial noted that unlike the North and the East, in Mississippi "every Negro citizen . . . has his own white friends. . . . [and] he can count on them for help."[50] Related observations appeared in a 1959 editorial in the *Jackson Clarion-Ledger*. Charles Diggs Sr., the well-known black U.S. representative from Michigan, had recently canceled a "March on Mississippi" to protest racial injustice in the state. The Jackson newspaper expressed regret that the march was called off and conjectured that instead of "savagery" the congressman would have witnessed "racial harmony" with no "signs of friction or ill will."[51] The *Vicksburg Evening Post* also weighed in, explaining that the marchers would have found no "animosity toward their race," no "discord between the races," and not "the slightest indication of tension."[52] Each of these assessments of race relations in the state and in the South contended that outsiders, whether civil rights leaders or the media, had gotten the story wrong, that they did not understand how blacks and whites interacted and that whites, as the *Jackson Clarion-Ledger* claimed, expressed "genuine affection" for black people.

Many other local narratives suggested that national misconceptions of the South obscured the true nature of race relations in the region. Erle Johnston Jr., who in 1957 was the editor of the *Scott County Times* in Forest, published an article about his encounter with a white editor he had met on a recent trip to Kansas. Johnston told the editor about a tribute to a principal at a black school that was published in his newspaper. The Kansas editor expressed disbelief that white people would pay tribute to a black man. Johnston told him that "Negroes mingle with the whites all over Forest. They shop side by side, they work together on community drives." After each description, the Kansas editor, Johnston tells the reader, reacted with surprise and noted that such interactions and cooperation did not happen in his town. Johnston then laid out the extent to which white people cared for their black citizens: "White folks in Mississippi won't let a Negro starve to death. . . . We even raised nearly $1000 to send a crippled Negro to a hospital. And every Christmas we look for needy Negro families and carry them food and fruit and toys for the children. Any time we know about a Negro in need, the white folks help out."[53] For Johnston, the Kansas editor stood in as a non-Southern white public that received its news about race relations in the South from the national media. Johnston's account used the Midwesterner's disbelief to emphasize regional difference in race relations. Echoing the accounts of white benevolence and paternalism in David Cohn's stories from the 1930s (see Chapter 2), Johnston's South was one of interracial intimacy. His central characters—the Negro citizen and the white citizen—consistently played the expected Jim Crow roles. The white people cared deeply for black people and acted mercifully toward them. The black people, meanwhile, appeared only as disadvantaged, less fortunate individuals in need of help. If this recounting of the visit with the Kansas editor was intended to illustrate how Johnston re-educated a non-Southern editor, in his local paper he was also educating his fellow Scott County citizens.

An emphasis on friendship and cooperation between the races also appeared in an article in the following year from the *Clinton News*. In a piece entitled "Negro Residents Are an Asset to Our Town," D. M. Nelson shared a series of vignettes about local black citizens, each meant to illustrate "how two distinct races can live together in peace and harmony." He mentioned "Uncle Bill Turner," who was "an honorable and respected Negro." He noted too that there had never been "a more humble and radiant Christian" than Timothy Tarvin, better known as "Uncle Tim." He turned to other black citizens in the town who displayed "an unfailing devotion and loyalty to those whom they delighted to serve," including Hammie Martin, "who proved to be faithful even unto death." Each individual mentioned by the author fit the familiar role of humility and faithfulness to whites. However, like many other accounts of mutual affection between the races during this period, the biographies were framed within larger concerns about desegregation. This article, for example, juxtaposed a vision of racial harmony, anchored by contented blacks, with a reference to another vision by people who have the impossible dream of "one world, one race, one religion," a vision that presumably was a reference to integration.[54] If the story read something like a tribute to these black individuals—albeit a tribute to their loyalty to whites—it ultimately functioned as counterevidence to an integrated world.

Many of the accounts of racial cooperation in this period focused in particular, and at times pointedly, on the things that white people had done for black Mississippians. With the interest in school desegregation, newspapers gave much coverage to the state funds spent on schools for black students. By the early 1950s, with many state officials aware that school segregation was in jeopardy, the legislature began to increase the budget for black schools, in part to try to get closer in fiscal practice to the idea of "separate but equal."[55] By the mid-1950s, the state had built a number of new schools for black students. Much of the coverage cited these expenditures to emphasize not only harmony but also the benevolence of whites in the state. For example, in 1959, the *Carrollton Conservative* reprinted a column for the *Jackson Clarion-Ledger* under the headline "Taxpayers in Mississippi Dig Deep to Assist Negro Race." The column, written by Gene Wirth, noted that "the white race in Mississippi pays approximately 90 percent of all taxes," and that based on current distributions of funds in the school equalization program, "Negroes" would receive $156 million while the funding for "white children" would be under $50 million. Following Wirth's column, the *Carrollton Conservative* writer asked, "How many states so critical of Mississippi and the South . . . can show better or fairer treatment of their Negro citizens?"[56] Numerous other newspapers similarly reported on the increases in state funding for black schools during this period.[57]

Stories of racial cooperation also regularly featured black protagonists expressing appreciation for white friendship and support. In 1955, the *Yazoo City Herald* reprinted a letter from a black minister in South Carolina. Under the tag "Says Live in Friendship," the minister cautioned blacks against supporting integration efforts or the NAACP. The Yazoo City editor included a note preceding the text of the letter, expressing hope that "every colored citizen reads the following letted [*sic*]."[58] That introduction suggests that these stories of racial harmony were being sent to both blacks and whites. Many other stories highlighted white people helping black people when they faced hardships. In June 1959, the *Jackson Daily News* carried a story about a fire in nearby Whitesand that destroyed the home of African

American Carsie Barnes. Barnes, according to the story, wanted the local newspaper, the *Prentiss Headlight,* to carry a story about the fire that would highlight the heroism of a white Baptist minister who had tried unsuccessfully to extinguish the fire. Barnes also noted the concern expressed by his white friends, and he wanted it to be known that "when Negroes in the South suffered misfortune, it was always the white people that come to their aid and not the NAACP."[59] Another story from the *Jackson Daily News* told of a local black woman named Ruth who sent a letter to the mayor thanking city officials for preventing home contractors from taking advantage of blacks in her neighborhood. The article quoted Ruth's letter in which she explained that "we can't get along without the aid and support of our white friends."[60] These narratives envisioned a world not only where blacks and whites coexisted but also one in which white people willingly supported black people and thus where white people continued to assume the part of benevolent masters.

In assessing Ruth's letter, the numerous articles on white support of black schools, or any of these other allusions to interracial interactions in the state, it is impossible to know how white readers interpreted these stories and whether or not they were persuaded to more aggressively support segregationist organizations and politicians. Nor can we know how African American readers would have interpreted these stories. What is clear, however, is that these public discourses about Mississippi race relations utilized a familiar racial language that was part of a larger narrative of interracial intimacy, white paternalism, and black loyalty. This language contradicted national images of conflict and violence and suggested even that segregation produced opportunities for whites to do good things and to act benevolently toward blacks. While these stories borrowed from nostalgic imaginings of a Southern past, other stories highlighted racial harmony by juxtaposing race relations in the South with race relations elsewhere.

Many of the stories on race relations focused on how much better relations were in the South than in other regions and subsequently on how much better off black Southerners were than black people outside the South. Sometimes that viewpoint came from white Northerners. For example, in May 1959, the *Jackson Clarion-Ledger* covered the commencement speech at the Piney Woods School for Negroes. The speaker, Dr. Preston Bradley, a pastor at a Chicago church, explained that harmony was "the answer to all this racial hatred." In an interview before the speech, Bradley spoke specifically about black people in Chicago, referring to them as a "public liability." He added, "A good Negro in the South is treated much better than a good Negro in the North."[61] Black narrators also regularly appeared in these stories that compared black progress across regional lines. The *Hattiesburg American*, for example, reprinted an article from Davis Lee, a black editor in New Jersey, that provided numerous examples of successful blacks in Mississippi and North Carolina and included references to Southern congressmen who had personally aided the black community.[62] An editorial in the *Meridian Star* cited a Georgia-born black archbishop from Harlem who referred to racial integration as "damnable for the Negro" and argued that blacks in the South were better off than those in Harlem.[63] Similarly, a story in the *McComb Enterprise-Journal* reported on a speech by Dr. J. H. White, an African American and the president of the Mississippi Vocational College for black students, and it ran under the headline "The Amazing Progress of Our Southern Negroes."[64] Each of these accounts contrasted with national stories suggesting that white Mississippi racism had kept blacks living in poverty, that blacks lived in fear of being killed by whites, and that they had few opportunities in a segregated system.

Some of these regional comparisons emphasized the conditions for African Americans outside the South. Mississippi newspapers often made this case in reference to schools. In 1957, an editorial in the Brookhaven newspaper contrasted the "ramshackle" schools in Harlem with "the fine new Negro schools" in the South. The editor then reasoned that New York schools were using all their resources to force blacks, Puerto Ricans, and whites into the same schools, instead of focusing on better (separate) facilities for each of these groups. The editorial concluded by reiterating that this deplorable situation was in "New York, the home of those who would reform the South."[65] In 1959, all three mainstream Jackson newspapers reported on a *New York Times* editorial about black parents in New York City sending their children to live with Southern relatives to attend Southern schools.[66] The *New York Times* qualified the report by noting that the number was "infinitesimal" and cautioning white Southerners that the students were headed to the South not because they preferred segregation but because of the horrible "slum conditions" of the schools in New York. That message, however, was lost on *Jackson State Times* editor Oliver Emmerich, who reasoned that Mississippi did not want New York's racial situation.[67] These various stories of regional racial experiences suggested that for African Americans, life was better and easier in the South than in other parts of the country.

One of the strangest examples of an alleged preference by African Americans for the South came in July 1957. Rumors circulated around Jackson that in response to unrest in Chicago, African Americans who had previously migrated to the city were now fleeing it and returning to Mississippi in large numbers. The *Jackson State Times*, an afternoon newspaper, investigated the claim and contacted a passenger agent of the Illinois Central Railroad, who denied the rumor and who knew of no dramatic increase in either direction.[68] Meanwhile, on the same day, the *Jackson Daily News*, an evening paper, published three photos of African Americans at the train station. Below the photos was the title "Coming Back Home to 'Home, Sweet Home.'" The caption explained that these passengers, "with lips quivering with fear," were "happy to be back in Dixie." It referred to them as "refugees from the reign of terror" and, contrary to the *State Times* story, claimed that on the previous day "only one Negro left," while in the evening "scores came back." The caption further explained that the unrest in Chicago was related to integrated picnics at a public park and that the city was on the verge of "an allout [*sic*] race war."[69] This six-sentence caption shifted the narrative of racial terror from the South to the North and then suggested that "quivering" black Southerners knew that as well. If the language was colorful and strange, especially compared to the *State Times* story, it was nonetheless consistent with other attempts to project Mississippi as a place of racial harmony embraced by both whites and blacks.

Whether the stories of racial harmony were delivered to local audiences or to national ones, blacks and whites in these stories consistently took on familiar Jim Crow roles, with whites characterized as kind, benevolent, and protective and blacks depicted as loyal, content, and grateful. This narrative theme was nothing new, but it was being put forth much more aggressively by the late 1950s as part of a larger effort to persuade national and Southern audiences, too, that integration threatened the racial harmony and intimacy between the races. Still, if these accounts tapped into the ways in which the nation had sometimes idealized the South and thought of the region as different, segregationists also sought ways to appeal to the public that emphasized commonality over regional difference.

To do that, they tapped into sentiments about black crime shared by white people across the country.

NARRATIVES OF BLACK CRIMINALITY AND DEVIANCE

On the surface, the notion that Mississippi segregationists in the 1950s spoke repeatedly about black deviance and especially warned of a black criminal threat may seem consistent with the image of the racial demagogue spewing hatred to mobilize white support. After all, many white Southerners had long told stories of black crime to justify larger racial systems around enslavement and segregation as well as particular practices such as lynching and disfranchisement.[70] Yet, as the homicide reports commissioned by Governor J. P. Coleman suggest, these crime narratives were different in that they adopted statistical and scientific language and dropped emotional appeals. This transition was not by accident. As officials sought to reach out to a national public, they drew on national racial discourses and increasingly talked about race and crime in ways that would be familiar to white populations in every region. These narrative performances positioned blacks and whites in very different roles from those that emphasized harmony and intimacy. In place of faithful blacks turning to loving whites for support were dangerous black individuals who committed crimes, spread diseases, and threatened the larger community. Meanwhile, benevolent white masters were replaced with white victims or with white individuals acting to defend the family, the community, and the nation from a nonwhite menace.

The basic narrative structure of these stories, one that repositioned white Southerners as victims instead of aggressors and that relied on reason and statistics over impassioned pleas, appeared in one of the first mailings produced by the Sovereignty Commission.[71] The four-page pamphlet, entitled *Don't Stone Her Until You Hear Her Side*, used figures from the 1954 homicide report and visuals to explain "her" side. The cartoon on the front page portrayed Mississippi as a white woman holding an infant (a symbol of the state's future) being threatened by "pressure groups"—national civil rights organizations—and by the national print media. Each of the men had dark hair and, compared to the woman, exaggerated noses. They appeared to be ambiguously ethnic, resembling perhaps street thugs or stereotypical images of members of a crime syndicate.[72] It is also possible that these caricatures, with their enlarged noses, were meant to be read as Jewish. The cartoon was an inversion of news photographs that regularly showed white Southerners—and especially white Southern men—attacking middle-class blacks. In this image, white Southerners were under attack from non-Southerners. The State of Mississippi, here white, feminized, and innocent, was depicted as the victim, with civil rights groups and the media as the aggressors. Below this image was a paragraph noting the "falsehoods" and "misrepresentations" of Mississippi and positioning the pamphlet as an opportunity to "present the facts to the nation."[73] The image on the front visually implied that white Southerners, not black Southerners, were the true victims, and that message was reinforced by other information in the pamphlet.

The written copy on the inside of the brochure extended the narrative attempt to invert the media depictions by noting four "falsehoods" perpetuated nationally, followed by corrective "facts" for each one. Among the falsehoods were references to Thurgood Marshall being threatened at a railroad station, the poverty rate among black Mississippians, and segregationists' interest in states' rights. The first "falsehood" in the pamphlet addressed the state's national image, noting the "untrue stories which imply a state of brutality and persecution . . . [that] have created the impression that white Mississippians constantly wear guns, ever-ready to shoot a Negro on the slightest provocation."[74] In the "facts" rebuttal to this accusation of white savagery toward blacks, the pamphlet could have countered with a story of racial harmony, of whites and blacks supporting each other, especially given that this theme appeared in other propaganda materials. Instead, the claim was refuted through the statistics from the 1954 homicide report. The facts section explained that "Negroes killed 8 whites; Negroes killed 182 Negroes; and whites killed only 6 Negroes."[75] With these three figures, only the last one directly addressed the accusation of white brutality toward blacks. The first one—Negroes who killed whites—could be interpreted as an effort to argue that interracial violence in general was relatively minimal in the state. But why, in refuting a claim that whites were attacking blacks, include the number of blacks killed by other blacks? This statistic was unrelated to the "falsehood," but, especially in positioning that number, 182, alongside the other numbers, 6 and 8, it served to replace a narrative of white violence with a narrative of black violence and to suggest that black crime was a potential threat. When coupled with the front cover cartoon of a white female and white

Don't Stone Her Until You Hear Her Side

All Mississippi Asks Is Fairness and a Chance to Present Its Side of the Case

Mississippi has been the target of more unfounded acrimonious and antagonistic falsehoods and/or misrepresentations—amounting to mass slander of all Mississippians—than any other state in history. Denied a voice with which to present the facts to the nation at large, Mississippians and Mississippi are turning to the grass-roots to obtain a fair hearing. We make no claim to being completely without fault—what state is? However, the continuation of utterly false accusations against our state and its people has led to the creation of a Public Relations Department of the State Sovereignty Commission to aid in the dissemination of the truth about Mississippi to fair-minded citizens of the nation.

(Please See Inside For Pertinent Examples)

The front page of the Mississippi State Sovereignty
Commission pamphlet entitled *Don't Stone Her Until You Hear Her Side*.
Courtesy of the Archives and Record Services Division, Mississippi
Department of Archives and History.

baby, the statistics on black crime alluded to a black threat to white women. And the mailing made that point about a black sexual threat to white women through statistics and without ever using the words "miscegenation," "interracial sex," or "rape."

The Sovereignty Commission was not alone in incorporating statistics on black crime into a defense of segregation. Other groups and individuals also turned to crime figures, often to make comparisons between the segregated South and the "integrated" North and West. John Bell Williams, a U.S. representative, a Citizens' Council member, and one of the most vocal segregationists in Mississippi, used criminal data extensively. In March 1956, speaking on the floor of the House, Williams asked, "What is the real effect of segregation with respect to the negro crime rate? Does the negro commit more crimes in integrated or segregated states?" In answering these questions, he relied on statistics from the Department of Justice with charts of prison rates and felony charges for thirteen "integrated" states and ten "segregated" states. For each state for the year 1950, the chart included the number of black prisoners admitted on felony charges, the rate per 100,000 black people, the same two categories for white people, and then a percentage showing how much higher the "Negro rate" was than the "White rate." For example, in California, the black crime rate was 516 percent higher than the white crime rate, and in Mississippi, the black crime rate was 279 percent higher. Overall, the black crime rate was 681 percent higher than the white crime rate in integrated states and 248 percent higher in segregated states. Elsewhere in the presentation, Williams displayed the prison rates broken down by felony charges and included the findings of the 1954 homicide report from his home state. This speech later became a Citizens' Council pamphlet, entitled *Where Is the Reign of Terror?*[76]

Williams's argument raised two points that would be a hallmark of the discussions of black criminality in this period. First, Williams used the numbers—from a seemingly objective source—to suggest that black people everywhere committed more crimes than white people. Never in the speech did he refer to blacks as inferior, but rather he deployed the statistics to make that case for him. Second, Williams used these statistics to argue that segregation kept black people and black crime in check. In this sense, the question in the title—where is the reign of terror?—was a response to media depictions of a lawless, barbaric South. Williams, citing data on criminal activity, argued that the reign of terror was not in the South and not in the form of white Southerners brutalizing black Southerners, but rather it was in integrated states where black people brutalized white populations. In redefining terror as black crime rather than Southern racial practices, and then in situating that terror primarily in the North and West, Williams narrated a story featuring black aggressors and white victims. His larger point was that white rule had prevented black crime, and that contention depended not only on proving that blacks were criminally inclined but also on showing that integration had allowed this behavior to flourish.

Other propaganda materials also adopted this comparative approach with crime data. A Citizens' Council mailing, for example, presented seventy "facts" about race. Fact number ten explained that "New York has approximately five times as many Negroes in its penal system as does the state of Mississippi," while the next one noted that "Mississippi has the second lowest crime rate in the Nation." Fact twenty-five cited FBI data to note that roughly half of all reported rape cases nationally "involve white female victims and male Negro attackers," with, according to the pamphlet, 90 percent of those cases in the North and the West, and with the South having "a lower incidence of criminal assault than any section of the Nation." Fact forty-six stated that the nation's "10.5% Negro minority" committed more than "half the nation's crime."[77] Collectively, these facts, like Williams's speech, used statistics in a way that could suggest that black criminality had been kept under control in the South. The Citizens' Council distributed its mailings primarily inside the region, so most likely this pamphlet was intended for white Southern audiences.[78] A similar approach, however, was taken by William J. Simmons when he spoke to non-Southern audiences.

Simmons was the director of the Citizens' Council from 1954 to 1967, and he was a central figure in the defense of segregation in Mississippi. He spoke on college campuses and elsewhere, including at the University of Notre Dame and Yale University and in Honolulu. His standard speech made numerous references to black criminality. In 1958 in Iowa, Simmons told of "the horrible stories of inter-racial crimes and violence in the integrated New York schools," which had prompted many of these schools to ask for police protection. He then explained that the school officials in the South had never needed the police to keep order in their schools.[79] Meanwhile, speaking to a Carleton College audience in Northfield, Minnesota, in 1962, Simmons remarked that the rate of "major crimes of violence" for blacks was three times that of the national average.[80] For Simmons and other segregationists, statistic-laden speeches and mailings marked a transition in how they talked about race. In a related move, many of these individuals also anchored their public conversations even more firmly in the sciences. In this regard, they were responding to changes in national racial discourses that characterized the post–World War II era.

For NAACP lawyers in the *Brown* case and in other legal battles over Jim Crow, the latest scientific research on race had played a central role in convincing the courts of the inherent inequalities of segregation. This reliance on science was related in part to the influence of Gunnar Myrdal's mammoth study of race relations, *An American Dilemma* (1944), which contributed to significant changes in how Americans thought about race and especially in dispelling beliefs in racial inferiority tied to biology.[81] Likely, because science had been marshaled to undermine Jim Crow practices, numerous segregationists sought out scholars who challenged these findings. In the late 1950s, Simmons, soon-to-be-governor Ross Barnett, Senator James Eastland, and Representative John Bell Williams each had ties with a group of scientists who aggressively made a case for fundamental differences between blacks and whites to contend that segregation was both natural and necessary.[82] Simmons worked this discussion into his standard speech to audiences outside the South, with ten of the twenty-five pages devoted to this scholarship. He summarized arguments from twenty-three academic studies and made a point of noting the academic homes of many of the authors, which included the University of Pennsylvania, Harvard University, the University of California, the University of London, and Columbia University—all schools with international reputations and none of them in the South. One of the reports had been produced for the United Nations Educational, Scientific, and Cultural Organization (UNESCO). The studies came from a range of disciplines, including sociology, psychology, and anthropology.[83] Simmons thus endeavored not only to give his case for segregation a scientific legitimacy but also to enhance its perceived objectivity by emphasizing the non-Southern credentials of the individuals he cited.

Beyond references to research universities, segregationists found other ways to highlight their sources on black deviance as objective, impartial, and not of Southern origin. For example, they referenced information from the Department of Justice and the FBI, among other federal sources.[84] An article appearing in the *Citizens' Council* newspaper entitled "Crime Figures Speak Louder Than Words" referenced figures from the Federal Bureau of Prisons to note that black individuals accounted for 66 percent of all federal executions in 1957.[85] Segregationists also valued evidence from the national media that seemed to support their defense of Jim Crow. In 1958, for instance, a number of Mississippi newspapers highlighted a report from *Time* magazine about the high crime rate among black populations in New York, Chicago, Detroit, Los Angeles, and San Francisco. Mississippi editors may have especially reveled in this news because *Time* had often been highly critical of racial violence in the South and specifically in Mississippi.[86] The *Morton Progress Herald*, a newspaper located east of Jackson, sardonically remarked that the magazine "finally discovers that Negroes commit far more crimes than their per capita population remotely permits."[87] A *Jackson Clarion-Ledger* editorial similarly expressed surprise that the publication had "at long last admitted that colored crime has become a serious problem."[88] In the same year, Theodore R. McKeldin, the governor of Maryland, commented critically on immorality among the black population in his own state. The *Clarion-Ledger* quoted extensively from the governor and informed its readers that McKeldin was a Republican and "ardent integrationist."[89] The following year, the *Jackson Daily News* reprinted an article from a Syracuse, New York, editor on the crime rate among blacks and Puerto Ricans in New York City. The Northern editor contended that "the crime record in Negro centers" was "the best argument for segregation."[90] Coming from non-Southerners, each of these assessments convinced Mississippi segregationists that talking about black crime could be effective in persuading a national white public of the necessity of segregation.

Even as segregationists embraced dispassionate empirical data, they did not completely abandon anecdotal evidence. However, most of the more graphic references came from sources outside the South, and incidents of alleged crimes committed by African Americans across the country regularly appeared in Mississippi newspapers and especially in the two Jackson newspapers owned by Citizens' Council members, the Hederman brothers. For instance, the *Jackson Daily News* picked up a wire service story from Detroit about a black man charged with raping a white teacher.[91] In an editorial, this newspaper also commented on a story from Philadelphia about a "savage gang" of black students who attacked three fifteen-year-old white girls on an "integrated streetcar" and attempted to "undress them."[92] A 1959 *Jackson Clarion-Ledger* editorial referenced reports of rampant racial violence from New York, Philadelphia, Chicago, Washington, D.C., Detroit, St. Louis, Boston, Los Angeles, and other cities. The story highlighted a statement from U.S. representative Charles C. Diggs Jr. about "a wolf pack" of black youth in Washington, D.C., who attacked a pedestrian. The editorial concluded, "No vicious 'wolf packs' rove the streets of Mississippi."[93] New York City, the headquarters of the NAACP and for many segregationists the symbolic center of liberals and civil rights agitation, was an especially popular target in this coverage. The *Jackson Clarion-Ledger*, for example, picked up a wire service story in August 1959 about nearly 300 African Americans in the Bronx who attacked two detectives trying to arrest a black couple.[94] In the same month, the newspaper published an editorial on racial problems with blacks and Puerto Ricans in New York and commented that "whites are on the streets at their own peril."[95] This editorial and others directly linked black crime in the city to integration.[96]

In addition to local newspaper coverage, the *Citizens' Council* newspaper, published in Jackson, also reported on black crime outside the South. In a front-page article from 1959, entitled "Big City Dwellers Quake under Negro Terrorism," the newspaper enumerated recent interracial crimes and racial disorders in Washington, D.C., Chicago, Baltimore, East Orange, New Jersey, New York City, St. Paul, Minnesota, and Seattle. Included in these incidents was the alleged rape of "a young white housewife" by a black man. The author also noted that in Harlem, where "Civil Rights" were strictly enforced, there had been 1,392 felonies committed, including twenty killings and thirty-four rapes, in the past seven months. More to the point, the writer reasoned that "increased racial tensions" were causing "riots, killings, [and] rapes" in New York and other Northern cities.[97] Whereas many of the statistical references targeted national audiences through speeches and mailings, the stories of black crime that appeared in Mississippi newspapers and the *Citizens' Council* newspaper had a primarily local or Southern readership. It seems likely that some of this coverage was intended simply to highlight national hypocrisy in showing that racial tensions existed all over the country. At the same time, though, such coverage could also have served the interests of white unity, reminding white readers of the need to stand strong against desegregation efforts or face the consequences of increased crime. Regardless of the intentions behind these stories, the effect was that white Mississippians were increasingly hearing about and reading about crime and race together, and conversations about crime were inevitably about race, even if that connection went unstated.

The public discourse around deviance was not limited to crime. It also encompassed other social and health concerns, including illegitimacy, venereal disease, and teen pregnancy. In the conversations with non-Southern audiences, many of these allusions, similar to the stories about crime, focused on integrated places outside the South and embraced statistics and seemingly objective sources. Reports about deviance in the black community also appeared in Mississippi newspapers, and those accounts serve as another indication that segregationists were attempting to solidify and unify white opinion within the region. Initially, given the immediate threat to segregation represented by the 1954 *Brown v. Board of Education* decision, these conversations focused in particular on public schools, and Washington, D.C., became a favorite target.

Prior to the *Brown* decision, the school system in Washington, D.C., was segregated. Early in the twentieth century, the black population in the district steadily increased, and white residents correspondingly moved into the Maryland and Virginia suburbs. As the influx of black residents continued, by the 1950s, the segregated black public schools in the district suffered from overcrowding. Within days after the announcement of the *Brown* ruling, the Washington, D.C., Board of Education made preparations for desegregation and then set the plan in motion in the fall. Schools reported numerous tensions between black students and white students.[98] Two years later in September 1956, the school district became the subject of a congressional subcommittee investigation and hearing. James Davis of Georgia headed the subcommittee, which also included Joey Broyhill of Virginia, Woodrow Wilson Jones of North Carolina, and Mississippi's John Bell Williams. All four of these representatives had signed the "Southern Manifesto" earlier in the year pledging to resist the *Brown* ruling with every legal means available.[99] The other two members of the subcommittee, A. L. Miller of Nebraska and Dewitt S. Hyde of Maryland—the only non-Southern members—refused to participate.[100] The NAACP protested the hearings.[101] The stated purpose of the probe was to learn the effects of school integration in Washington, D.C., and over the course of a week and a half, the Southern representatives queried fifty-five witnesses, many of them teachers and principals from the integrated schools.[102]

Some of the testimony focused on sexual relations between black males and white females in the schools. A high school principal testified that sex-related problems had resulted from integration, referring in particular to the sexual advances by black male students, whom he observed giving their telephone numbers to white female students.[103]

The same principal heard two black male students make "obscene remarks" to a white female student.[104] A junior high principal reported a problem with "boys feeling girls."[105] A high school teacher claimed that a black male student and a white female student were exchanging love letters and dating and that the white "girl was seen carving her initals [*sic*] with those of the Negro boy in the school cafeteria."[106] In terms of the interactions among students, these references tapped into fears of "miscegenation" and more pointedly of black boys/men having sex with white girls/women.

In addition to questions about interracial interactions, much of the testimony also focused specifically on the behavior and morals of the black students. Numerous school officials commented on pregnancies among black female students. One remarked, for example, that approximately a dozen black students had become pregnant, and another referenced a twelve-year-old black girl who was pregnant for the second time.[107] Meanwhile, an official from the Washington, D.C., health department cited statistics from the district to testify that one in four black children was illegitimate. This individual also reported that cases of venereal disease were higher among nonwhites than whites and that the rate of scalp ringworm in a recent year was at 10 percent in the white population and 90 percent in the black population.[108] Alongside these behavioral concerns, some of the witnesses discussed the lower academic achievement among black students compared to white students and expressed concern that the white students would suffer.[109] At least one teacher offered a different interpretation of the integration process, testifying that conditions were not as bad as had been previously suggested.[110] Overall, however, the hearing painted a picture of integration generally, and of black children in particular, as a threat to white people. The language, drawing on anecdotes from D.C. educators and on statistics, framed black students as a threat to white racial purity, to white academic achievement, and to white health conditions. The congressional hearing, while attracting national attention, did not lead to dramatic changes in the D.C. school district. The themes, however, were invoked repeatedly by Mississippi segregationists in the mid-1950s.

A few months before the D.C. hearings, Mississippi representative John Bell Williams had already turned his attention to the nation's capital. In his "Where Is the Reign of Terror?" speech detailing black crime in urban areas outside the South, Williams had also used a number of charts focused specifically on the district. These included racially specific data on felony arrests, reported cases of gonorrhea and other venereal diseases, and illegitimate births. Each showed significantly higher incidences in the black population than in the white population.[111] Judge Tom P. Brady, another prominent segregationist, referenced the hearing and Williams's earlier findings about the nation's capital in a 1957 speech in San Francisco. The speech then was reprinted in a Citizens' Council pamphlet. In it, Brady noted the "exhaustive study" of the D.C. schools, which, he claimed, showed that the white students' educational progress had been "retarded two to three years." He also made reference to illegitimacy, pregnancy, and venereal disease in the black community in D.C. The same speech cited statistics on murders, rapes, and burglaries committed by black individuals in the nation's capital.[112] In the same year, the *Citizens' Council* newspaper reported a "whopping increase [in illegitimacy] of 227 per cent among Negroes in Washington" from 1946 to 1955.[113] Much like the conversations about crime in New York and other "integrated" cities, segregationists talked about black immorality in D.C. in an attempt to prove that desegregation would not work. It was a traditional racial fear tactic backed now with data.[114] Nearly two years after the congressional hearings, a Mississippi newspaper focused attention on the behavior of the black community within the state.

In August 1958, the *Jackson Daily News* published an exposé detailing the rate of illegitimate births in the state under the headline "Sordid Record of Degradation No Longer a 'Quiet' Scandal." The layout included two charts. One showed the rate of illegitimate births in the state, broken down by race, for selected years from 1935 to 1957. In each instance, black illegitimacy vastly outpaced white illegitimacy. The second chart showed the same rates for thirty-three states, and it ran under the subheading "Immorality Barometer." The author of the article then drew two broad conclusions from these numbers. First, he cited this evidence as proof of black inferiority in a statement that wove together the narrative of racial harmony with one of black immorality: "With the patient help of white friends, the Negro has made rapid progress in the economic world, in educational standards, and on the political front. On an issue in which he and he alone is totally responsible and can govern and control, the Negro has racked up a record of shame and sin." The language was much stronger and more openly condescending than other reporting during this period, even for a staunchly prosegregation publication. It also hinted at how some white Southerners would transition from narratives of interracial cooperation and intimacy to stories rooted in animosity—in short, by putting the blame for any perceived social problems on black people themselves. The second point of this article was to show that black illegitimacy rates were higher outside the South in integrated societies. Here, the article connected what it called "bastard production" to World War II when integration was "practiced in the armed forces" and then "spread rapidly to Northern and Eastern cities."[115]

References to illegitimacy in the state also appeared in the propaganda materials of the Citizens' Council and the Sovereignty Commission. The Citizens' Council's *Racial Facts* mailing, for example, noted among its seventy facts that, in Leflore County, of 364 illegitimate births in 1962, "359 were Negro." A separate fact included the illegitimate birth rates for whites and blacks throughout the state, and another fact included the reported cases of venereal disease in the state, divided by race.[116] A Sovereignty Commission handout used some of these same numbers for illegitimate births and venereal disease.[117] Similar to the crime statistics, segregationists seemed to assume that these numbers would speak for themselves and would lead to the conclusion by the reader that integration was a bad idea. At least one prominent journalist in the state, however, offered a different interpretation of the numbers. Oliver Emmerich, a racial moderate who occasionally criticized the more extreme segregationist voices, published an editorial in the *McComb Enterprise-Journal* about the findings of a Chicago panel on racial conflict in 1958. Emmerich was on the panel with Roy Wilkins, the head of the NAACP. After another panelist cited the high black crime rate in North Carolina, Wilkins dismissed the numbers, observing that white Southerners used such figures to defend their racial practices. Emmerich, however, returned to the numbers, as well as to the statistics on illegitimacy and venereal disease among the black population in his own state, to argue not for continued segregation but rather for white Southerners to do something to reverse these numbers.[118] The suggestion was, in some respects, a call to live up to the paternalistic nurturing role whites had previously claimed. Few others in this era, however, cited the numbers in this context. Regardless, for Emmerich, as well as for those trying to save segregation, conversations about race were increasingly becoming conversations about black crime, illegitimacy, and other claims of social deviance.

As performative narratives, these articles, editorials, speeches, and propaganda pieces delineated particular roles for whites and blacks. Blacks played the part of dangerous criminals who were a threat to the white population, especially to white women and, given the concerns about school desegregation, white children. More than a criminal threat, as spreaders of disease who engaged in sex out of wedlock, they became a hygienic and moral threat to white civilization. These narratives of black immorality also rewrote the script for the white actors. In the areas identified as "integrated," white individuals became victims of black aggressors in schools and on the streets. These constructions were an important inversion of the media narratives that portrayed blacks as the victims and whites as the irrational aggressors. Meanwhile, in the areas where segregation remained, the role of the kind paternalist who nurtured and protected local blacks was replaced with the role of whites as the protectors of the white family and the white community.

It should be noted that these accounts of black immorality existed alongside and competed with the narratives of racial harmony and that each one tapped into its own version of a Southern exceptionalism. Racial harmony embraced the exceptionalist fiction of interracial intimacy where whites and blacks stayed in their place and loved each other, while stories of black immorality imagined an exceptional South where, unlike the urban North and West, white Southerners knew how to control black social deviance. In talking about race, especially nationally, the racial harmony narratives defied belief when seen alongside media images of whites attacking blacks. The black crime narratives, meanwhile, in their excessive emphasis on crime in the North, were likely to be read by many as disingenuous. A third narrative theme, however, drew on the notion of American civilization as superior and suggested a much smoother bridge to reunite white people across regional lines and win public support for a system that preserved white supremacy.

NARRATIVES OF GLOBAL WHITENESS

It is well known that Cold War politics influenced the civil rights movement. As U.S. officials delivered an international message of spreading democracy and freedom, they worried that images of violence, injustice, and racism in the South undermined their claims.[119] Within this context, media images of racial violence and injustice in the South positioned this region as an exception to American democracy. Civil rights organizations took advantage of this international dynamic, and these concerns often pushed a reluctant federal government into action.

It is less well known that a number of segregationists also took a keen interest in the global arena. Those interests fueled a variation on the black deviance narratives in which segregationists positioned non-whites outside and within U.S. borders as a threat to the nation. Cultural geographer Doreen Massey's conceptualization of the relationship between space and xenophobia is helpful here for understanding why foreigners, immigrants, and ethnic others became an important issue for Mississippi segregationists. Massey contends that "there is imagined to be the security of a [false] stability and an apparently reassuring boundedness. . . . Such understandings of the identity of places require them to be enclosures, to have boundaries and—therefore and most importantly—to establish their identity through negative counterpositions with the Other beyond the boundaries."[120] Xenophobia, in other words, helps to define a perimeter around a particular place, drawing a stark contrast between what is inside and what is outside that boundary. Segregationists, at a moment in which the South was being portrayed as a problem for the nation, deemphasized their regional difference and promoted instead a national identity around whiteness and Americanness. They tried to build a bridge across regional lines by evoking narratives that imagined nonwhites everywhere as a threat to white Americans.[121]

In March 1960, reports emerged out of South Africa that police officers in Sharpeville had opened fire on thousands of black demonstrators who were protesting an apartheid measure requiring them to carry passes. What became known as the Sharpeville massacre left sixty-seven people dead.[122] In the following months in the United States, with college students engaging in lunch counter sit-ins across the South, a few individuals made a direct correlation between South Africa and the U.S. South, seeing an analogy between the black protesters in each locale, as well as between the apartheid and Jim Crow regimes. *Jackson Clarion-Ledger* columnist Tom Ethridge took exception to these parallels and offered another perspective on the Sharpeville massacre. Ethridge chastised the State Department for decrying "the killing of a few riotous natives in South Africa" but remaining silent about the "wholesale rape and violence against whites in the

Congo." He then made his own link between international events and the U.S. South, criticizing State Department officials' hostility to segregation because they feared that the South's racial customs might "offend world opinion."[123] Ethridge's response was defensive, but it also was an attempt to replace a story about blacks under attack with one about whites under attack.[124] For Ethridge, the Belgians and the white Southerners had become the victims and the South African protesters and the Congolese had become the aggressors.

In addition to violence in South Africa, segregationists sought out other places in Africa that could be fashioned into metaphors for the United States. For example, Senator James Eastland made much of an independence movement in Southern Rhodesia initiated by a white minority, and he likened the leader of the rebellion to George Washington battling Indians in the early American "wilderness."[125] Most of the time, however, segregationist references to Africa focused on black Africans. In particular, they referenced problems in newly independent African nations as examples of black inferiority.[126] Within this context, a proposal for the Coordinating Committee for Fundamental American Freedoms, a national group with connections to numerous Mississippi officials, explained that its public relations materials should give "particular attention [to] the 'emerging' African nations, their obvious inability to govern themselves, their inherent inadequacies."[127]

At other times, segregationists referenced events in Africa specifically to counter reports of violence in the Jim Crow South. On November 19, 1960, in Batesville, a town on the eastern edge of the Delta about fifty miles south of Memphis, twelve-year-old Lynda Faye Kuykendall visited Sterling's Variety Store. Lynda Faye was the daughter of Willie Kuykendall, an African American who had recently attempted to vote. Not long after that attempt, someone fired shots into the Kuykendall house, and on a separate occasion, the family found a cross burning in the front yard. On this day, as Lynda Faye was leaving the store, the owner stopped her and accused her of shoplifting a Hershey's candy bar. He questioned her, and as he recalled later, she was "insolent and sassy." During the Jim Crow era, those two adjectives were regularly applied to African Americans who did not play the part of the happy, deferential servant before whites. "Sassy" was a term that was used in particular for black females not performing the expected role. According to the owner, after questioning the girl, he then called the town marshal, I. C. Seales. Details as to what happened next were disputed by the white individuals and the Kuykendalls. The storeowner and the marshal contended that Seales took her home unharmed. Willie Kuykendall, however, signed a statement claiming that the two men hit Lynda Faye, with the town marshal using a blackjack. A doctor who treated Lynda Faye's injuries confirmed that she had bruises across her face. Soon after the incident, the Kuykendalls left Mississippi for Gary, Indiana.[128]

Meanwhile, in southern California, television personality Steve Allen, who had become a popular national figure with the weekly variety program *The Steve Allen Show*, read about the incident in Batesville in a local newspaper. The article on the beating was another example of wire services and a national media narrating the South as a region where violent whites attacked black people, and even black children. Allen was an outspoken critic of segregation, and after reading the article, he penned a letter to Seales wherein he condemned the beating. When Sovereignty Commission agent Tom Scarbrough came to Batesville to investigate the matter, the town marshal informed him that he had received the letter and that Allen had expressed concern for the damage the incident had done to the United States internationally. Seales had not yet replied, but the Sovereignty Commission agent encouraged him to do so. Scarbrough suggested that Seales inform Allen of "the atrocities committed daily in California, Chicago and New York, as well as in the Congo, against the white people by the Negroes."

The agent also gave Seales a pamphlet to include with the letter to Allen. Produced by the Belgian government, the pamphlet detailed "the rapes and other brutal crimes committed by the Congolese Army against the white people in the Congo."[129] The report, which claimed that white nuns had been raped, was also being circulated nationally by the conservative religious leader Gerald L. K. Smith.[130] In the fall of 1960, the Congo region attracted much media attention in the United States. The former Belgian colony had gained its independence in June, and Patrice Lumumba had become the prime minister of the new Republic of the Congo. Amid Cold War concerns that the Congolese leader was seeking support from the USSR, the CIA aided in Lumumba's assassination in December. While U.S. involvement was unknown to the general public, reports of violence in the Congo were very much in the news in late 1960 and early 1961. Whether or not the agent believed Allen could be persuaded, the exchange underscores some of the ways in which segregationists were thinking about race at a moment when a national public was reading about the beating in Mississippi. Tactically, the references to crimes in the Congo attempted to deflect attention away from violence in Mississippi. More specifically, like the *Jackson Clarion-Ledger* columnist, Scarbrough referenced the Congo and other places in order to replace reports of white people attacking black people in Mississippi with reports of black people attacking white people in Africa.

References to newly independent African nations regularly appeared in the monthly publication of the Citizens' Council, including an entire issue devoted to African nations in 1962. In 1956, the newspaper reprinted an excerpt from *Time* magazine about Stuart Cloete's experiences in South Africa and Nigeria. Stuart Cloete was a French-born South African novelist who regularly claimed that native Africans across the continent were incapable of ruling themselves. In *Time* magazine, Cloete made reference to Nigerians eating a corpse, and the article noted that Cloete "finds that everywhere the savage past impinges on the present." As previously noted, many white Southerners considered *Time* magazine to be part of a liberal media regularly attacking segregation and the South, and thus the *Citizens' Council* newspaper made much of this assessment of Africa that agreed with its own.[131] It seems likely too that such reports from national publications would have encouraged segregationists that they could likewise find common racial ground in shared attitudes with whites outside the South.

Another popular touchstone for segregationists was Kenya, an east African nation also just emerging from European colonization. In the 1950s, the Mau Mau, a group of anticolonial forces, challenged British rule, and the British responded with brutal force, leaving thousands dead. References to Kenya frequently appeared in the *Citizens' Council* newspaper.[132] A January 1956 article referred to the British struggles against the "mumbo-jumbo terrorist Mau Mau" who were trying to rebuild a "voodoo movement." The article praised the efforts of "white" farmers in Kenya who were not cooperating with the Mau Mau.[133] Six months later, the newspaper cited a New York publication that referenced a British claim that Jawaharlal Nehru, the prime minister of India, was providing aid to the Mau Mau to help them "slaughter" white settlers.[134] These articles suggested that, internationally, nonwhite groups—Indians, indigenous Kenyans—were joining together to kill white people, in this case, the British and white settlers.

If the parallels to racial events in the South were implied, the newspaper connected the two places more directly in a 1958 editorial cartoon featuring a caricatured black man, barefoot, wearing only a grass skirt, with a bone in his nose, a spear in one hand, and a basic stone-and-wood ax in the other hand. The image, with exaggerated lips outlined in a lighter color, shared some attributes with the black minstrel character, and it also reflected a civilizationist perspective that positioned black Africans as savages.[135] This oversized caricature was about to trample over three white Americans, a "left-wing preacher," a judge carrying a briefcase with documents labeled "Ebony" and "moderation," and "Aunt Pussyfoot," adorned in outdated clothes and reminiscent of the stereotype of a hillbilly or a country bumpkin.[136] Aunt Pussyfoot, who made frequent appearances in the newspaper's cartoons, represented white Southerners who were not fully committed to defending segregation. The cartoon was in part a commentary on the lack of white unity in the South. It also, however, conflated the situation in Kenya with the situation in the U.S. South and by extension suggested that whites in both places were in danger of being overrun by savage blacks.

Numerous other global references appeared in the propaganda materials of both the Sovereignty Commission and the Citizens' Council. Erle Johnston Jr., who prepared the standard speech to be used in the agency's speakers' bureau for non-Southern audiences, also prepared a list of frequently asked questions and appropriate answers for those questions. If a member of the audience asked why the speaker believed the white race was superior, the speaker was instructed to remind the questioner of "the history and progress and achievements by nations governed by white people and compare this with nations governed by nonwhites."[137] More specific language appeared in the *Racial Facts* pamphlet distributed by the Citizens' Council, as both Haiti and the Congo were noted as places where blacks had taken control of "a white civilization," resulting in "chaos, poverty, and ignorance." Another fact observed that the "stronger nations," which included the "U.S., Great Britain, France, Germany, Australia, Canada and Russia," were "predominantly white."[138] Similar to Scarbrough's allusion to violence in the Congo, this pamphlet too suggested that nonwhites were a threat to whites everywhere unless white people ruled over them.

A prominent subtheme in these global references to race was miscegenation. Within the U.S. context, many white Southerners had

Cartoon on the front page of the *Citizens' Council* newspaper in November 1958.

regularly voiced their opposition to school desegregation by expressing fears that it would lead to increased sexual relations, marriages, and births between blacks and whites. A number of segregationists similarly invoked international examples of racial mixing as cautionary tales.[139] The *Racial Facts* pamphlet, for example, stated that miscegenation had contributed to the decline of civilizations "in Egypt, Greece, Rome, India, and Portugal."[140] John Satterfield made a related point in discussing the racial history of South America. Satterfield, a Mississippi native and prominent lay leader in the Methodist Church, served as president of the American Bar Association in the early 1960s and worked as a consultant for the Sovereignty Commission.[141] In 1958, he cautioned that if the South were integrated, it "would succumb to the fate of South America," and that fate, he explained, would be a population that was a single race.[142] For Satterfield, South America's history served as a warning against what would happen in the United States if desegregation efforts continued. Racial perceptions of Latin America similarly informed the thinking of William J. Simmons of the Citizens' Council. The well-traveled and highly educated man spent time in Trinidad in the 1930s, where, he later recalled, racial mixing "was so complicated that nobody could understand who was what."[143]

Within the segregationist literature, critiques of black or mixed race populations in Africa and South America were not limited to white segregationists. Rev. J. W. Jones, perhaps the most vocal black supporter of segregation in Mississippi, published a semimonthly newspaper that regularly defended segregation and pointed to the lawlessness of African Americans in Northern cities. The newspaper also made references to Africans. An editorial from 1957 commented that African Americans were no longer in the "jungles of Africa" and advised that blacks needed education "not to behave like savages."[144] A 1960 issue published a letter from a reader—racial identity unstated—who cautioned black Americans that the domestic issues of "race-mixing" and "special rights" were insignificant compared to the situation in Kenya, where the Mau Maus were committing "savage murders."[145] A year earlier, the newspaper had reprinted an article from the *South Deering Bulletin*—a Chicago-area publication vehemently opposed to integration—attributing the high rates of illegitimacy in Jamaica to the lack of laws against "race mixing."[146]

Whether the source was black or white, from the South or from outside the South, the language in these negative commentaries was relatively consistent, and it was somewhat different from the language in the references to crime and immorality among blacks in the urban North and West. This discourse on black populations outside the United States was far less subtle, and the claims of savagery were generally presented without scientific or statistical evidence. Even the Citizens' Council image of the Mau Mau was a much more exaggerated, more racialized depiction than the organization's images for U.S. blacks. One reason for this much stronger language was that segregationists could have counted on more support for these views nationally. Still, even if national audiences held similar opinions about Africa and South America, those audiences did not necessarily buy the narrative that employed African savagery as a metaphor for desegregation in the U.S. South. There was, however, another related way that segregationists tried to use a racial narrative to connect with U.S. whites outside the South and to achieve a boundedness around Americanness and whiteness. Those stories featured historical and contemporary non-white invaders in every region of the United States.

The aforementioned statistical and anecdotal references to crime in the urban North and West and the discussions of illegitimacy and venereal diseases in Washington, D.C., and other locations each implied that African Americans were potential invaders who threatened whites and white civilization. For many segregationists, this discourse could also be tailored to include additional nonwhite groups as a problem for white people in particular regions. The standard Sovereignty Commission speech that was created for non-Southern audiences reflected this consideration.[147] In soliciting material for the talk from segregationists across the state, Erle Johnston Jr. explained that "material for speakers should be reasonable and persuasive, without any reference, directly or indirectly, which could be construed as hatred or resentment."[148] A version of the speech from 1962 began with the speaker holding up a map of Mississippi with the counties where African Americans outnumbered whites shaded in. The speaker then noted that blacks outnumbered whites in more than one-third of the counties, and that, overall, blacks were 42 percent of the state's population. The audience learned that these demographics had "brought problems" that would be inconceivable in the North where the black population was smaller. The talk then launched into a discussion of how Mississippians had handled this problem by creating a system of "separation." The word "segregation" did not appear in the speech. Toward the conclusion, the speaker then attempted to relate Mississippi's situation to others around the country: "In Mississippi, we have made no attempt to solve the problems of the Mexicans in the Southwest, the Asiatics on the West Coast, the Indians in the Midwest, or Puerto Ricans on the East Coast." In this one sentence, the speaker laid out the boundaries of a whiteness and an Americanness in which those of Mexican, Asian, Indian, or Puerto Rican descent existed as problems to be solved by whites. The press release to accompany the visit included this same phrase.[149]

The references to various ethnic/racial groups in this speech, as well as other allusions to deviance and to nonwhite "problems," highlight one of the ways in which segregationists attempted to tap into an evolving national discourse about race. In the 1950s, concerns over juvenile delinquency mounted in cities throughout the nation. By the end of the decade, the media characterized this issue "as an urban problem with racial overtones."[150] Accordingly, growing fears of crime and disorder in the urban North and West provided a bridge for white Southerners. In playing up a nonwhite problem from inside and outside the nation, segregationists accentuated their shared racial fears and attitudes with other white Americans. Thus, while media coverage of the civil rights movement emphasized Southern exceptionalism around racist violence, Mississippi segregationists turned to examples that instead emphasized regional similarities in which nonwhites became a problem for whites everywhere.

William J. Simmons of the Citizens' Council also used the language of a "white problem" in his speeches to non-Southern audiences. In his 1962 talk at Carleton College in Minnesota, Simmons detailed the "problem" facing the North. He explained that a student had written and asked if Mississippi could set up reservations "for the Negroes as was done for the Indians." The Citizens' Council leader suggested that the student may have been thinking of how Minnesota had "handled its racial problem after Little Crow led the Sioux on a rampage."[151] As Simmons recalled later, this reference to whites massacring Indians seemed "to get across to them."[152] In addition, in his litany of academics who had made a case for racial difference, Simmons included a psychology professor from New York who had stated that "Negroes and American Indians are . . . to the same degree, inferior to whites in mental test performance." From that point, the speech suggested that "the problem" with the "Negro population" was coming soon to the North and West, with a steady migration of African Americans out of the South and a "soaring Negro birth rate," which, Simmons noted, had not declined, as had been the case with "other ethnic groups." The talk referenced race riots in the urban North and West and "gang wars in Harlem and other Negro slums."[153] Similar to Johnson's speech, the Simmons talk had lumped together various populations—the Sioux, blacks, and other ethnic groups—as challenges for whites.

These themes also appeared in the *Citizens' Council* newspaper, edited by Simmons. A 1956 article, for example, referenced Chinese populations in San Francisco and black populations in Harlem to illustrate that other parts of the country also engaged in segregation.[154] Meanwhile, the coverage of tensions in New York regularly noted criminal incidents not only among African Americans but also with other groups, including a reference to a "race war" between Puerto Ricans and Italian gangs in 1958.[155] On another occasion, the newspaper conflated domestic and international dilemmas for whites. In an article entitled "England Feeling Racial Problems," the newspaper observed that thousands of West Indians were "flooding" into the country akin to the rush of Puerto Ricans into New York and blacks into Chicago and Detroit. Similar arguments were made to local audiences, too. In 1955, for example, Robert Patterson, the founder of the Citizens' Council, speaking to the Lions Club in Yazoo City, noted the "Chinese problem" in California.[156] In each of these instances, references to West Indians and to Chinese Americans, like the references to Haitians and the Congolese, served as a parallel way to talk about African Americans and to appeal to whites throughout the country. In these constructions, whiteness and Americanness overlapped to exclude or marginalize blacks, naturalized citizens, and territorial citizens (Puerto Ricans) as not quite American.

The interest in nonwhite parallels was related to other narratives of the South circulating nationally. As segregationists and their materials ventured outside the South, they assumed they were meeting white people who had been misinformed about race relations in the South. Those audiences had been conditioned to see white Southerners as irrational, violent, and racist. Segregationists countered by trying to reposition the Southern narrative within a larger national racial discourse about black deviance and white superiority that had informed U.S. imperialism projects abroad and Jim Crow practices at home in the urban North and West. Within that national context, many white Mississippians tried to present segregation as another chapter in the story of white Americans repelling attacks on white people and white civilization. Beyond the appeal to whites, this approach to talking about race, one that merged global and domestic concerns, hinted at performative transformations in the scripted roles for blacks and whites. In place of a system of interracial intimacy in which blacks and whites lived in harmony was a narrated world of racial animosity. In that world, blacks were imagined not as servants, mammies, musicians, or entertainers, but as invaders who threatened white people with crime, disease, and social disorder. Whites, accordingly, played a defensive role, protecting not only themselves but also the community and the nation from this invasion.

In the late 1950s, Mississippi segregationists tried to shore up support from white Southerners and from whites nationally. Hoping in particular to undermine the national media image of a violent, racist South, these Mississippians espoused two very different public racial discourses. Both sets of stories, however, embraced elements that would have been familiar to white audiences everywhere. The narratives of interracial intimacy reflected a version of Southern exceptionalism prominent in national popular culture in which black people happily served white people. The black crime narratives, meanwhile, clothed in statistics and the social sciences, would have also been recognizable to a national public. Neither of these stories of race relations could supplant the media depictions of white Southerners violently attacking black Southerners. On a tactical level, then, these narratives represented a failure.

In another regard, though, the narratives of black criminality marked a critical transition in public dialogues about race. In a post–Jim Crow era, white Southerners and white people in every other region in the country talked about race and crime in quite similar ways, regularly referencing concerns for "law and order" and expressing fears of black crime, demonstrating, as Senator James Eastland had implied in 1955, that white people throughout the country were not so different in their racial thinking. At the same time, if the civil rights movement ultimately brought down Jim Crow in the South, the various transformations in practices and discourses pointed to how racism and white privilege would survive Jim Crow and influence everyday racial performances, not only in the South but throughout the nation. And all the narratives that had shaped the battles in the civil rights era—of Southern exceptionalism, interracial intimacy, and black criminality—would live on as well.

EPILOGUE

Living Post–Jim Crow

In December 2010, Mississippi governor Haley Barbour attracted a storm of national criticism for comments he made about the civil rights movement in his hometown of Yazoo City. The governor, who was born in 1947, explained, "I just don't remember it being that bad." He attributed the relative peace in his town to the Citizens' Council, which, he recalled, "passed a resolution that said anybody who started a chapter of the Klan would get their ass run out of town." As a result, he summarized, "we didn't have a problem with the Klan."[1] Scholars, critics, and others lambasted Barbour for speaking favorably about an organization dedicated to white supremacy and for downplaying the racism and violence of the civil rights years. While the comments represented a political misstep—they likely ended any thoughts of a presidential run for Barbour in 2012—they could also be read as the latest attempt by a Southerner to explain his region's race relations to a national audience.

The governor's remarks came seventy-three years after another Southerner, Richard Wright, sought to explain the interactions between black Southerners and white Southerners in his essay "The Ethics of Living Jim Crow."[2] Whereas Barbour had generally reduced racism to the overtly racist and violent actions of the Klan, Wright had instead portrayed Jim Crow as a pernicious and pervasive system that was virtually inescapable in daily life. While Barbour had suggested—as did many 1950s segregationists—that benevolent white leaders had acted to protect local black citizens, Wright instead contended that even the most routine of actions, such as boarding an elevator, involved tense negotiations that always had the potential to end in violence.

To be sure, these two depictions of Southern life emerged from quite different eras, and both Mississippi and the nation had witnessed significant transformations in the intervening years. Yet what unites these narratives across time and across major racial change is that in each account race relations hinged not on the dramatic moments of violence but on the mundane ones, with Wright highlighting the trauma of daily life and Barbour remembering that it was not "that bad." Both narratives point to the importance of interrogating the routines of the everyday realm in the Jim Crow South. Additionally, Barbour's 2010 recollections should lead us to ask about the racial practices and stories in the decades since Jim Crow's demise.

In exploring race relations in the late Jim Crow era—roughly from the time of Wright's essay through the time of Barbour's childhood—this book has emphasized the dramaturgical qualities of the daily racial routines. Jim Crow was a kind of theatrical production that depended on stages and props, on scripts and stage directions, and especially on actors and audiences. Laws, customs, and the manipulation of geography came together to establish performative expectations for blacks and for whites. Incumbent upon individuals to perform—to move, to talk, to gesture—in specific ways, Jim Crow had to be remade each day with each interaction. Accordingly, if living Jim Crow had something to do with lynchings and with vigilantes dressed in white hoods and robes, it also was defined through countless mundane experiences, from walking along the sidewalk, to boarding a bus, to shopping for clothes. Important too were the ways white people and black people made sense of this world in the stories they told about these interactions. In both the narrative performances and the physical ones, many white Mississippians hoped to make real a world of interracial intimacy where whites assumed the part of loving masters and paternalists and blacks took on the role of loyal servants. That vision was regularly disrupted and challenged by the performances from whites and blacks who did not follow the script.

Examining the racial routines also sheds light on how Jim Crow was changing in the 1950s. In response to local and national challenges and especially to the public performances of protest by African Americans and their allies, Mississippi officials adapted their racial practices and racial narratives in an attempt to save a system based on white supremacy. As the national media highlighted dramatic acts of white Southern racial violence, many Mississippi officials sought ways to conceal violence and racism from public view. They centralized their racial practices within the legal structure, including turning to race-neutral laws and expanding the role for police officers and other official agents of the state. New ways of talking about race accompanied these shifts, and the evolving language, like the more centralized methods of racial enforcement, represented another turn away from overt markers of racism.

These adjustments altered daily racial routines and contributed to a more formal system in which the legal structure and its agents would assume a greater role in the policing of racial lines. Accordingly, for Mississippi officials, the shift to a post–Jim Crow world was already well under way by the early 1960s as the state was just beginning to become a central battleground for national civil rights organizations.

In 1961, the Student Nonviolent Coordinating Committee (SNCC) set up a field office in McComb in the southwest region of the state to focus on voter registration efforts. Increasingly, local African Americans and their allies publicly protested Jim Crow practices.[3] In addition, grassroots organizing in local communities led to freedom schools and voter education programs.[4] In performative terms, these activities meant that black Mississippians were steadily playing new roles in their interactions with white authorities, such as in trying to register to vote. Even if the would-be voter was turned away, the attempt represented a very different interracial interaction from those that had involved, for instance, stepping off a sidewalk. Indeed, one indication that these enactments of equal citizenship represented a significant disruption of earlier routines was revealed in the ways that many white Mississippians attempted to make sense of the civil rights demonstrations occurring around them. Well into the 1960s, many argued that the protesters were overwhelmingly from out of state or that the local blacks who participated in the movement were being misled by agitators from somewhere else.[5] Thus, even as black Mississippians blatantly rejected the Jim Crow role, some whites found explanations that allowed them to cling to the racial harmony narratives that featured contented black Southerners.

Meanwhile, the national media continued to perpetuate its own narrative about the South by capturing a steady stream of performances of peaceful protest that met with white Southern violence. In 1962, the enrollment of James Meredith at the University of Mississippi, which came after much behind-the-scenes negotiating between Governor Ross Barnett and federal officials, led to rioting and violence on the campus. The next year, a gunman shot and killed civil rights leader Medgar Evers, and a year later, during Freedom Summer, three civil rights workers were murdered. Mississippi's place as a symbol of racism and violence became more entrenched with each act of brutality, and that reputation extended beyond the news coverage and into the national popular culture. The state's racial past and present became the focus of numerous songs, including Bob Dylan's "The Death of Emmett Till" (1963), Nina Simone's "Mississippi Goddamn" (1963), and Phil Ochs's "Too Many Martyrs" (1964).[6] In addition, Ochs's "Here's to the State of Mississippi" (1965) called out the entire state—the people, the schools, the cops, the judges, the government, the laws, and the churches—in ways reminiscent of Roy Wilkins's denouncement of the state a decade earlier after Till's death.

Lost in these narratives of dramatic Southern violence were the ways in which Mississippi officials continued to adjust. Law enforcement officials arrested and jailed thousands of demonstrators, and the expanding authority of the state highway patrol continued a shift in policing powers from local police officials to state-level officials.[7] Merging a language of law and order with more centralized practices, Mississippi governor Paul B. Johnson Jr. explained at the 1966 dedication of the Mississippi Law Enforcement Officers Training Academy that "the police officer stands his vigil to keep peace—to uphold the law. He stands—sometimes alone—between the rioter and the peaceful citizen—between the criminal and the law abiding citizen."[8] The society envisioned in Johnson's statement called for a greater role for the law and the officer of the law and a reduced role for the citizen. Nonetheless, in the short term, as performances on a national stage, these more centralized policing efforts were no match for the enactments of white Southern violence seen by a national audience, which ultimately contributed to federal action that altered some of Jim Crow's most prominent features.

The Civil Rights Act, passed by Congress and signed into law by President Lyndon Johnson in 1964, banned racial discrimination. In Mississippi, the results of these measures were initially mixed. Jackson mayor Allen Thompson, who had been an ardent defender of segregation, believed there was little point in challenging the federal act. Many places in Jackson and throughout the state desegregated without incident.[9] Still, some business owners resisted, and many restaurants, hotels, and other establishments in the state continued to refuse service to black customers. A number of owners preferred instead to pay the $500 fine, at least until demonstrators returned each day and the fines mounted.[10] By the end of the decade, most businesses had relented, and the protests and legislation had visibly altered the physical landscape. On the stage on which blacks and whites had previously performed Jim Crow roles, racial signs came down and black patrons and white patrons entered through the same doors and sat in the same sections. This transition came more slowly to rural areas in the South, and in some places racially separate spaces were still present in the 1980s.[11] Meanwhile, school desegregation proceeded slowly, until 1969, when a federal judge in the *Alexander v. Holmes County* decision called for the immediate desegregation of public schools. Similar to other places in the region, many white parents soon enrolled their children in segregation academies or other newly formed private schools, reproducing segregation.[12]

A year after passage of the Civil Rights Act, Lyndon Johnson signed the Voting Rights Act, which provided federal protections for voters. Television coverage of the voting rights march in Selma, Alabama, had been instrumental in pushing the president and legislators to take action. At a march that became known as "Bloody Sunday," cameras captured police officers attacking peaceful marchers and later showed images of battered and bloodied demonstrators.[13] In Mississippi, in the immediate aftermath of the Voting Rights Act, potential black voters continued to face intimidation and violence. Nonetheless, the number of registered black voters steadily climbed, and by 1967 white candidates were actively campaigning for black votes. That same year, Robert G. Clark Jr., of Holmes County, where Eddie Noel had shot three white men thirteen years earlier, became the first African American elected to the state legislature since the Reconstruction years.[14] Throughout the state, within a span of four years, the percentage of registered African American voters jumped from 7 percent to 59 percent. Across the South over the same period, the number of registered black voters rose from 2 million to 3.1 million. Perhaps more significant, the number of black elected officials in Mississippi increased from zero in 1965 to 521 in 1986, the largest number in the nation.[15] Unita Blackwell, who had recalled her fears of being killed by whites during the Jim Crow era, became the first black mayor of Mayersville in 1977.[16] These voting trends in Mississippi were similar across the region, and into the 1990s, the South continued to elect a substantial majority of the nation's black elected officials.[17]

The legal death of segregation and the changes in voting altered the daily racial routines between African Americans and whites. The legislation that protected voting rights and banned discrimination, like the various laws of the late nineteenth century, contributed to new scripts. Those measures signaled that the stage props—the signs and barriers marking off racial space—would change, too. And, of course, spaces would continue to be defined by how blacks and whites interacted each day. The defeat of Jim Crow indeed represented a dramatic difference in how blacks and whites moved, talked, and interacted in shared space. The legal scripts that defined these spaces—from schools to restaurants to the voting booth—marked them as spaces where blacks and whites engaged with each other as social equals. Some of the other scripts and narratives of interracial intimacy, such as whites referring to African Americans as "uncle" or "mammy" or "boy," slowly faded. These racial transformations that established new rules for interactions in shared space especially shaped the experiences of the black middle class, ultimately contributing to an expanding group of black professionals in the South, with many more African Americans appearing in courts as lawyers, on television as news anchors, and in legislative halls as politicians.[18]

In other respects, however, the successes of the civil rights movement in redefining spaces and daily performances were more modest, and these limits related in part to the performances of racism and violence that had captured national attention. The media's coverage that focused on white Southerners attacking black victims provided images that equated racism with blatant acts of violence, making it easier to overlook the subtler forms of racism, both in the South and throughout the nation.[19] The federal legislative efforts, while significant, concentrated narrowly on limiting violence, protecting voting rights, and desegregating public spaces. These measures did not address economic inequalities, and they depended on imagining racism as overt and visually horrific, as specific actions committed by individuals rather than as the by-products of a larger political and economic system. Certainly civil rights activists recognized that the mid-1960s federal victories were not the end of the struggle. In Mississippi, into the late 1960s, various groups continued working in communities to address inequalities in employment, housing, and education.[20] Yet the national public and the media, which had previously been powerful allies for civil rights organizations, had lost interest and moved on. Indeed, in the two years following the Voting Rights Act, violence in Mississippi persisted, including four murders related to movement activities.[21] However, these performances of white Southern aggression, which had once fueled public support for the struggle, now garnered comparatively little attention outside the South. Thus, one of the critical changes of the mid-1960s was that public interest in the Southern civil rights movement waned. Instead, the national public turned its attention to racial uprisings closer to home.

Jim Crow had always been a national racial system, but the process to dismantle it in the North and West unfolded differently from the South.[22] In the post–World War II years, civil rights activists in cities such as Philadelphia, New York City, and Oakland, California, had success in overturning some of the policies and practices of residential segregation, discrimination in employment, and racial separation in public spaces and places of business. Interracial efforts involving local black activists and white liberal sympathizers produced reforms, including expanded opportunities for the black middle class; but much like the civil rights movement in the South, reforms in the North and the West left unaddressed deeper structural inequalities, particularly for poor and working-class populations. In many communities, by the early 1960s, African Americans, frustrated with the slow and limited nature of reforms through biracial cooperation, turned away from liberal support and increasingly embraced empowerment and collective action within the black community.[23] In a number of ways, both the official and the public response to Black Power efforts in the North and the West bore a similarity to how segregationists had responded to civil rights challenges in Mississippi in the 1950s.

As happened in Mississippi, officials in the North and the West drew on national shifts in policing, including a greater reliance on modern equipment and an expansion of authority for police officers, which had been under way since the 1940s.[24] In urban areas outside the South in the mid-1960s, authorities responded to black public protest with a centralized effort tied to law enforcement agencies. Accordingly, when racial uprisings erupted in Watts, Newark, Harlem, and elsewhere, local authorities arrested those who protested.[25] National and local officials also went on the offensive, and these policing practices extended to campaigns against Black Power organizations. For example, with considerably more skill, training, and resources than the Sovereignty Commission had, the FBI infiltrated the Black Panther Party and numerous other organizations.[26] Reminiscent of Mississippi, Oakland patrolmen also carried lists of license plate numbers of known Black Panther members so they could regularly follow those cars. Local authorities then utilized arrest charges for moving violations and disturbing the peace to deplete the funds of the organization.[27] On the ground, one finds numerous parallels in how officials in the South and throughout the nation responded to dissent through a centralized response rooted in the law.

The national media, meanwhile, became important players in framing these protests in the urban North and West, and they told a story that was vastly different from their earlier narratives of black protest in the South. For roughly a decade, the media had depicted the civil rights movement as a Southern struggle, and its definition of racism—revolving around white individuals attacking innocent black individuals—had a distinctly Southern accent. In those accounts, white Southerners were irrational and violent and black Southerners were victims. Outside the South, however, the media characterized the black individuals in the streets not as innocent victims but as rioters and criminals. Additionally, the media told a broader story, not about racism, injustice, and worsening social conditions but instead about vandalism, arson, and theft.[28]

To be sure, the performance of "Black Power" was considerably different from the performances of nonviolent direct action that had been part of the earlier civil rights efforts both in the urban North and West and in the South. As many activists turned away from biracial reform efforts and toward community empowerment strategies, many also enacted more aggressive public postures. Whereas the media had previously captured images of quiet demonstrators sitting at lunch counters in the South, the media now focused on Black Power activists standing and raising a closed fist in the air. Furthermore, the Black Panther Party's image of men and women dressed in black, wearing berets, and publicly displaying large guns took center stage.[29] It represented a powerful performance, as unsettling for many white Americans as the Southern demonstrators had been for many white Southerners. In the South, racist and violent white Southerners became the villains. In cities outside the South, however, the villains were more likely to be the black protesters, not the police officers and troops who sought to quell disturbances or the politicians who condemned the demonstrations. Nationally, the narrative of racial uprisings framed these protests as a breakdown of law and order. And in that regard, challenges to racist practices once again collided with crime narratives, as they had in the South, suggesting a convergence across regional lines.

In the 1950s, statistics and stories about black crime and deviance were at the center of Mississippi segregationists' public response to civil rights threats. In the following decade, national narratives about crime became intertwined with the response to Black Power and to uprisings in the urban North and West. Conservatives and liberals alike criminalized Black Power and African Americans who took to the streets. Politicians played up FBI statistics showing an increase in crime nationally, and Republicans and Democrats turned to a language of law and order that blurred the lines between protesters, rioters, and criminals.[30] It was a message couched in a fear of black criminality that had never been exclusively confined to one region. In the 1960s and 1970s, that rhetoric contributed to Ronald Reagan's gubernatorial victory in California in 1967 and to Richard Nixon's presidential victories in 1968 and 1972.[31] While some have linked a coded rhetoric to a Southern strategy that appealed to white racists, it is more accurate to recognize this political strategy as a national one rooted in a long tradition. Thus, the conservative turn that embraced a law-and-order mentality did not represent a Southernization of the nation so much as it indicated that the regions had never been far apart in their racial ideologies.[32] Regardless of region, stories of a black criminal threat always accompanied the moments of crisis for white supremacy.

Since the 1960s, both the more centralized forms of policing and the narratives of black criminality influenced racial transformations in the South and throughout the nation. From the law-and-order rhetoric in the 1960s to a "war on drugs" in the 1980s to the tough-on-crime language of the 1990s, conservatives and liberals used fears of black crime to their political advantage.[33] In addition, as historian Heather Ann Thompson contends, the practices and the rhetoric of the post–civil rights years criminalized urban space and fueled the processes that produced mass incarceration and a prison-industrial complex.[34] As deindustrialization and middle-class migrations out of urban areas contributed to high unemployment, poverty, and municipal neglect, the prison system grew. Working-class and poor populations among African Americans and Latinos in urban areas were especially vulnerable and were the most likely to end up behind bars. Nonetheless, the highest rates of imprisonment have been in Southern states, including nine of the ten highest rates, with Louisiana leading the way and Mississippi coming in fifth.[35] Michelle Alexander has referred to this development as the "New Jim Crow," in which mass incarceration functions as a "racialized system of social control" and, like the old Jim Crow, produces disfranchisement, discrimination, and social exclusion.[36]

The legalistic turn has likewise been reflected in the daily racial routines and in the ways in which public spaces are monitored in the South and throughout the nation. The end of Jim Crow meant an end to a number of performative practices that had marked racial difference, including barring African American shoppers from trying on clothes before purchasing them and expecting African American passengers on a bus to give up their seats for white riders. However, other forms of surveillance and daily policing have replaced these routines. In stores, African American shoppers are often subtly or not so subtly followed as suspected shoplifters. On the roadways, African American drivers may be pulled over for "driving while black," and that has been especially true for black professionals driving expensive cars.[37] Both of these practices and others demonstrate that the law, arrests, and police officers have played a greater role in surveillance and in marking the differences between whiteness and blackness. If the Jim Crow stage production idealized African Americans as contented servants, the more recent staging has increasingly imagined African Americans as criminals. In addition, across the nation, African Americans are not—and historically have not been—the only "nonwhite" group to be criminalized within the larger culture, as these processes have also encompassed Latino/as, Asian Americans, and Native Americans.[38]

At the same time, police brutality and shootings have continued to preserve various forms of violence within the legal structure in ways that have shaped racial meanings throughout the nation. Within a post–Jim Crow system, narratives of black criminality have justified aggressive and violent reactions, producing well-known incidents, such as the 1992 beating of Rodney King in Los Angeles and the death of unarmed Guinean immigrant Amadou Diallo, who in 1999 was shot nineteen times by police officers after he reached for his wallet. Juries and commissions on policing have consistently supported the aggressive actions and strengthened the authority of law enforcement officials. Beyond the role of officers, these transformations have also at times extended to and expanded the role of citizens. The "stand your ground" law, for example, allows a citizen to use force in self-defense even when retreat is an option. In Florida, in 2012, that measure protected an act of vigilantism when George Zimmerman fatally shot an unarmed Trayvon Martin.[39] While the language of the stand your ground law is race neutral, many have expressed concern that its interpretation is firmly rooted in racial politics.[40]

Fueling all of these changes, from expanding the role of some citizens to use force to the rise of mass incarceration and excessive policing, are narratives of black criminality and deviance. And just as clothing and bold postures figured prominently in criminalizing Black Power in the 1960s, in the post–civil rights era, hoodies, sagging pants, and playing music loudly have been woven into the stories about black deviance. In this sense, the narratives and practices within the legal arena define appropriate and inappropriate racial performances for African Americans.

While national narratives of black criminality continue to shape racial meanings across regional lines, narratives of Southern exceptionalism persist within national racial discourses. Even after the transformations following the civil rights movement, including gains in the number of African Americans elected to political office in the South, nationally the South and especially Mississippi has consistently been imagined as the most racist and violent place in the nation. In Queens, in 1987, for example, following the murder of African American Michael Griffith, New York mayor Ed Koch reasoned that such episodes were expected in the Deep South but not in his city. In 1998, in Riverside, California, following the death of Tyisha Miller at the hands of police officers, a family member similarly likened the ordeal to Mississippi.[41] The narrative of an exceptionally racist and backward South lived on. Furthermore, officials regularly invoked Mississippi, not as a call to address racist practices in their locales but rather to mark specific racial incidents as exceptional, isolated moments. Accordingly, the racial narratives of the South continued to play a role in denying or downplaying the racism in other regions.

At the same time, the other version of Southern exceptionalism—the one that played up interracial intimacy—also survived Jim Crow.[42] With the emergence of the Sunbelt South, which saw an influx of migrants and corporate investment, many Southern places have marketed a bucolic past tied in part to interracial intimacy to attract tourists, with plantations in particular becoming a popular draw.[43] These stories of intimacy are often set in the past, and in this regard the interest in the past is reminiscent of other times (the 1950s, the 1890s) when many white Southerners fondly remembered earlier days of racial harmony, featuring African Americans as happy, faithful servants.[44] In the post–Jim Crow era, these tales have been kept alive especially through the image of the black domestic worker in the white home.

In reality, the black domestic worker steadily disappeared from white homes in the second half of the twentieth century, and by the 1980s, very few black women worked as domestics.[45] Increasingly, throughout the nation, Latinas and migrants from Latin America engaged in this work.[46] Of the remaining black domestic workers, compared to an earlier generation, they were now more likely to do only "day work" and to work for multiple families. As a result, they were spending much less time in white homes and much less time with a single white family that might think of the domestic worker as "like family." In the post–civil rights years, then, one of the bedrocks of interracial intimacy—the nurturing and loyal black mammy—virtually ceased to exist in the present. Variations on that figure, however, continued to live on in the memories of the past. These recollections, most often from white women, emphasized a mutual fondness across the racial line. As one white female recalled about the domestic workers she had employed, "There was no hard feelings, no hate. . . . We loved them."[47]

Similarly, Kathryn Stockett, who grew up in the 1970s, in Jackson, Mississippi, fondly remembered the domestic worker who raised her, and that relationship inspired her novel, *The Help*.[48] Significantly, though, Stockett's novel is not set during her childhood but a decade earlier, in the late 1950s and early 1960s. In a sense, like Haley Barbour superimposing his childhood memories on race relations in the civil rights era, Stockett drew on her memories (in the 1970s) to tell a story about the civil rights movement. Her best-selling novel revolves around a young white woman who loved the black women who worked in her home and who then used her connections in the literary world to tell their story and presumably to rescue them from the racial hatred of a few white employers. If the story follows a familiar Hollywood narrative of a "white savior" movie, this tale is also distinctively Southern and connected to earlier narratives about interracial intimacy. *The Help* bears some resemblance to the 1950s narratives about interracial intimacy, as it depicts cooperation and a special bond between black Southerners and white Southerners.[49] It is unclear if Stockett's story is meant to represent an homage to an imagined and irretrievable past of interracial intimacy or instead to suggest that some aspect of this racially harmonious past continues to mark the South as different. Nonetheless, it is worth noting that this story of intimacy, like so many of the previous ones, positioned African Americans as servants waiting on white people.

The narratives of both racial harmony and black criminality have demonstrated a special ability to survive across periods of sweeping transformations; they were present before Jim Crow developed in the late nineteenth century and they persist more than a century later. The performances of race encompassed in those narratives continue to justify and even produce racist practices. In the process, they obscure the ways in which racism and racist practices continue to infiltrate daily life.

This book followed the interactions of black Mississippians and white Mississippians across time from the 1930s through to the early 1960s, charting how race functioned in everyday life and how these practices changed as state-sanctioned segregation came to an end. Extending this query forward, we could no doubt identify a number of critical developments, including shifts in the political realm that led to the election of the nation's first African American president, economic and social changes that have expanded opportunities for black professionals, and changes in the public realm whereby public figures who make overtly racist statements are likely to be ostracized. All of these things suggest that the nation has moved a great distance away from an era that was characterized by lynchings, burning crosses, and "whites only" signs. Yet if a close examination of the quotidian in the Jim Crow era tells us anything, it is that often the most devastating aspects of an oppressive system are the ones that generally go unnoticed, appearing in the routines and the rhetoric that disguise racial expectations and disparities in stories and daily performances.

NOTES

ABBREVIATIONS USED IN THE NOTES

AMD-USM   Archives and Manuscript Department, William D. McCain Library and Archives, University of Southern Mississippi, Hattiesburg, Miss.

JHFHC   John Hope Franklin Historical Collections, Rare Book, Manuscript, and Special Collections Library, Duke University, Durham, N.C.

MDAH   Mississippi Department of Archives and History, Archives and Library Division, Jackson, Miss.

MOHP   Mississippi Oral History Program, University of Southern Mississippi, Hattiesburg, Miss.

MSSCR   Mississippi State Sovereignty Commission Records, Mississippi Department of Archives and History, Archives and Library Division, Jackson, Miss.

SHC   Southern Historical Collection, Wilson Library, University of North Carolina, Chapel Hill, N.C.

INTRODUCTION

1. The essay originally appeared in *American Stuff: An Anthology of Prose and Verse by Members of the Federal Writers' Project*. Richard Wright, "The Ethics of Living Jim Crow," 14, 15.

2. For an overview of Jim Crow, see Packard, *American Nightmare*. On the Jim Crow era in Mississippi, see McMillen, *Dark Journey*.

3. For an excellent earlier survey of the manifestations of Jim Crow in both the South and the North, see Charles S. Johnson, *Patterns of Negro Segregation*.

4. For an overview of the legal system of Jim Crow, see Klarman, *From Jim Crow to Civil Rights*. On Jim Crow as a cultural system, see Hale, *Making Whiteness*.

5. A critical exception is Joe Crespino's study of conservative politicians in Mississippi in the 1950s and 1960s, *In Search of Another Country*.

6. On imaginings of the South, and in particular Mississippi, as exceptionally violent and racist, see Crespino, "Mississippi as Metaphor"; and Griffin, "Southern Distinctiveness, Yet Again."

7. In examining the link between race and culture in the South, I am drawing especially on the work of Grace Elizabeth Hale, Robin D. G. Kelley, and Saidiya

Hartman. See Hale, *Making Whiteness*; Robin D. G. Kelley, *Race Rebels*; and Hartman, *Scenes of Subjection*.

8. On Jim Crow's origins and formative years, see Litwack, *Trouble in Mind*; Glenda Elizabeth Gilmore, *Gender and Jim Crow*; Dailey, *Before Jim Crow*; Ayers, *The Promise of the New South*; Kousser, *The Shaping of Southern Politics*; Cell, *The Highest Stage of White Supremacy*; and Woodward, *Origins of the New South*.

9. W. Fitzhugh Brundage observes, regarding lynching, that this practice varied a great deal by time and place and that those differences are important in understanding how lynching functioned in the South. One can make a related argument for examining the temporal and spatial variances in racial practices within the everyday realm. Kimberley Johnson also challenges the idea of an unchanging South in her study of black reformers and white reformers in the era before the civil rights movement, and in his study of Virginia, J. Douglas Smith highlights the importance of studying race relations in the 1920s and 1930s on their own terms. Brundage, *Lynching in the New South*; Kimberley Johnson, *Reforming Jim Crow*; J. Douglas Smith, *Managing White Supremacy*, 16.

10. Dailey, Gilmore, and Simon, "Introduction," 4.

11. Studies of racial practices beyond the South serve as excellent models for Mississippi. Rooted in the notion that racism was less overt in the North and the West, scholars of these regions have been accustomed to digging deep to uncover racist practices buried within the structure. Conversely, because so much attention has been devoted to the overt practices in the South—lynching, racial signage, disfranchisement—the more insidious workings of Jim Crow have often received far less attention. For non-Southern models, see Biondi, *To Stand and Fight*; Murch, *Living for the City*; Sugrue, *The Origins of the Urban Crisis*; Countryman, *Up South*; Self, *American Babylon*; and Satter, *Family Properties*. Similarly, studies of regions with multiple nonwhite populations also highlight sophisticated racial practices. See, for example, Foley, *The White Scourge*; and Kurashige, *The Shifting Grounds of Race*.

12. See, for example, Glenda Elizabeth Gilmore, *Defying Dixie*; Sullivan, *Days of Hope*; Jeffries, *Bloody Lowndes*; Brown-Nagin, *Courage to Dissent*; de Jong, *A Different Day*; Green, *Battling the Plantation Mentality*; Ransby, *Ella Baker and the Black Freedom Movement*; Theoharis and Woodard, *Freedom North*; and Sugrue, *Sweet Land of Liberty*. In response to the scholarly turn toward a Long Civil Rights Movement, some scholars have cautioned that the long civil rights movement framework obliterates distinctions within the black freedom struggle, blurring the lines between civil rights and Black Power and sacrificing the historical specificity of particular social movements. See Cha-Jua and Lang, "The 'Long Movement' as Vampire." For other overviews of civil rights scholarship, see Lawson, "Freedom Then, Freedom Now"; Payne, *I've Got the Light of Freedom*, 413–42; Eagles, "Toward New Histories of the Civil Rights Era"; Mattson, "Civil Rights Made Harder"; Hall, "The Long Civil Rights Movement"; and Theoharis, "Black Freedom Struggles."

13. Robin Kelley contends that individual, everyday acts of resistance within the black community had a cumulative effect contributing to a larger movement for social change. Robin D. G. Kelley, *Race Rebels*, 8.

14. Virginia senator Harry Byrd initially coined this term in reference to the *Brown* ruling against segregation in public schools. Central to his plan was a legal strategy of interposition, according to which states, not a federal court, would claim the right to make decisions about segregated schools. Scholars and others have also attached this term more loosely to white Southern resistance to desegregation in the civil rights era. On this term and the segregationist response, see Lewis, *Massive Resistance*. See also Bartley, *The Rise of Massive Resistance*.

15. Kruse, *White Flight*.

16. Lassiter, *The Silent Majority*.

17. In this regard, Joe Crespino identifies Governor J. P. Coleman and a few racially more moderate politicians in the state as "practical segregationists." Crespino, *In Search of Another Country*, 4, 19. Anders Walker also highlights the willingness of Coleman to compromise on some issues in order to save segregation. Anders Walker, *The Ghost of Jim Crow*. Elsewhere, Crespino argues that South Carolina politician and one time States' Rights/Dixiecrat presidential candidate Strom Thurmond was another prominent segregationist who successfully repositioned himself as part of a national New Right. Crespino, *Strom Thurmond's America*. On the complexities of the response of segregationist politicians stretching back to the 1930s, see Ward, *Defending White Democracy*; and Finley, *Delaying the Dream*.

18. For a narrative overview of how white Southerners responded to these changes, see Sokol, *There Goes My Everything*.

19. As Martha Biondi notes, from 1947 to 1952, New York City police officers killed forty-six unarmed African Americans and two whites. Biondi, *To Stand and Fight*. On the connections between policing and violence in New York, see also Marilynn S. Johnson, *Street Justice*. Meanwhile, according to Chris Lowen Agee, in San Francisco, centralization in local policing between 1950 and 1975 served to promote cultural, racial, and sexual democracy. Agee, *Streets of San Francisco*.

20. Murch, *Living for the City*, 58–61, 64. Related practices also developed on a national scale. Federal agencies such as the FBI and the Immigration and Naturalization Service (INS) expanded their reach by committing more resources to training, new equipment, and surveillance activities. Within the FBI, these efforts were well under way by the 1930s, as director J. Edgar Hoover sought to professionalize the bureau. For the INS in Los Angeles in the 1950s, under Operation Round-Up and Operation Wetback, more aggressive deportation efforts ensnared Mexicans and Mexican Americans, and both groups lived in fear every day of being picked up. O'Reilly, *Racial Matters*; Molina, *How Race Is Made in America*, 112–38.

21. At the same time, the criminalization of nonwhites emerged from earlier traditions that linked blackness and criminality. See Muhammad, *The Condemnation of Blackness*.

22. In this regard, the performance occurs at the intersection of race and culture.

23. Aware of the importance of "wearing the mask" for self-protection, many African Americans instructed their children in how to act around white people. See Ritterhouse, *Growing Up Jim Crow*; and Berrey, "Resistance Begins at Home." On the psychological effects of a white-constructed blackness, see Fanon, *Black Skins, White Masks*.

24. Doyle, *The Etiquette of Race Relations in the South*, 9. In the same era, sociologist John Dollard also alluded to African Americans performing in daily life. Dollard, *Caste and Class in a Southern Town*, 440.

25. Beyond the primarily historical references, performance studies scholar E. Patrick Johnson analyzes the performance of blackness within American culture and its relationship to the notion of an "authentic" blackness. His discussion includes an exploration of the racial performances of his grandmother, who was a domestic worker for a white family in 1960s North Carolina. E. Patrick Johnson, *Appropriating Blackness*.

26. Most of these allusions to performance are made in passing as succinct analogies intended to convey a sense of Jim Crow life from the perspective of African Americans. For example, in his focus on the early years of Jim Crow, Leon Litwack notes that the black Southerner was made to "perform the rituals expected of him and play the roles defined by whites, all of them equally dehumanizing, equally degrading, equally unrewarding." Litwack, *Trouble in Mind*, xiii. For a later period, David R. Goldfield also uses a theater metaphor to explain racial etiquette. Goldfield, *Black, White, and Southern*, 6. For Mississippi, Neil McMillen references the performance qualities of the expected racial etiquette for black individuals. McMillen, *Dark Journey*, 23–28.

In terms of how historical projects use performance as an analytical tool, two studies in particular have influenced my approach. In her examination of race relations during and after the period of enslavement, literature scholar Saidiya Hartman considered the ways in which whites manifested power by compelling enslaved individuals to entertain them. Thus, the performance of singing and "dancing for the master" constituted a psychological and symbolic form of violence. Hartman, *Scenes of Subjection*, 42. Robin D. G. Kelley also uses the metaphor of performance to examine Birmingham buses in the 1940s. He refers to these buses as "moving theaters" in which African American passengers regularly staged resistance in refusing to move for white passengers or in talking back to or fighting with white drivers and passengers. Robin D. G. Kelley, *Race Rebels*, 57.

27. Goffman, *The Presentation of Self in Everyday Life*, 22.

28. Ibid., 16.

29. Ibid., 58–66.

30. My exploration of the performative qualities of Jim Crow also draws on the ways in which folklorists discuss performances. Thus, language components such as pronunciation and intonation, as well as loudness and pitch, can be important. Non-vocal elements include facial expressions, bodily movements, gestures, and postures. Bauman, *Folklore, Cultural Performances, and Popular Entertainments*, 27.

31. An earlier indication of the importance of storytelling by African Americans is Ida B. Wells. In researching lynchings in the late nineteenth century, she challenged the popular narrative that lynchings were primarily responses to sexual assaults on white women by black men. See Bay, *To Tell the Truth Freely*.

32. Joel Williamson positions white Southerners within one of three ideological groups: radicals, who wanted to expel blacks; conservatives, who accepted blacks as long as they remained in a subordinate, accommodating position; and a few

liberals, who believed blacks could make progress. Williamson argues that the radical vision marked the origins of Jim Crow and that conservatives won out by 1915. The analysis is compelling and the categories are useful, although the emphasis on radicals in the early Jim Crow years understates the extent to which the "conservative" vision was written into the early laws. Indeed, in remaking a world of accommodating blacks, the conservatives and radicals complemented each other. Williamson, *The Crucible of Race*.

33. James R. Grossman contends that white Southerners needed to believe that African Americans were content and that they accepted their position as second-class citizens and as willing peasants. Laurie Green also references the master-slave relationship—which she conceptualizes through the term "plantation mentality"— in her study of the black freedom struggle in Memphis, and she uses that concept to explore how African Americans understood and talked about freedom. These constructions of racial roles emerged at least in part from nostalgic memories of a plantation past remembered as an era of faithful slaves and juxtaposed with fears of a more aggressive New Negro in the late nineteenth century. Grossman, "'Amiable Peasantry' or 'Social Burden,'" 235. Green, *Battling the Plantation Mentality*, 5. On nostalgia among white Southerners for the faithful slave, see Litwack, *Trouble in Mind*, 83–97; and Hale, *Making Whiteness*. For an extension of this nostalgia into national culture in the twentieth century, see McElya, *Clinging to Mammy*; and Manring, *Slave in a Box*.

34. In some of the work on segregation in metropolitan areas, there is an assumption that residential patterns in cities created distance—and thus less intimacy—between blacks and whites. Yet, even if blacks and whites lived in separate neighborhoods, culturally they were likely to interact regularly, such as on sidewalks, in stores, and in white homes, working as maids.

35. On the antecedents to the twentieth-century narratives of black deviance, see Fredrickson, *The Black Image in the White Mind*, 256–84; Williamson, *The Crucible of Race*, 111–23; and Wagner, *Disturbing the Peace*.

36. US Census Data, online, http://www.census.gov/population/www/documentation/twps0056/tab39.xls (accessed September 29, 2013).

37. Key, *Southern Politics in State and Nation*, 230.

38. On the complicated history of race relations in the Delta, see Cobb, *The Most Southern Place on Earth*.

39. On the lives of Eastland and Hamer in Sunflower County, see Asch, *The Senator and the Sharecropper*. For a biography of Hamer, see Lee, *For Freedom's Sake*; and Mills, *This Little Light of Mine*.

40. Key, *Southern Politics in State and Nation*, 230; Grantham, *The Life and Death of the Solid South*, 32–33.

41. See Rabinowitz, *Race Relations in the Urban South*.

42. In the 1940s and early 1950s, Percy Greene was one of the more vocal opponents of segregation in the state. Greene's tone changed in the mid-1950s, and the Sovereignty Commission provided some funding to the newspaper. On Greene and the complexities of his political positions, see Julius E. Thompson, *Percy Greene and the Jackson Advocate*, and Cooper, "Percy Greene and the *Jackson Advocate*."

43. Chalmers, *Backfire*, 55–56.

44. For an excellent autobiographical introduction to civil rights efforts along the Mississippi Gulf Coast, see Mason, *Beaches, Blood, and Ballots*.

45. Dittmer, *Local People*, 1–18. In addition to ibid., for an excellent account of the civil rights movement in the state, see Payne, *I've Got the Light of Freedom*. On one of the most influential civil rights leaders in the state, see Williams, *Medgar Evers*.

46. For accounts of organizing in local communities in Mississippi, see Moye, *Let the People Decide*; Crosby, *A Little Taste of Freedom*; and Hamlin, *Crossroads at Clarksdale*.

47. On the longer history of armed self-defense in Mississippi, see Umoja, *We Will Shoot Back*. On armed resistance as part of the movement story in other Southern states, see Hill, *The Deacons for Defense*; Wendt, *The Spirit and the Shotgun*; and Tyson, *Radio Free Dixie*. For an account of armed resistance in an earlier period in the South, see Woodruff, *American Congo*.

48. Scott, *Domination and the Arts of Resistance*, 18–19. Robin D. G. Kelley has applied this concept to the African American experience to explore resistance that sometimes existed outside organizations and outside of or on the margins of the civil rights movement. See Robin D. G. Kelley, *Race Rebels*.

49. As Alessandro Portelli notes, historical participants could not even remember the correct year of a particularly well-known death. Portelli, *The Death of Luigi Trastulli*, 1–2.

50. Estes, "Engendering Movement Memories," 290–312.

51. On the strengths and limitations of memory and oral histories in historical work, see Nora, "Between Memory and History"; Cubitt, *History and Memory*; Portelli, "The Peculiarities of Oral History"; Vansina, *Oral Tradition as History*; and Halbwachs, *On Collective Memory*.

52. Trouillot, *Silencing the Past*, 49.

53. Classen, *Watching Jim Crow*, 140–45.

54. Geoffrey Cubitt, for instance, references Ulrich Neisser's study of an interview with Richard Nixon staff member John Dean. Although Dean's memory included inaccuracies and inflated his own role in the events of the time, Neisser contended that Dean's memory captured overall impressions of the period. Cubitt, *History and Memory*, 85–86.

55. See, for example, Payne, *I've Got the Light of Freedom*, 204–9.

CHAPTER 1

1. Scott interview.

2. Ed Ayers notes that this law was intended as a compromise between white sensibilities and black civil rights, as legislators called for equal accommodations from railroad companies. Ayers, *The Promise of the New South*, 143. On the meanings of this law in Tennessee, see Cartwright, *The Triumph of Jim Crow*; and Folmsbee, "The Origins of the First 'Jim Crow' Law."

3. McMillen, *Dark Journey*, 8. On the legal changes in Mississippi during this early Jim Crow period, see ibid., 3–32.

4. On the physicality of signs and the industry that emerged around Jim Crow signage, see Abel, *Signs of the Times*, 62–102.

5. Dailey, *Before Jim Crow*, 103–31.

6. Litwack, *Trouble in Mind*, 184–86.

7. As Micki McElya notes, interest in looking back nostalgically to a faithful slave was becoming widespread throughout the nation by the turn of the twentieth century. McElya, *Clinging to Mammy*, 13.

8. Hale, *Making Whiteness*, 123, 128–29.

9. Ibid., 137–38.

10. Ayers, *The Promise of the New South*, 140.

11. Fredrickson, *White Supremacy*, 254. Leon Litwack likewise observes that during the Jim Crow era "the two races came into frequent contact"; and Jack Temple Kirby notes, in relation to labor and residential patterns, "Much of the southern countryside . . . was in a literal sense racially integrated throughout the age of segregation." J. Douglas Smith, who compares race relations in Jim Crow Virginia to a form of paternalism, also points out that this system depended on regular personal contact between blacks and whites. Litwack, *Trouble in Mind*, 20; Kirby, *Rural Worlds Lost*, 235; J. Douglas Smith, *Managing White Supremacy*, 15.

12. Massey, *For Space*, 154, 9.

13. Holt, "Marking," 3.

14. Ellison's larger point was to argue that the idea of the mask—of a "smart man playing dumb"—as being part of a Negro tradition was false, that it was more of a practical strategy within a specific contemporary context than some long-held tradition with roots in black folklore. Ellison, "Change the Joke," 57.

15. Charles S. Johnson, *Patterns of Negro Segregation*, 143.

16. Ibid.

17. For an overview of the legal developments in this period and extending throughout the Jim Crow era, see Klarman, *From Jim Crow to Civil Rights*. For a discussion of the origins of these segregation spaces, see Litwack, *Trouble in Mind*, 229–37.

18. Joel Williamson characterizes this early period as a struggle within the white political leadership among radicals wanting to expel and destroy blacks, paternalistic conservatives who believed the races could exist if blacks embraced an accommodating and inferior position, and a few liberals who believed that blacks might have some potential. Williamson focuses primarily on the first decades of Jim Crow (into the 1910s), but one could make the case that divisions within the white community between extremists and paternalists persisted throughout the Jim Crow era. Williamson, *The Crucible of Race*.

19. Referencing North Carolina governor Charles Aycock's observation at the turn of the twentieth century that every generation would have to "settle [the race question] for themselves," Jason Morgan Ward has also made the case for considering how manifestations of white supremacy shift across time within the political arena. Ward, *Defending White Democracy*, 2.

20. For an overview of lynching, see Dray, *At the Hands of Persons Unknown*. For a discussion of how lynching changed over time, see Brundage, *Lynching in the New South*.

21. That this world would have seemed settled relative to an earlier period, however, does not mean that race relations were actually static. As J. Douglas Smith observes, the most critical Jim Crow measures in Virginia emerged in the 1920s and 1930s. J. Douglas Smith, *Managing White Supremacy*, 16.

22. Litwack, *Trouble in Mind*, xvi, 378–403.

23. Charles S. Johnson, *Patterns of Negro Segregation*, 178.

24. Ayers, *The Promise of the New South*, 140–46.

25. Abel also illustrates the cost concerns with a Birmingham ordinance. An ordinance that forbade blacks and whites from eating in the same room in a restaurant was amended in 1930 to allow blacks and whites in the same room as long as these customers were "separated by a solid partition extending from the floor upward to a distance of seven feet or higher" and as long as they entered from the street through separate entrances. Abel, *Signs of the Times*, 161–63, 180.

26. In addition, as Stetson Kennedy noted, air travel had not been anticipated by early legislators, and thus seating on airplanes that traveled across "Southern" skies was not segregated by race. Stetson Kennedy, *Jim Crow Guide*, 179.

27. Charles S. Johnson, *Patterns of Negro Segregation*, 46.

28. Ibid., 48.

29. Ibid., 32.

30. Hale, *Making Whiteness*, 173.

31. Povall, *The Time of Eddie Noel*, 4–6.

32. Kirby, *Rural Worlds Lost*, 236.

33. Charles S. Johnson, *Patterns of Negro Segregation*, 32.

34. Ibid., 73–74.

35. Hale, *Making Whiteness*, 8.

36. Dahmer interview.

37. Packard, *American Nightmare*, 88. This exception had roots in the period of enslavement, when in many places enslaved individuals could ride with their masters in the stagecoach or railcar. Doyle, *The Etiquette of Race Relations in the South*, 58–59.

38. Cartwright, *The Triumph of Jim Crow*, 184.

39. Ibid., 166–67. Key made this observation in part to argue that "a neatly dressed well behaved colored person" should be allowed to ride in any car. On the legal discussion surrounding this Tennessee law, see Mack, "Law, Society, Identity."

40. Bertram Wilbur Doyle, citing Robert Parks, also noted in his study that a "colored nurse could ride, without exception, if she has a white baby in her arms." On at least one occasion in Louisiana in 1911, however, a judge ruled that under no circumstances could a black passenger occupy a Pullman berth. Doyle, *The Etiquette of Race Relations in the South*, 150, 233.

41. The South was not the only region that practiced a racial exclusion with exceptions for blacks playing the part of servants. As Bryant Simon shows, along the boardwalk in Atlantic City, New Jersey, African Americans were excluded as tourists but hired in service positions, with roles modeled on the Jim Crow characters of minstrel shows. He contends that being served, especially by a black individual, became an important marker of upward mobility for tourists rising into the middle

class. It also represents another example of the close connection between racial performance and the making of space. Simon, *Boardwalk of Dreams*, 13–14, 21, 39–41.

42. The wording of the statute actually allowed servants of either race employed by the other race to live on the premises of the other race. Stetson Kennedy, *Jim Crow Guide*, 73.

43. Similar measures were implemented in Jacksonville in 1929 and in Birmingham in 1930. Tindall, *The Emergence of the New South*, 146.

44. It is unclear how long this law was enforced or whether other states adopted it. Bryant Simon cites an incident from 1947 in South Carolina in which a white cabdriver was carrying a black passenger. Packard, *American Nightmare*, 89–90; Simon, "Race Reactions," 245–46.

45. I am drawing in large part here on photographs that show African Americans in these "whites only" spaces. See, for example, Gordon Parks's photograph of a black domestic worker in a white waiting room in Mobile in 1956 (http://lens .blogs.nytimes.com/2012/07/16/a-different-approach-to-civil-rights-images/) and Jack Moebes's photograph of a black man working behind the Greensboro lunch counter during the lunch counter sit-ins in 1960 (http://www.smithsonianmag .com/arts-culture/Courage-at-the-Greensboro-Lunch-Counter.html). According to an observer from 1956, "As every traveler knows, Negroes have been conspicuous for their absence in railroad trains, offices, and yards—except for waiters and porters in dining, parlor, and sleeping cars." Cited in Arnesen, *Brotherhoods of Color*, 4.

46. Joel Williamson, for example, identifies an earlier moment—the 1830s— when many white Southerners played up an image of the South as a harmonious place of masters as paternalists and slaves as content "sambos." Those accounts sought to justify and explain slavery in the face of counterevidence of black discontent expressed in the Nat Turner rebellion and the claims of abolitionists. Williamson, *The Crucible of Race*, 24–35.

47. Scholars have long debated whether new laws or long-standing racial customs formed the foundation of Jim Crow. C. Vann Woodward in *The Strange Career of Jim Crow* and *The Origins of the New South* made a case for the legal argument. Others have pointed to the black codes of the postemancipation era, which banned blacks from serving on juries, called for segregated schools, and allowed for the arrest of African Americans not working on plantations, as precedents for later legal measures. The postemancipation years though were uncertain, if violent, ones, and many of these black codes were overturned during Reconstruction. If Jim Crow drew on customs and the law, it also represented something new as racial lines hardened. For key texts on the origins of segregation and the development of Jim Crow, see Woodward, *The Strange Career of Jim Crow*; Woodward, *Origins of the New South*; Rabinowitz, "More Than the Woodward Thesis"; Wade, *Slavery in the Cities*; Williamson, *After Slavery*; Rabinowitz, *Race Relations in the Urban South*; Cell, *The Highest Stage of White Supremacy*; Ayers, *The Promise of the New South*; Glenda Elizabeth Gilmore, *Gender and Jim Crow*; Litwack, *Trouble in Mind*; and Hale, *Making Whiteness*. For a succinct discussion of these historiographical debates, see John David Smith, *When Did Southern Segregation Begin?*

48. Stetson Kennedy, *Jim Crow Guide*, 220–21.

49. Hunter, *To 'Joy My Freedom*, 108. White Southerners regularly referred to their relationships with their domestic workers as intimate ones. This idea of intimacy was uncommon in other regions. On the experiences of domestic workers in the homes of whites in the South, see Sharpless, *Cooking in Other Women's Kitchens*; and Clark-Lewis, *Living In, Living Out*. For domestic worker experiences outside the South, see Romero, *Maid in the U.S.A.*; and Hondagneu-Sotelo, *Doméstica*. For an overview of black women and labor in the South, see Jones, *Labor of Love*. For recollections of these experiences and relationships, see van Wormer, Jackson, and Sudduth, *The Maid Narratives*; and Childress, *Like One of the Family*.

50. See, for example, van Wormer, Jackson, and Sudduth, *The Maid Narratives*. In the 1930s, Hortense Powdermaker also documented white Mississippians expressing affection for the domestic workers and nurses who worked for them. Powdermaker, *After Freedom*, 31–32, 119.

51. For the extension of this mammy image into national culture, see McElya, *Clinging to Mammy*; Manring, *Slave in a Box*; and Wallace-Sanders, *Mammy*.

52. Stetson Kennedy, *Jim Crow Guide*, 218–20.

53. In a study of Claiborne County, Mississippi, historian Emilye Crosby similarly observes not only that some interracial interactions were defined by whites and by blacks in terms of kindness and friendship, but also that, because African Americans had virtually no economic or political power, they were especially dependent on white goodwill. Crosby, *A Little Taste of Freedom*, 35–36, 42.

54. Some white Southerners continued to make the case for expelling blacks. Fredrickson, *The Black Image in the White Mind*, 216–17.

55. Stetson Kennedy, *Jim Crow Guide*, 183.

56. Packard, *American Nightmare*, 100–106. Similar residential patterns developed in Los Angeles and other cities in the North and the West. Sánchez, *Becoming Mexican American*, 77; Sugrue, *Sweet Land of Liberty*, 202.

57. For a discussion of these roadway rules in mid-1930s Mississippi, see Powdermaker, *After Freedom*, 48–50. See also Seiler, "'So That We as a Race Might Have Something Authentic.'"

58. Ward interview.

59. Henry, *Aaron Henry*, 6. Despite the evidence of animosity between poor whites and African Americans, there is also evidence of much cultural interaction among these working-class populations in the South. See, for example, Daniel, *Lost Revolutions*.

60. Dollard, *Caste and Class in a Southern Town*, 75–79.

61. Cohn, *Where I Was Born and Raised*, 72–73. Conducting research in Mississippi during the same period, Hortense Powdermaker concluded that poor whites despised African Americans in part because they believed that white employers preferred black laborers. Powdermaker, *After Freedom*, 28–29.

62. Dollard, *Caste and Class in a Southern Town*, 7–8.

63. Leon Litwack notes that Jim Crow subordination affected "speech and body movements." We can also turn this around and ask how speech and movement defined subordination and, for whites, how their speech and movement defined privilege. Litwack, *Trouble in Mind*, 415.

64. Jane Dailey contends, regarding the emergence of Jim Crow in Virginia, that "the meaning of whiteness . . . lay mainly in the privileges accorded it. Strip whiteness of privilege and its meaning and boundaries became unclear." I am suggesting that those privileges emerged in part from the ways blacks and whites moved and waited. Dailey, *Before Jim Crow*, 149.

65. Spillers, "Mama's Baby, Papa's Maybe," 66.

66. Litwack, *Trouble in Mind*, 233.

67. Hall interview.

68. The racial identity of the sales clerk is unclear in Hall's account.

69. Love interview.

70. Hanchard, "Afro-Modernity," 263–64.

71. Gates interview.

72. Charles S. Johnson, *Patterns of Negro Segregation*, 47.

73. Parker interview.

74. Similarly, Elizabeth Abel references Cleveland Sellers's concern over language in references to whites sitting on a bus from the *front* and blacks from the *rear*. The term "rear" suggested a location and bodily designation different from the term "back." Abel, *Signs of the Times*, 128.

75. Grace Hale notes that, given the racial dynamics in general stores in the South, many African Americans turned to ordering products by mail as a way to move their consumption practices beyond local white control. Hale, *Making Whiteness*, 179. See also Ownby, *American Dreams in Mississippi*.

76. Ward interview.

77. Stetson Kennedy, *Jim Crow Guide*, 224–25.

78. Litwack, *Trouble in Mind*, 233. On Jim Crow shopping experiences of African Americans, see Hale, *Making Whiteness*, 179–97. For a description of these practices in Mississippi, see Ownby, *American Dreams in Mississippi*, 154.

79. Gates interview.

80. Here too a notion of time is being imposed on ideas about cleanliness and hygiene, with African Americans constructed not only as unclean but as temporally behind cleaner, more civilized, whites.

81. On how physical characteristics shaped the African American experience in Jim Crow theaters, see Abel, *Signs of the Times*, 117–48. Accordingly, theaters catering only to a black audience could become spaces for promoting racial pride and community. See Baldwin, *Chicago's New Negroes*, 91–120.

82. Dailey, *Before Jim Crow*, 108.

83. Ibid., 128–29. Sociologist Bertram Wilbur Doyle also observed that interactions between blacks and whites after emancipation were characterized by a sense of uncertainty. In this case and in others, it was in part the racial uncertainty that led to violence. W. Fitzhugh Brundage notes that in this regard some individuals conceived of segregation as an alternative to violence. Doyle, *The Etiquette of Race Relations in the South*, 109–35; Brundage, *Lynching in the New South*, 155.

84. Blackwell, *Barefootin'*, 33.

85. Franzetta W. Sanders interview.

86. This notion of movement does not necessarily contradict Spillers's conceptualization of a "powerful stillness." Rather, the racial positioning of African Americans could be demonstrated in lack of movement or in disruptive movements, both of which can be understood as counter to the flowing, undisturbed movements of white bodies.

87. Parker interview.

88. Many black Mississippians recalled that one of their earliest memories of racial difference was in walking to school and being passed by white children on a bus, who sometimes engaged in name-calling or threw things from the bus. One individual remembered a bus driver who sometimes swerved toward black children walking along the side of the road. See, for example, Robinson interview; Johnson interview; Scularkinterview; Leach interview; Scott interview; Giles interview; and Mathews interview. See also Ritterhouse, *Growing Up Jim Crow*, 172.

89. Leon Litwack notes that whites forced blacks to drink alcohol or to fight each other for the amusement of white spectators. Litwack, *Trouble in Mind*, 10.

90. Gooden interview.

91. Leach interview.

92. There is also evidence of this "entertainment" role in the early Jim Crow years in other parts of the South. In a study of race relations in the South at the turn of the century, journalist Ray Stannard Baker observed that whites did not like the "New Negro" but instead preferred black people to be "jolly and joking." Ray Stannard Baker, *Following the Color Line*, 46.

93. Cohn, *Where I Was Born and Raised*, 360.

94. Bryan Wagner argues that in the period after slavery and into the twentieth century, black culture and the police power were linked, with blackness being "imperceptible except for the presumed danger it pose[d] to public welfare." In this case, the depiction of Cohn's Moss as a wandering black man often in trouble with the law might suggest that he was dangerous. For Cohn, though, that threat was offset by his eagerness to entertain whites with his harmonica. Wagner, *Disturbing the Peace*, 7, 34.

95. Cohn, *Where I Was Born and Raised*, 363–64.

96. Baker interview.

97. Hudson, *Mississippi Harmony*, 21–22.

98. Meier and Rudwick, "The Boycott Movement against Jim Crow Streetcars in the South," 756–59. See also Blair L. M. Kelley, *Right to Ride*.

99. Stetson Kennedy, *Jim Crow Guide*, 181–84.

100. Historian Glenda Elizabeth Gilmore describes a similar incident involving Pauli Murray and her friend Adelene McBean in 1940 in Virginia. On a bus trip through Virginia, initially the only seat available in the "colored" section was over the wheel well. With their luggage in tow, they had little room and the seat was uncomfortable, Murray saw that in the white section many of the passengers were spread out, and she asked some of them to move forward and consolidate so she could have a more comfortable seat. The white passengers refused. At the next stop, a major shift in passengers allowed Murray and McBean to move to seats

with more room. This seat, however, was broken, so they moved to an empty row directly behind the farthest-back white passengers. The driver tried to maintain an empty row between these sections and asked them to move. They refused, the police came, and eventually they were arrested. Glenda Elizabeth Gilmore, *Defying Dixie*, 318–19.

101. Smith interview.

102. Barbour and Barbour interview.

103. Baker interview.

104. "Negro Students Boycott Bus Line," *Wilkamite Record*, November 29, 1946; "Mayor Leland Speed Says Best Relations between White and Negro Citizens Will Be Maintained in Jackson," *Jackson Advocate*, November 30, 1946.

105. Litwack, *Trouble in Mind*, 169.

106. Charles S. Johnson, *Patterns of Negro Segregation*, 143.

107. Stetson Kennedy, *Jim Crow Guide*, 219–20.

108. Sharpless, *Cooking in Other Women's Kitchens*, 142.

109. The relationship between white employers and nonwhite domestic workers in regions outside the South often reflected racial hierarchies and even included some elements of benevolence. For example, in Los Angeles, white employers sometimes offered used clothing, as well as maternal advice, to Latina domestic workers. Still, the notion that the domestic worker was "like family" was especially characteristic of the South. In fact, many of the black domestic workers who migrated from the South to Washington, D.C., in the first half of the twentieth century noted the different relationship in their new city and also expressed a strong desire to move from a "master-slave relationship" to an "employer-employee relationship." Hondagneu-Sotelo, *Doméstica*, 172; Clark-Lewis, *Living In, Living Out*, 5. On domestic service among Latinas, see Romero, *Maid in the U.S.A.* On domestic service involving Japanese migrants, see Glenn, *Issei, Nisei, War Bride*. For a firsthand account from a former black domestic worker, see Childress, *Like One of the Family*. On domestic service, see also Dill, *Across the Boundaries of Race and Class*; Rollins, *Between Women*; and Katzman, *Seven Days a Week*.

110. Van Wormer, Jackson, and Sudduth, *The Maid Narratives*, 15.

111. Bynum interview.

112. H. J. Williams interview.

113. Sharpless, *Cooking in Other Women's Kitchens*, xiv.

114. Jones, *Labor of Love*, 199–200.

115. E. Patrick Johnson, *Appropriating Blackness*, 108.

116. Austin interview.

117. Genovese, *Roll, Jordan, Roll*, 621.

118. Scott, *Domination and the Arts of Resistance*, 18–19.

119. Robin D. G. Kelley, for example, has situated the daily skirmishes on Birmingham buses in the 1940s within this framework. Robin D. G. Kelley, *Race Rebels*, 55–76.

120. Dailey, *Before Jim Crow*, 149.

121. Ayers, *The Promise of the New South*, 137–44.

122. Meier and Rudwick, "The Boycott Movement against Jim Crow Streetcars in the South," 758–59. See also McMillen, *Dark Journey*, 293–95.

123. Ray Stannard Baker, *Following the Color Line*, 31–35.

124. "Flora Soldier Arrested in Sun. Incident Here," *Jackson Advocate*, November 20, 1943.

125. These tensions were not limited to the South. A number of incidents of police brutality directed at black veterans and black men in uniform occurred during the World War II era in New York City. Biondi, *To Stand and Fight*, 60–78.

126. Jennifer Brooks notes that both black veterans and white veterans in Georgia returned from the war with a strong belief that they should be more involved in political life. Brooks, *Defining the Peace*, 5.

127. A 1943 article, for example, suggested that a black man in uniform symbolized a person who did not know his racial "place." "The Negro: His Future in America," *New Republic*, October 18, 1943, 541–45, cited in Bates, *Pullman Porters*, 183.

128. Robin D. G. Kelley, *Race Rebels*, 65. Similarly, John Dittmer has noted the strong presence of black veterans in the civil rights movement in Mississippi. Dittmer, *Local People*, 1–18.

129. On the Eleanor Clubs, see Tyler, "Blood on Your Hands."

130. Odum, *Race and Rumors of Race*, xxviii.

131. As James Sparrow contends, the desire for federal funding led many Southern political leaders, including South Carolina senator Strom Thurmond, to overlook that these spaces would be integrated ones. Sparrow, "A Nation in Motion."

132. Ward, *Defending White Democracy*, 41–42.

133. Hale, *Making Whiteness*, 225.

134. Dahmer interview.

135. On city buses in Birmingham, Alabama, for example, Robin D. G. Kelley found 176 reports and complaints related to interracial conflicts in 1941 and 1942, including 51 episodes in which blacks intentionally sat in the white section or refused to give up their seats to a white person. From those incidents, Kelley characterizes the Birmingham buses as "moving theaters" in which other African American passengers were an audience witnessing acts of resistance. Robin D. G. Kelley, *Race Rebels*, 57–59. Derek Catsam notes that the 1940s witnessed numerous challenges in interstate travel. Catsam, *Freedom's Mainline*, 13–46.

136. "Soldier Badly Beaten, Fined $25 for Criticizing Jim Crow Bus Here," *Jackson Advocate*, March 9, 1946.

137. Robin D. G. Kelley, *Race Rebels*, 57.

138. This incident led to a boycott, and eventually the driver was fired.

139. Peoples interview.

140. As several interviewees note, white people were much less likely to enforce Jim Crow customs if they were at even strength or outnumbered by African Americans.

141. Fairley, Phillips, and Phillips interview.

142. Johnson, *Patterns of Segregation*, 128.

CHAPTER 2

1. Marvin Carraway, Police Report on "Fatal Shooting of Orville Bailey," May 10, 1959, SCRID# 2-9-0-127-1-1-1, MSSCR; "Man Shot, Officers Slay Assailant," *Clarksdale Press Register*, May 11, 1959; "Clarksdale Negro Who Killed Man Is Slain," *Greenville Delta Democrat Times*, May 11, 1959; "Two Negroes Are Killed by Law Officers in Miss. Over Weekend," *Jackson Advocate*, May 16, 1959.

2. The following day the newspaper included Elnora's claim that the police shot her. "Man Shot, Officers Slay Assailant."

3. "Clarksdale Negro Who Killed Man Is Slain."

4. "Sharecropper Slays White Farmer," *Chicago Defender*, May 12, 1959.

5. "Clarksdale NAACP Urged FBI to Investigate Slaying of Negro," *Jackson Advocate*, May 23, 1959.

6. Ibid.

7. "Two Negroes Are Killed by Law Officers in Miss. Over Weekend."

8. "First Complaints Are Filed with 'Rights' Group Here," *Jackson Clarion-Ledger*, March 14, 1960.

9. Myrlie Evers remarks that for her, a map of Mississippi was "a reminder not of geography but of atrocities" and that she remembers "the years by the names of the victims." For 1959, she remembered Causey and Mack Charles Parker, who was lynched near Poplarville, after being accused of raping a white woman. Evers, *For Us, the Living*, 204.

10. The term "violence" is a weighted one, often implying negative connotations or connected to the adjectives "legitimate" or "illegitimate." I am less concerned with an objective definition of violence than with how whites and blacks defined violence on their own terms, and thus in this chapter I generally use the term "aggression" to refer to these acts. For more on definitions and theories of violence, see Galtung, "Cultural Violence"; James, *Resisting State Violence*; Wolff, "On Violence"; and Gordon, *Her Majesty's Other Children*.

11. See Williamson, *The Crucible of Race*, 111–23; and Fredrickson, *The Black Image in the White Mind*, 256–84. The black male rapist myth continued into the twentieth century. See Dorr, *White Women, Rape, and the Power of Race*. These narratives and the accompanying violence served to control not only black behavior but also the behavior of white women. Versions of this narrative around rape and the fear of rape proliferated throughout the Jim Crow era. Hall, *Revolt against Chivalry*, 150–51. Similarly, as Nancy MacLean observes, stories about sexual assault also served to obscure transgressive sexual behavior of white women. MacLean, "The Leo Frank Case Reconsidered."

12. As Amy Wood notes, "Stories of black crime and moral dereliction dominated southern newspapers, which further fueled racial fears." Jacquelyn Dowd Hall observes that even as newspaper editorials condemned lynchings, news stories in the same publications fostered hatred and encouraged a violent response. Wood,

Lynching and Spectacle, 6; Hall, *Revolt against Chivalry*, 220. See also Ayers, *The Promise of the New South*, 153, 155.

13. Muhammad, *The Condemnation of Blackness*, 5.

14. Interest in Jim Crow practices outside the South has coincided with interest in the black freedom struggle beyond regional boundaries. See Theoharis and Woodard, *Freedom North*; Sugrue, *Sweet Land of Liberty*; Countryman, *Up South*; and Biondi, *To Stand and Fight*.

15. As historian Mia Bay notes, Ida B. Wells was the first antilynching advocate to gain a large audience. Bay, *To Tell the Truth Freely*, 6.

16. As she explained in an 1892 editorial, "Nobody in this section of the country believes the old threadbare lie that Negro men rape white women." Wells-Barnett, *The Red Record*, 12.

17. Included in these alternative narratives are the findings of antilynching investigators Arthur Raper and Jessie Daniel Ames. On the role of Raper and Ames within the context of racial reform, see Kimberley Johnson, *Reforming Jim Crow*, 43–65. For a biography of Ames, see Hall, *Revolt against Chivalry*. For a biography of Raper, see Mazzari, *Southern Modernist*.

18. Muhammad, *The Condemnation of Blackness*, 9–10.

19. Ibid., 78. DuBois, however, sometimes used a "bourgeois-tinged rhetoric" in describing poor blacks and linking them to crime. Gaines, *Uplifting the Race*, 164–65.

20. See John W. Roberts, *From Trickster to Badman*.

21. Adam Gussow theorizes that even violence within the black community was a response to the lynching spectacle, and that black individuals sometimes attacked another black man when they really wanted to attack the white world. Gussow, *Seems Like Murder Here*, 4, 6.

22. Statistics provided by the archives at the Tuskegee Institute, available at http://law2.umkc.edu/faculty/projects/ftrials/shipp/lynchingyear.html (accessed June 5, 2011).

23. Payne, *I've Got the Light of Freedom*, 19, 28. Neil McMillen notes that in Mississippi by the 1930s, lynchings had become primarily "a rural–small town phenomenon." McMillen, *Dark Journey*, 230. The literature on lynching is vast. For two works that chart changes in lynching over time, see Wood, *Lynching and Spectacle*; and Brundage, *Lynching in the New South*.

24. Most Southerners and most Americans experienced lynchings and other episodes of racial violence secondhand in the retelling of stories shared in the community and through newspaper coverage and postcards. Grace Hale argues that the initial racialized narrative of lynching took shape in the 1890s, first through pamphlets detailing the main event and then through newspaper coverage, which similarly adopted a standardized and sensationalized format. Hale, *Making Whiteness*, 206.

25. While a few whites were also lynched during this period, it nonetheless quickly became a racially specific practice that delivered to black audiences a message of far-reaching white power. In addition, in the late nineteenth century, unlike the lynchings of African Americans, white victims were rarely lynched in

front of a large crowd, and, according to David Garland, there is no evidence of white victims being tortured or burned. Stephen Kantrowitz observes that in South Carolina white political elites publicly adopted a "carrot and stick" argument, claiming that blacks in their actions had a choice between white paternalism (the carrot) and violence (the stick). In reality, he argues, the advocates of white supremacy turned to violence whenever it was politically expedient. Garland, "Penal Excess and Surplus Meaning," 804; Kantrowitz, "One Man's Mob Is Another Man's Militia," 67–87.

26. One of the more vocal white Southerners to speak out against lynching was William J. Northen, a former governor of Georgia. Godshalk, "William J. Northen's Public and Personal Struggles against Lynching."

27. Ayers, *Vengeance and Justice*, 250–55.

28. Ray Stannard Baker, *Following the Color Line*, 199.

29. Illustrating the staying power of this narrative, in the late 1930s Hortense Powdermaker conducted a survey in Mississippi, which showed that 64 percent of whites believed that lynching was justifiable in cases of rape. Powdermaker, *After Freedom*, 389.

30. On the film's relationship to lynching, see Wood, *Lynching and Spectacle*, 147–77.

31. A much larger percentage in fact was tied to an accusation of homicide. Statistics provided by the archives at the Tuskegee Institute, available at http://law2 .umkc.edu/faculty/projects/ftrials/shipp/lynchingyear.html (accessed June 5, 2011).

32. Grace Hale argues that newspapers played a central role in framing the narrative of the Sam Hose lynching, to "civilize" the mob and to portray the lynching as upholding white civilization. Hale, *Making Whiteness*, 209–15. See also Brundage, *Lynching in the New South*, 82–84; Litwack, *Trouble in Mind*, 280–87; and Dray, *At the Hands of Persons Unknown*, 4–13.

33. Hale, *Making Whiteness*, 211.

34. Jacquelyn Dowd Hall notes, regarding the work of antilynching advocate Jessie Daniel Ames in the 1930s, that within the context of lynching, rape and rumors about rape constituted "a kind of acceptable folk pornography in the Bible Belt." In a similar vein, another researcher from the 1930s, Arthur Raper, observed the importance of the story—an exaggerated one—in fueling calls for a lynching. The details became exaggerated and in turn excited the mob. As Raper explained, "After a time, the various stories of the crime take on a sort of uniformity, the most horrible details of each version having been woven into a supposedly true account." Hall, *Revolt against Chivalry*, 150–51; Raper, *The Tragedy of Lynching*, 44.

35. See Dan T. Carter, *Scottsboro*.

36. Hale, *Making Whiteness*, 225. Kimberley Johnson notes that reformers interested in moderate changes also played a role in reframing lynchings not as acts tied to white womanhood and white supremacy but as examples of bad government and social disorder. Kimberley Johnson, *Reforming Jim Crow*, 45.

37. Cox, "The South and Mass Culture," 681. For a fuller discussion of this national imagining of the South, see Cox, *Dreaming of Dixie*. For other discussions of national popular culture constructions of the South, see McPherson,

Reconstructing Dixie; Duck, *The Nation's Region*; and Barker and McKee, *American Cinema and the Southern Imaginary*.

38. One of those consistencies across time was the narrative link between a lynching and a black criminal act. As W. Fitzhugh Brundage observes, "Even while the practice of lynching changed significantly, whites clung to the notion that lynchings were the predictable consequence of black crime, particularly sexual assaults." Brundage, *Lynching in the New South*, 53.

39. These details are based on an investigation by Jessie Daniel Ames, "Lynching at Oxford, Lafayette County, Miss., September 17, 1935," box 1, folder 7, Jessie Daniel Ames Papers, SHC.

40. Ibid.

41. Ibid.

42. As middle- and upper-class whites blamed poor whites, other rifts related to race also emerged within the white community. Kari Frederickson, for example, argues that the effects of the New Deal in the 1930s—providing assistance to working-class whites—fostered class tensions along economic lines. After two decades of New Deal benefits, working-class whites were less willing to turn against the federal government, as many segregationist leaders advocated. Perhaps related to the narratives of violence that placed the blame on poor whites, J. Wayne Flynt notes that in the 1930s much of the literature about the South—from William Faulkner, James Agee, and Erskine Caldwell—devoted attention to the degradation of poor whites. Frederickson, *The Dixiecrat Revolt*; Flynt, *Dixie's Forgotten People*, 75–78.

43. The two men were accused of robbing a white man and white woman. "Two Negroes Lynched by Mississippi Mob," *New York Times*, September 11, 1930.

44. "Dangerous," *Meridian Star*, May 4, 1930.

45. The Norfolk newspaper often took a liberal position on racial issues, including opposing Virginia segregationists' "Massive Resistance" strategy following the *Brown* decision in 1954. "Murder Parading as Justice," *Norfolk Pilot*, September 12, 1930; "Another Lynching Outrage," *New Orleans Times-Picayune*, September 12, 1930. On the *Norfolk Pilot* editor, see Leidholdt, *Standing before the Shouting Mob*.

46. On the political manifestations of this class-tinged rivalry between the Delta and the Hills, see Key, *Southern Politics in State and Nation*, 229–53; and Grantham, *The Life and Death of the Solid South*, 32–33.

47. David Oshinsky notes that Cohn and other intellectual elites in Greenville, including Walker Percy and Hodding Carter, characterized lynchings as "low-class affairs." Hortense Powdermaker, whose research was on Indianola in the Delta, also noted that poor whites resented blacks and the white elite and that poor whites were responsible for lynchings. Oshinsky, *Worse Than Slavery*, 102; Powdermaker, *After Freedom*, 20.

48. "Governor Hits Lynching of Two Negroes," *Jackson Clarion-Ledger*, October 13, 1942.

49. "The Bitter Fruit," *Meridian Star*, October 13, 1942.

50. "This Is a Crisis," *Laurel Leader-Call*, October 19, 1942.

51. "State Demands Prosecution of Jones County Mob Leaders," *Jackson Clarion-Ledger*, October 20, 1942.

52. Christopher Waldrep contends that the federal investigations of lynchings in the 1940s—after federal officials previously refused to intervene—were part of an expansion of a national administrative state, a recognition of certain national rights that federal authorities were constitutionally obligated to protect. Within the context of Jim Crow, federal intervention and the beliefs supporting intervention were an indication of a changing relationship between the federal government and the South. Waldrep, "National Policing, Lynching, and Constitutional Change."

53. Ibid.

54. "J. C. Sanford Shot Fatally," *Jackson Daily News*, January 2, 1940; "Deputy Dead, Two Shot by Negro Couple," *Jackson Daily News*, January 3, 1940; "'Guilty as Charged'—Negroes Sentenced to Hang Feb. 23rd," *Prentiss Headlight*, July 18, 1940.

55. "Hilton Fortenberry Pays with Life for Recent Crime," *Jackson Clarion-Ledger*, October 11, 1940.

56. A number of white people in Prentiss were angry with the governor because he had commuted James Franklin's sentence to life in prison. "Another Insult to the People by the Man in the Governor's Office," *Prentiss Headlight*, October 17, 1940; "Hilton Fortenberry Pays with Life for Recent Crime."

57. "Hilton Fortenberry Pays Supreme Penalty," *Prentiss Headlight*, October 17, 1942.

58. "Hilton Fortenberry Pays with Life for Recent Crime."

59. Unlike lynchings, executions were not a racially exclusive practice. Capital punishment, was, however, racially disproportionate. African Americans were far more likely to be executed, and more likely to be given a death sentence on lighter charges (such as robbery) than white defendants. Two of these 104 individuals were black females, sixteen were white males, one was listed as a Native American male, and one individual's identity was unknown. Statistics provided by Rob Gallagher from M. Watt Espy and John Ortiz Smykla, *Executions in the United States, 1608–1987: The ESPY FILE*, available at http://web.archive.org/web/20090326095005/http://users.bestweb.net/~rg/execution.htm (accessed May 31, 2012). These patterns persisted across the South. For example, of those executed in the South between 1870 and 1950 for the charge of rape, 701 of 771 executed were black; for the charge of robbery, 31 of 35 were black; and for the charge of burglary, 18 of 21 were black. Banner, *The Death Penalty*, 230. On the relationship between race and the death penalty in Jim Crow Mississippi, see Oshinsky, *Worse Than Slavery*, 206–9.

60. These two practices coexisted as functions of a Jim Crow State, and, as Ethan Blue observes regarding Texas in the 1930s, when lynching violence decreased, it was replaced by incarceration and legal execution. Blue, "A Dark Cloud Will Go Over," 11. See also Garland, "Penal Excess and Surplus Meaning," 793–833; Senechal de la Roche, "The Sociogenesis of Lynching," 75; and George C. Wright, *Racial Violence in Kentucky*.

61. George C. Wright, "By the Book," 251.

62. The performance and the recorded narratives of executions have a long history. In the seventeenth century, the publication of the last words of the

condemned and the sermon delivered at the event—a message to the assembled audience—followed the execution. Into the nineteenth century, public executions continued as highly performative affairs, with expectations for the roles played by the condemned, the officials, and the audience. From the 1830s to the 1930s, as executions moved indoors and beyond public view, newspapers assumed a primary role in being the eyes and ears of the public. These narratives continued to emphasize the central elements of the ritual—the condemned's behavior, the last words, and a vivid account of the details of the death. Masur, *Rites of Execution*, 93–116. See also Banner, *The Death Penalty*, 158–64; Linebaugh, *The London Hanged*; and Philip Smith, "Executing Executions." For an example of the performative elements of a slave execution, see Olwell, *Masters, Slaves, and Subjects*, 96–99. For a discussion of concerns about the condemned refusing to play their expected role, see Philip Smith, "Executing Executions." For the performative aspects of lynching, see Wood, *Lynching and Spectacle*, 62, 67; Garland, "Penal Excess and Surplus Meaning," 807–9; and Wiegman, *American Anatomies*, 81–114.

63. "Admits Slaying before Dying," *Meridian Star*, May 16, 1941.

64. Every other state that used the electric chair housed it in a single state prison. Banner, *The Death Penalty*, 193.

65. Ibid., 169–207.

66. "Admits Slaying before Dying." On Jimmy Thompson, see Oshinsky, *Worse Than Slavery*, 205–8.

67. Outside the South, concerns that public hangings were barbarous led many states to replace public executions with private ones as early as the 1830s. Related to similar concerns, in the late nineteenth century, many states moved away from public hangings to methods of death that seemed less painful and thus more modern and civilized. Toward this end, states shifted from hanging to electrocution to the gas chamber, and, much later, to lethal injection. These shifts came later in Southern states. See Banner, *The Death Penalty*, 112–207.

68. Hale, *Making Whiteness*, 203–4. On photographs and souvenirs at lynchings, see Allen, Als, Lewis, and Litwack, *Without Sanctuary*.

69. "Admits Slaying before Dying."

70. "Green Electrocuted Early Friday Morning," *Port Gibson Reveille*, June 26, 1941.

71. "Negro Man Electrocuted This A.M., Sam Porter Pays Extreme Penalty in Electric Chair," *McComb Enterprise*, January 7, 1943.

72. For example, in the 1898 lynching of Sam Hose, newspapers emphasized the orderliness of the mob. Hale, *Making Whiteness*, 212.

73. "Two Sentenced to Death on Armed Robbery Charge," *Jackson Advocate*, March 16, 1946.

74. Ultimately the governor decided against the execution of Augustine and White.

75. Jo Drake Arrington to Governor Fielding Wright, May 7, 1947, Sentence and Execution Files, 1948–52, Governors' Papers, MDAH.

76. Maurice B. Gatlin to Governor Fielding Wright, April 17, 1947, Sentence and Execution Files, 1948–52, Governors' Papers, MDAH.

77. "14- and 15-Year-Old Boys Sentenced to Death for Murder of Farmer," *Jackson Advocate*, March 23, 1946.

78. Mrs. Frances Tann Diamond to Governor Fielding Wright, November 27, 1946, Sentence and Execution Files, 1948–52, Governors' Papers, MDAH.

79. D. A. Spence to Governor Fielding Wright, December 29, 1946, Sentence and Execution Files, 1948–52, Governors' Papers, MDAH.

80. T. Price Dale to Governor Fielding Wright, January 6, 1947, Sentence and Execution Files, 1948–52, Governors' Papers, MDAH.

81. In December 1946, Governor Wright, perhaps in response to the letters and extensive national and international publicity, issued a stay of execution to allow time to review the case. He then received a telegram from a judge in Wilkinson County where the incident occurred, informing him that locals were upset with the governor's decision. The governor replied to the judge that the stay was only for him to review the record and that he fully expected to agree with the decision rendered by the jury. He also, however, commented on the "tender age" of these boys and explained that "even though they be colored," he wanted to have all the facts. Trudell and Lewis were executed in July 1947. Governor Fielding Wright to John T. Netterville, December 13, 1946, Sentence and Execution Files, 1948–52, Governors' Papers, MDAH.

82. Throughout the Jim Crow South, black individuals who had white support could get a lighter sentence, and pardons were more likely if the victim was black. Litwack, *Trouble in Mind*, 254–56, 265–70.

83. Oshinsky, *Worse Than Slavery*, 124–33.

84. Ibid., 128.

85. Dollard, *Caste and Class in a Southern Town*, 269. Hortense Powdermaker linked the higher crime rate among black Mississippians to white paternalism, noting that middle- and upper-class whites saw blacks as children, and thus within the law were more indulgent. Powdermaker, *After Freedom*, 172–74.

86. Cohn, *Where I Was Born and Raised*, 104.

87. Within the black community, however, a number of individuals expressed concern over the official neglect of crime in their community, including T. R. M. Howard. Beito and Beito, "T. R. M. Howard," 80.

88. The letter writing was part of a much larger national trend toward greater public involvement in the clemency process. Nationally, for much of the eighteenth century, most of the requests for clemency came from prominent individuals or a small group of local leaders. By midcentury, however, ordinary citizens were submitting petitions, often signed by hundreds or thousands. Banner, *The Death Penalty*, 162–68.

89. For early release at Parchman Farm, an inmate needed the support of the camp sergeant and the superintendent. The inmate would then need a published petition in a local community. At that point, local citizens and especially officials within the legal arena, such as sheriffs, attorneys, and judges, submitted letters to the governor favoring or opposing the request. On how letters in the clemency process worked in Mississippi, see Oshinsky, *Worse Than Slavery*, 179–204.

90. These conceptualizations had a long history rooted in the period of enslavement and with no direct connection to crime. During slavery, "bad

Negro" referred to enslaved individuals who challenged white authority. The "bad Negro" was a risk to run away and to disobey the master and, in disrespecting whites, served as a negative example to other enslaved individuals. In its most extreme form—encapsulated in figures such as Nat Turner, Gabriel Prosser, and Charles Deslondes—the "bad Negro" evoked fears of slave rebellions. What made these slaves "bad" was that, through their insubordination, they threatened to undermine the paternalistic master/slave relationship and more generally the basis of the system of labor control. As Eugene D. Genovese illustrates, enslaved people also used variations on this term, but with two entirely different meanings. For enslaved individuals, "bad nigger" referred to slaves who did harm to other blacks. Meanwhile, the term "ba-ad Nigger" (with emphasis on the pronunciation) was a positive reference to other slaves who "gave the white man hell." Litwack, *Been in the Storm So Long*, 154, 105; Genovese, *Roll, Jordan, Roll*, 625–26, 436–37. See also John W. Roberts, *From Trickster to Badman*, 177. On the uses of the term "bad nigger" by whites and by blacks, see Litwack, *Trouble in Mind*, 437–39.

91. M. L. Aldridge to Governor M. S. Connor, April 15, 1935, Pardon and Suspension Files, 1940–43, Governors' Papers, MDAH. The superintendent oversaw operations, and to "win an early release, an inmate had to have the backing of his camp sergeant and the Parchman superintendent." Oshinsky, *Worse Than Slavery*, 180.

92. W. H. White to Governor Paul B. Johnson, March 6, 1941, Pardon and Suspension Files, 1940–43, Governors' Papers, MDAH.

93. Dorothy Whitaker to Governor Fielding Wright, July 18, 1949, Sentence and Execution Files, 1948–52, Governors' Papers, MDAH.

94. Carl H. Everett to Walter Bullock, June 13, 1952, Penitentiary Papers, 1952–56, Governors' Papers, MDAH.

95. Report from Bill Harpole, December 10, 1956, Pardons, 1960–64, Governors' Papers, MDAH.

96. Report from S. B. Harrington, n.d., Pardons, 1960–64, Governors' Papers, MDAH.

97. Report on Lucious Evans, n.d., Pardons, 1960–64, Governors' Papers, MDAH.

98. Ibid. The board ruled in favor of Evans, and he was paroled. Report from Bill Harpole, October 12, 1956, Pardons, 1960–64, Governors' Papers, MDAH.

99. Jack Dickey to the Pardon and Parole Board, April 10, 1943, Executions, 1944–46, Governors' Papers, MDAH.

100. Citizens of Yazoo County to Governor Paul B. Johnson, August 23, 1940, Governors' Papers, MDAH; Citizens of Covington County to Governor Paul B. Johnson, n.d., Executions, 1944–46, Governors' Papers, MDAH.

101. W. U. Corley to Governor Paul B. Johnson, December 19, 1940, Executions, 1944–46, Governors' Papers, MDAH.

102. As Lisa Dorr contends, when whites showed mercy to African Americans, it could also reassure them that they were just and that Jim Crow was just. Dorr, *White Women, Rape, and the Power of Race*, 10.

103. Daisy R. Cochran to Governor Fielding Wright, November 26, 1946, Sentence and Execution Files, 1948–52, Governors' Papers, MDAH.

104. Another example is the children's rhyme "Ten Little Niggers," in which the black children are killed off one-by-one. *Ethnic Notions*, directed by Marlon T. Riggs (1986, San Francisco, Calif.: California Newsreel, 2004), DVD.

105. Cohn, *Where I Was Born and Raised*, 277–79. Similarly, South Carolina native W. J. Cash, in his critique of white paternalism, *The Mind of the South*, referenced a black man named Cuffey who would come to town on Saturday night and "swagger along the street in guffawing gangs which somehow managed to take up the whole breadth of the sidewalk, often to flash razors and pistols." Cash, *The Mind of the South*, 227.

106. William R. Newman Jr. to Governor Sennett Conner, February 12, 1935, Pardon and Suspension Files, 1940–43, Governors' Papers, MDAH.

107. Joe A. McFarland Jr. to Governor Fielding Wright, May 10, 1949, Sentence and Execution Files, 1948–52, Governors' Papers, MDAH.

108. African Americans also shared stories about survival, resistance, and trickery. Litwack, *Trouble in Mind*, 43–46.

109. See, for example, H. Williams interview; and Ruby Williams interview.

110. Bays interview.

111. Bowie interview.

112. Weston interview.

113. Leach interview; Love interview; Weston interview.

114. Blackwell, *Barefootin'*, 19–20.

115. Johnson interview.

116. Fleming interview.

117. See Litwack, *Trouble in Mind*, 34–46; and Berrey, "Resistance Begins at Home." For more on children in the Jim Crow South learning about race, see Ritterhouse, *Growing Up Jim Crow*; and DuRocher, *Raising Racists*.

118. Trudier Harris, *Exorcising Blackness*, 70, 94. Related to literary themes, Houston A. Baker Jr. argues that a "blues matrix" emerged from how African American cultural producers have negotiated an "economics of slavery" to "achieve a resonant, improvisational, expressive dignity." One could argue that a similar process is at work in the stories that African Americans told about violence, that these stories also had a function beyond the sharing of information. Houston A. Baker, *Blues, Ideology, and Afro-American Literature*, 4, 14.

119. Gussow is seeking in part to explain the presence of violence between African Americans within blues lyrics. Author emphasis. Gussow, *Seems Like Murder Here*, 15–16. Another example of communities talking about violence comes from lynching ballads. See Bruce E. Baker, "North Carolina Lynching Ballads," 219–20.

120. Bryan Wagner has also noted that African Americans often told their own narratives about aggression. In 1900, in New Orleans, after African American Robert Charles shot and killed a white police officer, setting off a race riot, blacks remembered the excessive violence perpetrated by the police and by the mob. Wagner, *Disturbing the Peace*, 45–49. On the black response to the Robert Charles incident, see Litwack, *Trouble in Mind*, 404–10.

121. In stories African Americans told about lynching, Amy Wood notes that African Americans portrayed white attackers as unholy and savage. Wood, *Lynching and Spectacle*, 46.

122. McMillen, *Dark Journey*, 225–26.

123. Each resulted in a violent response from whites. For the Tulsa race riot, see Ellsworth, *Death in a Promised Land*. For details on the conflict in Elaine and other incidents of armed resistance in Arkansas, see Woodruff, *American Congo*.

124. Tensions during World War II, as Howard Odum documented at the time, also produced many rumors of an aggressive black response, especially among veterans. Odum, *Race and Rumors of Race*.

125. Robin D. G. Kelley, *Race Rebels*, 65.

126. See O'Brien, *The Color of the Law*.

127. Charles Payne alludes to this tradition in 1960s Mississippi. Payne, *I've Got the Light of Freedom*. In addition, in 1946 a young veteran named Medgar Evers led a group of other veterans to the Decatur courthouse to register to vote, where they were met by a group of armed white men. The black veterans left and returned with their own guns before backing down. Dittmer, *Local People*, 1–2.

128. Lou Allen interview.

129. Frederick interview.

130. Love interview.

131. Lewis interview.

132. On the role of the "badman," a literary figure who outsmarted whites, see John W. Roberts, *From Trickster to Badman*, 171–220. On the literary figure "Stagolee," another version of the badman, see Levine, *Black Culture, Black Consciousness*, 414–15.

133. For example, in Mississippi, Laura McGhee kept a gun in the house, threatened a law enforcement official who came on her property, and even physically attacked a police officer. Payne, *I've Got the Light of Freedom*, 205, 208–18; Umoja, *We Will Shoot Back*, 100. Emilye Crosby also notes that the practice and ideology of self-defense had been an important part of the African American tradition in the state. Crosby, *A Little Taste of Freedom*, 169.

134. Ward interview.

135. Perhaps in this sense the code of silence that sometimes existed around sexual assault incidents played a role. For a fuller discussion of sexual assault and the code of silence within the black community, see McGuire, *At the Dark End of the Street*, 137, 346.

136. Collins, *Black Feminist Thought*, 46–52.

137. Litwack, *Trouble in Mind*, 343–47.

138. Estes argues that stretching from the black men's patriotic sacrifices during the World War II era to the civil rights and Black Power movements, ideas about manhood and militancy informed much of their activism and in some ways mirrored the manhood claims made by segregationists. Many black men, Estes notes, understood segregation as a challenge to their manhood, necessitating a masculine and aggressive response. Estes, *I Am a Man*, 8.

139. Jones interview.

140. Ibid.

141. Ibid.

142. Rosie Sanders interview.

143. Tommie Lee Williams Sr. interview.

144. Kornegay interview.

145. Franzetta W. Sanders interview.

146. Bailey interview.

147. "Three Holmes Men Dead, Two Seriously Injured by Negro Man Following Argument over Whiskey," *Lexington Advertiser*, January 14, 1954; "Jittery Shiners, Trigger-Happy Men Messed Up Holmes Manhunt," *Lexington Advertiser*, January 21, 1954; Hazel Brannon Smith, "Slayer of Three White Men Gives Up to Authorities Wednesday Night," *Lexington Advertiser*, January 28, 1954; "Eddie Noel Found Insane," *Lexington Advertiser*, May 27, 1954; Povall, *The Time of Eddie Noel*.

148. Smith was born in Alabama in 1914, and in 1935 she graduated from the University of Alabama with a degree in journalism. Soon after, she purchased a failing newspaper in Durant, Mississippi, and in 1943, she purchased the Lexington paper. She became more progressive on racial issues over time. Whalen, *Maverick among the Magnolias*. See also Whitt, *Burning Crosses and Activist Journalism*; Kaul, "Hazel Brannon Smith and the *Lexington Advertiser*"; and Weill, *In a Madhouse's Din*.

149. "Three Holmes Men Dead, Two Seriously Injured by Negro Man Following Argument over Whiskey." Many years later, in an article about the ordeal, Smith reiterated that the fight began after a black man "came into the store with bottles of whiskey sticking out of his pockets." Hazel Brannon Smith, "Separate but Unequal," n.d., www.aliciapatterson.org/APF0606/Brannon_Smith/Brannon_Smith .html (accessed January 18, 2005).

150. Julius E. Thompson, *The Black Press in Mississippi*, 26–30. The black newspaper with the largest circulation was the *Jackson Advocate*. It also played a key role in covering the shootings and, at least in 1954, had a reputation as a relatively progressive newspaper under Percy Greene.

151. "Noel Surrenders and Is Taken to Hinds Co. Jail," *Mississippi Enterprise*, January 29, 1954.

152. In 1946, in the small town of Pickens, a white man killed a black youth, Chenley Dennis, for no apparent reason. The shooter pretended to be drunk before pulling a gun on Dennis and shooting him in the back as he tried to escape. Three months after that incident, a white man, Jeff Dodd, accused African American Leon McTatie of stealing a horse saddle. McTatie was arrested but continued to proclaim his innocence. Dodd then took McTatie from the jail and, with several other men, beat him. Soon after, McTatie's dead body was found in the lake. Three men were charged with beating McTatie to death, and even though they admitted to the beating (but not the death), the jury acquitted them. Authorities later learned that McTatie had not stolen the saddle. In 1954, Sheriff Richard F. Byrd shot African American Harry Randle in the back, and Byrd justified his actions by arguing that Randle had yelled in the direction of the sheriff's car. "Killing of Youth at Pickens Called Most Cold Blooded Murder in Town's History," *Jackson Advocate*, April 27,

1946; "Five White Men Jailed for Murder of Holmes Negro Will Get Preliminary Hearing in Lexington Friday," *Lexington Advertiser*, August 1, 1946; Cobb, *The Most Southern Place on Earth*, 213; Murray Kempton, "What Have They Got to Live For?" *New York Post*, November 16, 1955.

153. Letter, *Lexington Advertiser*, January 14, 1954; Povall, *The Time of Eddie Noel*, 89.

154. These diverse reactions to the incident may have stemmed from feelings about Dickard's alleged relationship with Lu Ethel. It may also have been related to the knowledge that Eddie Noel was likely descended from a prominent "white" family in the state, which included former governor Edmund Noel, who served from 1908 to 1912. This last point was suggested to me by an individual who grew up near Lexington in the 1950s. To whatever extent influential whites were involved, however, it is clear from interviews and press coverage that Eddie Noel was considered "black" by both the black and the white communities.

155. "Jittery Shiners."

156. "Noel Surrenders, Trial Set First Monday in April," *Jackson Advocate*, February 6, 1954.

157. "Noel Surrenders and Is Taken to Hinds Co. Jail."

158. See John W. Roberts, *From Trickster to Badman*, 171–220.

159. "Bloodhounds, Armed Men Join Delta Man Hunt When Unidentified Negro Is Alleged Assaulter of Three White Men," *Jackson Advocate*, January 20, 1945.

160. "Eddie Noel Found Insane," *Lexington Advertiser*, May 27, 1954. Hazel Brannon Smith's coverage of this case led the Mississippi legislature to pass legislation requiring military officials to notify families of any mental health issues concerning a discharged soldier.

161. "Negro Veteran Slayer of Three," *Jackson Advocate*, January 16, 1954. Perhaps it is coincidental, but adjacent to that article is a photograph of a local African American army private stationed in Germany. The private is in uniform and holding a rifle.

162. Frederick interview.

163. Johnson also referred to the white posse as "a Ku Klux Klan mob." Youth of the Rural Organizing and Cultural Center, *Minds Stayed on Freedom*, 154–56.

164. Clayborn, Davis, and Davis interview.

165. Regarding the oral narrative, Richard Bauman notes that folktales are learned from multiple sources and produce "median versions" that throughout the process "maintain their thematic similarities." With the Eddie Noel stories, even forty years later, the theme of a black man outsmarting hundreds of whites persisted. Bauman, *Folklore, Cultural Performances, and Popular Entertainments*, 108–9.

CHAPTER 3

1. For an account of the confession told to journalist William Huie, see Roberts and Klibanoff, *The Race Beat*, 101–6. The scholarship on Emmett Till's death is voluminous. See especially Whitfield, *A Death in the Delta*; Till-Mobley and Benson,

Death of Innocence; Metress, *The Lynching of Emmett Till*; Feldstein, "I Wanted the Whole World to See"; and Houck and Grindy, *Emmett Till and the Mississippi Press*.

2. Scholars studying surveillance generally focus on "vision," which refers to the processes of watching, and/or "visibility," which refers to how those being watched are seen and how they respond. For an introduction to the field of surveillance studies, see Lyon, *Surveillance Studies*. See also Giddens, *The Nation-State and Violence*. For Michel Foucault's discussion of panoptic surveillance, see Foucault, *Discipline and Punish*, 195–229; and Mathiesen, "The Viewer Society."

3. The roots of Jim Crow surveillance can be found in practices from the slavery period, including those of masters, overseers, and slave patrols monitoring slave workers and the passes enslaved people needed to travel, which represented a form of bureaucratic surveillance. For an overview of surveillance in the slavery era, see Parenti, *The Soft Cage*, 13–42. See also Hadden, *Slave Patrols*. For the role of informants among enslaved individuals, see Genovese, *Roll, Jordan, Roll*, 19, 365–88.

4. Litwack, *Trouble in Mind*, 214–16.

5. Wiegman, *American Anatomies*, 13. The concept of panoptic surveillance was popularized by Michel Foucault and was likened to a prison panopticon, in which cells are arranged in a circle around a guard tower, from which a guard is potentially always watching any particular person. Foucault, *Discipline and Punish*, 201, 208.

6. On the pervasiveness of racial violence in Mississippi in the 1940s and 1950s, see Dittmer, *Local People*, 1–40; and Payne, *I've Got the Light of Freedom*, 7–66.

7. I am thinking here of Stuart Hall's contention that hegemony is hard work. Cited in Lipsitz, "The Struggle for Hegemony," 146.

8. Ray Stannard Baker, *Following the Color Line*, 28–35. For racial tensions and protests related to streetcars during this period, see Meier and Rudwick, "The Boycott Movement against Jim Crow Streetcars in the South"; and Blair L. M. Kelley, *Right to Ride*.

9. Robin D. G. Kelley, *Race Rebels*, 57. Other discussions of race relations in daily interactions, such as Bertram Wilbur Doyle's exploration of etiquette, also implicitly include an element of surveillance. Doyle, for example, defined racial etiquette as a behavior that was "expected and accepted," implying a watchfulness from those in a position to convey acceptance. Doyle, *The Etiquette of Race Relations in the South*, 1–11. See also Stetson Kennedy, *Jim Crow Guide*, 204–5. In addition, the rumors of black rebellion spread by white Southerners during World War II can be understood as products of a system in which white people at the local level were expected to be ever watchful for signs of impertinence from African Americans. On these rumors, see Odum, *Race and Rumors of Race*.

10. Abel, *Signs of the Times*, 265, 253.

11. Bodroghkozy, *Equal Time*, 4. These dynamics also influenced how the civil rights movement has been remembered nationally. See Morgan, "The Good, the Bad, and the Forgotten."

12. See Bodroghkozy, *Equal Time*; and Torres, *Black, White, and in Color*.

13. Dittmer, *Local People*, 65. On the relationship between television and civil rights in Mississippi, see Classen, *Watching Jim Crow*; and Mills, *Changing Channels*.

14. Woodward, *The Strange Career of Jim Crow*, 107.

15. On the link between surveillance and the spectacle lynching, see Wiegman, *American Anatomies*. See also Wood, *Lynching and Spectacle*. Much of the work on lynching has focused on spectacle lynchings, which were more characteristic of the earlier period.

16. As African Americans migrated to the North and the West, they encountered other forms of surveillance. In these regions, surveillance was often a product of blacks and whites inhabiting separate neighborhoods and urban spaces. In this system, to surveil the black population often meant that those watching had to cross borders into unfamiliar and predominantly black spaces, such as a black section of town. In the Progressive era, for example, white reformers in New York went "undercover" and visited black-owned clubs, looking for evidence of race mixing. A few years later, as federal and military officials worried about the loyalty of blacks during World War I, both the Bureau of Investigations and the Military Bureau of Investigations monitored editorials in the black press. In each of these cases, the surveillance meant that whites had to move into black spaces and eavesdrop on black conversations. While these forms of watching involved going into black spaces, others focused on keeping blacks out of white areas. Restrictive covenants in real estate contracts, for example, could stipulate that a property could not be sold to a black buyer. These practices transformed sellers, neighbors, and real estate agents into the guardians of racial lines. In this case, these individuals, backed by a legal document, watched white areas to keep blacks out. Fronc, *New York Undercover*; Ellis, *Race, War, and Surveillance*. For examples of racially restrictive covenants in areas outside the South, see Sugrue, *The Origins of the Urban Crisis*; Satter, *Family Properties*; and Sánchez, "What's Good for Boyle Heights Is Good for the Jews."

17. More than 1,100 African Americans were lynched across the South in the 1890s; in the 1930s, 123 African Americans were lynched. Statistics provided by the archives at the Tuskegee Institute, available at http://law2.umkc.edu/faculty/projects/ftrials/shipp/lynchingyear.html (accessed June 5, 2011). Brundage, *Lynching in the New South*, 28–29; Payne, *I've Got the Light of Freedom*, 19, 28.

18. Hale, *Making Whiteness*, 225.

19. For a discussion of Ames's antilynching work, see Hall, *Revolt against Chivalry*.

20. "Resume Lynching, Louisville, Mississippi," n.d., box 1, folder 4, Jessie Daniel Ames Papers, SHC.

21. "Mississippi, Louisville Lynching," n.d., box 1, folder 4, Jessie Daniel Ames Papers, SHC.

22. In many cases, the willingness of a white law enforcement official to intervene was often pivotal in whether or not a lynching was prevented. Griffin, Clark, and Sandberg, "Narrative and Event," 30.

23. "No Criticism Deserved," *Bolivar Democrat*, May 12, 1930, folder 811, Arthur Raper Papers, SHC; Griffin, Clark, and Sandberg, "Narrative and Event," 31–32.

24. Similarly localized systems may have existed in other parts of the South. In a study of Hancock County in rural Georgia, Mark Schultz notes that personal and face-to-face interactions were a key feature in local race relations. Schultz, *The Rural Face of White Supremacy*.

25. Dollard, *Caste and Class in a Southern Town*, 359.

26. Unita Blackwell worked with the Student Nonviolent Coordinating Committee to register black voters, and in 1964 at the Democratic National Convention in Atlantic City she served as a delegate for the Mississippi Freedom Democratic Party, a group that challenged the legitimacy of the Democratic Party's appointed delegates based on voter discrimination. Blackwell later became the first black woman to be elected mayor in the state. See her autobiography, Blackwell, *Barefootin'*.

27. Blackwell interview.

28. Blackwell, *Barefootin'*. 34.

29. Aaron Henry's activism began in 1946 when, after returning home from serving in World War II, he registered to vote. Henry later served as president of the Mississippi NAACP, organized boycotts, and, like Blackwell, was a Mississippi Freedom Democratic Party delegate in 1964. Payne, *I've Got the Light*, 56–66; Dittmer, *Local People*, 75, 120–21. On Henry's life, see his autobiography, *Aaron Henry*.

30. Henry, *Aaron Henry*, 28.

31. Until very recently, most of the scholarly and popular discussions of sexual assault in the segregated South referred to *white* women and were linked to lynching—that is, the frequency with which the charge of rape or attempted rape of a white woman served as the justification for a lynching (just over 25 percent of the time). One possible reason for this discrepancy relates to sources. Lynching was an intentionally public event that generated large crowds, media attention, and, ultimately, massive national publicity. Sexual assaults, however, tended to be carried out in privates spaces, often concealed from white wives, from the media, and from a larger public. The historical record for lynching then is much more voluminous than it is for rape. Another reason for the scholarly discrepancies between lynching and rape relates to how these acts are coded. Lynching is bound up with race, understood almost exclusively as a racial act and primarily as a Southern event throughout most of the Jim Crow era. It is difficult to imagine a Jim Crow study neglecting to mention lynching. Rape on the other hand does not connote racial or regional specificity. And thus even when evidence of sexual assault against black women appears in the historical record, its centrality to the black Southern experience is often overlooked. A recent exception is the work of historian Danielle McGuire, who positions the rape of black women at the center of the civil rights movement narrative. McGuire, *At the Dark End of the Street*. On sexual assault and its relationship to white women and black men, see Dorr, *White Women, Rape, and the Power of Race*.

32. Danielle McGuire has found that many black women were quite open in discussing acts of sexual assault by white men. Many of them spoke out publicly and even in some cases—especially during the civil rights era—testified to being sexually assaulted by a white man. At the same time, it is safe to assume that for all those who spoke out and who challenged the system in court, thousands more—indeed

an unknown number—kept quiet. The reasons for their silences could range from a sense of shame to hopelessness that a white man would ever be convicted to fear that an accused attacker might retaliate. At the same time, black women also could draw on a long history of sharing accounts of being sexually exploited. McGuire, *At the Dark End of the Street*, xviii–xx. From her interviews with former black domestic workers, Elizabeth Clark-Lewis also observes that young black women in the rural South had to be especially careful around white men. Clark-Lewis, *Living In, Living Out*, 48–49. See also van Wormer, Jackson, and Sudduth, *The Maid Narratives*, 181–84.

33. Hudson, *Mississippi Harmony*, 21.

34. Holland, *From the Mississippi Delta*, 90.

35. Ibid.

36. In some respects, these interactions between white men and black women can be likened to what Saidiya Hartman referred to during the period of enslavement as "dancing for the master." Entertaining the slave owner represented one of the ways in which the hierarchical relations of domination were maintained. Hartman, *Scenes of Subjection*, 42.

37. Holland, *From the Mississippi Delta*, 90.

38. Important exceptions would include the presence of black informants or, in the case of black schools, white superintendents and school board members. Even still, these observations were generally not firsthand observations in the fashion of the daily face-to-face interactions. See Brundage, "The Roar on the Other Side of Silence." On beauty shops as sites of resistance, see Gill, *Beauty Shop Politics*.

39. See Crespino, "Mississippi as Metaphor"; and Griffin, "Southern Distinctiveness, Yet Again."

40. Abel, *Signs of the Times*, 253, 265.

41. Fleming, *Soon We Will Not Cry*, 113. On the role of clothing in the civil rights movement, see Ford, "SNCC Women, Denim, and the Politics of Dress."

42. Martin A. Berger contends that the media emphasis on capturing white violence left blacks in the role of passive victims, obscuring their agency and bravery. While there is much validity to that claim—especially in recognizing that the focus on peaceful protesters obscured more radical black voices in the movement—there is little question that civil rights activists took advantage of this framing. Renee Romano makes a related point regarding the public memory of the 1963 Birmingham church bombing that emphasizes white heroes and black victims. Berger, *Seeing through Race*, 19; Romano, "Narratives of Redemption," 102–5.

43. See, for example, Torres, *Black, White, and in Color*; Abel, *Signs of the Times*; Bodroghkozy, *Equal Time*; Martin A. Berger, *Seeing through Race*; McCarthy, *The Citizen Machine*; Maurice Berger, *For All the World to See*; Raiford, *Imprisoned in a Luminous Glare*; and Kasher, *The Civil Rights Movement*.

44. Hale, *Making Whiteness*, xi. On national reunification, tied especially to how the Civil War was remembered, see Blight, *Race and Reunion*.

45. Myrdal, *The Negro Problem*, 48.

46. Cox, "The South and Mass Culture," 681.

47. In other ways, white Southerners played a direct role in these depictions. For example, in the 1920s and 1930s, white Southerners were responsible for numerous successful Broadway productions that portrayed nonthreatening blacks in the South. Glenda Elizabeth Gilmore, *Defying Dixie*, 26–28.

48. As James Cobb notes, by the 1950s and 1960s, the media had long been depicting the white South as especially savage. Cobb, *Away Down South*, 198.

49. One of those moments was in 1931, when nine African American teenagers were falsely charged and convicted of raping two white women in Alabama. On national perceptions of Southern culture and the Southern past in the 1930s and 1940s, see Hale, *Making Whiteness*, 85–120; McPherson, *Reconstructing Dixie*, 39–94; and Cox, *Dreaming of Dixie*. On the Scottsboro case, see Dan T. Carter, *Scottsboro*.

50. Matthew Lassiter and Joseph Crespino argue that the idea of a South that was racially exceptional was a myth that allowed the nation to preserve a story of racial innocence. Lassiter and Crespino, "Introduction."

51. In some cases, a growing federal defense industry in the South quietly disrupted traditional Jim Crow employment practices. See Sparrow, "A Nation in Motion." Although Cold War politics could at times work to the advantage of civil rights activists, it nonetheless had a debilitating effect on some civil rights organizations in the post–World War II era. For example, through the rhetoric and politics of anticommunism, civil rights groups in the United States, which during the World War II years had strengthened ties to anticolonial movements in Asia and Africa, were forced to break those connections during the Cold War years. Thus, when a mass movement emerged in the late 1950s and early 1960s, national civil rights groups couched their protests within a domestic milieu instead of attaching the movement to anticolonial struggles throughout the African diaspora. Von Eschen, *Race against Empire*. On connections between communists and Southern radicals, see Glenda Elizabeth Gilmore, *Defying Dixie*; and Robin D. G. Kelley, *Hammer and Hoe*. On the impact of Cold War pressures, see Dudziak, *Cold War Civil Rights*; and Plummer, *Rising Wind*.

52. Lassiter and Crespino, "Introduction," 3–5.

53. In the World War II years, as Jason Morgan Ward contends, a segregationist movement began to emerge in response to looming threats. See Ward, *Defending White Democracy*.

54. That interest included the 1942 lynchings of Charlie Lang and Ernest Green. Payne, *I've Got the Light of Freedom*, 13–19. A report within Arthur Raper's papers on his investigation of this lynching also indicates that as a direct result of the negative publicity, local whites agreed that in the future such efforts should be handled more secretly and by a smaller group of men. "Lynching and Murder in Canton, Mississippi, 1938, 1939," folder 1062, Arthur F. Raper Papers, SHC.

55. "Another Negro Is Jailed in Assault Case Investigation," *Laurel Leader-Call*, November 4, 1945. It is unclear if McGee had assaulted Hawkins, the white woman. Both McGee and Hawkins were married. McGee claimed that they were in a consensual relationship, and around Laurel rumors spread that the two of them were

having an affair. Hawkins later testified that she did not scream when McGee entered her room because she was lying next to a sleeping child. For more on the case, see Zaim, "Trial by Ordeal"; and Heard, *The Eyes of Willie McGee*.

56. "Negro to Pay with Life Is Court Edict," *Laurel Leader-Call*, December 7, 1945.

57. "Federal Judge Hears Plea to Stay McGee's Execution," *Jackson Daily News*, May 7, 1951.

58. The Civil Rights Congress had formed in 1946 to call international attention to racial violence in the United States, including producing the United Nations petition "We Charge Genocide," which held the U.S. government responsible for lynchings and continuing racial discrimination. On the Civil Rights Congress and its involvement in the case, see Horne, *Communist Front?*

59. "Giant Rally Hears Wife of Willie McGee," *Jackson Advocate*, July 15, 1950.

60. Dittmer, *Local People*, 21–22.

61. W. C. Shoemaker, "Switch Was Pulled and the Generator Struggled, Then the Throng Quieted," *Jackson Daily News*, May 8, 1951.

62. By way of contrast, officials had a much different reaction to court cases targeting segregation in Southern schools. As court cases challenging school inequality mounted in the early 1950s, a number of Mississippi officials embraced proposals to increase funding for black schools and to build new facilities in the hope of getting closer to meeting the "separate-but-equal" measure. Despite these efforts, as of 1962, Mississippi was spending $21.77 per black student compared to $81.86 per white student. Dittmer, *Local People*, 35–36; Bolton, *The Hardest Deal of All*, 87.

63. As Sasha Torres notes, reporters from across the nation came to Mississippi and covered the trial, initiating a new beat for journalists around civil rights and race coverage. Torres, *Black, White, and in Color*, 26. On the impact of journalists coming to the South to cover the trial, see Roberts and Klibanoff, *The Race Beat*, 86–87.

64. On the preparation of Till's casket, on how it ended up in Chicago, and on Mamie Till Bradley's decision to have an open casket—all of which served to graphically illustrate the violence African Americans in Mississippi faced, see Suzanne E. Smith, *To Serve the Living*, 124–28. For a gendered analysis of the role of Mamie Till Bradley in events after her son's death and its relationship to constructions of motherhood, see Feldstein, "I Wanted the Whole World to See."

65. Maurice Berger, *For All the World to See*, 98–110.

66. Abel, *Signs of the Times*, 265.

67. Martin A. Berger argues that the media's focus on violence shifted the focus "away from historically rooted inequities in public accommodation, voting rights, housing policies, and labor practices." Berger, *Seeing through Race*, 47.

68. Houck and Grindy, *Emmett Till and the Mississippi Press*.

69. Stephen Whitfield notes that initially both the governor and the local press expressed support for a conviction. Whitfield, *A Death in the Delta*, 25–26.

70. "Mississippi Hard Hit by the Slaying of Till," *Jackson Advocate*, September 10, 1955.

71. Houck and Grindy, *Emmett Till and the Mississippi Press*, 20–22.

72. "A Just Appraisal," *Greenwood Commonwealth*, September 2, 1955. Houck and Grindy, in *Emmett Till and the Mississippi Press*, imply that Roy Wilkins is partially or even equally to blame for the acquittals based on his critique. That point is less compelling, given that it is tied primarily to counterfactual evidence, including projecting a different outcome if Wilkins had not issued his denouncement of the state.

73. Houck and Grindy, *Emmett Till and the Mississippi Press*, 26–30; "Indict Two for Murder in Till Slaying as Doubts Arise over Identity of Victim's Body," *Jackson Advocate*, September 10, 1955.

74. Segregationists were especially sensitive to the NAACP leader's remarks in part because the NAACP had stepped up school integration efforts in the state in the summer of 1955. NAACP school petitions were circulating in several communities. Thus, at the moment that a national NAACP official condemned the state, segregationists had identified the organization as the primary threat to segregation (with the U.S. Supreme Court and the press outside the South close behind). "School Board Files Petition from Local NAACP Unit," *Clarksdale Press Register*, August 12, 1955; "Letter to Board Is Signed by 53 Negroes," *Yazoo City Herald*, August 18, 1955; "Negro Says Name Forged to NAACP Petition," *Natchez Democrat*, July 24, 1955.

75. Some newspapers acknowledged that the two men were perhaps guilty but that the case had not been proven. Houck and Grindy, *Emmett Till and the Mississippi Press*, 107–10.

76. "The Till Case in Retrospect," *Jackson Advocate*, November 26, 1955. The editorial was initially published in the *McComb Enterprise-Journal*, November 21, 1955.

77. "About Till's Father," *Jackson Daily News*, October 15, 1955.

78. Anders Walker, in focusing on changes instituted by Governor J. P. Coleman—including increasing the power of the state police—connects these centralizing efforts to the national response to the Till murder. While Coleman played an important role, I contend that his actions were part of a much larger movement in Mississippi and nationally toward centralization. Anders Walker, *The Ghost of Jim Crow*, 27–31. See also Anders Walker, "The Violent Bear It Away."

79. McMillen, *The Citizens' Council*, 16–19, 22, 27.

80. On the Hederman brothers and the Mississippi press in relation to the civil rights movement, see Dittmer, *Local People*, 64–67; and Roberts and Klibanoff, *The Race Beat*, 82–85. See also Davies, *The Press and Race*; and Weill, *In a Madhouse's Din*.

81. McMillen, *The Citizens' Council*, vii–viii, 22.

82. Ibid., 22–23.

83. James O. Eastland, "We've Reached Era of Judicial Tyranny," speech at the Citizens' Council Statewide Convention, December 1, 1955, reprinted as a pamphlet, box 1, folder 29, Citizens' Council/Civil Rights Collection, AMD-USM. Eastland was one of the most vocal segregationists in the state. On his life, see Asch, *The Senator and the Sharecropper*.

84. McMillen, *The Citizens' Council*, 209. Local chapters often relied on economic pressure to thwart integration efforts, including getting suspected activists
fired from their jobs or getting banks to deny them credit. Within the state, not
everyone believed the Citizens' Council rhetoric. Hodding Carter Jr., editor of the
Delta Democrat Times (Greenville, Miss.) and a racial moderate, referred to the
group as an "uptown Ku Klux Klan." Silver, *Mississippi*, 36.

85. While I am emphasizing the similarities in terms of racial practices and discourses of the Citizens' Council and the Mississippi State Sovereignty Commission,
relations between these two groups were often tense. The Citizens' Council had not
endorsed J. P. Coleman for governor, and after he won the election he distrusted
it and imagined the Sovereignty Commission as an agency that could balance the
Citizens' Council. Meanwhile, the Sovereignty Commission received little funding
under Coleman's administration, and throughout the agency's history a number
of state politicians questioned its purpose and its use of funds. On the relationship between these two groups and their relationship with state officials, see Irons,
Reconstituting Whiteness, 35–62. For a detailed history of the Sovereignty Commission, see Katagiri, *The Mississippi State Sovereignty Commission*. See also
Rowe-Sims, "The Mississippi State Sovereignty Commission."

86. The spying activities emerged in the late 1950s and then increased significantly under Ross Barnett's administration. Joseph Crespino situates the first
few years of the Sovereignty Commission within the more moderate "practical
segregation" approach of Governor J. P. Coleman. Crespino, *In Search of Another
Country*, 26.

87. Ibid., 26–27.

88. The FBI also had a number of civil rights activists under surveillance, including Fannie Lou Hamer. Outside of Mississippi, the police chief in Albany, Georgia,
also relied on surveillance, including putting police officers inside black churches
and obtaining inside information from African Americans. O'Reilly, *Racial Matters*,
1–3, 116. See also McKnight, *The Last Crusade*; and Garrow, *The FBI and Martin
Luther King, Jr.*

89. Smead, *Blood Justice*, 147–48; O'Reilly, *Racial Matters*, 179.

90. "Report to the Mississippi State Legislature on Activities of the State Sovereignty Commission," SCRID# 7-3-0-5-7-1-1, MSSCR; "Facts about Mississippi Sovereignty Commission," Associated Press Report, March 18, 1998.

91. Of these groups, relatively little is known about the surveillance of law
enforcement officials or the Citizens' Councils. There are few surviving records of
these activities, and many of these efforts were probably not documented at the
time. However, from the Sovereignty Commission records, one gets a very detailed
picture of its surveillance as well as an indication that these other groups were
actively involved in surveillance.

92. Tom Scarbrough, "Leflore County—Johnnie Barbour—Negro male; Lois
Ware—Negro female—tag #588-322 and tag #589-018," May 24, 1961, SCRID#
2-45-1-37-2-1-1, MSSCR; Albert Jones, "Check with Mr. Conwell Sykes," May 9,
1961, SCRID# 2-44-1-44-1-1-1, MSSCR; Tom Scarbrough, memo to "Members,
State Sovereignty Commission," June 5, 1961, SCRID# 7-4-0-7-1-1-1, MSSCR.

93. An earlier example of this type of bureaucratic surveillance was Walter Plecker's activities in Virginia. As the state's first registrar of vital statistics in the 1920s, Plecker attempted to get every citizen to report his or her racial status in order to monitor and limit interracial marriage. Pascoe, *What Comes Naturally*, 140–54.

94. Such was the case for William Higgs, who was followed from a civil rights meeting, and for Peter Stoner, who was continually harassed and arrested several times. Both are discussed in Chapter 4. "Higgs and Group Arrested, Threatened," *Mississippi Free Press*, June 30, 1962; Peter Stoner, "Report of SNCC Worker Pete Stoner on Experiences in Hattiesburg from January 7 to May 21, 1964," Peter Stoner Papers, AMD-USM.

95. As an indication of the Sovereignty Commission's interests, the agency kept files on both local individuals and prominent national figures, including Robert F. Williams, Martin Luther King Jr., Ella Baker, and Harry Belafonte.

96. Tom Scarbrough, "Rev. P. R. Watkins . . . ," September 26, 1960, SCRID #2-61-1-23-1-1-1 to 5-1-1, MSSCR; Scarbrough, "Washington County, Hayes Haynes, Negro Male," June 18, 1963, SCRID# 2-44-1-79-1-1-1, MSSCR; anonymous letter, December 22, 1957, SCRID# 1-0-0-16-1-1-1, MSSCR.

97. Tom Scarbrough, "NAACP activities, Sunflower, Bolivar, Coahoma, Tunica, DeSoto, and Tate Counties," August 10, 1960, SCRID# 2-61-1-19-1-1-1, MSSCR; "E. M. Gregory, Negro Minister, Bolivar County, Shaw, Mississippi," August 24, 1960, SCRID# 2-6-0-51-1-1-1 to 2-1-1, MSSCR.

98. "E. M. Gregory, Negro Minister."

99. "Negro Says Name Forged on Petition," *Natchez Democrat*, July 24, 1955.

100. Coleman's response was consistent with his stance on segregation when he became governor, as he continued to seek some compromises in the interest of preserving the system of segregation. See Walker, *The Ghost of Jim Crow*, 11–48; and Crespino, *In Search of Another Country*, 18–48.

101. "Citizens' Council Organized after Appeal from Brady," *Clarksdale Press Register*, August 17, 1955; "Unity or Integration, Says Brady at Rally," *Natchez Times*, August 5, 1955.

102. Citizens' Council advertisement, *Yazoo City Herald*, August 25, 1955.

103. Henry, *Aaron Henry*, 92.

104. "Negro Says Name Forged to NAACP Petition," *Natchez Democrat*, July 24, 1955; "Only 288 Names Now Remain on NAACP-Sponsored Petition," *Clarksdale Press Register*, August 18, 1955.

105. "School Board Files Petition from Local NAACP Unit," *Clarksdale Press Register*, August 12, 1955.

106. "Three More Negroes Ask School Board to Disregard Names," *Yazoo City Herald*, September 8, 1955; "Letter to Board Is Signed by 53 Negroes," *Yazoo City Herald*, August 18, 1955. On the petitions within the context of movement strategies of the NAACP in Mississippi, see Dittmer, *Local People*, 43–46, 50–52.

107. "Citizens' Council Organized after Appeal from Brady," *Clarksdale Press Register*, August 17, 1955; "Unity or Integration, Says Brady at Rally," *Natchez Times*, August 5, 1955; "Random Thoughts," *Yazoo City Herald*, September 22, 1955.

108. Ruby Hurley to Roy Wilkins, "Economic Pressure in Southeast Region," October 7, 1955, microfilm, Papers of the NAACP (Frederick, Md.: University Publications of America, 1990), film 17, 417, part 18, series C, reel 13.

109. Dittmer, *Local People*, 83–84. On the Mack Charles Parker lynching, see Smead, *Blood Justice*.

110. "Report to the Mississippi State Legislature on the Activities of the State Sovereignty Commission," December 3, 1959, SCRID# 7-3-0-5-7-1-1, MSSCR.

111. See also Katagiri, *The Mississippi State Sovereignty Commission*, 36–63; and Anders Walker, "The Violent Bear It Away," 485–92.

112. Blackwell, *Barefootin'*, 5.

113. Ruby Hurley to Roy Wilkins, "Economic Pressure in Southeast Region"; Zack J. Van Landingham, "Negro Anti-NAACP Organization," May 21, 1959, SCRID# 2-61-1-9-1-1-1, MSSCR; "Progressive Voters' League," August 25, 1959, SCRID# 2-61-1-10-1-1-1, MSSCR; Zack J. Van Landingham to Governor Ross J. Barnett, January 25, 1960, SCRID# 2-2-0-54-1-1-1, MSSCR.

114. After investigating the informant (checking criminal records and interviewing his acquaintances) and determining that he was, as one white official put it, "a white man's Negro," the agency agreed to allot the informant $100 per month for three months to explore the possibility of creating "a secret underground organization of Negroes." Zack Van Landingham to file 9-9, January 15, 1959, SCRID# 9-9-0-11-1-1-1, MSSCR.

115. Zack J. Van Landingham to Director, Sovereignty Commission, March 9, 1959, SCRID# 9-9-0-20-1-1-1, MSSCR; Katagiri, *The Mississippi State Sovereignty Commission*, 48–49.

116. "Diggs to See President about Delta Situation," *Mississippi Free Press*, April 4, 1963.

117. Carson, *The Eyes on the Prize Civil Rights Reader*, 178.

118. Zack J. Van Landingham, "NAACP, Shaw, Mississippi," October 13, 1959, SCRID# 2-6-0-42-1-1-1, MSSCR.

119. A. L. Hopkins, "NAACP Activities in Bolivar County, Miss.," July 11, 1960, SCRID# 2-6-0-45-1-1-1 to 5-1-1, MSSCR.

120. Charles E. Snodgrass, "Negro Meeting, Clarksdale, Mississippi," February 13, 1962, SCRID# 1-16-1-61-1-1-1 to 7-1-1, MSSCR.

121. Zack J. Van Landingham to file 9-17, December 4, 1959, SCRID# 9-17-0-16-1-1-1, MSSCR.

122. O'Reilly, *Racial Matters*, 179.

123. See ibid.

124. William J. Simmons of the Citizens' Council wanted to have King arrested, but the Jackson chief of police believed this would be played up in the national media. It was then decided that taping the meeting was a better option. Katagiri, *The Mississippi State Sovereignty Commission*, 51–53.

125. "Kickoff of Drive to Get Negroes to Vote Scheduled in Clarksdale Sunday Afternoon," *Clarksdale Press Register*, December 6, 1957.

126. Sheila Michaels, August 29 to September 28, 1962, diary, Sheila Michaels Papers, AMD-USM.

CHAPTER 4

1. Arsenault, *Freedom Rides*, 140–62. For more on the Freedom Riders in Mississippi, see Dittmer, *Local People*, 90–99. For two excellent accounts of the Freedom Rides from the perspective of the participants, see Farmer, *Lay Bare the Heart*, 195–223; and Forman, *The Making of Black Revolutionaries*.

2. Bob Pittman, "Ross Says Law Will Be Upheld," *Jackson Daily News*, May 25, 1961; Dittmer, *Local People*, 92–95.

3. "Citizens' Council Urges 'Let Authorities Handle,'" *Jackson Clarion-Ledger*, May 24, 1961; Bill Coppenbarger, "Mayor Says Law Will Prevail Here," *Jackson Daily News*, May 22, 1961; "Ross Promises Nonstop Rides," *Jackson Daily News*, May 22, 1961; Bob Pittman, "Ross Asks Public to Stay Calm," *Jackson Daily News*, May 24, 1961; "Police Waiting Probe of Fight to Make Charge," *Jackson Clarion-Ledger*, May 24, 1961.

4. "Freedom Rider Cases Appealed in Hinds County Court, General Criminal Docket, Book 8," box M337, folder 5, Albert F. Gordon Freedom Rider Collection, AMD-USM.

5. The death toll in the late 1950s and early 1960s included Emmett Till, George Lee, Lamar Smith, Tim Holman, Matthew Crawford, Clinton Melton, Charles Brown, Jessie Shelby, Ed Duckworth, Woodrow Wilson Daniels, Mack Charles Parker, Jonas Causey, William Roy Prather, Lover Stapleton, Herbert Lee, Eli Brumfield, Medgar Evers, James Chaney, Michael Schwerner, and Andrew Goodman. In terms of beatings, the *Worker*, an alternative newspaper published in New York, counted forty-three incidents of direct physical violence against black Mississippians from January 1961 through March 1963. "Mississippi Terror Traced to Officials, War on Negro Voters," *Worker*, April 21, 1963, copy of article in folder "CORE, 1962–1967," J. B. Matthews Papers, JHFHC.

6. Silver, *Mississippi*.

7. Dittmer, *Local People*, 19–40; Payne, *I've Got the Light of Freedom*, 29–66.

8. While Northern cities are often credited with having the first police forces in the nation, modeled on London's force, Rousey observes that similar forces emerged at least as early in Southern cities. Rousey, *Policing the Southern City*, 3. For a survey of the history of policing, prisons, and criminal justice in the United States, see Samuel Walker, *Popular Justice*. For other studies on policing in the Jim Crow era, see Carl V. Harris, "Reforms in Government Control of Negroes in Birmingham"; and Watts, "The Police in Atlanta."

9. Sally Hadden observes that the earliest organized law enforcement took the form of slave patrols targeting slaves, merging race and policing. Wagner, *Disturbing the Peace*, 60; Hadden, *Slave Patrols*, 4. On the relationship between the Ku Klux Klan and the police, see Dubber, *The Police Power*.

10. For an examination of the relationship between the police and lynching, see Griffin, Clark, and Sandberg, "Narrative and Event."

11. Anders Walker notes that Coleman also sought to institute new standards for local justices of the peace, many of whom had little training and charged exorbitant fees. As Walker contends, Coleman's efforts were important in centralizing authority at the state level. Anders Walker, *The Ghost of Jim Crow*, 27–28.

12. "Arrest Two Negroes at Railroad Station," *Jackson Clarion-Ledger*, January 29, 1956; "Jackson Has Sit-In Demonstrations," *Jackson Advocate*, April 1, 1961; "More 'Riders' Arraigned in County Court," *Jackson Clarion-Ledger*, September 7, 1961.

13. "Jackson Youths Parade Despite 'Illegal to Demonstrate' Injunction," *Mississippi Free Press*, June 15, 1963; Williams, *Medgar Evers*, 254.

14. Hine, Hine, and Harrold, *The African American Odyssey*, 512, 518. Arrests were also not an obvious reaction in Greensboro, North Carolina, to the four college students who attempted to integrate the Woolworth's lunch counter on February 1, 1960. A police officer was in the business, but because the students were not disruptive, he could not find a reason to arrest them. Goldfield, *Black, White, and Southern*, 119–20. On the Greensboro sit-ins, see Chafe, *Civilities and Civil Rights*.

15. Among the more extreme measures in the mid-1950s, Alabama outlawed the NAACP. Mississippi legislators considered a similar bill, but they ultimately decided against it. It is unclear why Mississippi officials did not ban the organization. John Dittmer speculates that legislators decided that it would be easier to track the group's activities in the state if it was operating in the open. Regardless, the decision not to ban the NAACP foreshadowed a less direct approach that would become more common in the legal measures passed near the end of the decade. This was not the only time states had tried to use a legal approach to respond to a court challenge to Jim Crow. In 1944, following the *Smith v. Allwright* decision, which disallowed the all-white primary, South Carolina responded by removing every law—130 of them—related to primaries. By taking the primary off the legal books, officials had hoped to transform the political party into a private club that would not have to follow the Supreme Court mandate. Sitkoff, *The Struggle for Black Equality*, 27; Dittmer, *Local People*, 450 n. 49; Simon, "Race Reactions." For a fuller description of the laws passed by various states during this period, see Bartley, *The Rise of Massive Resistance*, 67–81.

16. Walker, *The Ghost of Jim Crow*, 40. On state officials' response to desegregation in schools, see Bolton, *The Hardest Deal of All*.

17. Dittmer, *Local People*, 59; Bartley, *The Rise of Massive Resistance*, 55–56, 77–78.

18. Another legal option, nullification, represented a much stronger position that had not been invoked since the antebellum era. This legal argument rested on the assertion that state governments had the right to nullify any federal decision they deemed unconstitutional. Mississippi was one of seven states that had passed an interposition resolution by the end of 1956. Despite the attention these options received in 1956, by 1958 both had been abandoned by most politicians. See Bartley, *The Rise of Massive Resistance*, 126–40.

19. As George Lewis notes, a lack of analysis of the various strategies has often left us with a portrayal of segregationists "as monolithic, one-dimensional reactionaries possessing little guile and even less intelligence in their attempts to cling on to their segregationist way of life." Lewis, *Massive Resistance*, 4. On the origins of the term and strategy known as "Massive Resistance," see ibid., 1–5. On Southern politicians' responses to desegregation during this period, see also Wilhoit, *The Politics of*

Massive Resistance; Newby, *Challenge to the Court*; Black, *Southern Governors and Civil Rights*; Webb, *Massive Resistance*; and J. Douglas Smith, *Managing White Supremacy*.

20. A number of scholars have noted the passage of new laws, but often this activity is presented as an example of widespread defiance. Little attention, however, has been paid to what happened to those laws and to how they were or were not put into practice. For recent studies making the case for a complex segregationist response during these years, see Lassiter, *The Silent Majority*; Kruse, *White Flight*; Crespino, *In Search of Another Country*; Anders Walker, *The Ghost of Jim Crow*; Lassiter and Lewis, *The Moderates' Dilemma*; and Webb, *Massive Resistance*.

21. Klarman, *From Jim Crow to Civil Rights*, 60.

22. McMillen, *Dark Journey*, 9–10. Similarly, George Lipsitz notes that prior to the 1960s, laws had not been needed to enforce racial discrimination and to keep African Americans from voting. Even if an African American citizen attempted to vote, white registrars were in place to prevent that from happening. Lipsitz, *The Possessive Investment in Whiteness*, 214.

23. Risa Goluboff contends that before the *Brown* decision, the civil rights movement could have gone in any number of legal directions, such as focusing on labor concerns, but *Brown* pushed the movement toward school and public desegregation and left many other issues unchallenged. Goluboff, *The Lost Promise of Civil Rights*, 13. On the legal history of Jim Crow and on *Brown*, see Klarman, *From Jim Crow to Civil Rights*; and Kluger, *Simple Justice*.

24. In Mississippi, Governors Fielding Wright and Hugh L. White initially pursued a plan to bring funding for black schools closer to the level of funding for white schools. Dittmer, *Local People*, 36, 38. See Ward, *Defending White Democracy*, 135.

25. Regarding motivations for consumer boycotts during the civil rights era, Ted Ownby contends that African Americans "saw shopping as a potentially democratic experience" and that they sought "pleasure and dignity in the experience." Similar desires to be full-fledged consumers may also have informed other protests. Ownby, *American Dreams in Mississippi*, 154.

26. "Arrest Two Negroes at Railroad Station." For a firsthand account of the leading role of the Women's Political Council in initiating a boycott, see Robinson, *The Montgomery Bus Boycott*.

27. Regarding the lunch counter sit-ins in Greensboro, North Carolina, in 1960, David Goldfield also noted that both the appearance and the behavior of the protesters challenged Jim Crow–related notions "of what blacks ought to look and behave like." Goldfield, *Black, White, and Southern*, 122.

28. "Arrest Two Negroes at Railroad Station."

29. Laws of the State of Mississippi, 1956 (chaps. 258, 259).

30. Ibid. (chap. 260).

31. However, this is not the "breach of peace" law that would be used in the early 1960s against the Freedom Riders and other activists. A revised law was passed in 1960. Ibid. (chap. 256).

32. Ibid. (chap. 257).

33. Ibid. (chaps. 239, 241, 253–61, 265, 273, 288, 365, 443, 466, 475).

34. Anders Walkers suggests that even as some Southern politicians compromised, it was still important to them to convey to voters that they had done everything in their power to preserve segregation. Anders Walker, *The Ghost of Jim Crow*, 126.

35. "Says He Won't Test Mix Law," *Jackson State Times*, November 16, 1958.

36. Hal C. DeCell to Governor J. P. Coleman, August 18, 1958, SCRID# 1-20-0-1-1-1-1, MSSCR.

37. Charles Dunagin, "Race Law Violator Is Freed," *Jackson State Times*, August 17, 1958; "Says He Won't Test Mix Law."

38. "Says He Won't Test Mix Law."

39. Laws against interracial marriage existed in every region of the country. Policing these cases, though, often proved difficult in part because the law depended on precise definitions of race and on whether, for example, an individual was at least 1/16th "Negro." On interracial marriage, see Pascoe, *What Comes Naturally*; Randall Kennedy, *Interracial Intimacies*; Moran, *Interracial Intimacy*; and Greg Carter, *The United States of United Races*. For an example from Mississippi of the complications of determining one's legal racial definition in a miscegenation case, see Bynum, " 'White Negroes' in Segregated Mississippi."

40. "New Segregation Law Struck Down," *Jackson Clarion-Ledger*, December 16, 1958.

41. This claim was made by the grandson of an attorney involved in the case. See https://sites.google.com/site/jessewshankssrabiography/home (accessed June 15, 2013). See also "Court to Hear Woman's Appeal," *Jackson Daily News*, November 17, 1958.

42. "Cohabitation Statute Called Unconstitutional," *Jackson Daily News*, November 24, 1958.

43. "Man Serving Prison Term for Unlawful Cohabitation with White Woman Freed by Judge," *Laurel Leader Call*, December 17, 1958.

44. Laws of the State of Mississippi, 1956 (chap. 239).

45. Walker, *The Ghost of Jim Crow*, 41–42, 175 n. 150.

46. Laws of the State of Mississippi, 1958 (chap. 651).

47. Ibid. (chaps. 311, 194).

48. Douglas Starr, "House Passes New Segregation Bill," *Jackson Clarion-Ledger*, February 17, 1956; John Herbers, "Mississippi Prepares New Subversive List," *Jackson Clarion-Ledger*, December 18, 1955.

49. For more on the investigative work of the agency, see Irons, *Reconstituting Whiteness*. For an overview of the agency's history, see Katagiri, *The Mississippi State Sovereignty Commission*.

50. Tom Scarbrough, "Rev. P. R. Watkins . . . Bolivar County . . . Negro Baptist," September 26, 1960, SCRID# 2-61-1-23-1-1-1 to 5-1-1, MSSCR.

51. Ibid. It is not clear what the next step would have been if Watkins had not left town.

52. The belief by many whites that African Americans preferred segregation persisted throughout the Jim Crow era. The protests of the civil rights era thus had the potential to undermine those beliefs. See Sokol, *There Goes My Everything*, 56–113.

53. Tom Scarbrough, "Carroll County & Opal Anderson, a colored female [. . .]," April 20, 1961, SCRID# 2-104-0-14-1-1-1 to 3-1-1, MSSCR.

54. See, for example, Dittmer, *Local People*, 79–83; Oshinsky, *Worse Than Slavery*, 231–33; Henry, *Aaron Henry*, 135–36; Evers, *For Us, the Living*, 214–25; and Katagiri, *The Mississippi State Sovereignty Commission*, 55–61.

55. In agreeing to speak with Kennard, several local black leaders presented the agency with a list of demands, which included opening a junior college for African Americans in the area. These individuals met with Kennard but were unable to persuade him to withdraw his application. Walker, *The Ghost of Jim Crow*, 34–35.

56. Zack J. Van Landingham, "M. C. Parker; Civil Rights—Violence," May 4, 1959, SCRID# 5-3-1-19-1-1-1, MSSCR.

57. Zack J. Van Landingham to Governor J. P. Coleman, September 21, 1959, SCRID# 1-27-0-40-1-1-1 to 6-1-1, MSSCR.

58. Ibid. Van Landingham remarked to Governor Coleman that the officers claimed that Kennard had left his car unlocked and that they found the whiskey in it while they were waiting for Kennard to return. Van Landingham checked with campus security officials, who had watched Kennard park and then lock his car. Thus, the agent and the security guard knew that the officers were lying, although neither made this information public.

59. Another moment in which segregationists in the state disagreed about how to respond to a civil rights event involved NAACP head Roy Wilkins visiting Jackson in 1958. A Citizens' Council member obtained a warrant to have Wilkins and Medgar Evers arrested. It took the attorney general, Joe Patterson, and the Sovereignty Commission's Zack Van Landingham to convince the head of the local chapter that the arrest would create bad publicity for the state. Walker, *The Ghost of Jim Crow*, 29–30.

60. Ibid.; "Kennard Guilty in Forrest Court," *Jackson Daily News*, September 29, 1959.

61. "The History of Clyde Kennard," *Mississippi Free Press*, September 8, 1962.

62. Conversely, the defendant accused of actually stealing the feed was given a five-year suspended sentence. In one of the saddest and most troubling episodes in an era full of tragedies, while in prison Kennard learned that he had cancer. Despite a medical report recommending immediate parole, he remained in prison and continued to work in the fields at the prison. In addition, his medical checkups were canceled. After numerous appeals to the governor, Kennard was finally released from prison in 1963 shortly before he died. Oshinsky, *Worse Than Slavery*, 232.

63. On Henry's life, see Henry, *Aaron Henry*.

64. Payne, *I've Got the Light of Freedom*, 56–66; Dittmer, *Local People*, 75, 120–21; Aaron Henry to Governor Ross Barnett, November 27, 1960, SCRID# 2-106-0-12-2-1-1, MSSCR.

65. Tom Scarbrough, "Washington County," May 17, 1961, SCRID# 1-70-0-10-1-1-1 to 4-1-1, MSSCR; Scarbrough, "Attala, Sunflower, Tallahatchie, Leflore, Coahoma, and Bolivar County," May 9, 1962, SCRID# 2-38-1-40-1-1-1 to 4-1-1, MSSCR; Scarbrough, "Coahoma County," January 4, 1963, SCRID# 1-16-1-62-1-1-1 to 2-1-1, MSSCR.

66. "Henry Jailed; Trumped-Up Charge," *Mississippi Free Press*, March 10, 1962.

67. Henry, *Aaron Henry*, 124–25.

68. Erle Johnston Jr. to W. D. McCain, March 2, 1963, SCRID# 1-70-0-24-1-1-1, MSSCR.

69. D. B. Crockett, "Information on [. . .]," June 10, 1964, box 115, folder 11, Paul B. Johnson Family Papers, AMD-USM.

70. On how the Red Scare altered the black freedom struggle in the United States, see especially Von Eschen, *Race against Empire*. See also Dudziak, *Cold War Civil Rights*; Borstelmann, *The Cold War and the Color Line*; and Plummer, *Window on Freedom*.

71. "Senator Eastland and the Negro Soldier," *Southern Frontier*, July 1945, box 4, folder 46, Jessie Daniel Ames Papers, SHC; Asch, *The Senator and the Sharecropper*, 132–66.

72. "It Happened in Mississippi," *Southern Patriot*, September 1950, box 24, folder "Printed Material, 1950," Lucy Randolph Mason Papers, JHFHC.

73. On the relationship between segregationists and anticommunism, see Woods, *Black Struggle, Red Scare*; and Lewis, *The White South and the Red Menace*.

74. William J. Simmons to J. B. Matthews, September 6, 1955, box 680, folder "Simmons, W. J.," J. B. Matthews Papers, JHFHC.

75. Kenneth Toler, "Mississippians Are Linked in Red 'Infiltrated' Groups," *Memphis Commercial Appeal*, November 19, 1959.

76. Zack J. Van Landingham, "Gulf Coast World," September 18, 1959, SCRID# 2-127-0-1-1-1-1, MSSCR.

77. "City Police Arrest Group at Station," *Jackson Daily News*, May 24, 1961; Pittman, "Ross Says Law Will Be Upheld"; "'Riders' Here Have Past Police Records," *Jackson Clarion-Ledger*, May 25, 1961.

78. W. C. Shoemaker, "Soviets Planned 'Freedom Rides,'" *Jackson Daily News*, June 29, 1961.

79. "Eastland's Speech Hits 'Riders' Chief," *Jackson Clarion-Ledger*, May 26, 1961.

80. Tom Scarbrough, "Humphreys County," October 12, 1960, SCRID# 2-53-0-6-1-1-1 to 2-1-1, MSSCR; Tom Scarbrough, "Investigation of NAACP Activities in Clay County, Mississippi," June 20, 1960, SCRID# 2-88-0-23-1-1-1 to 2-1-1, MSSCR; Erle Johnston Jr., "Schedule of Violations Which Can Be Use[d] with General Affidavit," n.d., box 135, folder 1, Paul B. Johnson Family Papers, AMD-USM. For example, a 1956 bill prohibited "any person, firm, partnership, corporation, group, organization, or association" from providing any funds to a person involved in a court proceeding. Two months later, the legislature approved a bill that would require any out-of-state attorneys to get approval from the state board to appear in a Mississippi court. Both of these measures were intended to make it more difficult for the NAACP or any other civil rights organization to bring a lawsuit against segregation within the state or to aid any local citizens who might be using the courts to challenge segregation. Laws of the State of Mississippi, 1956 (chaps. 253, 255); "Bill Is Aimed against NAACP," *Jackson Clarion-Ledger*, January 25, 1956.

81. Consistency was also more likely with a more centralized state police force. Walker, *The Ghost of Jim Crow*, 5.

82. See, for example, "Four More Arrested at Counter," *Jackson Clarion-Ledger*, July 14, 1961; "Picketing Negro Free on Bond," *Memphis Commercial Appeal*, August 29, 1961.

83. Laws of the State of Mississippi, 1956 (chap. 256).

84. "Mississippi Code Section 2087.5," copy in box M337, folder 4, Albert F. Gordon Freedom Rider Collection, AMD-USM.

85. Perhaps no white official in the South better understood the critical role of the media and the performance of the police than Laurie Pritchett, the police chief in Albany, Georgia. Pritchett instructed his police officers that there would be no violence or dogs, explaining, "We're going to out-nonviolent them [the protesters]." Hampton and Fayer, *Voices of Freedom*, 106.

86. W. C. Shoemaker, "Tougaloo Students Arrested for Entering White Library," *Jackson Daily News*, March 27, 1961; "Negro Woman's Appeal," *Jackson Clarion-Ledger*, May 24, 1961; "Four More Arrested at Counter," *Jackson Clarion-Ledger*, July 14, 1961; W. C. Shoemaker, "Jackson Negroes Reject 'Cool Off,'" *Jackson Daily News*, May 27, 1961.

87. A. L. Hopkins, "Summary Report for Month of October, 1961," November 1, 1961, SCRID# 7-4-0-48-1-1-1, MSSCR.

88. "Arrest 6 Clarksdale Youths for Littering," *Mississippi Free Press*, July 27, 1963; "81 Negroes Held in Clarksdale City Jail," *Mississippi Free Press*, August 10, 1963.

89. "Negro Girls Turned Away from Church," *Jackson Clarion-Ledger*, October 14, 1963; "12 Arrested at Churches Here Sunday," *Jackson Clarion-Ledger*, October 21, 1963.

90. "Bus-Rider Negro Hit in Winona," *Jackson Clarion-Ledger*, August 28, 1960; "Negro Remains in Jail in Winona Disturbance," *Jackson Clarion-Ledger*, August 29, 1960.

91. Albany, Georgia, police chief Laurie Pritchett, who was also concerned about the presence of the media, relied on the charges of breach of the peace and unlawful assembly. Goldfield, *Black, White, and Southern*, 131.

92. "Negro Refused Admittance at MSC, Then Arrested," *Hattiesburg American*, September 15, 1959; "Two Negroes Found Guilty," *Jackson Clarion-Ledger*, May 20, 1962; Congressional Record, "Council of Confederated Organizations," 13517–18; "Police Harassment Noticed in Jackson," *Mississippi Free Press*, April 28, 1962; Joanne Grant, "Racist Terror Spreads in Mississippi," *National Guardian*, October 1, 1962; "State NAACP Head Hits Clarksdale Arrests Saturday," *Jackson Advocate*, April 6, 1963; Tom Scarbrough, "Coahoma County," January 4, 1963, SCRID# 2-62-2-13-1-1-1 to 2-1-1, MSSCR.

93. Tom Scarbrough, "Coahoma County," November 9, 1962, SCRID# 2-62-2-11-1-1-1 to 3-1-1, MSSCR.

94. "Tupelo Youths May Face Death Penalty," *Jackson Advocate*, November 28, 1958; Congressional Record, "Council of Federated Organizations," 16509; "Has Been Offered Bond, Negro Remains in Winona Prison," *Jackson Clarion-Ledger*,

August 29, 1960; "Mississippi Terror Traced to Officials, War on Negro Voters," *Worker*, April 21, 1963; Aaron Henry to Governor Ross Barnett, November 27, 1960, SCRID# 2-106-0-12-1-1-1, MSSCR; Edmund Noel, "Trip from Meridian Quiet under Escort," *Jackson Clarion-Ledger*, May 25, 1961; "Negro Refused Admittance at MSC, Then Arrested," *Hattiesburg American*, September 15, 1959; Tom Scarbrough, "Panola County," April 17, 1962, SCRID# 2-106-0-33-1-1-1 to 2-1-1, MSSCR; Tom Scarbrough, "Bolivar County—Aaron Henry and James Bevel," June 13, 1962, SCRID# 2-61-1-78-1-1-1 to 3-1-1, MSSCR; "Mississippi—Type Cases," January 31, 1956, microfilm, Papers of the NAACP (Frederick, Md.: University Publications of America, 1990), film 17, 412, part 18, series C, reel 12; "Two Negroes Found Guilty," *Jackson Clarion-Ledger*, May 20, 1962.

95. A. L. Hopkins to Aubrey Bell, "Bob Moses," April 19, 1963, SCRID# 1-71-0-1-1-1-1 to 5-1-1, MSSCR.

96. Tom Scarbrough, "Sunflower County," November 9, 1962, SCRID# 2-38-1-49-1-1-1 to 3-1-1, MSSCR.

97. Zack J. Van Landingham, "NAACP, Humphreys, Mississippi," January 27, 1959, SCRID# 2-53-0-3-1-1-1, MSSCR.

98. In Scarbrough's report, the agent referred to the twenty-one-year-old Eckles as a "Negro boy." Scarbrough further remarked that Eckles "was totally lacking in ability as well as character to qualify as a citizen to participate in any election. His reputation was bad and his education very limited." Tom Scarbrough, "Panola County."

99. On the media depictions of civil rights activists, see Bodroghkozy, *Equal Time*, 4; and Abel, *Signs of the Times*, 265.

100. "Negro Claims Was Beaten," *Jackson Clarion-Ledger*, March 15, 1962; "Mississippi Terror Traced to Officials, War on Negro Voters," *Worker*, April 21, 1963, box 165, folder "CORE, 1962–1967," J. B. Matthews Papers, JHFHC; Henry, *Aaron Henry*, 106–7.

101. Carson, *The Eyes on the Prize Civil Rights Reader*, 178; Payne, *I've Got the Light of Freedom*, 228–29.

102. Dan Berger contends that during the civil rights era the prison became an important symbol for both segregationists and black activists. For segregationists, it was an extension of their police power; for activists, the prison became a site of liberation. Dan Berger, "The Jailhouse in Freedom Land: Civil Rights and Civil Disobedience in the Carceral South, 1955–1966," draft of essay in author's possession.

103. W. C. Shoemaker, "Higgs Complains to Rights Group," *Jackson Daily News*, June 19, 1962; "Group Arrested Studying Race Relations in State Launch Probe," *Jackson Advocate*, June 23, 1962; "Higgs and Group Arrested, Threatened," *Mississippi Free Press*, June 30, 1962.

104. Peter Stoner, "Report of SNCC Worker Pete Stoner on Experiences in Hattiesburg from January 7 to May 21, 1964," Peter Stoner Papers, AMD-USM.

105. The reliance on laws could also be read as an attempt to create two extremes—vigilantes on one side and activists on the other—that would make state officials appear to represent the moderate voice of reason. That may especially have

been the case in Atlanta, where in 1961 Bill Cody, a member of the American Nazi Party, was arrested while trying to disrupt a school desegregation attempt. Like many civil rights activists, Cody was arrested and charged with disorderly conduct. Kruse, *White Flight*, 155.

106. Tom Scarbrough, "Coahoma County—Wade Walker—Negro male barber [. . .]," July 17, 1961, SCRID# 2-62-1-54-1-1-1 to 3-1-1, MSSCR.

107. On the Louvenia Knight case, see Katagiri, *The Mississippi State Sovereignty Commission*, 135–38.

108. A. L. Hopkins and Tom Scarbrough, "Meeting with the West Jasper County School Board [. . .]," August 22, 1960, SCRID# 3-81-0-5-1-1-1 to 4-1-1, MSSCR.

109. Because Davis Knight's parents, grandparents, and great-grandfather were listed as white, for him to qualify legally as a "negro" (at least "one eighth 'negro' blood") his great-grandmother, Rachel Knight, would have to have been "pure African." One man testified that Rachel had "negroid" features; three others testified that she could not have been "pure African" based on her skin color and features. Nonetheless, the jury deliberated for fifteen minutes before returning with a guilty verdict. Davis Knight was sentenced to five years in the state penitentiary. "Davis Knight vs. The State of Mississippi, Brief on behalf of Appellant," n.d., SCRID# 3-81-0-1-1-1-1 to 27-1-1, MSSCR; Erle Johnston, "Knight Case," November 27, 1963, SCRID# 3-81-0-8-1-1-1 to 2-1-1, MSSCR. On the Davis Knight case, see Bynum, "'White Negroes' in Segregated Mississippi."

110. In addition, they discovered that Louvenia had a sister near Laurel and a first cousin in Jackson, all of whose children attended white schools. Also, according to the agents' reports, Louvenia's sons were most likely about "1/32 negro," as defined by the law.

111. Erle Johnston Jr., "Louvenia Knight," November 26, 1963, SCRID# 3-81-0-6-1-1-1, MSSCR; Tom Scarbrough and Virgil Downing, "Jasper County (Louvenia Knight and her farher [*sic*], Otho Knight)," November 27, 1963, SCRID# 3-81-0-7-1-1-1 to 4-1-1, MSSCR; Erle Johnston Jr., "Director's Report to Sovereignty Commission Members—December 1963," box 135, folder 4, Paul B. Johnson Family Papers, AMD-USM.

112. Erle Johnston Jr., "Louvenia Knight, described on her birth certificate [. . .]," December 12, 1963, SCRID# 7-4-0-108-1-1-1 to 4-1-1, MSSCR.

113. A. L. Hopkins and Erle Johnston Jr., "Further Investigation of Louvenia Knight Case," December 19, 1963, SCRID# 3-81-0-15-1-1-1 to 3-1-1, MSSCR.

114. Erle Johnston Jr., "Louvenia Knight, described."

115. Erle Johnston Jr. to Louvenia Knight, January 24, 1964, SCRID# 3-81-0-18-1-1-1 to 2-1-1, MSSCR.

116. Erle Johnston Jr. to Governor Paul B. Johnson and Lieutenant Governor Carroll Gartin, February 14, 1964, SCRID# 3-81-0-29-1-1-1 to 2-1-1, MSSCR.

117. Katagiri, *The Mississippi Sovereignty Commission*, 170.

118. Tom Scarbrough, "Humphreys County."

119. "Man Wants Trial, City Would Like to Forget Case," *Mississippi Free Press*, April 27, 1963.

CHAPTER 5

1. J. P. Coleman to Ney M. Gore, September 11, 1956, SCRID# 10-5-0-1-1-1-1, MSSCR; Ney M. Gore to J. P. Coleman, February 19, 1957, SCRID# 10-5-0-106-1-1-1, MSSCR. In asking Gore to compile these statistics, Coleman noted that the previous study had been "a most telling piece of information."

2. An additional death in the "colored" category included one Indian killed by another Indian.

3. Gore to Coleman, February 19, 1957. Of the fifty-one white homicides, thirty-five were killed by other whites, two by blacks, two by officers, one by a railroad company, four by the legal institution, and one by suicide. Five homicides were listed as unsolved.

4. According to the 1954 study, blacks had killed eight whites, whites had killed six blacks, and blacks had killed 183 blacks.

5. For an example of a religious defense of segregation, see *A Christian View on Segregation*, Citizens' Council pamphlet, Paul B. Johnson Family Papers, AMD-USM. For two opposing views on the relationship between religion and the movement, see Chappell, *A Stone of Hope*; and Dailey, "The Theology of Massive Resistance." On Cold War and anticommunism defenses of segregation, see Woods, *Black Struggle, Red Scare*; Dudziak, *Cold War Civil Rights*; and Lewis, *The White South and the Red Menace*.

6. Kruse, *White Flight*, 163.

7. Lassiter, *The Silent Majority*, 122–23.

8. Joe Crespino uses the term "practical segregationist" to describe Coleman. Anders Walker likens Coleman's more moderate, compromising approach to segregation to North Carolina governor Luther Hodges and Florida governor LeRoy Collins. Crespino, *In Search of Another Country*; Anders Walker, *The Ghost of Jim Crow*.

9. David L. Cohn's tale of a razor-wielding black woman threatening a black man, for example, positioned black crime as white entertainment. Cohn, *Where I Was Born and Raised*, 360–64, 277–79. For other considerations of the role of black crime in the formation of Jim Crow, see Williamson, *The Crucible of Race*, 111–39; Fredrickson, *The Black Image in the White Mind*, 273–75; Litwack, *Trouble in Mind*, 210; and Ayers, *The Promise of the New South*, 153–55.

10. For examples from earlier periods of how these narratives shaped discourses around race and gender, see Brown, *Foul Bodies*; Lyons, *Sex among the Rabble*; Kramer, *The Blood of Government*; Shah, *Contagious Divides*; and Chávez-García, *States of Delinquency*.

11. Those assumptions were based on the ways in which crime data were collected. Crime among immigrant groups in urban areas was absorbed into the category "white," which then suggested that black individuals were more likely to commit crime than other urban dwellers. Muhammad, *The Condemnation of Blackness*. Not coincidentally, at roughly the same time, race in the United States was being reduced to color and specifically to black and white. Guterl, *The Color of Race in America*, 189.

12. On racial liberalism and how national thinking about race changed in the Jim Crow era, see Lee D. Baker, *From Savage to Negro*. On the ways in which segregationists understood these changes, see Jackson, *Science for Segregation*.

13. James O. Eastland, "We've Reached Era of Judicial Tyranny," speech at the Citizens' Council Statewide Convention, December 1, 1955, reprinted as a pamphlet, box 1, folder 29, Citizens' Council/Civil Rights Collection, AMD-USM.

14. Although Eastland emphasized race in his appeal to a national public, at least some segregationists in the South thought they should downplay race in their arguments for segregation. James Kilpatrick in Virginia, for example, made the case for focusing on interposition and the legal implications surrounding desegregation. Thorndike, "The Sometimes Sordid Level of Race and Segregation," 52.

15. Portraying the desegregation battle as exclusively Southern meant that similar fights outside the South received very little media attention. As Matthew Lassiter and Joseph Crespino note, for example, just two weeks prior to the crisis in Little Rock, a violent confrontation over an attempt to desegregate an all-white neighborhood in Levittown, Pennsylvania, attracted relatively little media attention. Lassiter and Crespino, "Introduction," 5. Negative images of white Southerners appeared regularly in the news, and in film, too, white Southerners were being portrayed as villains. See Graham, *Framing the South*.

16. Abel, *Signs of the Times*, 265.

17. In the South, these constructions emerged at least in part from nostalgic memories of a plantation past remembered as an era of faithful slaves and juxtaposed with fears of a more aggressive "New Negro" in the late nineteenth century. See Litwack, *Trouble in Mind*, 83–97. For the role of this nostalgia in national culture in the twentieth century, see McElya, *Clinging to Mammy*; and Cox, *Dreaming of Dixie*.

18. As Tara McPherson contends, the theme of happy contented black Southerners is most pronounced in pre–civil rights narratives in films such as *Gone with the Wind*. McPherson, *Reconstructing Dixie*, 45. On Southern racial images in film, see Duck, *The Nation's Region*; and Barker and McKee, *American Cinema and the Southern Imaginary*.

19. Anna McCarthy contends that the group's use of the term "citizen" came at a moment in which the idea of citizenship was being used by various groups to lend legitimacy to their cause. For the Citizens' Council, it put a "'respectable' public face [on] segregationism." The group's name might then also suggest an interest in appealing to a larger national audience. Similarly, Todd Moye notes that the use of the term "citizen" was not coincidental but rather reflected segregationists' claims to "good citizenship" during this era. McCarthy, *The Citizen Machine*, 14; Moye, *Let the People Decide*, 25.

20. The Sovereignty Commission initially gave the Citizens' Council $20,000 and then gave the group $5,500 per month. The state agency continued to make monthly donations (although they were reduced in 1962) until 1964, by which time the state had contributed $193,500 to the Citizens' Council. McMillen, *The Citizens' Council*, 35–36, 38–39, 337; Classen, *Watching Jim Crow*, 37–38, 111.

21. "State Sovereignty Commission," July 13, 1959 (date stamped), SCRID# 7-0-1-56-1-1-1, MSSCR.

22. Some of the mailings were created from research carried out by the agency; others came from reprints of reports and articles from segregationist circles; a few were critiques of integration from African Americans, including *Jackson Advocate* editor Percy Greene, an anticommunist perspective by Manning Johnson, and a criticism of school integration from Zora Neale Hurston. Collectively, these propaganda materials attacked integration from various perspectives, including legal and judicial concerns over federal power and states' rights and claims of a communist infiltration of the civil rights movement. "After Integration Repeal, What?" reprint from *Jackson Advocate*, SCRID# 99-111-0-2-1-1-1, MSSCR; "A Negro Deplores Integration Idea," SCRID# 99-111-0-7-1-1-1 to 3-1-1, MSSCR; Manning Johnson, "Wanted! Another Booker T. Washington," SCRID# 99-111-0-9-1-1-1 to 6-1-1, MSSCR; "The Montgomery Advertiser," SCRID# 10-0-2-2-1-1-1 to 56-1-1, MSSCR; "Government of Laws or of Men?" SCRID# 99-111-0-10-1-1-1 to 6-1-1, MSSCR; "In the Interest of Better Understanding," SCRID# 99-111-0-11-1-1-1 to 3-1-1, MSSCR; "Let the Facts Speak, . . ." SCRID# 99-111-0-5-1-1-1 to 2-1-1, MSSCR; *Don't Stone Her Until You Hear Her Side*, SCRID# 99-111-0-13-1-1-1 to 4-1-1, MSSCR; "State Sovereignty Commission: Report to the Members of the Senate and House of Representatives of the State of Mississippi," n.d., SCRID# 99-111-0-1-1-1-1, MSSCR.

23. Judge Tom P. Brady, "Segregation and the South," October 4, 1957, reprinted as a pamphlet, box 1, folder 29, Citizens' Council/Civil Rights Collection, AMD-USM.

24. W. D. McCain, Address to the Pro-American Forum, Chicago, September 9, 1960, box 135, folder 2, Paul B. Johnson Family Papers, AMD-USM.

25. According to historian Yasuhiro Katagiri, Jones volunteered for the Sovereignty Commission's speakers' bureau to give talks to audiences outside the South, and he may have prepared this statement hoping it would improve his chances of being selected for the bureau. He never was. At least one African American, Joseph Albright, who was an informant for the Sovereignty Commission, spoke at Columbia University as part of the speakers' bureau, even though the agency's board voted against sending him. "Rev. J. W. Jones, pastor of a Baptist church in New Albany and editor of the Community Citizen," n.d., SCRID# 99-111-0-8-1-1-1, MSSCR; Katagiri, *The Mississippi State Sovereignty Commission*, 78–79; Irons, *Reconstituting Whiteness*, 74–76.

26. William J. Simmons, "The Mid-West Hears the South's Story," February 3, 1958, box 680, folder "Simmons, W. J.," J. B. Matthews Papers, JHFHC.

27. Hal C. DeCell to Sir, n.d., SCRID# 99-111-0-14-1-1-1, MSSCR.

28. John Herbers, "State Survey Shows Negro Land and Business Ownership Is Increasing," *Tupelo Journal*, April 18, 1959.

29. Tisdale, "'Don't Stone Her Until You See Her Side.'"

30. Those numbers were likely based on new schools being built for black students, a last-ditch effort to get closer materially to the "separate but equal" doctrine. But throughout the Jim Crow era the State of Mississippi spent far more on education for whites than for blacks. *Racial Facts*, box 1, folder 29, Citizens' Council/Civil Rights Collection, AMD-USM; Bolton, *The Hardest Deal of All*, 87. See also

McMillen, *Dark Journey*, 72–108. On education in the Jim Crow South, see James D. Anderson, *The Education of Blacks in the South.*

31. Robert Webb, "Dramatic Behind-Scenes Story: Power-Packed Truth Marketed to Nation by State Sovereignty Commission Skill," *Jackson State Times*, May 12, 1956.

32. Hal C. DeCell to Ney M. Gore, March 14, 1957, SCRID# 10-0-1-103-1-1-1, MSSCR.

33. Aniko Bodroghkozy notes that at the beginning of the civil rights movement, television networks sought a certain ideological balance in their coverage. For example, if a network produced a documentary featuring ardent segregationists in a community, they also interviewed white moderates in that community. Ney M. Gore to Governor J. P. Coleman, March 26, 1957, SCRID# 10-1-0-1-1-1-1, MSSCR; "Shooting of Gus Courts, NAACP Branch President, Keeps State in Spotlight as Observers See New Crisis in Race Relations," *Jackson Advocate*, December 3, 1955; McCarthy, *The Citizen Machine*, 191–92; Bodroghkozy, *Equal Time*, 42.

34. Hal C. DeCell to Ney Gore, May 20, 1957, SCRID# 10-0-1-106-1-1-1, MSSCR; Hal C. DeCell to Ney Gore, June 12, 1957, SCRID# 10-0-1-108-1-1-1, MSSCR; Katagiri, *The Mississippi State Sovereignty Commission*, 13–15.

35. "The Message from Mississippi," box 9, folder 5, Erle E. Johnston Jr. Papers, AMD-USM.

36. Katagiri, *The Mississippi State Sovereignty Commission*, 80–84.

37. The NAACP learned of the visit in advance and provided journalists with sample questions they could ask about segregation. For additional details on the tour, see Tisdale, "'Don't Stone Her Until You See Her Side'"; Katagiri, *The Mississippi State Sovereignty Commission*, 15–17; and Irons, *Reconstituting Whiteness*, 64–65.

38. "Visiting Editors Voice Sharply Opposed Views," *Jackson Clarion-Ledger*, October 11, 1956.

39. "Editors Interview State Negroes in Catfish Alley," *Jackson Clarion-Ledger*, October 9, 1956.

40. "Governor Lauds Visit of Editors," *Jackson Clarion-Ledger*, October 18, 1956.

41. "Visiting Editors Voice Sharply Opposed Views."

42. "Editor Disputes Negro's Desire for Integration," *Jackson Clarion-Ledger*, October 19, 1956.

43. Bartley, *The Rise of Massive Resistance*, 13, 14.

44. In Mississippi in 1964, the Jackson Chamber of Commerce encouraged compliance with the new civil rights law, fearful that noncompliance would hurt future business prospects. Eskew, *But for Birmingham*, 13; Dittmer, *Local People*, 275. Also see Jacoway and Colburn, *Southern Businessmen and Desegregation.*

45. Kruse, *White Flight*, 106–7.

46. Lassiter, *The Silent Majority*, 70; Sokol, *There Goes My Everything*, 121–22.

47. In Mississippi, for example, Governor J. P. Coleman believed the state should be prepared to compromise on some issues to save the larger segregation system. Some politicians in other states took a similar stance. Crespino, *In Search of Another Country*, 11. See also Anders Walker, *The Ghost of Jim Crow.*

48. Holland, *From the Mississippi Delta*, 202.

49. On mainstream press coverage in the state during this period, see Weill, *In a Madhouse's Din*. On the black press, see Julius E. Thompson, *The Black Press in Mississippi*.

50. "Trust and Understanding," *West Point Daily Times Leader*, October 26, 1957.

51. "A 'March on Mississippi' Would Have Opened Their Eyes to Facts," *Jackson Clarion-Ledger*, November 2, 1959.

52. A portion of the editorial was included in the *Jackson Clarion-Ledger* editorial. Ibid.

53. "Midwestern Editor Amazed at Report on Situation in South by Editor of Scott County Times at Forest," *Houston Times Post*, October 24, 1957.

54. D. M. Nelson, "Negro Residents Are an Asset to Our Town," *Clinton News*, July 25, 1958.

55. Dittmer, *Local People*, 35–37.

56. "Taxpayers in Mississippi Dig Deep to Assist Negro Race," *Carrollton Conservative*, January 16, 1959.

57. See, for example, "Pupils of Both Races May Look with Hope to Mississippi Future," *Jackson State Times*, September 30, 1957; "Huge Equal School Plan Is Approved," *Jackson Daily News*, November 25, 1957; "Jackson County School Program Receives Funds," *Gulfport-Biloxi Daily Herald*, April 14, 1958; "State Pays 18–20 Million Annually to Teachers," *Brookhaven Leader Times*, April 30, 1958; untitled, *West Point Daily Times Leader*, October 1, 1958; "Negro College Gets Biggest Funds Slice," *Jackson State Times*, April 23, 1959; "Negro Colleges Head Funds List; More Than Whites," *Sardis Sovereign Reporter*, April 23, 1959; and "Spending More per Student for Negroes," *Jackson Clarion-Ledger*, April 25, 1959.

58. "Says Live in Friendship . . . Negro Pastor against Integration," *Yazoo City Herald*, September 29, 1955.

59. "Fire Victim Says Whites 'True Friends' of Negroes," *Jackson Daily News*, June 11, 1959.

60. "Negro Woman Writes Praise of Drive to Curb 'Fleecers,'" *Jackson Daily News*, December 16, 1958.

61. "Clergyman Urges Harmony of Races," *Jackson Clarion-Ledger*, May 19, 1959.

62. "Facts," *Hattiesburg American*, September 12, 1957.

63. "A Courageous Man," *Meridian Star*, September 1, 1957.

64. "The Amazing Progress of Our Southern Negroes," *McComb Enterprise-Journal*, October 13, 1958.

65. Untitled editorial, *Lincoln County Advertiser* (Brookhaven), November 7, 1957.

66. "Exodus of Negro Children Reported in New York," *Jackson State Times*, September 1, 1959; "Negroes Sending Children South," excerpt from the *New York Times*, *Jackson Daily News*, September 15, 1959; "Do They Support School Segregation?" *Jackson Clarion-Ledger*, September 3, 1959.

67. "Exodus of Negro Children Reported in New York."

68. The *State Times* began operations in early 1955, and it took a more moderate position on racial issues compared to the two other Jackson newspapers, both owned by the Hederman brothers. "ICRR Claims No Hike in Immigration," *Jackson State Times*, July 31, 1957; "Coming Back Home to 'Home, Sweet Home,'" *Jackson Daily News*, July 31, 1957. On editor Oliver Emmerich and other racially moderate editors in Mississippi during the civil rights era, see Davies, *The Press and Race*.

69. "Coming Back Home."

70. At least some white politicians in the South were steadily referencing black crime and immorality in the 1940s as a defense of segregation, including Stuart Landry in New Orleans. In addition, Landry was also linking his arguments to science. Ward, *Defending White Democracy*, 86. Jackson, *Science for Segregation*, 70–72. See Landry, *The Cult of Equality*.

71. Mississippians were not the only ones trying to challenge the national media narrative of the South. In Little Rock, during the integration of Central High School, Arkansas governor Orville Faubus tried unsuccessfully to turn the events into a story about the federal troops taking young white girls into custody and questioning them without the knowledge of their parents. Karen S. Anderson, "Massive Resistance, Violence, and Southern Social Relations," 211.

72. Tisdale, "'Don't Stone Her Until You See Her Side.'"

73. Ibid.

74. Ibid.

75. Ibid.

76. "Where Is the Reign of Terror?—Rep. John Bell Williams, speech in the U.S. House of Reps.," box 1, folder 29, Citizens' Council/Civil Rights Collection, AMD-USM.

77. *Racial Facts*, box 1, folder 29, Citizens' Council/Civil Rights Collection, AMD-USM.

78. While the organization claimed to send mailings to every state, the bulk of its materials went to Southern states. McMillen, *The Citizens' Council*, 35–36.

79. Simmons, "The Mid-West Hears the South's Story."

80. William J. Simmons, "The Race Problem Moves North," Carleton College, Northfield, Minnesota, May 15, 1962, box 141, folder 7, Paul B. Johnson Family Papers, AMD-USM.

81. Franz Boas and a number of anthropologists played a central role in debunking mainstream beliefs in biological constructions of race. See Lee D. Baker, *From Savage to Negro*, 168–207.

82. As governor, Ross Barnett declared a "Race and Reason Day" in the state in 1961 to honor Carleton Putnam's prosegregation book, *Race and Reason*. Lesseig, "Roast Beef and Racial Integrity"; Jackson, *Science for Segregation*, 119.

83. Simmons, "The Race Problem Moves North."

84. Other segregationists in the South also emphasized crime and statistics in cities outside the South. South Carolina senator Strom Thurmond, for example, suggested in 1958 that integration was responsible for a higher crime rate in New York schools. A year later, he referenced a published report on crime in Northern cities. Crespino, *Strom Thurmond's America*, 95.

85. "Crime Figures Speak Louder Than Words," *Citizens' Council*, April 1957, at http://www.citizenscouncils.com.

86. Just a few months after this report, *Time* reported on the trial of the sheriff in Yalobusha County who was charged with the beating death of Woodrow Wilson Daniels. The sheriff was acquitted by an all-white jury. "Justice in Water Valley," *Time*, August 18, 1958.

87. "*Time* Magazine Backs Up," *Morton Progress Herald*, April 24, 1958.

88. "Those Who Criticized South Now Begin to Understand Problem," *Jackson Clarion-Ledger*, May 4, 1958.

89. "An Integrationist Offers Timely Words of Advice to Colored Race," *Jackson Clarion-Ledger*, October 11, 1958.

90. "Crime Record Tells Why Negro Is 'Second Class,'" *Jackson Daily News*, December 10, 1959.

91. "Teacher Attacked in Mixed 'Jungle,'" *Jackson Daily News*, March 16, 1960.

92. "Civil Rights for White Girls?" *Jackson Daily News*, March 4, 1960.

93. "No Wolf Packs Rove Mississippi Streets," *Jackson Clarion-Ledger*, August 26, 1959.

94. "Negro Mob Jumps Cops in Bronx," *Jackson Clarion-Ledger*, August 10, 1959.

95. "New York Continues to Sit on Racial Dynamite, Reports Show," *Jackson Clarion-Ledger*, August 12, 1959.

96. See also "Two More People Are Dead," *Jackson Clarion-Ledger*, January 17, 1960.

97. "Big City Dwellers Quake under Negro Terrorism," *Citizens' Council*, August 1959, box 63, folder 5, Will D. Campbell Papers, AMD-USM.

98. On school desegregation efforts in Washington, D.C., see Wolters, *The Burden of* Brown.

99. The "Southern Manifesto" was a 1956 document expressing opposition to desegregation efforts. It was signed by ninety-nine Southern politicians. See Finley, *Delaying the Dream*, 142–54.

100. The hearings received little national attention, but Mississippi newspapers covered the proceedings extensively. In addition, the Citizens' Council of Mississippi issued a twenty-page report on the congressional hearings. Jackson, *Science for Segregation*, 76–77.

101. "NAACP against Probe of Schools," *Yazoo City Herald*, September 13, 1956.

102. "Mixed Washington Schools Prove Integration a Failure," *Yazoo City Herald*, October 11, 1956; "Williams Says Probers Don't Intend to Smear," *Jackson Clarion-Ledger*, September 19, 1956; "Promise No Reprisals for School Testimony," *Jackson Clarion-Ledger*, September 25, 1956.

103. "D.C. Schools' Sex Problems Told Probers," *Jackson Clarion-Ledger*, September 20, 1956.

104. Ibid.

105. "Tales of Delinquency Feature School Probe," *Jackson Clarion-Ledger*, September 21, 1956.

106. "School Probe to Continue, States Solon," *Jackson Clarion-Ledger*, September 27, 1956.

107. "D.C. Schools' Sex Problems Told Probers"; "School Probe to Continue, States Solon."

108. "School Integration Termed Too Hasty," *Hattiesburg American*, September 28, 1956.

109. "Witnesses State Whites Injured by Integration," *Jackson Clarion-Ledger*, September 26, 1956.

110. "Principal Says Negroes' I.Q. Lower than Whites," *Hattiesburg American*, September 21, 1956.

111. "Where Is the Reign of Terror?"

112. Judge Tom T. Brady, "Segregation and the South."

113. "Negro Illegitimacy in D.C. Rises 227 Pct. in 9 Years," *Citizens' Council*, April 1957, at http://www.citizenscouncils.com.

114. Another vocal proponent of segregation, James Kilpatrick in Virginia, also referenced statistics on illegitimacy, venereal disease, and crime as a defense of segregation. Ward, *Defending White Democracy*, 148.

115. "Sordid Record of Degradation No Longer a 'Quiet' Scandal," *Jackson Daily News*, August 29, 1958. Anders Walkers notes that some segregationists believed that if they abolished the common marriage law, many blacks would not join in legal marriage, which turned out to be untrue. Anders Walker, *The Ghost of Jim Crow*, 41–43.

116. *Racial Facts*.

117. "Information Sheet on Mississippi's Racial Situation," SCRID# 99-139-0-8-1-1-1 to 3-1-1, MSSC.

118. "Positive Program for South," *Jackson State Times*, December 27, 1957.

119. Following World War II, the politics of the Cold War centrally influenced the nature of the black freedom struggle. In the early 1950s, many of the most radical individuals, who were linking racism in the United States to colonialism in Africa and Asia, had become targets of anticommunism crusaders. Many were arrested, discredited, and silenced. While nationally the Red Scare peaked in the early 1950s, a number of Southern politicians, most notably Mississippi senator James Eastland, turned to claims of communist infiltration to discredit the civil rights movement. If some truly believed that the Communist Party was behind the integration efforts, others turned to anticommunism for pragmatic reasons. The interest in communism became another way for segregationists to try to disguise their racial intentions. George Lewis contends that a reliance on the tactics of anticommunism was particularly popular among segregationists because it drew on traditional Southern ideologies, including a distrust of outsiders and a belief that the South represented the ultimate bastion of Americanness. See Von Eschen, *Race against Empire*; Lewis, *The White South and the Red Menace*.

120. Massey, *Space, Place, and Gender*, 169.

121. In explaining connections between anticommunism and the segregationist defense, Jeff Wood contends that white Southern leaders mixed regional separatism

and patriotic Americanism to appeal to a larger national audience. Woods, *Black Struggle, Red Scare*, 2.

122. Leonard Thompson, *A History of South Africa*, 210–11.

123. Tom Ethridge, "Mississippi Notebook," *Jackson Clarion-Ledger*, September 14, 1960.

124. In his inauguration speech in 1963 as governor of Alabama, George Wallace also made reference to the Belgian survivors in the Congo. Dan T. Carter, *Politics of Rage*, 108–9.

125. Rhodesia gained independence from Great Britain in 1963 and became Zambia. In Southern Rhodesia, the British-descended Ian Smith led a group of whites requesting and later declaring their independence from Zambia. In this part of the country, whites constituted 5 percent of the population. While Great Britain and the United States officially refused to recognize Smith's declaration, Eastland and other segregationists voiced their support, and numerous organizations in the United States, most of them in the South, formed to show support for Smith and Rhodesia. Eastland traveled to Rhodesia in 1969. Asch, *The Senator and the Sharecropper*, 262–66.

126. Florence Sillers Ogden also referenced African nations in making a case for segregation. Noer, "Segregationists and the World," 142. On Southern segregationists and foreign policy, see also Ziker, "Race, Conservative Politics, and U.S. Foreign Policy." On the role of white women in defense of white supremacy during this era, see McRae, "White Womanhood, White Supremacy, and the Rise of Massive Resistance," 181–202.

127. Undated proposal, box 142, folder 4, Paul B. Johnson Family Papers, AMD-USM.

128. Willie Kuykendall to State Sovereignty Commission, n.d., SCRID# 2-106-0-14-1-1-1, MSSC; Aaron Henry to Governor Ross Barnett, November 27, 1960, SCRID# 2-106-0-12-1-1-1, MSSC; Governor Ross Barnett to Aaron Henry, December 1, 1960, SCRID# 2-106-0-13-1-1-1, MSSC; "Governor Refuses to Act in 'Beating,'" *Jackson Daily News*, December 6, 1960; Tom Scarbrough, "Investigation of Allegedly [*sic*] Beating of Lynda Fay Kuykendall, Negro, Female, age 12, Batesville, MS," December 9, 1960, SCRID# 2-106-0-15-1-1-1 to 10-1-1, MSSC; Tom Scarbrough, "Panola County," January 30, 1961, SCRID# 2-106-0-22-1-1-1 to 2-1-1, MSSC.

129. Scarbrough, "Panola County." Similarly, in a speech before the Citizens' Council in Florence, South Carolina, in 1963, Paul B. Johnson Jr., who would be elected governor the following year in Mississippi, referred to the events in the Congo and other new African nations as "a stern warning for whites." Address by Paul B. Johnson, April 22, 1963, box 91, folder 10, Paul B. Johnson Family Papers, AMD-USM.

130. Noer, "Segregationists and the World," 143–45; Scarbrough, "Panola County."

131. "Time Magazine Offers a Note on African Culture," *Citizens' Council*, February 1956, at http://www.citizenscouncils.com.

132. Noer, "Segregationists and the World," 143.

133. "Foreign Notes," *Citizens' Council*, January 1956, at http://www .citizenscouncils.com.

134. "Nehru Aiding Terrorism," *Citizens' Council*, July 1956, at http://www .citizenscouncils.com.

135. Like the discourses of black criminality, discourses of race and civilization had a history that began long before the postcolonial period. For an example from the early twentieth century, see Bederman, *Manliness and Civilization*.

136. "The Mau Maus Are Coming!" *Citizens' Council*, November 1958, at http:// www.citizenscouncils.com.

137. "Questions Asked, and Answers Given," SCRID# 99-139-0-7-1-1-1 to 5-1-1, MSSC.

138. *Racial Facts*.

139. White Southerners' international interests had an earlier history that predated the civil rights era. When the United States intervened in Haiti in 1915, a number of white Southerners played a leading role in the intervention, referencing their handling of their own "race problem" as instructive. Glenda Elizabeth Gilmore, *Defying Dixie*, 21–26.

140. *Racial Facts*.

141. Elsewhere, Satterfield had expressed an interest in an "anthropological" approach that would draw on academic research to inform the public of "the differences between the races." Undated proposal, box 142, folder 4, Paul B. Johnson Family Papers, AMD-USM.

142. James Featherston, "Denies Segregation Is Un-Christian Attitude," *Jackson Daily News*, March 18, 1958.

143. After graduating from college in 1937, Simmons studied French literature in France, where, as he later recalled, he took note of tensions between Senegalese migrants and the French. A few years later, he also traveled in Cuba and Dutch Guiana. Simmons interview.

144. "A Real Negro Problem," *Community Citizen*, July 23, 1957.

145. "Letter to Editor Jones," *Community Citizen*, May 26, 1960.

146. "News from Here and There," *Community Citizen*, March 26, 1959.

147. On the Sovereignty Commission's speakers' bureau, see Irons, *Reconstituting Whiteness*, 72–85; and Katagiri, *The Mississippi State Sovereignty Commission*, 74–82.

148. "Operation: The Message from Mississippi," box 135, folder 2, Paul B. Johnson Family Papers, AMD-USM.

149. Ibid.; "Suggested News Article for Speakers Press Kit," SCRID# 99-140-0-9-1-1-1 to 2-1-1, MSSC.

150. Flamm, *Law and Order*, 14.

151. Simmons, "The Race Problem Moves North."

152. Simmons interview.

153. Simmons, "The Race Problem Moves North."

154. "Reform Begins at Home, Magazine Tells Yankees," *Citizens' Council*, June 1956, at http://www.citizenscouncils.com.

155. "More New York Trouble," *Citizens' Council*, August 1958, at http://www
.citizenscouncils.com.

156. "Patterson Tells Lions Club," *Yazoo City Herald*, September 8, 1955.

EPILOGUE

1. Andrew Ferguson, "The Boy from Yazoo City," *Weekly Standard*, December 27,
2010; Michael D. Shear, "Discussing Civil Rights Era, a Governor Is Criticized," *New
York Times*, December 20, 2010.

2. Richard Wright, "The Ethics of Living Jim Crow," 39–52.

3. See Dittmer, *Local People*; and Payne, *I've Got the Light of Freedom*.

4. For excellent local case studies in Mississippi during these years, see Moye,
Let the People Decide; Crosby, *A Little Taste of Freedom*; and Hamlin, *Crossroads
at Clarksdale*.

5. Irons, *Reconstituting Whiteness*, 164.

6. Crespino, "Mississippi as Metaphor," 103. See also Griffin, "Southern
Distinctiveness, Yet Again."

7. As Anders Walker notes, the strengthening of the state highway patrol began
during the administration of Governor J. P. Coleman, who wanted to wrest some
of the policing authority away from local groups in the Delta in particular. Anders
Walker, "The Violent Bear It Away," 480–81.

8. Paul B. Johnson Jr., "Dedication of the MS Law Enforcement Officers Training Academy," box 126, folder 8, Paul B. Johnson Family Papers, AMD-USM.

9. Sokol, *There Goes My Everything*, 197–98.

10. Payne, *I've Got the Light of Freedom*, 320.

11. For an overview of white Southern local responses to the end of legal segregation in the 1960s and 1970s, see Sokol, *There Goes My Everything*, 182–237.

12. Crespino, *In Search of Another Country*, 186–88.

13. The ABC television network interrupted prime-time programming to show
images of Alabama state troopers in gas masks beating and gassing marchers.
Martin A. Berger notes that the media could have focused on a number of themes,
such as the courage of the marchers, but instead journalists made it a story about
spectacular violence. Garrow, *Protest at Selma*, 163; Berger, *Seeing through Race*, 4.
On the coverage of "Bloody Sunday" in Selma as an influential television moment,
see Bodroghkozy, *Equal Time*, 115–51.

14. Dittmer, *Local People*, 415–16.

15. Grantham, *The Life and Death of the Solid South*, 164. As of 2012, Mississippi
continued to have more black elected officials than any other state. Gene Dattel,
"Beyond Black and White in the Mississippi Delta," *New York Times*, December 1,
2012.

16. Dittmer, *Local People*, 484n.

17. On the voting changes during the civil rights era, see Lawson, *Black Ballots*.
On voting transformations in the South since the 1960s related to the Voting Rights
Act, see Davidson and Grofman, *Quiet Revolution in the South*.

18. Dittmer, *Local People*, 425–26; Cobb, *The South and America*, 192.

19. On the role of these visual images in creating a narrative of the movement and shaping ideas about racism, see Martin A. Berger, *Seeing through Race*.

20. Payne, *I've Got the Light of Freedom*, 361.

21. Ibid., 397–98. These incidents included the deaths of Vernon Dahmer in Hattiesburg in 1966; of Ben Chester White in 1966 and Wharlest Jackson in 1967, both in Natchez; and of Benjamin Brown in Jackson in 1967. Also in 1967 in Jackson, George Metcalfe narrowly survived a car bombing.

22. For overviews of the civil rights struggle outside the South, see Theoharis and Woodard, *Freedom North*; and Sugrue, *Sweet Land of Liberty*.

23. See, for example, Biondi, *To Stand and Fight*; Murch, *Living for the City*; Sugrue, *The Origins of the Urban Crisis*; Countryman, *Up South*; and Self, *American Babylon*.

24. Murch, *Living for the City*, 64; Flamm, *Law and Order*, 14.

25. For a discussion of the official response to the Watts uprising, see Horne, *Fire This Time*.

26. See O'Reilly, *Racial Matters*.

27. Murch, *Living for the City*, 148. Peniel Joseph has also referenced the numerous arrests of activists involved in the Black Power movement. Joseph, *Waiting 'Til the Midnight Hour*.

28. Acham, *Revolution Televised*, 29.

29. Although guns were a steady presence throughout the rural South, and even though a number of armed resistance groups formed in the region, guns did not became attached to the popular narrative of the civil rights movement in the South. That is in part because individuals such as Robert Franklin Williams who advocated armed self-defense were ostracized by the national media, national organizations, and others. On Williams, see Tyson, *Radio Free Dixie*. On the role of clothing in the civil rights movement, see Ford, "SNCC Women, Denim, and the Politics of Dress."

30. Flamm, *Law and Order*, 4.

31. McGirr, *Suburban Warriors*, 203–5; Flamm, *Law and Order*, 178.

32. Writing in the 1970s at a moment when many Southerners were thinking about how their region had changed in the wake of the civil rights movement, John Egerton argued that the South and the nation were becoming more like one another, but mostly in the worst ways, including in terms of racial and class divides. See Egerton, *The Americanization of Dixie*.

33. Michael Flamm, however, notes that, especially in the 1960s and 1970s, conservatives spoke the language of law and order more clearly and more successfully than liberals did. Meanwhile, Heather Thompson notes that the embrace of mass incarceration was not simply part of a Republican or conservative strategy but rather it reflected a rightward shift for the nation. Flamm, *Law and Order*, 124; Heather Ann Thompson, "Why Mass Incarceration Matters," 730–31.

34. These patterns of black criminalization were not new to the civil rights era but, rather, emerged from longer national traditions of stigmatizing black populations in urban areas as deviant. See Muhammad, *The Condemnation of Blackness*. Heather Ann Thompson, "Why Mass Incarceration Matters," 707–8. On the emergence of

mass incarceration and its relationship to race, see Ruth Wilson Gilmore, *Golden Gulag*; Davis, *Are Prisons Obsolete*; and Alexander, *The New Jim Crow*.

35. U.S. Department of Justice, Office of Justice Programs, Bureau of Justice Statistics, "Prisoners in 2008," by William J. Sabol, Heather C. West, and Matthew Cooper, NCJ 228417 (n.p.: Office of Justice Programs, December 2009), http://www.bjs.gov/index.cfm?ty=pbdetail&iid=1763.

36. Alexander, *The New Jim Crow*, 4, 13.

37. For a discussion of policing practices on roads in the contemporary United States, see Epp, Maynard-Moody, and Haider-Markel, *Pulled Over*.

38. By the same token, historically and in the present, African Americans have not been the only "nonwhite" group to be criminalized within the larger culture. See, for example, Lui, *The Chinatown Trunk Mystery*; Wu, *The Color of Success*; Ross, *Inventing the Savage*; Molina, *How Race Is Made in America*; Rios, *Punished*; and Chávez-García, *States of Delinquency*.

39. The racial politics and meanings of the case are somewhat complicated by Zimmerman's racial identity. He is of Peruvian and German American descent. Clearer, however, are the ways in which Trayvon, as a young black male wearing a hoodie, fit mainstream cultural imaginings of a criminal.

40. For example, in 2010, African American Marissa Alexander fired a gun in the air during a fight with her ex-husband. In that case, the judge denied the "stand your ground" defense and sentenced Alexander to twenty years in prison. Billy Kenber, "Marissa Alexander Case in Spotlight after Zimmerman Trial," *Washington Post*, July 15, 2013.

41. Griffin, "Southern Distinctiveness, Yet Again," 11. Joseph Crespino contends that, within the national imagination, since the civil rights era, the state has served as a metaphor for one of three tropes: as Southern exceptionalism defined by violence and racism, as a synecdoche for the rest of the nation, or as a scapegoat (embraced especially by segregationists pointing to Northern hypocrisy). Crespino, "Mississippi as Metaphor," 100.

42. In terms of physical intimacy—that is, of regular interactions between blacks and whites—it is likely the case that those encounters are more common in the urban South than in other parts of the country. A 2001 report, for example, noted that the South contained eight of the ten least segregated metropolitan areas in the nation. Cobb, *Away Down South*, 264.

43. Since the 1970s, many of the migrants to the South have been African Americans. Interest in the past within the tourism industry has often fueled tensions between white Southerners and black Southerners over what part of the past is remembered and how it is remembered, and these conflicts are nothing new. As W. Fitzhugh Brundage observes, "The enduring presence of white memory in the South's public space and blacks' resistance to it . . . is a central theme of the southern past." Cobb, *Away Down South*, 263; Brundage, *The Southern Past*, 7. On the economic development of the Sunbelt South, see Cobb, *The Selling of the South*; and Schulman, *From Cotton Belt to Sunbelt*.

44. In the late 1950s, for example, C. Vann Woodward noted that as Southern institutions began to crumble, white Southerners turned to myths about their past.

Woodward, *The Burden of Southern History*, 12. On these stories in the 1890s, see Litwack, *Trouble in Mind*, 183–97; and McElya, *Clinging to Mammy*, 207–52.

45. In 1940, 59.5 percent of employed African American women worked in domestic service. By 1960, that figure was 36.2 percent, and by 1980 it had dropped to 7.4 percent. As historian Rebecca Sharpless notes, throughout the twentieth century, black women steadily took advantage of other employment opportunities in order to avoid domestic work for whites. Sharpless, *Cooking in Other Women's Kitchens*, 179.

46. Ibid. On the politics of domestic service in the contemporary United States, see Ehrenreich and Hochschild, *Global Woman*.

47. Tucker, "Telling Memories among Southern Women," 49.

48. Stockett, *The Help*.

49. *The Help* is somewhat similar in this regard to Margaret Mitchell's 1936 novel *Gone with the Wind*, which also features a special, familial bond between a black domestic worker and the protagonist Scarlett O'Hara.

BIBLIOGRAPHY

MANUSCRIPT AND ARCHIVAL MATERIAL

Chapel Hill, N.C.
  Southern Historical Collection, Wilson Library, University of North Carolina
    Jessie Daniel Ames Papers
    Arthur F. Raper Papers
Durham, N.C.
  John Hope Franklin Historical Collections, Rare Book, Manuscript, and
      Special Collections Library, Duke University
    J. B. Matthews Papers
    Lucy Randolph Mason Papers
Hattiesburg, Miss.
  Archives and Manuscript Department, William D. McCain Library and
      Archives, University of Southern Mississippi
    Will D. Campbell Papers
    Citizens' Council/Civil Rights Collection
    Albert F. Gordon Freedom Rider Collection
    Paul B. Johnson Family Papers
    Erle E. Johnston Jr. Papers
    Lucy Komisar Collection
    Sheila Michaels Papers
    Peter Stoner Papers
Jackson, Miss.
  Margaret Walker Alexander Research Center, Jackson State University
    Mississippi Lynching Collection
  Mississippi Department of Archives and History, Archives and Library Division
    Governors' Papers
    Mississippi State Sovereignty Commission Records
    Mississippi newspapers

UNPUBLISHED INTERVIEWS

Durham, N.C.
  Behind the Veil: Documenting African-American Life in the Jim Crow South,
      John Hope Franklin Historical Collections, Rare Book, Manuscript, and
      Special Collections Library, Duke University
    Lou Allen, interview by Paul Ortiz, tape recording, Greenwood, Miss.,
      July 25, 1995

George Bailey, interview by Doris Dixon, tape recording, Indianola, Miss., July 25, 1995

Georgia Bays, interview by Doris Dixon, tape recording, Indianola, Miss., July 25, 1995

Eura Bowie, interview by Paul Ortiz, tape recording, Moorhead, Miss., August 9, 1995

Rosie Bynum, interview by Paul Ortiz, tape recording, Leland, Miss., July 26, 1995

Arthur Clayborn Jr., William Earl Davis, and Arnette Davis, interview by Mausiki Scales and Doris Dixon, tape recording, Yazoo City, Miss., August 7, 1995

Cora Fleming, interview by Paul Ortiz, tape recording, Indianola, Miss., August 7, 1995

Booker Frederick, interview by Mausiki Scales, tape recording, Itta Bena, Miss., August 2, 1995

Alice Giles, interview by Paul Ortiz, tape recording, Indianola, Miss., August 8, 1995

John (Henry) Johnson, interview by Mausiki Scales, tape recording, Greenwood, Miss., August 2, 1995

Johnny Jones, interview by Mausiki Scales, tape recording, Itta Bena, Miss., August 2, 1995

Herman Leach, interview by Doris Dixon, tape recording, Yazoo City, Miss., August 8, 1995

Hettie Love, interview by Doris Dixon, tape recording, Itta Bena, Miss., August 2, 1995

David Mathews, interview by Paul Ortiz, tape recording, Indianola, Miss., August 5, 1995

James Robinson, interview by Mausiki Scales, tape recording, Itta Bena, Miss., August 10, 1995

Rosie Sanders, interview by Doris Dixon, tape recording, Greenwood, Miss., August 3, 1995

H. Scott, interview by Mausiki Scales, tape recording, Yazoo City, Miss., August 8, 1995

Walter Sculark, interview by Paul Ortiz, tape recording, Cleveland, Miss., August 2, 1995

Alma Ward, interview by Doris Dixon, tape recording, Itta Bena, Miss., July 31, 1995

Minnie Weston, interview by Paul Ortiz, tape recording, Moorhead, Miss., August 8, 1995

H. J. Williams, interview by Mausiki Scales, tape recording, Yazoo City, Miss., August 8, 1995

Ruby Williams, interview by Paul Ortiz, tape recording, Clarksdale, Miss., July 31, 1995

Hattiesburg, Miss.

Civil Rights Movement in Mississippi, William D. McCain Library and Archives, University of Southern Mississippi

Constance Baker, interview by Kim Adams, transcript, Hattiesburg, Miss., April 3, 1995

Unita Blackwell, interview by Mike Garvey, transcript, Mayersville, Miss., April 1, 1977

J. C. Fairley, Mamie Phillips, and Charles Phillips, interview by Charles Bolton, transcript, Hattiesburg, Miss., June 24, 1998

Bennie Gooden, interview by Homer Hill, transcript, Clarksdale, Miss., March 15, 1994

Mrs. Pinkey Hall, interview by Kim Adams, transcript, place unknown, December 13, 1995

Nathaniel H. Lewis, interview by Tom Healy, transcript, McComb, Miss., October 24, 1978

Mississippi Oral History Program, University of Southern Mississippi

Gladys Austin, interview by Kim Adams, transcript, Laurel, Miss., May 2, 1995

Ellie J. Dahmer, interview by Orley B. Caudill, transcript, Hattiesburg, Miss., July 2, 1974

Eva Gates, interview by Pic Firmin, transcript, November 30, 1999

Charlie Parker, interview by Orley B. Caudill, transcript, Laurel, Miss., July 22, 1981

William J. Simmons, interview by Orley B. Caudill, transcript, Jackson, Miss., June 26, 1979

E. Hammond Smith, interview by Orley B. Caudill, transcript, Hattiesburg, Miss., April 8, 1982

Jackson, Miss.

Recollections of the Civil Rights Movement, Margaret Walker Alexander Research Center, Jackson State University

John Peoples, interview by Alferdteen Harrison, transcript, February 23, 1994

Tougaloo, Miss.

Civil Rights Documentation Project, L. Zenobia Coleman Library, Tougaloo College

Reverend Johnny Barbour Jr. and Clara M. Barbour, interview by Donald Williams, transcript, Jackson, Miss., January 25, 1999

Hobert Kornegay, interview by Don Williams, transcript, Meridian, Miss., January 6, 1999

Franzetta W. Sanders, interview by Stephanie Scull Millet, transcript, Moss Point, Miss., May 17, 2000

Tommie Lee Williams Sr., interview by Donald Williams, transcript, Vicksburg, Miss., August 20, 1999

PERIODICALS

American Mercury

Bolivar Democrat

Brookhaven Leader Times

Carrollton Conservative

Chicago Defender

Citizens' Council (Jackson, Miss.)

Clarksdale Press Register

Clinton News

Community Citizen (New Albany, Miss.)

Greenville Delta Democrat Times

Greenwood Commonwealth
Gulfport-Biloxi Daily Herald
Hattiesburg American
Houston (Miss.) Times-Post
Jackson Advocate
Jackson Clarion-Ledger
Jackson Daily News
Jackson State Times
Laurel Leader-Call
Lexington Advertiser
Lincoln County Advertiser
  (Brookhaven)
McComb Enterprise
McComb Enterprise-Journal
Memphis Commercial Appeal
Meridian Star
Mississippi Enterprise (Jackson, Miss.)
Mississippi Free Press (Jackson, Miss.)
Morton Progress Herald

Natchez Democrat
Natchez Times
National Guardian
New Orleans Times-Picayune
New York Post
New York Times
Norfolk (Va.) Pilot
Port Gibson Reveille
Prentiss Headlight
Sardis Sovereign Reporter
Southern Frontier
Southern Patriot
Tupelo Journal
Washington Post
Weekly Standard
West Point Daily Time-Leader
Wilkamite Record
Worker
Yazoo City Herald

BOOKS, ARTICLES, AND DISSERTATIONS

Abel, Elizabeth. *Signs of the Times: The Visual Politics of Jim Crow*. Berkeley: University of California Press, 2010.

Acham, Christine. *Revolution Televised: Prime Time and the Struggle for Black Power*. Minneapolis: University of Minnesota Press, 2004.

Agee, Christopher Lowen. *Streets of San Francisco: Policing and the Creation of a Cosmopolitan Liberal Politics, 1950–1970s*. Chicago: University of Chicago Press, 2014.

Alexander, Michelle. *The New Jim Crow: Mass Incarceration in the Age of Colorblindness*. New York: New Press, 2010.

Allen, James, Hilton Als, John Lewis, and Leon F. Litwack. *Without Sanctuary: Lynching Photography in America*. Santa Fe: Twin Palms Publishers, 2000.

Anderson, James D. *The Education of Blacks in the South, 1860–1935*. Chapel Hill: University of North Carolina Press, 1988.

Anderson, Karen S. "Massive Resistance, Violence, and Southern Social Relations." In *Massive Resistance: Southern Opposition to the Second Reconstruction*, edited by Clive Webb, 203–20. New York: Oxford University Press, 2005.

Arnesen, Eric. *Brotherhoods of Color: Black Railroad Workers and the Struggle for Equality*. Cambridge: Harvard University Press, 2001.

Arsenault, Raymond. *Freedom Rides: 1961 and the Struggle for Racial Justice*. New York: Oxford University Press, 2006.

Asch, Christopher Myers. *The Senator and the Sharecropper: The Freedom Struggles of James O. Eastland and Fannie Lou Hamer*. Chapel Hill: University of North Carolina Press, 2011.

Ayers, Edward L. *The Promise of the New South: Life after Reconstruction*. New York: Oxford University Press, 1992.

———. *Vengeance and Justice: Crime and Punishment in the Nineteenth Century American South*. New York: Oxford University Press, 1984.

Baker, Bruce E. "North Carolina Lynching Ballads." In *Under Sentence of Death: Lynching in the South*, edited by W. Fitzhugh Brundage, 219–46. Chapel Hill: University of North Carolina Press, 1997.

Baker, Houston A., Jr. *Blues, Ideology, and Afro-American Literature: A Vernacular Theory*. Chicago: University of Chicago Press, 1984.

Baker, Lee D. *From Savage to Negro: Anthropology and the Construction of Race, 1896–1954*. Berkeley: University of California Press, 1998.

Baker, Ray Stannard. *Following the Color Line: An Account of Negro Citizenship in the American Democracy*. New York: Doubleday, Page, 1908.

Baldwin, Davarian L. *Chicago's New Negroes: Modernity, the Great Migration, and Black Urban Life*. Chapel Hill: University of North Carolina Press, 2007.

Banner, Stuart. *The Death Penalty: An American History*. Cambridge: Harvard University Press, 2001.

Barker, Deborah, and Kathryn McKee, eds. *American Cinema and the Southern Imaginary*. Athens: University of Georgia Press, 2011.

Bartley, Numan V. *The Rise of Massive Resistance: Race and Politics in the South during the 1950s*. Rev. ed. Baton Rouge: Louisiana State University Press, 1997.

Bates, Beth Tompkins. *Pullman Porters and the Rise of Protest Politics in Black America, 1925–1945*. Chapel Hill: University of North Carolina Press, 2001.

Bauman, Richard. *Folklore, Cultural Performances, and Popular Entertainments*. New York: Oxford University Press, 1992.

Bay, Mia. *To Tell the Truth Freely: The Life of Ida B. Wells*. New York: Hill and Wang, 2009.

Bederman, Gail. *Manliness and Civilization: A Cultural History of Gender and Race in the United States, 1880–1917*. Chicago: University of Chicago Press, 1995.

Beito, David T., and Linda Royster Beito. "T. R. M. Howard: Pragmatism over Strict Integrationist Ideology in the Mississippi Delta, 1942–1954." In *Before Brown: Civil Rights and White Backlash in the Modern South*, edited by Glenn Feldman, 68–95. Tuscaloosa: University of Alabama Press, 2004.

Berger, Martin A. *Seeing through Race: A Reinterpretation of Civil Rights Photography*. Berkeley: University of California Press, 2011.

Berger, Maurice. *For All the World to See: Visual Culture and the Struggle for Civil Rights*. New Haven: Yale University Press, 2010.

Berrey, Stephen A. "Resistance Begins at Home: The Black Family and Lessons in Survival and Subversion in Jim Crow Mississippi." *Black Women, Gender, and Families* 3 (Spring 2009): 65–90.

Biondi, Martha. *To Stand and Fight: The Struggle for Civil Rights in Postwar New York City*. Cambridge: Harvard University Press, 2003.

Black, Earl. *Southern Governors and Civil Rights: Racial Segregation as a Campaign Issue in the Second Reconstruction*. Cambridge: Harvard University Press, 1976.

Blackwell, Unita, with JoAnne Prichard Morris. *Barefootin': Life Lessons from the Road to Freedom*. New York: Crown Publishers, 2006.

Blight, David W. *Race and Reunion: The Civil War in American Memory*. Cambridge: Harvard University Press, 2001.

Blue, Ethan. "'A Dark Cloud Will Go Over': Pain, Death, and Silence in Texas Prisons in the 1930s." *Humanities Research* 14 (2007): 5–24.

Bodroghkozy, Aniko. *Equal Time: Television and the Civil Rights Movement*. Urbana: University of Illinois Press, 2012.

Bolton, Charles C. *The Hardest Deal of All: The Battle over School Integration in Mississippi, 1870–1980*. Jackson: University Press of Mississippi, 2005.

Bonilla-Silva, Eduardo. *Racism without Racists: Color-Blind Racism and the Persistence of Racial Inequality in America*. 4th ed. Lanham, Md.: Rowman and Littlefield, 2013.

Borstelmann, Thomas. *The Cold War and the Color Line: American Race Relations in the Global Arena*. Cambridge: Harvard University Press, 2001.

Brooks, Jennifer E. *Defining the Peace: World War II Veterans, Race, and the Remaking of Southern Political Tradition*. Chapel Hill: University of North Carolina Press, 2004.

Brown, Kathleen M. *Foul Bodies: Cleanliness in Early America*. New Haven: Yale University Press, 2009.

Brown-Nagin, Tomiko. *Courage to Dissent: Atlanta and the Long History of the Civil Rights Movement*. New York: Oxford University Press, 2011.

Brundage, W. Fitzhugh. *Lynching in the New South: Georgia and Virginia, 1880–1930*. Urbana: University of Illinois Press, 1993.

———. "The Roar on the Other Side of Silence: Black Resistance and White Violence in the American South, 1880–1940." In *Under Sentence of Death: Lynching in the South*, edited by W. Fitzhugh Brundage, 271–91. Chapel Hill: University of North Carolina Press, 1997.

———. *The Southern Past: A Clash of Race and Memory*. Cambridge: Harvard University Press, 2005.

Bynum, Victoria E. "'White Negroes' in Segregated Mississippi: Miscegenation, Racial Identity, and the Law." *Journal of Southern History* 64 (May 1998): 247–76.

Carter, Dan T. *Politics of Rage: George Wallace, the Origins of the New Conservatism, and the Transformation of American Politics*. Baton Rouge: Louisiana State University Press, 1996.

———. *Scottsboro: A Tragedy of the American South*. Baton Rouge: Louisiana State University Press, 1969.

Carter, Greg. *The United States of United Races: A Utopian History of Race Mixing*. New York: New York University Press, 2013.

Cartwright, Joseph H. *The Triumph of Jim Crow: Tennessee Race Relations in the 1880s*. Knoxville: University of Tennessee Press, 1976.

Cash, W. J. *The Mind of the South*. New York: Vintage Books, 1991.

Catsam, Derek Charles. *Freedom's Mainline: The Journey of Reconciliation and the Freedom Rides*. Lexington: University Press of Kentucky, 2009.

Cell, John W. *The Highest Stage of White Supremacy: The Origins of Segregation in South Africa and the American South*. Cambridge: Cambridge University Press, 1982.

Chafe, William H. *Civilities and Civil Rights: Greensboro, North Carolina, and the Black Freedom Struggle*. New York: Oxford University Press, 1981.

Cha-Jua, Sundiata Keita, and Clarence Lang. "The 'Long Movement' as Vampire: Temporal and Spatial Fallacies in Recent Black Freedom Studies." *Journal of African American History* 92 (Spring 2007): 265–88.

Chalmers, David. *Backfire: How the Ku Klux Klan Helped the Civil Rights Movement*. Lanham, Md.: Rowman and Littlefield, 2003.

Chappell, David L. *A Stone of Hope: Prophetic Religion and the Death of Jim Crow*. Chapel Hill: University of North Carolina Press, 2004.

Chávez-García, Miroslava. *States of Delinquency: Race and Science in the Making of California's Juvenile Justice System*. Berkeley: University of California Press, 2012.

Childress, Alice. *Like One of the Family: Conversations from a Domestic's Life*. Boston: Beacon Press, 1986.

Clark-Lewis, Elizabeth. *Living In, Living Out: African American Domestics in Washington, D.C., 1910–1940*. Washington, D.C.: Smithsonian Institution Press, 1994.

Classen, Steven D. *Watching Jim Crow: The Struggles over Mississippi TV, 1955–1969*. Durham: Duke University Press, 2004.

Cobb, James C. *Away Down South: A History of Southern Identity*. New York: Oxford University Press, 2005.

———. *The Most Southern Place on Earth: The Mississippi Delta and the Roots of Regional Identity*. New York: Oxford University Press, 1992.

———. *The Selling of the South: The Southern Crusade for Industrial Development, 1936–1990*. 2nd ed. Urbana: University of Illinois Press, 1993.

Cohn, David L. *Where I Was Born and Raised*. South Bend: University of Notre Dame Press, 1967.

Collins, Patricia Hill. *Black Feminist Thought: Knowledge, Consciousness, and the Politics of Empowerment*. 2nd ed. New York: Routledge, 2000.

Cooper, Caryl A. "Percy Greene and the *Jackson Advocate*." In *The Press and Race: Mississippi Journalists Confront the Movement*, edited by David R. Davies, 55–84. Jackson: University Press of Mississippi, 2001.

Countryman, Matthew J. *Up South: Civil Rights and Black Power in Philadelphia*. Philadelphia: University of Pennsylvania Press, 2006.

Cox, Karen L. *Dreaming of Dixie: How the South Was Created in American Popular Culture*. Chapel Hill: University of North Carolina Press, 2011.

———. "The South and Mass Culture." *Journal of Southern History* 75 (2009): 677–90.

Crespino, Joseph. *In Search of Another Country: Mississippi and the Conservative Counterrevolution*. Princeton: Princeton University Press, 2007.

———. "Mississippi as Metaphor: Civil Rights, the South, and the Nation in the Historical Imagination." In *The Myth of Southern Exceptionalism*, edited by Matthew D. Lassiter and Joseph Crespino, 99–120. New York: Oxford University Press, 2010.

———. *Strom Thurmond's America*. New York: Hill and Wang, 2012.

Crosby, Emilye. *A Little Taste of Freedom: The Black Freedom Struggle in Claiborne County, Mississippi*. Chapel Hill: University of North Carolina Press, 2005.

Cubitt, Geoffrey. *History and Memory*. Manchester, U.K.: Manchester University Press, 2007.

Dailey, Jane. *Before Jim Crow: The Politics of Race in Postemancipation Virginia*. Chapel Hill: University of North Carolina Press, 2000.

———. "The Theology of Massive Resistance: Sex, Segregation, and the Sacred after *Brown*." In *Massive Resistance: Southern Opposition to the Second Reconstruction*, edited by Clive Webb, 151–80. New York: Oxford University Press, 2005.

Dailey, Jane, Glenda Elizabeth Gilmore, and Bryant Simon. "Introduction." In *Jumpin' Jim Crow: Southern Politics from Civil War to Civil Rights*, edited by Jane Dailey, Glenda Elizabeth Gilmore, and Bryant Simon, 3–6. Princeton: Princeton University Press, 2000.

Daniel, Pete. *Lost Revolutions: The South in the 1950s*. Chapel Hill: University of North Carolina Press, 2000.

Davidson, Chandler, and Bernard Grofman, eds. *Quiet Revolution in the South: The Impact of the Voting Rights Act, 1965–1990*. Princeton: Princeton University Press, 1994.

Davies, David R., ed. *The Press and Race: Mississippi Journalists Confront the Movement*. Jackson: University of Mississippi Press, 2001.

Davis, Angela Y. *Are Prisons Obsolete?* New York: Seven Stories Press, 2003.

De Jong, Greta. *A Different Day: African American Struggles for Justice in Rural Louisiana, 1900–1970*. Chapel Hill: University of North Carolina Press, 2002.

Dill, Bonnie Thornton. *Across the Boundaries of Race and Class: An Exploration of Work and Family among Black Female Domestic Servants*. New York: Garland, 1994.

Dittmer, John. *Local People: The Struggle for Civil Rights in Mississippi*. Urbana: University of Illinois Press, 1994.

Dollard, John. *Caste and Class in a Southern Town*. 3rd ed. Garden City: Doubleday Anchor, 1957.

Dorr, Lisa Lindquist. *White Women, Rape, and the Power of Race in Virginia, 1900–1960*. Chapel Hill: University of North Carolina Press, 2004.

Doyle, Bertram Wilbur. *The Etiquette of Race Relations in the South: A Study in Social Control*. Chicago: University of Chicago Press, 1937.

Dray, Philip. *At the Hands of Persons Unknown: The Lynching of Black America*. New York: Random House, 2002.

Dubber, Markus Dirk. *The Police Power: Patriarchy and the Foundations of American Government*. New York: Columbia University Press, 2005.

Duck, Leigh Anne. *The Nation's Region: Southern Modernism, Segregation, and U.S. Nationalism*. Athens: University of Georgia Press, 2006.

Dudziak, Mary L. *Cold War Civil Rights: Race and the Image of American Democracy*. Princeton: Princeton University Press, 2000.

DuRocher, Kristina. *Raising Racists: The Socialization of White Children in the Jim Crow South*. Lexington: University Press of Kentucky, 2011.

Eagles, Charles W. "Toward New Histories of the Civil Rights Era." *Journal of Southern History* 66 (November 2000): 815–48.

Egerton, John. *The Americanization of Dixie: The Southernization of the United States*. New York: Harper's Magazine Press, 1974.

Ehrenreich, Barbara, and Arlie Russell Hochschild, eds. *Global Woman: Nannies, Maids, and Sex Workers in the New Economy*. New York: Henry Holt, 2002.

Ellis, Mark. *Race, War, and Surveillance: African Americans and the United States Government during World War I*. Bloomington: Indiana University Press, 2001.

Ellison, Ralph. "Change the Joke and Slip the Yoke." In *Shadow and Act*, 45–59. 1964. Reprint, New York: Vintage, 1995.

Ellsworth, Scott. *Death in a Promised Land: The Tulsa Race Riot of 1921*. Baton Rouge: Louisiana State University Press, 1992.

Epp, Charles R., Steven Maynard-Moody, and Donald P. Haider-Markel. *Pulled Over: How Police Stops Define Race and Citizenship*. Chicago: University of Chicago Press, 2014.

Eskew, Glenn T. *But for Birmingham: The Local and National Movements in the Civil Rights Struggle*. Chapel Hill: University of North Carolina Press, 1997.

Estes, Steve. "Engendering Movement Memories: Remembering Race and Gender in the Mississippi Movement." In *The Civil Rights Movement in American Memory*, edited by Renee C. Romano and Leigh Raiford, 290–312. Athens: University of Georgia Press, 2006.

———. *I Am a Man! Race, Manhood, and the Civil Rights Movement*. Chapel Hill: University of North Carolina Press, 2005.

Evers, Myrlie, with William Peters. *For Us, the Living*. Jackson: University Press of Mississippi, 1967.

Fanon, Frantz. *Black Skins, White Masks*. New York: Grove Weidenfeld, 1967.

Farmer, James. *Lay Bare the Heart: An Autobiography of the Civil Rights Movement*. New York: Arbor House, 1985.

Feldstein, Ruth. "'I Wanted the Whole World to See': Race, Gender, and Constructions of Motherhood in the Death of Emmett Till." In *Not June Cleaver: Women and Gender in Postwar America, 1945–1960*, edited by Joanne Meyerowitz, 263–303. Philadelphia: Temple University Press, 1994.

Finley, Keith M. *Delaying the Dream: Southern Senators and the Fight against Civil Rights, 1938–1965*. Baton Rouge: Louisiana State University Press, 2008.

Finnegan, Terence. "Lynching and Political Power in Mississippi and South Carolina." In *Under Sentence of Death*, edited by W. Fitzhugh Brundage, 189–218. Urbana: University of Illinois Press, 1993.

Flamm, Michael W. *Law and Order: Street Crime, Civil Unrest, and the Crisis of Liberalism in the 1960s*. New York: Columbia University Press, 2005.

Fleming, Cynthia Griggs. *Soon We Will Not Cry: The Liberation of Ruby Doris Smith Robinson*. New York: Rowman and Littlefield, 1998.

Flynt, J. Wayne. *Dixie's Forgotten People: The South's Poor Whites*. Bloomington: Indiana University Press, 1979.

Foley, Neil. *The White Scourge: Mexicans, Blacks, and Poor Whites in Texas Cotton Culture*. Berkeley: University of California Press, 1997.

Folmsbee, Stanly J. "The Origins of the First 'Jim Crow' Law." *Journal of Southern History* 15 (May 1949): 235–47.

Ford, Tanisha C. "SNCC Women, Denim, and the Politics of Dress." *Journal of Southern History* 79 (August 2013): 625–58.

Forman, James. *The Making of Black Revolutionaries*. 1972. Reprint, Washington, D.C.: Open Hand Publishing, 1985.

Foucault, Michel. *Discipline and Punish: The Birth of the Prison*. Translated by Alan Sheridan. New York: Vintage Books, 1977.

Frederickson, Kari. *The Dixiecrat Revolt and the End of the Solid South, 1932–1968*. Chapel Hill: University of North Carolina Press, 2001.

Fredrickson, George M. *The Black Image in the White Mind: The Debate on Afro-American Character and Destiny, 1817–1914*. New York: Harper and Row, 1971.

———. *White Supremacy: A Comparative Study in American and South African History*. New York: Oxford University Press, 1981.

Fronc, Jennifer. *New York Undercover: Private Surveillance in the Progressive Era*. Chicago: University of Chicago Press, 2009.

Gaines, Kevin K. *Uplifting the Race: Black Leadership, Politics, and Culture in the Twentieth Century*. Chapel Hill: University of North Carolina Press, 1996.

Galtung, Johan. "Cultural Violence." *Journal of Peace Research* 27 (1990): 291–305.

Garland, David. "Penal Excess and Surplus Meaning: Public Torture Lynchings in Twentieth-Century America." *Law and Society Review* 39 (2005): 793–833.

Garrow, David J. *The FBI and Martin Luther King, Jr.: From "Solo" to Memphis*. New York: W. W. Norton, 1981.

———. *Protest at Selma: Martin Luther King, Jr., and the Voting Rights Act of 1965*. New Haven: Yale University Press, 1978.

Genovese, Eugene D. *Roll, Jordan, Roll: The World the Slaves Made*. New York: Vintage, 1974.

Giddens, Anthony. *The Nation-State and Violence*. Cambridge, U.K.: Polity Press, 1985.

Gill, Tiffany. *Beauty Shop Politics: African American Women's Activism in the Beauty Industry*. Urbana: University of Illinois Press, 2010.

Gilmore, Glenda Elizabeth. *Defying Dixie: The Radical Roots of Civil Rights, 1919–1950*. New York: W. W. Norton, 2008.

———. *Gender and Jim Crow: Women and the Politics of White Supremacy in North Carolina, 1896–1920*. Chapel Hill: University of North Carolina Press, 1996.

Gilmore, Ruth Wilson. *Golden Gulag: Prisons, Surplus, Crisis, and Opposition in Globalizing California*. Berkeley: University of California Press, 2007.

Glenn, Evelyn Nakano. *Issei, Nisei, War Bride: Three Generations of Japanese American Women in Domestic Service*. Philadelphia: Temple University Press, 1988.

Godshalk, David F. "William J. Northen's Public and Personal Struggles against Lynching." In *Jumpin' Jim Crow: Southern Politics from Civil War to Civil Rights*, edited by Jane Dailey, Glenda Elizabeth Gilmore, and Bryant Simon, 140–61. Princeton: Princeton University Press, 2000.

Goffman, Erving. *The Presentation of Self in Everyday Life*. Garden City: Doubleday, 1959.

Goldfield, David R. *Black, White, and Southern: Race Relations and Southern Culture, 1940 to the Present*. Baton Rouge: Louisiana State University Press, 1990.

Goluboff, Risa L. *The Lost Promise of Civil Rights*. Cambridge: Harvard University Press, 2007.

Gordon, Lewis R. *Her Majesty's Other Children: Sketches of Racism from a Neocolonial Age*. Lanham, Md.: Rowman and Littlefield, 1997.

Graham, Allison. *Framing the South: Hollywood, Television, and Race during the Civil Rights Struggle*. Baltimore: Johns Hopkins University Press, 2001.

Grantham, Dewey W. *The Life and Death of the Solid South: A Political History*. Lexington: University Press of Kentucky, 1988.

Green, Laurie B. *Battling the Plantation Mentality: Memphis and the Black Freedom Struggle*. Chapel Hill: University of North Carolina Press, 2007.

Griffin, Larry J. "Southern Distinctiveness, Yet Again, or, Why America Still Needs the South." In *Southern Cultures: The Fifteenth Anniversary Reader, 1993–2008*, edited by Harry L. Watson and Larry J. Griffin, 3–21. Chapel Hill: University of North Carolina Press, 2008.

Griffin, Larry J., Paula Clark, and Joanne C. Sandberg. "Narrative and Event: Lynching and Historical Sociology." In *Under Sentence of Death: Lynching in the South*, edited by W. Fitzhugh Brundage, 24–47. Chapel Hill: University of North Carolina Press, 1997.

Grossman, James R. "'Amiable Peasantry' or 'Social Burden': Constructing a Place for Black Southerners." In *American Exceptionalism? U.S. Working-Class Formation in an International Context*, edited by Rick Halpern and Jonathan Morris, 221–43. New York: St. Martin's, 1997.

Gussow, Adam. *Seems Like Murder Here: Southern Violence and the Blues Tradition*. Chicago: University of Chicago Press, 2002.

Guterl, Matthew Pratt. *The Color of Race in America, 1900–1940*. Cambridge: Harvard University Press, 2001.

Hadden, Sally E. *Slave Patrols: Law and Violence in Virginia and the Carolinas*. Cambridge: Harvard University Press, 2001.

Halbwachs, Maurice. *On Collective Memory*. Chicago: University of Chicago Press, 1992.

Hale, Grace Elizabeth. *Making Whiteness: The Culture of Segregation in the South, 1890–1940*. New York: Vintage Books, 1998.

Hall, Jacquelyn Dowd. "The Long Civil Rights Movement and the Political Uses of the Past." *Journal of American History* 91 (March 2005): 1233–63.

————. *Revolt against Chivalry: Jessie Daniel Ames and the Women's Campaign against Lynching*. Rev. ed. New York: Columbia University Press, 1993.

Hamer, Fannie Lou. "To Praise Our Bridges." In *The Eyes on the Prize Civil Rights Reader: Documents, Speeches, and Firsthand Accounts from the Black Freedom Struggle*, edited by Clayborne Carson, David J. Garrow, Gerald Gill, Vincent Harding, and Darlene Clark Hine, 176–78. New York: Penguin, 1991.

Hamlin, Françoise N. *Crossroads at Clarksdale: The Black Freedom Struggle in the Mississippi Delta after World War II*. Chapel Hill: University of North Carolina Press, 2012.

Hampton, Henry, and Steven Fayer, with Sarah Flynn. "Albany, Georgia, 1961–1962." In *Voices of Freedom: An Oral History of the Civil Rights Movement from the 1950s through the 1980s*, edited by Henry Hampton and Steve Fayer, with Sarah Flynn, 97–114. New York: Bantam, 1990.

Hanchard, Michael. "Afro-Modernity: Temporality, Politics, and the African Diaspora." In *Alter/Native Modernities*, edited by Dilip Parameshwar Gaonkar, 245–68. Durham: Duke University Press, 2001.

Harris, Carl V. "Reforms in Government Control of Negroes in Birmingham, Alabama, 1890–1920." *Journal of Southern History* 38 (1972): 567–600.

Harris, Trudier. *Exorcising Blackness: Historical and Literary Lynching and Burning Rituals*. Bloomington: Indiana University Press, 1985.

Hartman, Saidiya V. *Scenes of Subjection: Terror, Slavery, and Self-Making in Nineteenth-Century America*. New York: Oxford University Press, 1997.

Heard, Alex. *The Eyes of Willie McGee: A Tragedy of Race, Sex, and Secrets in the Jim Crow South*. New York: Harper, 2010.

Henry, Aaron, with Constance Curry. *Aaron Henry: The Fire Ever Burning*. Jackson: University Press of Mississippi, 2000.

Hill, Lance. *The Deacons for Defense: Armed Resistance and the Civil Rights Movement*. Chapel Hill: University of North Carolina Press, 2004.

Hine, Darlene Clark, William C. Hine, and Stanley Harrold. *The African American Odyssey*. Upper Saddle River: Prentice Hall, 2000.

Holland, Endesha Ida Mae. *From the Mississippi Delta*. New York: Simon and Schuster, 1997.

Holt, Thomas C. "Marking: Race, Race-Making, and the Writing of History." *American Historical Review* 100 (February 1995): 1–20.

Hondagneu-Sotelo, Pierrette. *Doméstica: Immigrant Workers Cleaning and Caring in the Shadows of Affluence*. Berkeley: University of California Press, 2001.

Horne, Gerald. *Communist Front?: The Civil Rights Congress, 1946–1956*. Rutherford: Fairleigh Dickinson Press, 1988.

————. *Fire This Time: The Watts Uprising and the 1960s*. Charlottesville: University Press of Virginia, 1995.

Houck, Davis W., and Matthew A. Grindy. *Emmett Till and the Mississippi Press*. Jackson: University Press of Mississippi, 2008.

Hudson, Winson, with Constance Curry. *Mississippi Harmony: Memoirs of a Freedom Fighter*. New York: Palgrave Macmillan, 2002.

Hunter, Tera W. *To 'Joy My Freedom: Southern Black Women's Lives and Labors after the Civil War*. Cambridge: Harvard University Press, 1997.

Irons, Jenny. *Reconstituting Whiteness: The Mississippi State Sovereignty Commission*. Nashville: Vanderbilt University Press, 2010.

Jackson, John P., Jr. *Science for Segregation: Race, Law, and the Case against Brown v. Board of Education*. New York: New York University Press, 2005.

Jacoway, Elizabeth, and David R. Colburn, eds. *Southern Businessmen and Desegregation*. Baton Rouge: Louisiana State University Press, 1982.

James, Joy. *Resisting State Violence: Radicalism, Gender, and Race in U.S. Culture*. Minneapolis: University of Minnesota Press, 1996.

Jeffries, Hasan Kwame. *Bloody Lowndes: Civil Rights and Black Power in Alabama's Black Belt*. New York: New York University Press, 2009.

Johnson, Charles S. *Patterns of Negro Segregation*. New York: Harper, 1943.

Johnson, E. Patrick. *Appropriating Blackness: Performance and the Politics of Authenticity*. Durham: Duke University Press, 2003.

Johnson, Kimberley. *Reforming Jim Crow: Southern Politics and State in the Age before Brown*. New York: Oxford University Press, 2010.

Johnson, Marilynn S. *Street Justice: A History of Police Violence in New York City*. Boston: Beacon Press, 2003.

Jones, Jacqueline. *Labor of Love, Labor of Sorrow: Black Women, Work, and the Family from Slavery to the Present*. New York: Vintage Books, 1985.

Joseph, Peniel E. *Waiting 'Til the Midnight Hour: A Narrative History of Black Power in America*. New York: Henry Holt, 2006.

Kantrowitz, Stephen. "One Man's Mob Is Another Man's Militia: Violence, Manhood, and Authority in Reconstruction South Carolina." In *Jumpin' Jim Crow: Southern Politics from Civil War to Civil Rights*, edited by Jane Dailey, Glenda Elizabeth Gilmore, and Bryant Simon, 67–87. Princeton: Princeton University Press, 2000.

Kasher, Steven. *The Civil Rights Movement: A Photographic History, 1954–1968*. New York: Abbeville Press, 1996.

Katagiri, Yasuhiro. *The Mississippi State Sovereignty Commission: Civil Rights and States' Rights*. Jackson: University Press of Mississippi, 2001.

Katzman, David M. *Seven Days a Week: Women and Domestic Service in Industrializing America*. New York: Oxford University Press, 1978.

Kaul, Arthur J. "Hazel Brannon Smith and the *Lexington Advertiser*." In *The Press and Race: Mississippi Journalists Confront the Movement*, edited by David R. Davies, 233–64. Jackson: University of Mississippi Press, 2001.

Kelley, Blair L. M. *Right to Ride: Streetcar Boycotts and African American Citizenship in the Era of Plessy v. Ferguson*. Chapel Hill: University of North Carolina Press, 2010.

Kelley, Robin D. G. *Hammer and Hoe: Alabama Communists during the Great Depression*. Chapel Hill: University of North Carolina Press, 1990.

———. *Race Rebels: Culture, Politics, and the Black Working Class*. New York: Free Press, 1996.

Kennedy, Randall. *Interracial Intimacies: Sex, Marriage, Identity, and Adoption*. New York: Vintage Books, 2003.

Kennedy, Stetson. *Jim Crow Guide: The Way It Was.* 1959. Reprint, Boca Raton: Florida Atlantic University Press, 1990.

Key, V. O., Jr. *Southern Politics in State and Nation.* New York: Alfred A. Knopf, 1949.

Kirby, Jack Temple. *Rural Worlds Lost: The American South, 1920–1960.* Baton Rouge: Louisiana State University Press, 1987.

Klarman, Michael J. *From Jim Crow to Civil Rights: The Supreme Court and the Struggle for Racial Equality.* New York: Oxford University Press, 2004.

Kluger, Richard. *Simple Justice: The History of* Brown v. Board of Education *and Black America's Struggle for Equality.* New York: Alfred A. Knopf, 1975.

Kousser, J. Morgan. *The Shaping of Southern Politics: Suffrage Restriction and the Establishment of the One-Party South, 1880–1910.* New Haven: Yale University Press, 1974.

Kramer, Paul A. *The Blood of Government: Race, Empire, the United States, and the Philippines.* Chapel Hill: University of North Carolina Press, 2006.

Kruse, Kevin M. *White Flight: Atlanta and the Making of Modern Conservatism.* Princeton: Princeton University Press, 2005.

Kurashige, Scott. *The Shifting Grounds of Race: Black and Japanese Americans in the Making of Multiethnic Los Angeles.* Princeton: Princeton University Press, 2010.

Landry, Stuart Omar. *The Cult of Equality: A Study of the Race Problem.* New Orleans: Pelican, 1945.

Lassiter, Matthew D. *The Silent Majority: Suburban Politics in the Sunbelt South.* Princeton: Princeton University Press, 2006.

Lassiter, Matthew D., and Joseph Crespino. "Introduction: The End of Southern History." In *The Myth of Southern Exceptionalism,* edited by Matthew D. Lassiter and Joseph Crespino, 3–22. New York: Oxford University Press, 2010.

Lassiter, Matthew D., and Andrew B. Lewis. *The Moderates' Dilemma: Massive Resistance to School Desegregation in Virginia.* Charlottesville: University Press of Virginia, 1998.

Lawson, Steven F. *Black Ballots: Voting Rights in the South, 1944–1969.* Lanham, Md.: Lexington Books, 1999.

———. "Freedom Then, Freedom Now: The Historiography of the Civil Rights Movement." *American Historical Review* 96 (April 1991): 456–71.

Lee, Chana Kai. *For Freedom's Sake: The Life of Fannie Lou Hamer.* Urbana: University of Illinois Press, 1999.

Leidholdt, Alexander S. *Standing before the Shouting Mob: Lenoir Chambers and Virginia's Massive Resistance to Public-School Integration.* Tuscaloosa: University of Alabama Press, 1997.

Lesseig, Corey T. "Roast Beef and Racial Integrity: Mississippi's 'Race and Reason Day,' October 26, 1961." *Journal of Mississippi History* 56 (February 1994): 1–15.

Levine, Lawrence W. *Black Culture, Black Consciousness: Afro-American Folk Thought from Slavery to Freedom.* New York: Oxford University Press, 1977.

Lewis, George. *Massive Resistance: The White Response to the Civil Rights Movement.* London: Hodder Arnold, 2006.

――. *The White South and the Red Menace: Segregationists, Anticommunism, and Massive Resistance, 1945–1965*. Gainesville: University Press of Florida, 2004.

Linebaugh, Peter. *The London Hanged: Crime and Civil Society in the Eighteenth Century*. 2nd ed. London: Verso, 2003.

Lipsitz, George. *The Possessive Investment in Whiteness: How White People Profit from Identity Politics*. Rev. ed. Philadelphia: Temple University Press, 2006.

――. "The Struggle for Hegemony." *Journal of American History* 75 (June 1988): 146–50.

Litwack, Leon F. *Been in the Storm So Long: The Aftermath of Slavery*. New York: Vintage, 1980.

――. *Trouble in Mind: Black Southerners in the Age of Jim Crow*. New York: Alfred A. Knopf, 1998.

Lui, Mary Ting Yi. *The Chinatown Trunk Mystery: Murder, Miscegenation, and Other Dangerous Encounters in Turn-of-the-Century New York City*. Princeton: Princeton University Press, 2005.

Lyon, David. *Surveillance Studies: An Overview*. Cambridge, U.K.: Polity Press, 2007.

Lyons, Clare A. *Sex among the Rabble: An Intimate History of Gender and Power in the Age of Revolution, Philadelphia, 1730–1830*. Chapel Hill: University of North Carolina Press, 2006.

Mack, Kenneth W. "Law, Society, Identity, and the Making of the Jim Crow South: Travel and Segregation on Tennessee Railroads, 1875–1905." *Law and Social Inquiry* 24 (Spring 1999): 377–409.

MacLean, Nancy. "The Leo Frank Case Reconsidered: Gender and Sexual Politics in the Making of Reactionary Populism." In *Jumpin' Jim Crow: Southern Politics from Civil War to Civil Rights*, edited by Jane Dailey, Glenda Elizabeth Gilmore, and Bryant Simon, 183–218. Princeton: Princeton University Press, 2000.

Manring, M. M. *Slave in a Box: The Strange Career of Aunt Jemima*. Charlottesville: University Press of Virginia, 1998.

Mason, Gilbert R. *Beaches, Blood, and Ballots: A Black Doctor's Civil Rights Struggle*. Jackson: University Press of Mississippi, 2000.

Massey, Doreen. *For Space*. London: Sage, 2005.

――. *Space, Place, and Gender*. Minneapolis: University of Minnesota Press, 1994.

Masur, Louis P. *Rites of Execution: Capital Punishment and the Transformation of American Culture, 1776–1865*. New York: Oxford University Press, 1991.

Mathiesen, Thomas. "The Viewer Society: Michel Foucault's Panopticon Revisited." *Theoretical Criminology* 1 (1997): 215–34.

Mattson, Kevin. "Civil Rights Made Harder." *Reviews in American History* 30 (December 2002): 663–70.

Mazzari, Louis. *Southern Modernist: Arthur Raper from the New Deal to the Cold War*. Baton Rouge: Louisiana State University Press, 2006.

McCarthy, Anna. *The Citizen Machine: Governing by Television in 1950s America*. New York: New Press, 2010.

McElya, Micki. *Clinging to Mammy: The Faithful Slave in Twentieth-Century America*. Cambridge: Harvard University Press, 2007.

McGirr, Lisa. *Suburban Warriors: The Origins of the New American Right*. Princeton: Princeton University Press, 2001.

McGuire, Danielle L. *At the Dark End of the Street: Black Women, Rape, and Resistance—A New History of the Civil Rights Movement from Rosa Parks to the Rise of Black Power*. New York: Alfred A. Knopf, 2010.

McKnight, Gerald D. *The Last Crusade: Martin Luther King, Jr., the FBI, and the Poor People's Campaign*. Boulder: Westview Press, 1998.

McMillen, Neil R. *The Citizens' Council: Organized Resistance to the Second Reconstruction, 1954–1964*. Urbana: University of Illinois Press, 1971.

———. *Dark Journey: Black Mississippians in the Age of Jim Crow*. Urbana: University of Illinois Press, 1989.

McPherson, Tara. *Reconstructing Dixie: Race, Gender, and Nostalgia in the Imagined South*. Durham: Duke University Press, 2003.

McRae, Elizabeth Gillespie. "White Womanhood, White Supremacy, and the Rise of Massive Resistance." In *Massive Resistance: Southern Opposition to the Second Reconstruction*, edited by Clive Webb, 181–202. New York: Oxford University Press, 2005.

Meier, August, and Elliott Rudwick. "The Boycott Movement against Jim Crow Streetcars in the South, 1900–1906." *Journal of American History* 55 (March 1969): 756–75.

Metress, Christopher, ed. *The Lynching of Emmett Till: A Documentary Narrative*. Charlottesville: University of Virginia Press, 2002.

Mills, Kay. *Changing Channels: The Civil Rights Case That Transformed Television*. Jackson: University Press of Mississippi, 2004.

———. *This Little Light of Mine: The Life of Fannie Lou Hamer*. New York: Plume, 1993.

Molina, Natalia. *How Race Is Made in America: Immigration, Citizenship, and the Historical Power of Racial Scripts*. Berkeley: University of California Press, 2014.

Moran, Rachel F. *Interracial Intimacy: The Regulation of Race and Romance*. Chicago: University of Chicago Press, 2001.

Morgan, Edward P. "The Good, the Bad, and the Forgotten: Media Culture and Public Memory of the Civil Rights Movement." In *The Civil Rights Movement in American Memory*, edited by Renee C. Romano and Leigh Raiford, 137–66. Athens: University of Georgia Press, 2006.

Moye, J. Todd. *Let the People Decide: Black Freedom and White Resistance Movements in Sunflower County, Mississippi, 1945–1986*. Chapel Hill: University of North Carolina Press, 2004.

Muhammad, Khalil Gibran. *The Condemnation of Blackness: Race, Crime, and the Making of Modern America*. Cambridge: Harvard University Press, 2010.

Murch, Donna Jean. *Living for the City: Migration, Education, and the Rise of the Black Panther Party in Oakland, California*. Chapel Hill: University of North Carolina Press, 2010.

Myrdal, Gunnar. *The Negro Problem and Modern Democracy.* Vol. 1 of *An American Dilemma.* New York: Harper and Row, 1944.

Newby, I. A. *Challenge to the Court: Social Scientists and the Defense of Segregation, 1954–1966.* Baton Rouge: Louisiana State University Press, 1969.

Noer, Thomas. "Segregationists and the World: The Foreign Policy of the White Resistance." In *Window on Freedom: Race, Civil Rights, and Foreign Affairs, 1945–1988,* edited by Brenda Gayle Plummer, 141–62. Chapel Hill: University of North Carolina Press, 2003.

Nora, Pierre. "Between Memory and History: *Les Lieux de Mémoire.*" *Representations* 26 (Spring 1989): 7–24.

O'Brien, Gail Williams. *The Color of the Law: Race, Violence, and Justice in the Post–World War II South.* Chapel Hill: University of North Carolina Press, 1999.

Odum, Howard W. *Race and Rumors of Race: The American South in the Early Forties.* Baltimore: Johns Hopkins University Press, 1997.

Olwell, Robert. *Masters, Slaves, and Subjects: The Culture of Power in the South Carolina Low Country, 1740–1790.* Ithaca: Cornell University Press, 1998.

Omi, Michael, and Howard Winant. *Racial Formation in the United States: From the 1960s to the 1990s.* 2nd ed. New York: Routledge, 1994.

O'Reilly, Kenneth. *"Racial Matters": The FBI's Secret File on Black America, 1960–1972.* New York: Free Press, 1989.

Oshinsky, David M. *"Worse Than Slavery": Parchman Farm and the Ordeal of Jim Crow Justice.* New York: Free Press, 1996.

Ownby, Ted. *American Dreams in Mississippi: Consumers, Poverty, and Culture, 1830–1998.* Chapel Hill: University of North Carolina Press, 1999.

Packard, Jerrold M. *American Nightmare: The History of Jim Crow.* New York: St. Martin's, 2002.

Parenti, Christian. *The Soft Cage: Surveillance in America from Slavery to the War on Terror.* New York: Basic Books, 2003.

Pascoe, Peggy. *What Comes Naturally: Miscegenation Law and the Making of Race in America.* New York: Oxford University Press, 2009.

Payne, Charles M. *I've Got the Light of Freedom: The Organizing Tradition and the Mississippi Freedom Struggle.* Berkeley: University of California Press, 1995.

Plummer, Brenda Gayle. *Rising Wind: Black Americans and U.S. Foreign Affairs, 1935–1960.* Chapel Hill: University of North Carolina Press, 1996.

———, ed. *Window on Freedom: Race, Civil Rights, and Foreign Affairs, 1945–1988.* Chapel Hill: University of North Carolina Press, 2003.

Portelli, Alessandro. *The Death of Luigi Trastulli and Other Stories: Form and Meaning in Oral History.* Albany: State University of New York Press, 1991.

———. "The Peculiarities of Oral History." *History Workshop* 12 (Autumn 1981): 96–107.

Povall, Allie. *The Time of Eddie Noel.* Concord, N.C.: Comfort Publishing, 2010.

Powdermaker, Hortense. *After Freedom: A Cultural Study in the Deep South.* New York: Viking Press, 1939.

Rabinowitz, Howard N. "More Than the Woodward Thesis: Assessing *The Strange Career of Jim Crow*." *Journal of American History* 75 (December 1988): 842–56.

———. *Race Relations in the Urban South, 1865–1890*. New York: Oxford University Press, 1978.

Raiford, Leigh. *Imprisoned in a Luminous Glare: Photography and the African American Freedom Struggle*. Chapel Hill: University of North Carolina Press, 2011.

Ransby, Barbara. *Ella Baker and the Black Freedom Movement: A Radical Democratic Vision*. Chapel Hill: University of North Carolina Press, 2003.

Raper, Arthur F. *The Tragedy of Lynching*. Chapel Hill: University of North Carolina Press, 1933.

Rios, Victor M. *Punished: Policing the Lives of Black and Latino Boys*. New York: New York University Press, 2011.

Ritterhouse, Jennifer. *Growing Up Jim Crow: How Black and White Southern Children Learned Race*. Chapel Hill: University of North Carolina Press, 2006.

Roberts, Gene, and Hank Klibanoff. *The Race Beat: The Press, the Civil Rights Struggle, and the Awakening of a Nation*. New York: Alfred A. Knopf, 2006.

Roberts, John W. *From Trickster to Badman: The Black Folk Hero in Slavery and Freedom*. Philadelphia: University of Pennsylvania Press, 1989.

Robinson, Jo Ann Gibson. *The Montgomery Bus Boycott and the Women Who Started It*. Knoxville: University of Tennessee Press, 1987.

Rollins, Judith. *Between Women: Domestics and Their Employers*. Philadelphia: Temple University Press, 1985.

Romano, Renee C. "Narratives of Redemption: The Birmingham Church Bombing Trials and the Construction of Civil Rights Memory." In *The Civil Rights Movement in American Memory*, edited by Renee C. Romano and Leigh Raiford, 96–134. Athens: University of Georgia Press, 2006.

Romero, Mary. *Maid in the U.S.A.* New York: Routledge, 1992.

Ross, Luana. *Inventing the Savage: The Social Construction of Native American Criminality*. Austin: University of Texas Press, 1998.

Rousey, Dennis C. *Policing the Southern City: New Orleans, 1805–1889*. Baton Rouge: Louisiana State University Press, 1996.

Rowe-Sims, Sarah. "The Mississippi State Sovereignty Commission: An Agency History." *Journal of Mississippi History* 61 (Spring 1999): 29–58.

Sánchez, George J. *Becoming Mexican American: Ethnicity, Culture, and Identity in Chicano Los Angeles, 1900–1945*. New York: Oxford University Press, 1993.

———. "'What's Good for Boyle Heights Is Good for the Jews': Creating Multiracialism on the Eastside during the 1950s." *American Quarterly* 56 (September 2004): 633–61.

Satter, Beryl. *Family Properties: Race, Real Estate, and the Exploitation of Black Urban America*. New York: Metropolitan Books, 2009.

Schulman, Bruce J. *From Cotton Belt to Sunbelt: Federal Policy, Economic Development, and the Transformation of the South, 1938–1980*. New York: Oxford University Press, 1991.

Schultz, Mark. *The Rural Face of White Supremacy: Beyond Jim Crow*. Urbana: University of Illinois Press, 2005.

Scott, James C. *Domination and the Arts of Resistance: Hidden Transcripts*. New Haven: Yale University Press, 1992.

Seiler, Cotten. "'So That We as a Race Might Have Something Authentic to Travel By': African American Automobility and Cold-War Liberalism." *American Quarterly* 58 (December 2006): 1091–1117.

Self, Robert O. *American Babylon: Race and the Struggle for Postwar Oakland*. Princeton: Princeton University Press, 2003.

Senechal de la Roche, Roberta. "The Sociogenesis of Lynching." In *Under Sentence of Death: Lynching in the South*, edited by W. Fitzhugh Brundage, 48–76. Chapel Hill: University of North Carolina Press, 1997.

Shah, Nayan. *Contagious Divides: Epidemics and Race in San Francisco's Chinatown*. Berkeley: University of California Press, 2001.

Sharpless, Rebecca. *Cooking in Other Women's Kitchens: Domestic Workers in the South, 1865–1960*. Chapel Hill: University of North Carolina Press, 2010.

Silver, James W. *Mississippi: The Closed Society*. New York: Harcourt, Brace, and World, 1964.

Simon, Bryant. *Boardwalk of Dreams: Atlantic City and the Fate of Urban America*. New York: Oxford University Press, 2004.

———. "Race Reactions: African American Organizing, Liberalism, and White Working-Class Politics in Postwar South Carolina." In *Jumpin' Jim Crow: Southern Politics from Civil War to Civil Rights*, edited by Jane Dailey, Glenda Elizabeth Gilmore, and Bryant Simon, 239–59. Princeton: Princeton University Press, 2000.

Sitkoff, Harvard. *The Struggle for Black Equality*. Rev. ed. New York: Hill and Wang, 1993.

Skinner, Reginald, and Jackie Collins. "Mr. T. C. Johnson: The Dirt Farmers Started the Movement." In *Minds Stayed on Freedom: The Civil Rights Struggle in the Rural South, an Oral History*, edited by Youth of the Rural Organizing and Cultural Center, 143–58. Boulder: Westview Press, 1991.

Smead, Howard. *Blood Justice: The Lynching of Mack Charles Parker*. New York: Oxford University Press, 1986.

Smith, J. Douglas. *Managing White Supremacy: Race, Politics, and Citizenship in Jim Crow Virginia*. Chapel Hill: University of North Carolina Press, 2002.

Smith, John David. *When Did Southern Segregation Begin?* Boston: Bedford/ St. Martin's, 2002.

Smith, Philip. "Executing Executions: Aesthetics, Identity, and the Problematic Narratives of Capital Punishment Ritual." *Theory and Society* 25 (1996): 235–61.

Smith, Suzanne E. *To Serve the Living: Funeral Directors and the African American Way of Life*. Cambridge: Harvard University Press, 2010.

Sokol, Jason. *There Goes My Everything: White Southerners in the Age of Civil Rights, 1945–1975*. New York: Vintage, 2006.

Sparrow, James T. "A Nation in Motion: Norfolk, the Pentagon, and the Nationalization of the Metropolitan South, 1941–1953." In *The Myth of Southern Exceptionalism*, edited by Matthew D. Lassiter and Joseph Crespino, 167–89. New York: Oxford University Press, 2009.

Spillers, Hortense J. "Mama's Baby, Papa's Maybe: An American Grammar Book." *Diacritics* 17 (Summer 1987): 64–81.

Stockett, Kathryn. *The Help*. New York: Amy Einhorn Books, 2009.

Sugrue, Thomas J. *The Origins of the Urban Crisis: Race and Inequality in Postwar Detroit*. Princeton: Princeton University Press, 1996.

———. *Sweet Land of Liberty: The Forgotten Struggle for Civil Rights in the North*. New York: Random House, 2008.

Sullivan, Patricia. *Days of Hope: Race and Democracy in the New Deal Era*. Chapel Hill: University of North Carolina Press, 1996.

Theoharis, Jeanne F. "Black Freedom Struggles: Re-imagining and Redefining the Fundamentals." *History Compass* 4 (February 2006): 348–67.

Theoharis, Jeanne F., and Komozi Woodard, eds. *Freedom North: Black Freedom Struggles Outside the South, 1940–1980*. New York: Palgrave Macmillan, 2003.

Thompson, Heather Ann. "Why Mass Incarceration Matters: Rethinking Crisis, Decline, and Transformation in Postwar America." *Journal of American History* 97 (December 2010): 703–34.

Thompson, Julius E. *The Black Press in Mississippi, 1865–1985*. Gainesville: University Press of Florida, 1993.

———. *Percy Greene and the Jackson Advocate: The Life and Times of a Radical Conservative Black Newspaperman, 1897–1977*. Jefferson, N.C.: McFarland, 1994.

Thompson, Leonard. *A History of South Africa*. 3rd ed. New Haven: Yale University Press, 2001.

Thorndike, Joseph J. "'The Sometimes Sordid Level of Race and Segregation': James J. Kilpatrick and the Virginia Campaign against *Brown*." In *The Moderates' Dilemma: Massive Resistance to School Desegregation in Virginia*, edited by Matthew D. Lassiter and Andrew B. Lewis, 51–71. Charlottesville: University Press of Virginia, 1998.

Till-Mobley, Mamie, and Christopher Benson. *Death of Innocence: The Story of the Hate Crime That Changed America*. New York: Random House, 2003.

Tindall, George B. *The Emergence of the New South, 1913–1945*. Baton Rouge: Louisiana State University Press, 1967.

Tisdale, John R. "'Don't Stone Her Until You See Her Side': New England Editors and the Mississippi State Sovereignty Commission's Public Relations Campaign of 1956." *Journal of Mississippi History* 64 (Fall 2002): 169–88.

Torres, Sasha. *Black, White, and in Color: Television and Black Civil Rights*. Princeton: Princeton University Press, 2003.

Trouillot, Michel-Rolph. *Silencing the Past: Power and the Production of History*. Boston: Beacon Press, 1995.

Tucker, Susan. *Telling Memories among Southern Women: Domestic Workers and Their Employers in the Segregated South*. Baton Rouge: Louisiana State University Press, 1988.

Tyler, Pamela. "'Blood on Your Hands': White Southerners' Criticism of Eleanor Roosevelt during World War II." In *Before Brown: Civil Rights and White Backlash in the Modern South*, edited by Glenn Feldman, 96–115. Tuscaloosa: University of Alabama Press, 2004.

Tyson, Timothy B. *Radio Free Dixie: Robert F. Williams and the Roots of Black Power*. Chapel Hill: University of North Carolina Press, 1999.

Umoja, Akinyele Omowale. *We Will Shoot Back: Armed Resistance in the Mississippi Freedom Movement*. New York: New York University Press, 2013.

Vansina, Jan. *Oral Tradition as History*. Madison: University of Wisconsin Press, 1985.

Van Wormer, Katherine, David W. Jackson III, and Charletta Sudduth. *The Maid Narratives: Black Domestics and White Families in the Jim Crow South*. Baton Rouge: Louisiana State University Press, 2012.

Von Eschen, Penny M. *Race against Empire: Black Americans and Anticolonialism, 1937–1957*. Ithaca: Cornell University Press, 1997.

Wade, Richard C. *Slavery in the Cities: The South, 1820–1860*. New York: Oxford University Press, 1964.

Wagner, Bryan. *Disturbing the Peace: Black Culture and the Police Power after Slavery*. Cambridge: Harvard University Press, 2009.

Waldrep, Christopher. "National Policing, Lynching, and Constitutional Change." *Journal of Southern History* 74 (August 2008): 589–626.

Walker, Anders. *The Ghost of Jim Crow: How Southern Moderates Used* Brown v. Board of Education *to Stall Civil Rights*. New York: Oxford University Press, 2009.

———. "The Violent Bear It Away: Emmett Till and the Modernization of Law Enforcement in Mississippi." *San Diego Law Review* 46 (Spring 2009): 459–502.

Walker, Samuel. *Popular Justice: A History of American Criminal Justice*. 2nd ed. New York: Oxford University Press, 1998.

Wallace-Sanders, Kimberly. *Mammy: A Century of Race, Gender, and Southern Memory*. Ann Arbor: University of Michigan Press, 2008.

Ward, Jason Morgan. *Defending White Democracy: The Making of a Segregationist Movement and the Remaking of Racial Politics, 1936–1965*. Chapel Hill: University of North Carolina Press, 2011.

Watts, Eugene J. "The Police in Atlanta, 1890–1905." *Journal of Southern History* 39 (1973): 165–82.

Webb, Clive, ed. *Massive Resistance: Southern Opposition to the Second Reconstruction*. New York: Oxford University Press, 2005.

Weill, Susan. *In a Madhouse's Din: Civil Rights Coverage by Mississippi's Daily Press, 1948–1968*. Westport, Conn.: Praeger, 2002.

Wells-Barnett, Ida B. *The Red Record*. Milwaukee: Garvey Ali University Publishing, 2011.

Wendt, Simon. *The Spirit and the Shotgun: Armed Resistance and the Struggle for Civil Rights*. Gainesville: University Press of Florida, 2007.

Whalen, John A. *Maverick among the Magnolias: The Hazel Brannon Smith Story*. Philadelphia: Xlibris, 2002.

Whitfield, Stephen J. *A Death in the Delta: The Story of Emmett Till*. New York: Free Press, 1988.

Whitt, Jan. *Burning Crosses and Activist Journalism: Hazel Brannon Smith and the Mississippi Civil Rights Movement*. Lanham, Md.: University Press of America, 2009.

Wiegman, Robyn. *American Anatomies: Theorizing Race and Gender*. Durham: Duke University Press, 1995.

Wilhoit, Francis M. *The Politics of Massive Resistance*. New York: G. Braziller, 1973.

Williams, Michael Vinson. *Medgar Evers: Mississippi Martyr*. Fayetteville: University of Arkansas Press, 2011.

Williamson, Joel. *After Slavery: The Negro in South Carolina during Reconstruction, 1861–1877*. New York: W. W. Norton, 1965.

———. *The Crucible of Race: Black-White Relations in the American South since Emancipation*. New York: Oxford University Press, 1984.

Wolff, Robert Paul. "On Violence." *Journal of Philosophy* 66 (October 1969): 601–16.

Wolters, Raymond. *The Burden of Brown: Thirty Years of School Desegregation*. Knoxville: University of Tennessee Press, 1984.

Wood, Amy Louis. *Lynching and Spectacle: Witnessing Racial Violence in America, 1890–1940*. Chapel Hill: University of North Carolina Press, 2009.

Woodruff, Nan Elizabeth. *American Congo: The African American Freedom Struggle in the Delta*. Cambridge: Harvard University Press, 2003.

Woods, Jeff. *Black Struggle, Red Scare: Segregation and Anti-Communism in the South, 1948–1968*. Baton Rouge: Louisiana State University Press, 2004.

Woodward, C. Vann. *The Burden of Southern History*. 3rd ed. Baton Rouge: Louisiana State University Press, 1993.

———. *Origins of the New South*. Baton Rouge: Louisiana State University Press, 1971.

———. *The Strange Career of Jim Crow*. Commemorative ed. New York: Oxford University Press, 2002.

Wright, George C. "By the Book: The Legal Executions of Kentucky Blacks." In *Under Sentence of Death: Lynching in the South*, edited by W. Fitzhugh Brundage, 250–70. Chapel Hill: University of North Carolina Press, 1997.

———. *Racial Violence in Kentucky, 1865–1940: Lynchings, Mob Violence, and "Legal Lynchings."* Baton Rouge: Louisiana State Press, 1990.

Wright, Richard. "The Ethics of Living Jim Crow: An Autobiographical Sketch." In *Uncle Tom's Children*. New York: Harper Perennial, 2004.

Wu, Ellen D. *The Color of Success: Asian Americans and the Origins of the Model Minority*. Princeton: Princeton University Press, 2013.

Zaim, Craig. "Trial by Ordeal: The Willie McGee Case." *Journal of Mississippi History* 65 (2003): 215–47.

Ziker, Ann Katherine. "Race, Conservative Politics, and U.S. Foreign Policy in the Postcolonial World, 1948–1968." Ph.D. diss., Rice University, 2008.

INDEX

Page references referring to photographs and illustrations are in *italics*.

164–65; segregationist concerns over media attention and, 139, 146, 147, 163, 165, 168, 169, 173, 174; segregation laws and, 142–50; space and, 165; as tactic in North and West, 7, 224, 226, 233 (n. 19); for walking, 43. *See also* Police and policing

Arrington, Elsie, 147–48

Asian and Asian Americans, 214, 227. *See also* Chinese and Chinese Americans

Association of Southern Women for the Prevention of Lynching (ASWPL), 70

Atlanta, Ga., 6, 32, 67, 178, 187, 274 (n. 105)

Atlantic City, N.J., 238 (n. 41)

Audience, 56; aggression narratives and, 65, 83; arrests and, 163–64, 165–67; arrests without, 167–68; in civil rights movement surveillance, 125–26; investigations and, 159; lynching and, 107–8; media coverage and, 10, 105, 113–20, 137, 139, 147, 163, 165, 221; narrative performances and, 64; national public as, 10, 64, 68, 70, 77, 78, 103, 105, 113–20, 175, 194, 210, 223, 277 (n. 14); performance and, 8–10; on sidewalks, 45; surveillance and, 103–4, 125–26, 136; unexpected performances and, 56–57; of white citizens watching blacks, 102–3, 123–30. *See also* Performance; Surveillance

Augustine, John, 76

"Aunt Pussyfoot," 211

Austin, Gladys, 50–51

Automobiles, 29–30, 32–33. *See also* Roadways

Avoidance, as a racial performance, 58–59, 241 (n. 75), 242 (n. 92)

Aycock, Charles, 237 (n. 19)

Ayers, Ed, 236 (n. 2)

Bailey, Orville, 61–64

Baker, Constance, 44–45, 47–48

Baker, Ella, 265 (n. 95)

Baker, Houston A., 253 (n. 118)

Baker, Josephine, 116

Baker, Ray Stannard, 52, 66–67, 242 (n. 92)

Balconies, theater, 25, 28, 40

Baltimore, Md., 201

Barbour, Haley, 218

Barbour, Johnny, 46

Barnes, Carsie, 191

Barnett, Ross, 121, 138, 158–59, 178, 199, 220, 264 (n. 86), 281 (n. 82)

Barrett, Eddie, 80

Barriers: on buses, 45, 46, 57–58; force and, 55–56; segregation and, 19, 20, 24, 25–26, 27, 29, 32, 36, 37, 41, 46, 221–22; on trains, 20, 26, 29, 32, 37

Bases, military, 53–54

Batesville, Miss., 208–9

Bauman, Richard, 256 (n. 165)

Bay, Georgia, 84

Belafonte, Harry, 265 (n. 95)

Benevolence: clemency and, 65, 82; and domestic servants, 243 (n. 109); executions as, 74, 75; media coverage and, 99, 100; narrative of, 70, 73, 101; paternalism and, 179, 180–94; performance of, 77. *See also* Paternalism

Berger, Dan, 274 (n. 102)

Berger, Martin A., 260 (n. 42), 262 (n. 67), 286 (n. 13)

Berger, Maurice, 117

Bevel, James, 139

Biloxi, Miss., 14, 163

Biondi, Martha, 233 (n. 19)

Birdsong, T. B., 159

Birmingham, Ala., 28, 104, 138, 141, 260 (n. 42)

Birth of a Nation (film), 67

Black codes, 20, 31, 239 (n. 47)

Black Panther Party, 224–25

plantations, 79; rape fears and, 196; segregation and, 7, 177–78, 197–98, 199–201; statistics, 177–78, 194–98, 199–200, 276 (nn. 3–4), 281 (n. 84). *See also* Deviance; Murder; Rape

Crisis in the South (film), 185

Crosby, Emilye, 240 (n. 53)

Crudup, Big Boy, 171

Customer lines, 36–38

Customers, African Americans as, 36–40

Customs, 30–33

Cutting in line, 36–38, 54–55

Dahmer, Ellie, 29, 54–55

Dahmer, Vernon, 54–55, 287 (n. 21)

Dailey, Jane, 5, 241 (n. 64)

"Dancing for the master," 260 (n. 36)

Daniels, Woodrow Wilson, 267 (n. 5), 282 (n. 86)

Danville, Va., 41

Davis, James, 202

Davis, Ossie, 116

"Death of Emmett Till, The" (Dylan), 221

Death penalty. *See* Capital Punishment; Executions

DeCell, Hal, 146, 183, 185, 186

Defense industry employment, 261 (n. 51)

Deference, 6, 22, 31, 50, 151, 80. *See also* Humility, racial roles in

Delta, 12–13, 34, *39*

"Delta Negro" (Cohn), 10, 79, 118

Democracy, cutting in line and, 38

Democratic Party, 116, 259 (n. 26)

Demographics, in Mississippi, 12

Dennis, Chenley, 255 (n. 152)

Desegregation, 6, 221–22; arrests over, 144; as breach of peace, 163; of education, 128–29, 133–34, 144, 150–51, 153–55, 156–57, 172–74, 184, 190, 202–4, 263 (n. 74), 281 (n. 71); of military, 115; of railroads, 144–45. *See also* Integration

Desegregation, white Southerners' responses to, 6, 178, 180, 181–82, 277 (n. 14), 282 (n. 99); after the Civil Rights Act of 1964, 221–22; and arrests, 146, 160–75; in Atlanta, 6, 178, 274–75 (n. 105); among business leaders, 279 (n. 44); in Charlotte, 6, 178; and divisions in the white community, 6, 187; involving interracial cohabitation, 146, 172–73; and massive resistance, 142–43; in legislation, 160–75, 268 (n. 15), 269 (n. 20), 274–75 (n. 105); in schools, 190, 202–3; and narratives of black crime, 194–206, 283 (n. 114); and racial mixing in South America, 212–13; references to race relations in the North and West, 201, 202–3. *See also* Arrest(s); Interposition; Massive resistance; Nullification; Violence

Deslondes, Charles, 252 (n. 90)

Detroit, Mich., 200

Deviance, 11–12, 194–206. *See also* Crime

Diallo, Amadou, 227

Dickard, Willie, 93–101, 256 (n. 154)

Diggs, Charles, Sr., 188, 200–201

Dining cars, on trains, 37

Disfranchisement, of black voters, 3, 64, 114, 115, 142, 146, 178, 194, 222, 226, 232 (n. 11), 259 (n. 26), 269 (n. 22)

Distance, segregation and, 235 (n. 34)

Disturbance, arrests for, 145–46. *See also* Breach of the peace

Dittmer, John, 268 (n. 15)

Dixon, Thomas, 67

Documentaries, 185

Dodd, Jeff, 255 (n. 152)

Dollard, John, 34–35, 79, 108–9

Domestic servants, 26, 29, 31–32, 48–50, 228–29, 238 (n. 40), 240 (n. 49), 243 (n. 109), 289 (n. 45)

Don't Stone Her Until You Hear Her Side (pamphlet), 194–96, *196*

Doors, 19
Dorr, Lisa, 252 (n. 102)
Doyle, Bertram Wilbur, 8, 238 (n. 40),
   241 (n. 83), 257 (n. 9)
Draughn, Tom Allen, 82
"Driving while black," 227. *See also*
   Roadways
DuBois, W. E. B., 65
Duckworth, Ed, 267 (n. 5)
Dunbar, Paul Laurence, 8

Eastland, James, 12, 121, 157, 180, 199,
   263 (n. 83), 277 (n. 14), 283 (n. 119)
East Orange, N.J., 201
Eckford, Elizabeth, 184
Eckles, Samuel, 167, 274 (n. 98)
Egerton, John, 287 (n. 32)
Einstein, Albert, 116
Elaine, Ark., 86
"Eleanor Clubs," 53
Electric chair, 74–76
Elevators, 1–2, 28
Ellison, Ralph, 8, 22, 237 (n. 14)
Emmerich, Oliver, 119, 192–93
Employees, domestic servants as,
   49–50, 243 (n. 109)
Employment, in defense industry,
   261 (n. 51)
Entertainment, as related to Jim Crow
   racial roles, 44, 82–83, 178,
   234 (n. 26), 242 (n. 92), 253 (n. 105),
   260 (n. 36)
Entranceways, 19
Ephraim, LaVerne, 144–45
Estes, Steve, 90, 254 (n. 138)
Ethel, Lu, 256 (n. 154)
"Ethics of Living Jim Crow, The"
   (Wright), 1, 218
Ethridge, Tom, 207–8
Etiquette, surveillance and, 257 (n. 9)
Evans, Lucious, 81
Everett, Carl H., 80–81
Evers, Medgar, 4, 62, 140–41, 158, 220,
   254 (n. 127), 267 (n. 5), 271 (n. 59)
Evers, Myrlie, 245 (n. 9)

Everyday realm, significance of, 2, 4, 5,
   6, 15, 22, 35, 218, 219, 230,
   232 (n. 9)
Evolution, 115
Executions, 73–78, 116, 249 (nn. 59, 62),
   250 (n. 67); similarities between
   lynching and, 73–74. *See also*
   Capital punishment

Fair Employment Practices
   Commission (FEPC), 157
Family, domestic workers in, 26, 31–32,
   48–49, 229, 243 (n. 109)
Faubus, Orville, 281 (n. 71)
Faulkner, William, 116, 248 (n. 42)
FBI. *See* Federal Bureau of
   Investigation
FCC. *See* Federal Communications
   Commission
Federal Bureau of Investigation (FBI),
   122, 125, 132, 224, 233 (n. 20),
   264 (n. 88)
Federal Communications Commission
   (FCC), 16
Federal government: black soldiers
   and, 53–54; civil rights movement
   and, 5, 115, 141, 146, 220, 221, 222,
   223, 249 (n. 52); defense industry
   employment and, 261 (n. 51);
   lynching and, 72, 249 (n. 52); New
   Deal and, 248 (n. 42); in South, 53,
   244 (n. 131)
Films, nostalgia and, 68
Flamm, Michael, 287 (n. 33)
Fleming, Cora, 85, 86
Flora, Miss., 52–53
Florida, 227
Flynt, J. Wayne, 248 (n. 42)
Folktales, 65, 256 (n. 165)
Following the Color Line (Baker), 52,
   66–67
Forest, Miss., 188
Fortenberry, Hilton, 72–73
Foucault, Michel, 257 (n. 5)
France, 285 (n. 143)

Franklin, James, 72
Frazier, Johnny, 164–65
Frederick, Booker, 87–88, 99
Frederickson, Kari, 248 (n. 42)
Fredrickson, George, 22
Freedom Riders, 15, 138–39, 141, 159, 163, *170*
Freedom Summer, 220
Friendship, in racial harmony narratives, 189, 190–91

Gaines v. Canada, 144
Garland, David, 247 (n. 25)
Gates, Eva, 37, 39, 46
Gatlin, Maurice, 77
Genovese, Eugene D., 252 (n. 90)
Georgia, 54. *See also specific cities*
Gilmore, Glenda Elizabeth, 5, 242 (n. 100)
God Shakes Creation (Cohn), 82–83
Goffman, Erving, 8–9
Golden, Allen, 81
Goldfield, David, 269 (n. 27)
Goluboff, Risa, 269 (n. 23)
Gone with the Wind (film), 68, 114–15, 277 (n. 18), 289 (n. 49)
Gooden, Bennie, 43, 44, 45
Goodman, Andrew, 4, 113, 267 (n. 5)
"Good Negro/bad Negro" categories, 80–81, 251 (n. 90)
Gordon, Marcell, *166*
Gore, Ney M., Jr., 177, 276 (n. 1)
Grand Central Station (Houston), 26–27
Great Britain, 216
Great Depression, 26
Green, Ernest, 71, 261 (n. 54)
Green, Laurie, 235 (n. 33)
Green, Roosevelt, 76
Greene, Percy, 235 (n. 42), 278 (n. 22)
Greensboro, N.C., 268 (n. 14), 269 (n. 27)
Greenville Delta Democrat Times (newspaper), 61–62
Gregory, E. M., 127, 133, 136

Griffith, D. W., 67
Griffith, Michael, 228
Grindy, Matthew A., 117
Grossman, James R., 235 (n. 33)
Gulf Coast, 14
Gulf Coast World (newspaper), 158–59
Gulfport, Miss., 14, 127
Guns, 14, 86, 89, 92, 100, 225, 254 (nn. 127, 133), 287 (n. 29)
Gussow, Adam, 85–86, 246 (n. 21)

Hadden, Sally, 267 (n. 9)
Haiti, 211, 285 (n. 139)
Hale, Grace Elizabeth, 21, 28, 54, 68, 231 (n. 7), 241 (n. 75), 246 (n. 24), 247 (n. 32)
Hall, Jacquelyn Dowd, 245 (n. 12), 247 (n. 34)
Hall, Pinkey, 36, 46
Hamer, Fannie Lou, 12, 168–69, 264 (n. 88)
Hanchard, Michael, 37
Hancock County, Ga., 259 (n. 24)
Handshakes, 31, *35*
Hanging, public, 73–74. *See also* Executions; Lynching(s)
Harlem, N.Y., 192, 201, 215
Harris, Dave, 108
Harris, Trudier, 85–86
Hartman, Saidiya, 231 (n. 7), 234 (n. 26), 260 (n. 36)
Hats, 19, 31
Hattiesburg, Miss., 46, 134, 156–57, 287 (n. 21)
Hattiesburg American (newspaper), 192
Hawkins, Willette, 116, 261 (n. 55)
Hederman, Robert, 121, 182, 200, 263 (n. 80), 281 (n. 68)
Hederman, Thomas, 121, 182, 200, 263 (n. 80), 281 (n. 68)
Help, The (Stockett), 229, 289 (n. 49)
Henry, Aaron, 62, 109–10, 112, 131, 134–35, 135–36, 155–56, *156*, 259 (n. 29)
Herbers, John, 183–84

"Here's to the State of Mississippi" (Ochs), 221

"Hidden transcripts," 14–15, 51

Hierarchy, segregation and, 21

Higginbotham, Elwood, 70

Higgs, William, 169, 265 (n. 94)

Highway patrol, 140, 157, 159, 167, 169, 221, 286 (n. 7). *See also* Police and policing

Hill, Donald, 171–72

Hitler, Adolf, 71

Holland, Endesha Ida Mae, 111, 112

Holman, Tim, 267 (n. 5)

Holmes County, Miss., 93–94, 222

Holt, Thomas C., 22

Homes, white, 48–50

Homicide. *See* Murder

Homosexuality, allegations of, 156–57

Hoover, J. Edgar, 132, 233 (n. 20)

Hopkins, A. L., 172

Hose, Sam, 67–68, 247 (n. 32)

Houck, Davis W., 117

Houston, Tex., 26

Hudson, Winson, 45, 110–11, 112

Huie, William, 256 (n. 1)

Humility, racial roles and, 80, 81, 83, 189. *See also* Deference

Humphreys County, Miss., 167

Hunton, Alphaeus, 157

Hurd, Frank, 88–89

Hurley, Ruby, 158

Hurston, Zora Neale, 278 (n. 22)

Hyde, Dewitt S., 202

Illegitimate children, 148–49, 204–6

Immigration and Naturalization Service (INS), 233 (n. 20)

Incrimination, 150–60

India, 210

Indianola, Miss., 34–35, 120, 248 (n. 47)

Informants, 130–32, 260 (n. 38), 266 (n. 114), 278 (n. 25)

Integration: black crime and, 197–202, 203–4, 215; black crime and deviance and segregation arguments against, 177–78, 194–206; miscegenation and, 211–13; performance of, 144–45; public opinion on, 187; resistance to, 142–43. *See also Brown v. Board of Education*; Desegregation

International Commerce Commission (ICC), 144, 145

Interposition, 142, 233 (n. 14), 268 (n. 18), 277 (n. 14)

Interracial intimacy, 10–11, 235 (n. 34), 288 (n. 42); compared to regions outside South, 240 (n. 49)

Interracial marriage, 147–49, 173, 265 (n. 93), 270 (n. 39)

Intimacy: customs and, 31; domestic servants and, 31–32, 48–49, 50, 229, 240 (n. 49); interracial, 10–11, 235 (n. 34), 288 (n. 42); lynching and, 107–8; performances of racial roles and, 48–50; post–Jim Crow narratives of the South and, 228–30; racial harmony and, 181; segregation and, 19–20, 21, 59–60; in segregationist discourses, 180–94; space and, 19–20, 22. *See also* Narrative(s); Performance

Intimidation, 150–60, 167, 168–69

Investigations, 150–60, 172

Invisible Man (Ellison), 8

Itta Bena, Miss., 87

Jackson, Miss., 15–16, 47–48, 52, 56–57, 134, 138–39, 144–45, 146–47, 163, 221, 266 (n. 124), 271 (n. 59)

Jackson, Wharlest, 287 (n. 21)

Jackson Advocate (newspaper), 13, 55–56, 62, 97–98, 255 (n. 150)

Jackson Clarion-Ledger (newspaper), 72, 121, 149, 159, 182, 188, 190, 200, 207–8

Jackson Daily News (newspaper), 13, 97, 98, 121, 169, 182, 190–91, 204

Jackson State Times (newspaper), 193, 281 (n. 68)

Jamaica, 213
Jim Crow: as "balancing act," 5, 9;
   compared to post–Jim Crow racial
   practices, 7, 217, 219–30; definition
   of 2–3; everyday routines and, 2, 4,
   5, 6, 15, 22–23, 35, 37, 39, 90, 106,
   123, 141–42, 144, 218, 219, 220,
   222, 227, 232 (n. 9); as national
   racial system, 3, 5, 6–7, 12, 115, 157,
   224–28, 179; Northern and Western
   forms of, 6–7, 115, 157, 224, 226,
   232 (n. 11), 233 (n. 19), 244 (n. 125),
   277 (n. 15); origins of, 24, 25,
   235–36 (n. 32), 236, (n. 2),
   239 (n. 47). *See also*
   Disfranchisement; Lynching(s);
   Segregation
Johnson, Charles S., 23–24, 37, 48
Johnson, E. Patrick, 50, 234 (n. 25)
Johnson, John, 85, 86
Johnson, Kimberley, 232 (n. 9),
   247 (n. 36)
Johnson, Lyndon, 221, 222
Johnson, Manning, 278 (n. 22)
Johnson, Paul, Sr., 72, 173
Johnson, Paul B., Jr., 221, 284 (n. 129)
Johnson, T. C., 99–100
Johnson County, N.C., 27
Johnston, Erle, Jr., 156–57, 173, 188–89,
   211, 214
Jones, Johnny, 90–91
Jones, J. W., 183, 213, 278 (n. 25)
Jones, Woodrow Wilson, 202
Juke joint, 27, *28*
Juvenile delinquency, 214–15

Kantrowitz, Stephen, 247 (n. 25)
Katagiri, Yasuhiro, 278 (n. 25)
Kelley, Robin D. G., 53, 104, 231 (n. 7),
   232 (n. 13), 243 (n. 119), 244 (n. 135)
Kennard, Clyde, 153–55, 161,
   271 (nn. 55, 62)
Kennedy, Robert F., 138
Kennedy, Stetson, 31, 238 (n. 26)
Kenya, 210, 211, *212*, 213

Key, David, 29, 30, 238 (n. 39)
Key, V. O., Jr., 71
Kilpatrick, James, 277 (n. 14),
   283 (n. 114)
King, Martin Luther, Jr., 131, 132, 141,
   158, 265 (n. 95), 266 (n. 124)
King, Rodney, 227
Kirby, Jack Temple, 237 (n. 11)
Kitchen, 48
Klarman, Michael, 143
Knight, B. W., 61–64
Knight, Davis, 172–73, 275 (n. 109)
Knight, Louvenia, 172–74, 275 (n. 110)
Knight, Rachel, 275 (n. 109)
Koch, Ed, 228
Kornegay, Hobert, 92
Kosciusko, Miss., 186
Ku Klux Klan: Citizens' Council vs.,
   121; Freedom Riders and, 138;
   as isolated phenomenon, 168; in
   southwestern Mississippi, 14
Kuykendall, Lynda Faye, 208
Kuykendall, Willie, 208

Landry, Stuart, 281 (n. 70)
Lang, Charles, 71, 261 (n. 54)
Language: aggression narratives
   and, 65; buses and, 241 (n. 74); in
   folklore, 234 (n. 30); in law, 148,
   149, 161, 162, 165; in media, 117,
   204–5; profane, 174
Lassiter, Matthew, 261 (n. 50),
   277 (n. 15)
Latinos and Latinas, 226, 229
Laurel, Miss., 50–51, 71–72, 116,
   261 (n. 55)
Laurel Leader-Call (newspaper), 72
Leach, Herman, 43–44, 85
Lee, George, 267 (n. 5)
Lee, Herbert, 267 (n. 5)
Leniency, in criminal justice, 79–82,
   251 (nn. 88–89)
Levittown, Pa., 115, 277 (n. 15)
Lewis, George, 268 (n. 19), 283 (n. 119)
Lewis, James, 77–78, 251 (n. 81)

Lewis, Nathaniel, 88–89
Lexington, Miss., 93–94
Lexington Advertiser (newspaper),
    94–95, 96, 97
Liberalism, 115, 179
Lines (queues): for buses, 45; in stores,
    36–38, 54–55
Lipsitz, George, 269 (n. 22)
Little Rock, Ark., 115, 150, 180, 184,
    281 (n. 71)
Litwack, Leon, 21, 104, 234 (n. 26),
    237 (n. 11), 240 (n. 63)
"Long civil rights movement," 5,
    232 (n. 12)
Look (magazine), 102, 256 (n. 1)
Los Angeles, Calif., 200, 227, 233 (n. 20),
    240 (n. 56), 243 (n. 109)
Louisville, Ky., 32
Louisville, Miss., 107
Love, Hettie, 36, 85, 87–88, 89
Lover, Jasper, 171
Lula, Miss., 109
Lumumba, Patrice, 209
Lynching(s): aggression of blacks
    and, 66–67; audience and, 107–8;
    black aggression and, 246 (n. 21);
    concerns of white savagery and,
    54, 68, 70, 73, 77, 195; crime and,
    248 (n. 38); death penalty and,
    73–78; decline in, 24; federal
    government and, 72, 249 (n. 52);
    intimacy and, 107–8; justification
    of, 66, 112; legislation against,
    143–44; media coverage of, 69–70,
    73, 108, 247 (n. 32); music and,
    85–86; narratives of, 66–78, 112,
    246 (n. 24); as performance, 66,
    75–76; police and, 258 (n. 22);
    rape and, 66–67, 259 (n. 31); rise
    in, 66–67; similarities between
    executions and, 73–74; social class
    and, 71, 248 (n. 47); as spectacles,
    66, 104; statistics on, 66, 258 (n. 17);
    surveillance and, 104, 106–13;
    variations by time and place and, 66,

232 (n. 9), 246 (n. 23), 248 (n. 38);
    of whites, 246 (n. 25); whites and,
    68–73; in writing, 85–86. *See also*
    Violence

Maddox, Lester, 178
Mail delivery, 38
Mail order shopping, 241 (n. 75)
Mallory, Arenia C., 96
"Mammy" figure, 48–49
Mangurian, David, 171–72
Marriage: common law, 148–49,
    283 (n. 115); interracial, 147–49,
    173, 265 (n. 93), 270 (n. 39)
Marshall, Thurgood, 195
Martin, Hammie, 189
Martin, Trayvon, 227, 288 (n. 39)
Massey, Doreen, 22, 50, 207
Mass incarceration, 18, 226,
    287 (nn. 33–34)
Massive resistance: as general term
    for segregation defense, 6, 142; as
    strategy, 6, 142, 233 (n. 14),
    248 (n. 45), 268 (n. 19)
Matthews, J. B., 158
Mau Mau, 210, *212*, 213
Mayersville, Miss., 222
Mayfield, Julian, 116
McBean, Andrew, 242 (n. 100)
McCain, William D., 154, 156–57,
    182–83
McCarthy, Anna, 277 (n. 19)
McComb, Miss., 164, *166*, 220
McComb Enterprise (newspaper), 76,
    118, 119, 192
McDowell, Fred, 171
McDowell, Lee, 107
McElya, Micki, 237 (n. 7)
McGee, Willie, 116, 157, 261 (n. 55)
McGhee, Laura, 254 (n. 133)
McGuire, Danielle, 259 (nn. 31–32)
McKeldin, Theodore R., 200
McMillen, Neil, 86
McPherson, Tara, 277 (n. 18)
McTatie, Leon, 95, 255 (n. 152)

Media coverage: audience and, 105; benevolence and, 99, 100; of civil rights activism, 113–14, 128–29; of execution, 75, 76, 116; language in, 117, 204–5; of lynching, 69–70, 73, 108, 247 (n. 32); of McGee case, 116; NAACP in, 118–19; by Northern journalists invited to South, 185–86; outside South, 224–25; racial harmony in, 185–94; of racial issues in Jackson, 15–16; of South, 7, 10, 68, 103, 179, 180–81, 220–21; surveillance and, 105, 108, 128–29; of Till case, 116–20, 263 (n. 72); of violence, 10, 61–62, 67, 69–70, 94–99, 245 (n. 12); of white Southerners as racist and violent, 7, 54, 105, 114–15, 120, 175, 215, 216, 217, 225, 228

Melton, Clinton, 267 (n. 5)

Men: black militancy and, 16–17, 89–92; segregation and, 254 (n. 138)

Mendenhall, Miss., 57

Meredith, James, 220

Meridian, Miss., 36–37

Meridian Star (newspaper), 71, 74, 75, 192

Message from Mississippi, The (film), 185

Metcalfe, George, 287 (n. 21)

Mexicans and Mexican Americans, 214, 227, 233 (n. 20)

Michaels, Sheila, 134–36

Micou, Rueben, 107

Migration: in racial harmony narrative, 193; report of return migration from Northern cities, 192–93; from South, 7, 215; surveillance and, 258 (n. 16); to Washington, D.C., 243 (n. 109)

Milam, J. W., 102, 117, 119

Militancy, in black community, 86–93

Military bases, 53–54

Military integration, 115

Military uniforms, 53–54, 56, 86, 118, 244 (nn. 125, 127), 256 (n. 161). *See*

also Soldiers, African Americans as; Veterans

Miller, A. L., 202

Miller, Tyisha, 228

Mims, Jasper, 129

Miscegenation, 173, 211–13. *See also* Interracial marriage

Mississippi Enterprise (newspaper), 95–96, 97–98

Mississippi Freedom Democratic Party, 29, 259 (n. 26)

Mississippi Free Press (newspaper), 134, 154

"Mississippi Goddamn" (Simone), 221

Mississippi State Sovereignty Commission, 2–3, *124*, 131, 132, 146, 158, *166*; Citizens' Council and, 264 (n. 85), 277 (n. 20); illegitimate children and, 205; investigations by, 150–61, 265 (n. 95); racial harmony narrative and, 181–82, 185, 186–87, 194–96; surveillance and, 106, 121–27, 131–33

Mississippi-Yazoo Delta, 12–13

Moebes, Jack, 239 (n. 45)

Money, Miss., 102–3

Montgomery, Ala., 141

Montgomery Bus Boycott, 144, 175, 180

Morton Progress Herald (newspaper), 200

Moss, Joe, 44, 45, 242 (n. 94)

Movement, segregation and, 52–53, 242 (n. 86)

Movie theaters, 25, 28, 29, 40

Moye, Todd, 277 (n. 19)

Muhammad, Khalil, 179, 276 (n. 11)

Murch, Donna, 7

Murder: African Americans as perpetrators of, 96, 177–78, 276 (n. 3); African Americans as victims of, 79, 96, 118; in crime narrative, 195–96; lynching and, 247 (n. 31); by whites, 102–3. *See also* Crime; Lynching(s)

Murray, Pauli, 242 (n. 100)

Music, 85–86, 171, 221, 253 (n. 119)
Mutilation, lynching and, 67, 75–76, 104
Myrdal, Gunnar, 23, 114, 199

NAACP. *See* National Association for
    the Advancement of Colored People
Narrative(s): of African deviance
    and crime, 207–11, 213–14;
    of aggression, told by blacks,
    63–65, 83–93; arrests in, 141; of
    benevolence, 65, 70, 73, 74–78,
    82, 99, 100, 101, 189–93, 218,
    243 (n. 109); of black crime, 7,
    12, 17, 63–65, 78–84, 100, 178–79,
    194–206, 217, 226, 227–28, 230;
    of black male as savage beast and
    rapist, 54, 64, 68, 119, 254 (n. 121);
    of black militancy, 86–93; of black
    servants and white masters, 10, 11,
    23, 29–33, 38, 44, 48, 49, 50, 59,
    65, 68, 79, 80, 84, 86, 93, 101, 112,
    137, 174, 179, 181, 187, 191, 194, 208,
    216, 217, 219, 228, 229, 238 (n. 41),
    239 (n. 46), 240 (n. 49), 243 (n. 109);
    of deviance, 194–206; of global
    whiteness, 206–17; of lynching,
    64–65, 66–78, 85–86, 112,
    246 (n. 24); of Eddie Noel, 93–101;
    of nonwhites as a problem for
    whites, 179, 192, 197, 200, 201–4,
    206–17; performance, 10, 63–64;
    of race nationally, 5, 115, 179, 198,
    213, 214, 217, 225–26, 228; of racial
    animosity, 17, 205, 206, 216; of
    racial harmony, 185–94; of slavery,
    84–85; of South, 10, 11, 68, 79, 105,
    114–15, 116, 117, 120, 121, 137, 184,
    194, 225–26, 228, 260 (n. 42),
    286 (n. 13); of state executions,
    73–78, 249 (n. 62). *See also*
    Performance
Nashville, Tenn., 27
Natchez, Miss., 14, 52, 287 (n. 21)
National Association for the
    Advancement of Colored People

(NAACP), *124*, 279 (n. 37);
    blocking of efforts of, 272 (n. 80);
    Causey case and, 62; in civil rights
    movement, 5; investigations of, 149,
    158–59; in media, 118–19; outlawing
    of, in Alabama, 268 (n. 15); race
    science and, 199; school integration
    and, 128, 202, 263 (n. 74);
    surveillance of, 123–26, 152
National perceptions of South, 11, 68,
    105, 114–15, 117, 120, 184, 194, 228,
    261 (n. 49), 277 (n. 17)
Native Americans, 214, 215, 227
Nehru, Jawaharlal, 210
Nelson, D. M., 189
Neshoba County, Miss., 113
New Deal, 248 (n. 42)
"New Negro," 21, 277 (n. 17)
New Orleans, La., 253 (n. 120)
Newspapers. *See* Media coverage
New York, N.Y., 7, 116, 192–93, 198,
    200, 201, 215–16, 228, 233 (n. 20),
    240 (n. 56), 243 (n. 109), 281 (n. 84)
New York Times (newspaper), 192
Nigeria, 210
Nixon, Richard, 226
Noel, Eddie, 15, 66, 93–101, 256 (n. 154)
Noel, Edmund, 256 (n. 154)
Northen, William J., 247 (n. 26)
Northfield, Minn., 198, 215
Nostalgia, 68, 277 (n. 17)
Nullification, 268 (n. 18)
Nurses, 29, 238 (n. 40)

Oakland, Calif., 7, 224
Observation, 103. *See also* Surveillance
Ochs, Phil, 221
Odum, Howard W., 53
Oliver, Paul, 171
Operation Round-Up, 233 (n. 20)
Operation Wetback, 233 (n. 20)
Oral histories, 15–17
Oshinsky, David, 248 (n. 47)
Outnumbered, whites as, 57, 244 (n. 140)
Ownby, Ted, 269 (n. 25)

Oxford, Miss., 69
Oxford Eagle (newspaper), 69

Pace, Miss., 151–53
Panopticon, 257 (n. 5)
Parchman Farm, 80, 251 (n. 89)
Pardons, 79–83
Parks, Gordon, 239 (n. 45)
Parker, Charlie, 42
Parker, Mack Charles, 14, 130,
    245 (n. 9), 267 (n. 5)
Parks, Robert, 238 (n. 40)
Parks, Rosa, 141
Parlor room, 48
Parole, 65, 81
Pascagoula, Miss., 52
Paternalism: "bad Negro" and,
    252 (n. 90); benevolence and, 107,
    179, 189; black crime and, 205,
    251 (n. 85); childlike conceptions
    of blacks and, 82–83, 253 (n. 105);
    counternarratives from blacks
    and, 88–89; education and, 184;
    line cutting and, 54–55; lynchings
    and, 106–7; in narratives of South,
    114–15, 181; performances of
    whiteness and, 10, 11, 23, 33, 54,
    63, 68, 79, 81–82, 83, 182, 184, 206,
    219, 239 (n. 46); poor whites and,
    34; racial harmony and, 182–83;
    relations with blacks and, 117–18,
    121, 182, 189, 191, 237 (n. 11);
    roadways and, 32–33; Southern
    exceptionalism and, 179–80;
    unexpected performance of, 54–55.
    See also Benevolence
Patterns of Negro Segregation
    (Johnson), 23–24
Patterson, Joe, 172, 271 (n. 59)
Patterson, Robert, 120, 123, 216
Payne, Charles, 89, 254 (n. 127)
Peoples, John, 56–57, 58
Percy, Walker, 248 (n. 47)
Performance: aggression narratives
    and, 86–87; arrests as, 141, 160–75;

audience and, 2, 8–10, 56; avoidance
    as, 58–59, 242 (n. 92); black
    convicts and, 80–83; perceptions
    of black immorality and, 153–57;
    "Black Power" as, 225; of blacks as
    servants, 30, 174, 238–39 (n. 41);
    buses and, 4645–47, 55–58, 164–65,
    244 (n. 135); as concept, 3–4,
    8–9, 219; daily routine and, 3–4;
    domestic servants and, 26, 31,
    48–50, 229, 234 (n. 25), 240 (n. 49),
    243 (n. 109); Erving Goffman and,
    8–9; as evasive tactic, 1–2, 44; in
    everyday life, 3–4, 8–9, 136–37,
    174, 219, 234 (n. 24); independent
    African Americans and, 33;
    intimacy and, 10–12, 17, 31–32, 33,
    48–50, 136, 137, 180–94, 205, 216,
    217, 219, 223, 228, 229; lynching
    and, 66, 75–76; military uniforms
    and, 53–54, 56, 86, 244 (nn. 125,
    127), 256 (n. 161); narrative, 10,
    11, 64; poor whites and, 33–34;
    physical, 9–10; public protest as,
    3, 6, 8, 11, 105, 144–45, 150, 160,
    164–65, 167, 175, 219, 220, 225,
    269 (n. 27); racial difference and,
    33, 40, 227; of racial harmony for
    the media, 185–94; Richard Wright
    and, 1–3; references to the black
    experience and, 8, 234 (nn. 24, 25);
    sidewalks and, 41–45, 52–53; space
    and, 50–52; stillness and, 35–37;
    surveillance and, 125–26, 136–37;
    unexpected, 50–59, 152, 165, 174; of
    violence by white Southerners, 11,
    130, 137, 139, 150, 174, 228,
    273 (n. 85), 286 (n. 13); waiting
    in lines and, 36–37; of whites as
    masters, 174. *See also* Audience;
    Narrative(s)
Philadelphia, Pa., 200
Phillips, Mamie, 57–58
Photographs, in Till case, 117, 118, 119
Physical performance, 9–10

Physical space, 19. *See also* Space(s)

Pickens, Miss., 255 (n. 152)

Plantation store, *39*

Plecker, Walter, 265 (n. 93)

Police and policing, 242 (n. 94); brutality, 7, 52–53, 62–63, 227, 233 (n. 19), 244 (n. 125); civil rights activism and, 117; since civil rights movement, 226–28; daily life and, 174, 175, 220, 224; fear of, 135–36; history of, 140; investigations, 150–60; "legalistic," 7; lynchings and, 258 (n. 22); in North and West, 6–7, 224, 226, 233 (n. 19), 244 (n. 125); racial concerns and, 140; state, 140; state government and, 140; surveillance and, 106, 108, 135–36, 264 (n. 88). *See also* Arrest(s)

Poor whites, 33–34, 240 (n. 59); blame for racial hatred and violence and, 70, 71, 72, 73, 78, 100, 118, 121, 168, 240 (n. 61), 248 (nn. 42, 47)

Population, in Mississippi, 12

Port Gibson Reveille (newspaper), 76

Powdermaker, Hortense, 79, 247 (n. 29), 248 (n. 47), 251 (n. 85)

Prather, William Roy, 267 (n. 5)

Prentiss, Miss., 72

Prentiss Headlight (newspaper), 191

Price, Willie, 80, 81

Prison, 130, 131, 140, 141, 274 (n. 102); civil rights activists and 169, 170; segregation defense and, 197, 199. *See also* Mass incarceration

Pritchett, Laurie, 91, 273 (nn. 85, 91)

Profane language, 174

Public hanging, 73–74. *See also* Executions; Lynching(s)

Puerto Ricans, 192, 200, 201, 214, 215, 216

Putnam, Carleton, 281 (n. 82)

Queens, N.Y., 228

Queues: for buses, 45; in stores, 36–38, 54–55

"Race and Reason Day," 281 (n. 82)

Racial criminalization, 6–7, 18, 23, 64, 79, 150–56, 177–78, 179, 194–206, 225–26, 233 (n. 21), 276 (n. 11), 281 (nn. 70, 84), 287 (n. 34); outside South, 6–7, 224, 226, 232 (n. 11), 233 (n. 19)

Racial difference: domestic workers and, 49; performance and, 40, 227; scientific justification of, 199; segregation and, 21; temporal experiences and, 37

Racial Facts (pamphlet), 184, 205, 211, 212

Racial harmony, 181, 182–94, 220

Racial practices in urban North and West, 7, 64–65, 225, 226, 232 (n. 11), 246 (n. 14)

Racial protest: aggression and, 88–89; arrests over, 140–42, 144–45, 155–56, 161–75; beatings for, 169–70; as breach of the peace, 161–63; communism and, 157–59; disturbance arrests and, 145–46; in early Jim Crow period, 52, 104–5; importance of clothing and, 105, 160, 228; killings connected to, 267 (n. 5); media coverage of, 113–14; outside South, 224–25; performance of, 175; police and, 117; respectability and, 113–14, 160; surveillance of, 123–26, *124*, 128–30, 133–34, 135. *See also* Black Power; Civil rights movement; Integration

Railroads: integration of, 144–45; segregation on, 20, 26, 29, 30, 32, 37, 236 (n. 2); waiting on, 37

Ramsey, Susie, 144–45

Rand, Roena, *162*

Randle, Harry, 255 (n. 152)

Randolph, A. Philip, 115

Rape, 245 (n. 9); black women's fears of, 89–90, 106; crime and fear of, 196; lynchings and fear of, 66–67,

248 (n. 38), 259 (n. 31); scholarship
of Jim Crow South and, 259 (n. 31);
sidewalks and fear of, 45; silence
on, 259 (n. 32); surveillance and,
106–13; white fear of, 64, 66–67,
234 (n. 31); whites as victims of,
67–68
Raper, Arthur, 68, 246 (n. 17),
247 (n. 34), 261 (n. 54)
Ratcliff, Daisy, 147–48
Reagan, Ronald, 226
Real estate, 258 (n. 16)
Red Scare, 157–58
Regional Council of Negro Leadership,
133–34
Reservations, for African Americans, 215
Resistance: as concept related to
domination and social movements,
14–15, 51; as response to domination
in everyday life, 14–15, 51–52, 85–86,
232 (n. 13), 234 (n. 26), 236 (n. 48),
244 (n. 135), 253 (n. 108)
Respectability, 113–14, 160
Restaurants, segregation in, 19–20, 26
Rhodesia, 208, 284 (n. 125)
Richmond, Va., 32, 41, 248 (n. 45)
Riverside, Calif., 228
Roadways, 32–33, 227
Robbery, death penalty for, 76–77
Roberts, Glen, 70
Robeson, Paul, 157
Rogers, W. T., 81
Romano, Renee, 260 (n. 42)
Roosevelt, Eleanor, 53
Roosevelt, Franklin D., 115
Rose, Mary, 148
Routine, as term, 3–4

St. Louis, Mo., 200
St. Paul, Minn., 201
Sanders, Franzetta W., 41, 43, 89, 92
Sanders, Rosie, 91, 92
Sanford, J. C., 72
San Francisco, Calif., 200, 204, 215,
233 (n. 19)

Sartre, Jean-Paul, 116
Satterfield, John, 212–13, 285 (n. 141)
Scarbrough, Tom, 123, 151–53, 171, 172,
209, 210, 274 (n. 98)
School buses, 43
Schools: desegregation of, 128–29,
133–34, 144, 150–51, 153–55,
156–57, 172–74, 184, 190, 202–4,
263 (n. 74), 281 (n. 71); deviance
and, 202–4; paternalism and, 184;
segregation in, 25, 142, 262 (n. 62);
in Washington, D.C., 202–4. See
also *Brown v. Board of Education*
Schultz, Mark, 259 (n. 24)
Schwerner, Michael, 4, 113, 267 (n. 5)
Science: crime and, 64, 179; race and,
198–99, 213
Scooba, Miss., 70
Scopes monkey trial, 115
Scott, H. A., Sr., 19–20, 22, 25, 58
Scott, James C., 14, 51
Scott, Joe, 148
Scott County Times (newspaper), 188
Scottsboro, Ala., 68
Seales, I. C., 208–9
Seattle, Wash., 201
Segregation: adherence to, 24; arrests
and, 142–50; barriers and, 25–26;
breach of the peace and, 162–63; on
buses, 45–48, 55–58; citizenship and,
277 (n. 19); crime and, 7, 177–78,
197–98, 199–201; difference and,
21; distance and, 235 (n. 34); early
laws on, 143; in education, 25, 142,
262 (n. 62); exceptions to, 29–30;
financial costs of, 26, 238 (n. 25);
incrimination and, 153–55; in
informal settings, 24; intimacy and,
19–20, 21, 59–60; manhood and,
254 (n. 138); movement and, 52–53,
242 (n. 86); new laws in, 142–50;
in North and West, 6–7, 115, 157,
224, 226, 232 (n. 11), 233 (n. 19),
244 (n. 125), 277 (n. 15); origins of,
24, 25, 235–36 (n. 32), 236, (n. 2),

239 (n. 47); as preferred by African Americans, 153, 270 (n. 52); on railroads, 20, 26, 30, 32, 236 (n. 2); in restaurants, 19–20, 26; scientific study of, 199; space and, 19–21, 22; stillness and, 35–37; in theaters, 40; violence vs., 241 (n. 83). *See also* Desegregation; Integration; Jim Crow

Segregation and the South (film), 185

Segregationists, portrayals of, 4, 6, 142–43, 149, 178, 268 (n. 19). *See also* Segregation

Selective Service Act, 159, 169

Sellers, Cleveland, 241 (n. 74)

Selma, Ala., 222, 286 (n. 13)

Senegal, 285 (n. 143)

Servitude, space and, 29–30

Sexual assault, 45, 106–13, 259 (n. 13); as threat for black women, 89; white rumors of, 53. *See also* Rape

Sharpeville massacre, 207–8

Sharpless, Rebecca, 49, 289 (n. 45)

Shaw, Miss., 127, 131

Shelby, Jessie, 267 (n. 5)

Shopping, 269 (n. 25)

Shubuta, Miss., 71

Sidewalks, 41–45, 52–53

Silver, James W., 139

Simmons, William J., 158, 183, 198, 213, 266 (n. 124), 285 (n. 143)

Simon, Bryant, 5, 53, 238 (n. 41)

Simone, Nina, 221

Sioux, 215

Slavery: "good Negro / bad Negro" and, 251 (n. 90); narratives of, 84–85; surveillance and, 257 (n. 3)

Smith, E. Hammond, 46

Smith, Gerald L. K., 209

Smith, Hazel Brannon, 94–95, 96, 99, 255 (nn. 148–49)

Smith, Ian, 284 (n. 125)

Smith, J. Douglas, 232 (n. 9), 237 (n. 11), 238 (n. 21)

Smith, Lamar, 118, 267 (n. 5)

Smith, Virgil, 76–77

Smith v. Allwright, 115, 144, 268 (n. 15)

Socioeconomic status: lynching and, 71, 248 (n. 47); New Deal and, 248 (n. 42); racial roles and, 33–34

Soldiers, African Americans as, 52–54, 55–57, 244 (n. 125)

Song of the South (film), 68

South: African Americans in, 25; as behind rest of nation, 105, 197; changing conceptions of, 115; crime and, 79; exceptionalism of, 179–80; federal government and, 53–54; in media, 7, 68, 103, 179, 180–81, 220–21; narratives of, 10, 68, 79, 105, 114–15; nostalgia and, 68, 277 (n. 17); public opinion on, 114–15; racial harmony narrative in, 182–94; as Sunbelt South, 228; surveillance of, 105, 113–20. *See also* National perceptions of South

South Africa, 207–8, 210

South America, 212–13

South Carolina, 268 (n. 15)

Southern Conference for Human Welfare, 5

"Southern Manifesto," 202, 282 (n. 99)

Southern Rhodesia, 208, 284 (n. 125)

Southwestern Mississippi, 13–14

Space(s): arrests and, 165; barriers in, 25–26; blacks and whites together in, 28–29; breach of the peace and, 161–63; on buses, 46–47; customs and, 30–31; cutting in line and, 38; force and, 55–56; intimacy and, 19–20, 22; modification of, 58, 59; physical forms under segregation, 24–26; racially exclusive, 24–25; segregation and, 19–21, 22, 24–26; servitude and, 29–30; sidewalks and, 41–45; stillness and, 40; surveillance and, 106, 258 (n. 16); verbal responses and, 57; white homes as, 48–50

Spillers, Hortense, 35, 37, 242 (n. 86)
"Stand your ground" law, 227,
    288 (nn. 39–40)
Stapleton, Lover, 267 (n. 5)
Starr, Douglas, 149
State police. *See* Highway patrol
State Sovereignty Commission. *See*
    Mississippi State Sovereignty
    Commission
States' Rights Party, 116
Steve Allen Show, The (television
    program), 209
Stillness, and segregation, 35–37, 40,
    242 (n. 86)
Stockett, Kathryn, 229
Stoner, Peter, 169–70, *170*
Stools, 19–20
Store(s): avoiding, 241 (n. 75); clerks
    in, 39–40; clothing, 39–40; country,
    27; plantation, *39*; waiting in line
    in, 36–38, 54–55
Streetcars, 45, 52, 104. *See also* Buses
"Street tax," 43–44
Student Nonviolent Coordinating
    Committee (SNCC), 220, 259 (n. 26)
Sturdivant, Bozie, 171
Sunbelt South, 228
Surveillance: audience concept and,
    103–4, 125–26, 136; by blacks,
    130–32, 260 (n. 38), 266 (n. 114);
    on buses, 104–5; centralization of,
    105–6, 120–37; Citizens' Council
    and, 120–21, 127–30, 133–34; of
    civil rights activism, 123–26, *124*,
    128–30, 133–34, 135; defined, 103;
    etiquette and, 257 (n. 9); everyday,
    106–13; fear and, 109–10, 134–35;
    in Foucault, 257 (n. 5); intimacy
    and, 107–8, 112, 136; lynching and,
    104, 106–13; media coverage and,
    105, 108, 128–29; of Mississippi,
    116; Mississippi State Sovereignty
    Commission and, 106, 121–27,
    131–33; of NAACP, 123–26, *124*,
    128; in New York, N.Y., 258 (n. 16);

in Oakland, Calif., 224; panoptic,
    257 (n. 5); performance and, 125–
    26; police and, 106, 108, 135–36,
    264 (n. 88); public opinion and,
    113–20; rape and, 106–13, 110–12,
    113; real estate and, 258 (n. 16);
    respectability and, 113–14; roots of,
    257 (n. 3); slavery and, 257 (n. 3); of
    South, 105, 113–20; space and, 106,
    258 (n. 16); technology, 132–33;
    Till case and, 116–20; vigilance and,
    104; violence and, 106, 113–20;
    vision in, 257 (n. 2); by white
    citizens, 102–3, 123–30
Sweatt v. Painter, 144
Syracuse, N.Y., 200

Tarvin, Timothy, 189
Taxicabs, 30, 239 (n. 44)
Technology, surveillance and, 132–33
Television, 15, 105, 117, 181, 185, 222,
    279 (n. 33), 286 (n. 13). *See also*
    Media coverage
Temple, Johnny, 171
Temporal stillness, and segregation,
    37, 40
Tennessee, 20, 25, 29, 115. *See also*
    specific cities
Texas, 32
Textbooks, 43
Theaters, 28, 29, 40
Thompson, Allen, 221
Thompson, Heather Ann, 226,
    287 (n. 33)
Thompson, Jimmy, 75
Thompson, Julius, 95
Thompson, Louberta, 80
Thurmond, Strom, 233 (n. 17), 281 (n. 84)
Till, Emmett, 4, 15, 102–3, 116–20, 136,
    144, 180, 185, 256 (n. 1), 262 (n. 64),
    263 (nn. 72, 78), 267 (n. 5)
Time, stillness and, 37
"Too Many Martyrs" (Ochs), 221
Torres, Sasha, 262 (n. 63)
"Tougaloo 9," 140

Index 329

Whiteness, global, 206–17
Whitesand, Miss., 190–91
Whitfield, Stephen, 262 (n. 69)
Wiegman, Robyn, 104
Wilbur, Betram, 8
Wilkins, Roy, 118–19, 130, 205, 221,
  263 (n. 72), 271 (n. 59)
Williams, H. J., 49
Williams, John Bell, 121, 197–98, 199,
  202, 203–4
Williams, Robert F., 265 (n. 95),
  287 (n. 29)
Williams, Tommie Lee, Sr., 92, 93
Williamson, Joel, 234 (n. 32),
  237 (n. 18), 239 (n. 46)
Winona, Miss., 168–69
Winston County Journal (newspaper),
  107
Wirth, Gene, 190
Women: aggression narratives and, 89;
  "dancing for the master" and,
  260 (n. 36); as domestic servants,
  29, 31–32, 48–50, 53, 238 (n. 40),
  240 (n. 49), 289 (n. 45); as
  "mammy" figure, 48–49; responses

of, 89; surveillance and, 110. *See
  also* Rape; Sexual assault
Women's Political Council, 144
Wood, Amy, 245 (n. 12), 254 (n. 121)
Wood, Jeff, 283 (n. 121)
Woodward, C. Vann, 106, 239 (n. 47),
  288 (n. 44)
Woolworth's lunch counter, 268 (n. 14),
  269 (n. 27)
Work, Monroe, 65
World War II, impact on race relations,
  7, 14, 49–50, 53–54, 55–56, 79, 86,
  97, 115
Wright, Fielding, 76, 116, 251 (n. 81),
  269 (n. 24)
Wright, Richard, 1–2, 9, 20, 59–60,
  102, 144, 218

Xenophobia, 207

Yazoo City, Miss., 19, 128–29, 216, 218
Yazoo City Herald (newspaper), 190

Zambia, 284 (n. 125)
Zimmerman, George, 227, 288 (n. 39)

MIX
Paper from
responsible sources
FSC® C013483
www.fsc.org